Surviving Death

CARL G. HEMPEL LECTURE SERIES

Surviving Death

MARK JOHNSTON

PRINCETON UNIVERSITY PRESS   PRINCETON & OXFORD

Copyright © 2010 by Princeton University Press

Published by Princeton University Press, 41 William Street,
Princeton, New Jersey 08540
In the United Kingdom: Princeton University Press, 6 Oxford
Street, Woodstock, Oxfordshire OX20 1TW

All Rights Reserved

LIBRARY OF CONGRESS CATALOGING-IN-PUBLICATION DATA
Johnston, Mark, 1954–
Surviving death / Mark Johnston.
    p.   cm. — (Carl G. Hempel lecture series)
Includes bibliographical references and index.
ISBN 978-0-691-13012-5 (hardcover : alk. paper)   1. Death.
2. Future life.   I. Title.
BD444.J5546 2010
129—dc22   2009034147

British Library Cataloging-in-Publication Data is available

This book has been composed in Minion

Printed on acid-free paper. ∞

press.princeton.edu

Printed in the United States of America

10 9 8 7 6 5 4 3 2 1

Dedicated to the memory of

JOSEPH HENRY JOHNSTON
(July 1919–June 1992)

and

JOSEPH LESLIE JOHNSTON
(January 2008–May 2008)

Contents

Preface

I am grateful to many people who have helped me in this project, and in philosophy more generally. In particular, I would like to express my debt to my doctoral supervisors from long ago, Saul Kripke and David Lewis, who showed me what it was to aim at something in the subject.

I should also mention Anthony Appiah, Paul Benacerraf, Alexander Nehamas, and Joyce Carol Oates, each of whom prepared kind introductions to the various lectures; Daniel Garber, who had earlier alerted me to several details in the tradition of Christian mortalism; and, of course, the two hundred or so people who kept attending, despite the almost exponential increase in the difficulty of the philosophical material.

Because of what subsequently happened to the younger Joseph I concluded that it had become obscene for me to be associated with this topic. The lectures were about to go in the trash bin, along with so much else. But then, as in so many other cases, Sarah-Jane spoke good sense to me, and got me to listen.

So here they are.

Surviving Death

Chapter One

Is Heaven a Place *We* Can Get To?

Having shaken off the yoke of being chair of the department (after seven years) it is a great honor to be invited by my colleagues to give these lectures. It is also a particular delight. For this lecture series celebrates the memory of our wonderful former colleague, Carl Gustav "Peter" Hempel.

Like all those who knew him, I remember Peter as a very good and kind man. To mention just one small kindness—a single example among so many—one Princeton summer, long ago, Peter offered his magnificent office in McCosh to my then fellow graduate student Alison McIntyre and me, with the encouragement that we look into his library. It provided a great education in the long history of positivism, especially in the often unnoticed practical idealism of that movement, which appeared so forcefully in the many early pamphlets associated with its formation, pamphlets that Peter still kept on hand. One of those pamphlets contained a partial translation of August Comte's *Système de politique positive,* in which I found an idea that I shall return to in the last lecture. I wonder what Peter would have made of it.

So now to begin on the lectures, I should say that I am very conscious of the awkwardness of my topic. To speak in this kind of academic context about whether we survive death is widely regarded as a form of bad

Many people have made enormously helpful comments on these lectures. Sarah-Jane Leslie's objections and suggestions throughout the rewriting of the lectures were indispensible and made for many improvements. Special thanks to Michael Forster for his very insightful and quite detailed written comments, and to Anthony Appiah, Paul Boghossian, Alex Byrne, Stanley Corngold, Adam Crager, Ebet Dudley, Adam Elga, Dan Garber, Gordon Graham, Paul Guyer, John Haldane, Caspar Hare, Elizabeth Harman, Gilbert Harman, John Hawthorne, Desmond Hogan, Cheng Kai-Yuan, Thomas Kelly, Boris Kment, Eden Lin, Hendrik Lorenz, Angela-Adeline Mendelovici, Carla Merino-Rajme, Colin McGinn, Jeff McMahon, Stephen Neale, Alexander Nehamas, Christopher Peacocke, Philip Pettit, Gideon Rosen, Kim Lane Scheppele, John Searle, John Haven Spencer, Michael Smith, Nicholas Stang, Jeff Stout, Rahel Villinger, and Dean Zimmerman.

taste. When I first announced the topic of these lectures, many of my friends in the department visibly flinched. And I believe that they are still a little nervous on my behalf. Why is this? Perhaps it is because there seem to be only two ways of proceeding, both bad ones at that. You either rehearse a scientifically established materialism about life and death, or you preach.

To do the first, to rehearse materialism, roughly the claim that the mind is merely the functioning of the brain and nervous system, so that a mind cannot survive the death of its brain, is just to insult peoples' cherished religious beliefs, and their consequent hopes that they and their loved ones are not obliterated by death. And that is not very helpful, is it?

Besides rehearsing the consequences of materialism, the only other option may seem to be apologetics or preaching; in effect, special pleading on behalf of *particular* religious beliefs. That is obviously out of court in an academic context. So how can you decently talk, in an academic context, about whether or not we survive death?

Well, we don't talk about it, or if we do, we talk about it under the arcane guise of what is called the philosophy of personal identity. This academic reticence on the question of life after death has at least two bad effects.

One effect is on the culture at large. Because there is something of a taboo on serious discussion of the topic, many people suppose that they have the right to believe anything they like about death and survival. So we get a good deal of second- or third-hand religiosity, mixed in with the whims of New Age wishful thought. Here as elsewhere, freedom of thought is confused with a license to believe anything. Philosophy is one of the few things that still enforces that disappearing distinction.

Another effect is to be found in the intellectual content of a major idée fixe of the day, namely the incessant discussion of the alleged compatibility or, as it might be, *in*compatibility of something called "religion" and something called "science." (As if Spiritualism and neurophysiology stood in the same relation as Unitarianism and, say, cosmology.) One reason why such discussions often seem like so much shadowboxing is that the crux of supernaturalist religious belief, the status of the afterlife, is not taken up in any detailed and concerted way.

One upshot of these lectures will be that dwelling on the *generic* motif of science versus religion misses something crucial. As we shall see, various supernaturalisms, particularly the Protestant and the exoteric Catholic theologies of death, have obscured a striking consilience between certain implications of the naturalistic philosophical study of the self and a central salvific doctrine found in Judaism, Christianity, Buddhism, and Vedanta.

The Popularity of the Other World

In 2003, the Barna Research Group conducted an extensive survey of the attitudes of Americans on the question of surviving death. Here is their own "executive summary" of their findings.

- Belief in life after death, like belief in God, is widely embraced. Not only do 81 percent of Americans believe in an afterlife of some sort, but another 9 percent said life after death may exist, but they were not certain.
- Moreover, a large majority of Americans (79 percent) agreed with the statement "Every person has a soul that will live forever, either in God's presence or absence."
- In fact, belief in the afterlife seems to be more popular than belief in the existence of God. Half of all self-described atheists and agnostics say that every person has a soul, that heaven and hell exist, and that there is life after death.

The Barna survey also explored Americans' particular conceptions of heaven and hell.

- In all, 76 percent believe that heaven exists, while nearly the same proportion said that there is such a thing as hell (71 percent).

While there is no dominant view of hell, two particular opinions seem widespread.

- Four out of ten adults believe that hell is "a state of eternal separation from God's presence" (39 percent) and one-third (32 percent) says it is "an actual place of torment and suffering where people's souls go after death." A third proposition, which one in eight adults will assent to, is that "hell is just a symbol of an unknown bad outcome after death."

The popular view of where we are going after death appears to ignore, even to reverse, the consistent and ominous biblical warning: "Narrow is the gate to salvation, but wide is the road that leads to perdition." For just one-half of 1 percent of Americans think that they will go to hell upon their death.

By the way, this is roughly the proportion of Americans who in other surveys are prepared to avow Satanism, or report that Satan is likely to be the highest power. So the level of anticipation of *effective* damnation, in the sense of ending up in *the wrong place*, may be considerably lower than half of 1 percent.

What Does Death Threaten?

It is the kind of survey of American attitudes that shows that we need to significantly amend Nietzsche's best-known aphorism. God is dead; but only in Australia, Scandinavia, and parts of Western Europe! In these "godless" countries, and the old country, Australia, it seems, is one of the more godless, much lower levels of belief in the afterlife are found.

These stark differences in levels of professed belief in an afterlife persist, even when we statistically correct for the difference in churchgoing as between, say, the United States and Australia. Here is a tempting speculation about the persistent difference between Americans and Australians. In Australia, for whatever reason, saying that you believe in God and the afterlife is *not* a speech act required of you in order to count as a conventionally good person. By contrast, *one* of the things American respondents are doing in announcing their beliefs in God and the afterlife is declaring themselves on the side of the good. (If that is right, then we should not expect that a significant increase in scientific literacy would automatically alter the rate of such avowals.) Like it or not, in this country, the present conventions are such that to openly avow atheism and materialism is thereby to create the presumption that you are a reprobate, a morally unprincipled person. You will then have, for example, little chance of being elected sheriff, let alone congressman, senator, or president.

Is this why atheists are now "coming out"—in part to erode these conventions?

Convention aside, is there any intelligible connection between allegiance to the good and belief in life after death? I think there is. Death confronts us with a threefold threat. For the person who is dying death threatens the loss of life with others, as well as the end of presence, the end of conscious awareness. As a generic phenomenon, death also threatens what we might call the importance of goodness. Belief in a life after death, where people get their just deserts, explicitly addresses this last threat. (Of course, it also promises the restoration of life with others and the persistence of conscious awareness.)

DEATH AND THE IMPORTANCE OF GOODNESS

How does death threaten the importance of goodness? To start with the more inchoate versions of the thought: Death is the great leveler; if the good and the bad alike go down into oblivion, if there is nothing about reality itself that shores up this basic moral difference between their lives, say by providing what the good deserve, then the distinction between the good and the bad is less important. So goodness is less important.

It is an argument with an ancient pedigree. Qoheleth, perhaps better known as Ecclesiastes, the "one who has gathered many things," writing sometime after 450 BCE, famously makes this argument in the case of one prized form of goodness, namely wisdom.

> So I turned to consider wisdom and folly.... Then I saw that wisdom excels over folly as light excels over darkness. The wise have eyes in their heads, but the fools walk in darkness. But then I remembered that the same fate befalls us all, wise and foolish alike. And I said to myself, "What happens to the fool will happen to me also. Why then have I been *so very wise?*" And I came to see that this wisdom also is vanity. There is no enduring remembrance of the wise or of the fools, for in the days to come all will have been long forgotten. The wise die just like the fools....
>
> So I hated life, because what is done under the sun was grievous to me; for all is vanity and a chasing after wind. (Eccl. 2:12–17)

And again:

> Everything that confronts them is vanity, for the same fate comes to them all, to the just and the unjust, to the good and the evil, to

the clean and the unclean, to those who sacrifice and to those who do not sacrifice. (Eccl. 9:2–3)

The argument is not (or not *yet*) that the distinctions between the wise and the foolish, the just and the unjust, and the clean and the unclean are *obliterated* by the fact that they all face the same fate, the supposed nothingness of the grave. Rather it is that the distinctions lose their importance. The struggle to be wise, or just, or good, or clean is so much vain effort, given what death is.

This is not an isolated thought in the Jewish tradition.[1] *The Wisdom of Solomon*, written by a Hellenized Jew probably at the end of the first century BCE, rather than promoting Qoheleth's argument directly, offers a more telling conceit. The author has the wicked or "the ungodly" invoke their ally Death to vindicate their wickedness, by what is in effect a radicalized version of Qoheleth's argument.

The ungodly by their words and deeds summoned Death;
considering him a friend, they pined away
and made a covenant with him,
because they are fit to belong to his company.
For they reasoned unsoundly, saying to themselves,
"Short and sorrowful is our life,
and there is no remedy when a life comes to its end,
and no one has been known to return from Death.
For we were born by mere chance,
and hereafter we shall be as though we had never been,
for the breath in our nostrils is smoke,
and reason is a spark kindled by the beating of our hearts;
when it is extinguished, the body will turn to ashes,
and the spirit will dissolve like empty air.
Come, therefore, let us enjoy the good things that exist,
and make use of creation to the full, as in youth.
Let us take our fill of costly wine and perfumes,
and let no flower of spring pass us by.
Let us crown ourselves with rosebuds before they wither.
Let none of us fail to share in revelry."

[1] Notwithstanding the fact that the tradition is now somewhat divided about the afterlife, and in particular about the old Pharisaic doctrine of the resurrection of the dead.

So far, so good; we seem to have a sensible Epicurianism; there is nothing in itself wicked here. But now the reasoning of the wicked takes a nasty turn.

> "Let us oppress the righteous poor man;
> let us not spare the widow
> or regard the gray hairs of the aged.
> But let our might be our law of right,
> for what is weak proves itself to be useless."

In so reasoning, the wicked "reason *unsoundly*," as the New Revised Standard Version of the Apocrypha has it; and it is clear from the surrounding text that the argument of the wicked is explicitly presented by the author as unsound, *but not invalid*. The author of the *Wisdom of Solomon* is telling us that if it were the case that the righteous and the wicked alike go down into the nothingness of Death, then one could validly infer that everything is permitted. But the argument of the wicked employs a false premise about death. On the author's view, the righteous are saved by the goodness of God. As he says:

> For the souls of the righteous are in the hands of God and no torment shall ever touch them ... for though in the sight of men they were punished, their hope is full of immortality. (*Wisdom* 3:1–4)

And we might add, *righteousness* is thereby saved; its importance is preserved even in the face of death.

CAN THE THREAT BE DISMISSED?

Among contemporary philosophers, it is widely held that a few elementary considerations in moral philosophy will suffice to expose the confusion in this sort of thinking. Many moral philosophers would say that the wicked described in the *Wisdom of Solomon* are reasoning *invalidly*. The dominant view would be that it *doesn't* follow from the supposed fact that all alike go down into the nothingness of the grave that righteousness or goodness is less important.

For example, modern moral rationalists would make the following points. Moral goodness is a normative property that attaches to acts because of the kinds of acts they are, and independently of whether those acts are rewarded. Moral badness is a normative property that attaches to acts because of the kinds of acts that *they* are, and independently of whether *those* acts are punished. Whatever the merely self-interested or prudential point of view might tell you about the importance of the distinction between goodness and badness in the face of the nothingness of death, the moral point of view represents that distinction as *categorically* important; that is, important in a way that is not at all conditioned by your finding it in your self-interest to pursue the good. This is so even if we extend the notion of self-interest to cover your eternal salvation or damnation as meted out by a just God.

More than this, moral considerations *override* the considerations of self-interest; they place *absolute side constraints* on the pursuit of ends. In this sense they have an absolutely *preemptory authority* over anything we might desire. Therefore the force of moral considerations as reasons to act and prefer is independent of any desire-based incentive that the afterlife might offer. So much is just the content of the moral point of view, according to our modern moral rationalist.

That seems all very well as far as it goes, but it does not go far enough. In thus ensuring the hardness of the moral "must," our modern moral rationalists have thereby left morality all too brittle. For we can ask about the importance of the moral point of view itself, given that reality—as depicted by secular naturalism—is indifferent to the very distinction that point of view treats as so important. It is internal to the moral point of view that great injustice cries out for punishment, and that great sacrifice in the name of the good cries out for reward. But if the world itself is deaf to these cries then it can be rational to care less about the deliverances of the moral point of view.

Compare a corresponding attack on the importance of the prudential point of view; a point of view that presents the pursuit of one's own long-term self-interest as a fundamental principle of rationality. From the prudential point of view, the pursuit of your long-term self-interest is *categorically* important; that is, the *force* of reasons of self-interest does not depend on your having antecedent desires to promote your self-interest. So from the prudential point of view, one can be criticized for not caring *enough* about oneself and one's future. So young smokers and heavy drinkers are often criticized from the point of view of prudence alone, even when it is clear that they lack present desires to now act to satisfy their anticipatable future desires not to be in pain or misery.

How stable is such criticism in the face of certain truths about the world? Suppose I now remind myself that I am just one of the immense horde of humanity. There they are, the enveloping mass of humanity, billions of them, *teeming* around me. Each member in the horde takes himself so very seriously, but no individual matters that much. So how much then can I matter? Why should I take what is in my self-interest so seriously?

Or suppose I contemplate the fathomless extent of the universe and of my own miniscule place within it. The universe is much too vast, and I am much too small, for there to be any conceivable cosmic drama with me playing the role of Everyman. Or forget Everyman; I am too minis-cule to be even a torch carrier in the back row of any conceivable drama played out on the vast cosmic stage. Seeing all this, it can reasonably seem to me that the pursuit of my self-interest doesn't matter much, precisely because I don't matter much. The effort and seriousness that it takes to prudently manage my own life is just not worth it.

Notice that I am not here adopting the *moral* point of view, and argu-ing from that point of view that prudence matters less. It's rather that in my practical reasoning I have access to a standpoint from which I can consider just how much prudence and morality matter, how important they in fact are. Moral and prudential reasons have a categorical *force*, but that does not settle their weight or importance. Compare the reasons of etiquette; like the reasons deriving from prudence and morality they do not have the force of reasons conditional on what you want to do. They are categorical, they tell you what you *should* do, whatever you may *want* to do. The rule is "Put the fork on the left, and the knife on the right" not "If you feel like it, put the fork on the left, and the knife on the right." Yet many of us, at the end of the day, find the demands of etiquette not to be too important, especially those that are not mere expressions of the requirements of considerateness. That is why we swap the knife and the fork for left-handers.

When I consider the question of the *importance* of the reasons deriv-ing from morality, the nature of the universe seems highly relevant. The importance of prudence and of morality is not wholly settled from in-side their respective points of view. Otherwise, we would expect some consensus as to how to comparatively weigh the reasons of self-interest and the reasons of morality. And despite enormous theoretical reflection on these two sources of reasons, no consensus has emerged or is emerging. Within certain limits, it seems that reasonable people, who grasp the force of both sources of reason, may disagree. This itself suggests that the respective standpoints, even when taken together, do not themselves settle how important the reasons they deliver are.

If that is right, the categorical and preemptory character of moral reasons does not invalidate the threat of death to the importance of (moral) goodness.

Let us try another way to make the threat come alive. Consider Qoheleth's remark, "The battle does not always go to the strong, nor the race to the swift, nor wealth to men of understanding." Compare Ogden Nash's ditty, which indicates something of the actual character of human life:

> The rain it raineth every day
> On the just and the unjust fellas,
> But mainly on the just because,
> The unjust have stolen their umbrellas.

We can go further than Qoheleth and the ditty, and imagine a quasi-demonic scenario in which the signs are unequivocally reversed; where goodness is systematically punished, and wickedness systematically rewarded: Rwanda, Kosovo, Moscow after the collapse of the Soviet Union, parts of Iraq under Saddam, and, sadly, parts of Iraq to this very day. Now we understand perfectly well what morality requires of us in such a scenario; it requires that we soldier on in the name of the good, whatever punishments the demons deliver. This is moral heroism, and deeply admirable as such. But it is also clear that the quasi-demonic scenario is *morally* repellent: It is one that a moral being, just because of what morality is, should hope never to inhabit.

It is hard to resist the further conclusion that a moral being should hope for more than just this. Besides hoping that he not inhabit a morally incoherent universe, he should hope that the universe he inhabits is actually morally coherent. That is, he should hope that it is a universe in which the cries of great injustice to be punished, and the cries of great sacrifice in the name of the good to be rewarded, do not just echo in the void.

In saying that I mean to align myself with Immanuel Kant's conclusions about what we are *rationally required* to hope for in the face of death. In various places in his writings, Kant presents three related worries about the relation between death and moral goodness, or "virtue" as he calls it. For Kant, being virtuous is being *worthy* of happiness, and this fact imposes a further moral requirement, namely that we all will the realization of a state, the so-called Highest Good, in which virtue and happiness converge. We have no reason to think that that virtue and happiness will converge in our lifetimes, or indeed in this world. Yet we are rationally required to believe in the possibility of realizing the objects of our will. So given the facts about this life, we are rationally required to hope for another life in which virtue is properly rewarded.

Kant's second thought is that without this hope we are naturally and rationally subject to moral discouragement. This is, anyway, how many do in fact react. When faced with the contrast between the professional torturer who dies calmly in his sleep at a ripe old age surrounded by his adoring family, and the nurse who, for her whole adult life, cared for the dying only to herself die young and alone from a horribly painful and degrading illness, people do tend to fall into despair over the importance of goodness. Unless, that is, they have hope or faith.

In the third *Critique*, Kant illustrates his concern over moral discouragement by the example of Spinoza; in Kant's view a paradigm of a just man, one who actively revered the moral law, and so needed no promises or threats in order to be motivated to follow its commands. Yet Spinoza had no belief in individual immortality (Kant supposes) and, a fortiori, no belief that our earthly lives would be judged in the afterlife by a just God. So, according to Kant, Spinoza was susceptible to having his unselfish resolve to bring about the good rationally undermined by considering the lives of other virtuous people and the manifest fact that "No matter how worthy of happiness they may be, nature, which pays no attention to that, will subject them all to the evils of deprivation, disease and untimely death" (*Critique of Judgment*, 452–43).

We can understand Kant's concern here if we consider that a good will cannot be a practically irrational will, not even conditionally or counterfactually. That is, a good will ought to be able to rationally maintain itself as the disposition that it is, even in the face of any relevant fact. But Kant is supposing that a good will, without irrationality, might not maintain itself in the face of the naturalistic picture of death that he takes Spinoza to have defended.

Kant allows himself a third variant on his theme of justice and the afterlife, perhaps the variant that is most relevant in an age in which the world financial system is run on principles of naked power and legalized theft. Kant's third thought is that absent final justice, obedience to the moral law may simply turn the just into fodder for the predatory unjust. In the *Lectures on Ethics*, we find this extraordinary aperçu: "We are obliged to be moral. Morality implies a natural promise: otherwise it could not impose any obligation upon us. We owe obedience only to those who can protect us. Morality alone cannot protect us."[2] (And yet virtue, which on Kant's view consists in acting in accord with the moral law, must be its own reward; the thing we will have to see is just how that reward can also be some kind of *protection*.)

Despite these various anxieties about death and moral goodness, Kant himself never endorses the stronger conclusion drawn by the author of the *Wisdom of Solomon*, namely that if the cries of goodness to be rewarded and the cries of evil to be punished do simply echo in the void, then everything is permitted.

Even so, to follow Kant as far as he goes is enough, in a very abstract way, to render intelligible something like the conventional American expectation that one should confess to some kind of belief in God and the afterlife as part of signaling one's allegiance to the good. As in the case of Kant, this need not rest upon the base idea of the afterlife as the *incentive* to be moral, but on the better idea that morality by its nature requires the support of the afterlife.

It is a distinction that we would do well to keep in mind. William James, who seems to have mistaken Kant as proposing the afterlife as an *incentive* to be moral, referred to Kant's philosophical theology as "the uncouth part" of his philosophy. We repeat something like James's confusion when we indulge in the idea that our self-declared enemies, the suicide killers, must be relying on the imagined incentive of the "doe-eyed houris" of the next world. Instead, in many cases, the next life seems to function more as a guarantor of justice, which intensifies the would-be suicide killers' sense of injustice in this world. That, of course, is *much* more worrying, for the sense of injustice is in certain ways more robust than the appeal of the doe-eyed houris.

---

[2]Immanuel Kant, *Lectures on Ethics*, trans. Louis Infield (Hackett, 1981), 82. In thinking about Kant on this topic, I have learned much from David Sussman's very illuminating discussion of Kant's anthropology in *The Idea of Humanity* (Routledge, 2001), and from Paul Guyer and Desmond Hogan, who made extremely helpful suggestions along the way.

THE AIM OF THESE LECTURES

More to our purpose here, there seems to be little point in defending any response to death unless that response addresses the threat of death to the importance of goodness. For this reason, I shall simply ignore the classical refutation of death proffered by Epicurus, namely that death is nothing to us, because we do not live to experience the event of our death; for we are then dead, and so suffer neither it nor its consequences. Whatever other defects there are in his view, what Epicurus says is simply not designed to address the threat death makes to the importance of goodness.

I shall also simply ignore cryonics, endless tissue transplantation, and similar proposed methods of life extension. These are devices available only to the financial elite in advanced technological cultures. (Though apparently the promoters of deep-freezing of still-warm bodies are trying to penetrate a wider, less upscale market. Instead of freezing your whole body for $170,000, you can simply have your head frozen for a mere $80,000, a plausible option given that any future civilization sophisticated enough to revive a frozen head will probably be able to provide it with a prosthetic body!)

As such absurdities suggest, cryonics and the like are not the sort of things that could even begin to address the threat of death to the importance of goodness. At best, they represent speculative forms of life extension that would only postpone death for relatively few people. But the threat is a general threat that looms over the moral aspirations of all of us. Therefore the answer to the threat, if there is one, must lie in some possibility that *already* exists in human life, and indeed in any mortal and fragile form of life that finds itself under moral demands.

In the *Phaedo*, Socrates is pressed by his friends to explain why he is so calm in the face of his own impending death. He replies in perfectly measured terms: "I am in hope that there is something for us in death, and as was claimed from old, something better for the good than there is for the bad" (*Phaedo* 63c).[3]

This is the constraint that I take myself to be under, namely to show that there is something in death that is better for the good than for the bad. The interest of what I have to say may lie in the fact that in doing this I shall have no recourse to any supernatural means. I shall take us to

[3]See *Plato, Complete Works*, ed. John M. Cooper and D. S. Hutchinson (Hackett, 1997).

be wholly constituted by our bodies. I shall find that there is no separate self or soul that could survive without the body or be reincarnated in another body. I shall argue that the idea of the resurrection of the body after its corruption is not, in the end, a coherent idea. Still, I shall maintain that the good, but not the bad, can overcome death, in part by seeing through it. And this, in its turn, will help us understand what goodness, the goodness that survives the threat of death, is.

Socrates' division between the good and the bad is not fine-grained enough for our purposes. People are better and worse; they are good to various degrees. "Overcoming death" will mean diminishing the threat of death to the one who is dying. Overcoming death will be a matter of degree, and will correlate with the degree to which one has a good will.

The conception of goodness that I have in mind is one shared by the best forms of Judaism, Christianity, and Buddhism. The good person is one who has undergone a kind of death of the self; as a result he or she lives a transformed life driven by entering imaginatively into the lives of others, anticipating their needs and true interests, and responding to these as far as is reasonable. The good person is thus a caretaker of humanity, in himself just as in others. By living this way, the good person encounters himself objectively, as just another, but one with respect to which he has a special trust.

To the extent that they *are* good, the good can see through death, and as a result death is less of a threat to them. Once we understand just how that is so, we will understand how the importance of goodness is vindicated even in the face of death.

But there is also a threshold of goodness at which the good person has forged a different kind of identity. And here, certain discoveries in the arcane subject known as the philosophy of personal identity will help us see how this new identity is not a mere metaphor but a basis for survival in what John Stuart Mill called "the onward rush of Mankind."

The one who is good in this sense is the one who follows the command of what the New Testament styles *agape*, and so has arrived at a thoroughly objective relationship with the human being he finds himself to be. He thereby sheds a certain kind of self-delusion, as it were the practical counterpart of the delusion of an enduring superlative self, and so finds that the death of a particular human being is so much less important to him than the onward rush of humankind that continues after his death. He is more identified with that and with its rich magnificence, so much so that he can find the end of his own individual personality to be a final release from the centripetal force that continued through his life to pull him back into his smaller self. Such a person's pattern of identification has given him a new identity, one that is not obliterated by the death of his body and the consequent end of his individual personality.

Those remarks, which on their face express what seems to be an all too abrupt transition between identification and identity, would be both metaphorical and misleading, were it not for certain surprising facts that will emerge in the later lectures.

Woody Allen famously remarked, "I don't want to achieve immortality through my work, I want to achieve it by not dying." No doubt that is how many of us feel when we hear of a naturalistic surrogate for surviving death. We don't want the surrogate, we want our own selves, and our own individual personalities, to live through death; or even better, we want not to die at all.

I am not offering a naturalistic surrogate for that kind of thing, though I will explain how a good person *quite literally* survives death. My central concern is to respond to the threat that, from the naturalistic point of view, is posed by death to the importance of goodness. However, along the way, we will encounter certain surprising philosophical discoveries about what matters in survival, discoveries which show that the typical structure of concern for one's own continued existence, understood as the continued existence of one's self and one's individual personality, is deeply incoherent.

As I say, in all this there will be no reliance on supernatural means. The commitment to naturalism is a constraint on method; in responding to the threat that death makes to the importance of goodness, I shall have no recourse to the other world, but only to this world properly conceived.

The proper conception in question, the central part of which is wholly novel, will take some work to grasp, I'm afraid. It will require attention over several afternoons of extended argument, with the payoff coming only at the end. You will be happy to hear that there will be some comic relief. But this will not be a distraction from the real philosophy; it will be an essential part of the real philosophy. We will have to go through a lot of real philosophy to get to our destination, and throughout each

lecture I shall be throwing some red meat to the professional philosophers in the audience, particularly the local tigers, who are even now
baring their fangs.

Nevertheless, I have some hope that a good deal of what I have to say
will be accessible and worthwhile to those without any arcane philosophical training. And maybe, just maybe, you might come to see that
philosophy is something to look into a little further.

THE PASSAGE OF THE SOUL

Why take the trouble, why not simply acquiesce in faith in the importance of goodness? Why not indeed? I have nothing but admiration for
a serene, unelaborated, yet tested faith to the effect that death cannot
threaten the importance of goodness. The trouble is that such a simple
faith hardly ever exists. Either self-deception clouds the real fact of death,
or some theological or quasi-theological elaboration gets in the way, an
elaboration that involves supernatural means, means that carry with
them extraneous psychological benefits that fatally distort the understanding of what goodness requires of us.

As a point of clarification, let me say that I am not *dogmatically* anti-
supernaturalist. Supernaturalism is an empirical thesis about the extent
of the world and about the way it operates. In my estimation it has turned
out that the preponderance of the evidence counts against this thesis.
However, my basic commitment to naturalism is methodological. I take
the right starting point in the foundations of ethics and the philosophy
of religion to involve questions like this: Is it possible to ransom any
genuinely salvific ideas found in the major religions from their supernaturalist captivity, and what price do we have to pay for the ransom?
Asking that question might lead us to see just what supernaturalism
would do for us, if it *were* true in one or another of its religious forms.

The foundational question of whether the ransom is possible is forced
upon us by our need for salvation and the fact that believing the epis-
temically dodgy claims of supernaturalism cannot be, morally and religiously speaking, necessary (let alone sufficient) for salvation.

To reject supernaturalism and yet talk of our need for salvation is
likely to provoke more or less everyone in the misbegotten debate between religion and science. But I also take it that the claim that we need

salvation is an empirical thesis, one that is also overwhelmingly supported by the available evidence. It is a thesis that can be explained to the naturalist, and if he is not dogmatic he will come to see the widespread evidence for it.[4] There are certain large-scale structural defects in human life that no amount of ordinary psychological adjustment and no degree of the resultant natural virtues of prudence, courage, moderation, just dealing, and so on, can adequately address or overcome. These large-scale structural defects include arbitrary and meaningless suffering, the decay of aging, untimely death, our profound ignorance of our condition, the destructiveness produced by our tendency to demand premium treatment for ourselves, and the vulnerability of everything we cherish to chance and to the massed power of states and other institutions. A truly religious or redeemed life is one in which these large-scale defects are somehow finally healed or addressed or overcome or rendered irrelevant.

Shouldn't it then be an urgent question whether any part of such a life is available within a naturalistic framework?

Furthermore, we can be methodological naturalists and yet admit that there could be supernaturalist narratives that would remain right in some fundamental sense, even if they are false to the historical facts and to the actual extent of the world. Perhaps the redeeming virtues can *at first* only be adequately depicted through compelling examples presented within a supernaturalist frame that invokes a God in another, prior or posterior, world.

Here is an example, deliberately drawn from a very mundane context, of being able to come to see what is there only by at first seeing what is not actually there. The correct way to begin to master pocket billiards involves seeing a white "ghost ball" touching your object ball at the point farthest from the intended pocket. You then shoot the cue ball directly at the ghost ball, and the object ball rolls into the pocket. (You hope.) This is the correct way to begin, even though there is no ghost ball, and even though seeing it actually gives the wrong aiming point on the object ball.[5] If you do not have an extraordinary natural talent, you won't really be

---

[4]For a detailed naturalistic discussion of the fallen condition of humanity, and of our corresponding need for salvation, even given the naturalistic point of view, see my *Saving God: Religion after Idolatry* (Princeton University Press, 2009).

[5]The ghost ball method is an inaccurate method of aiming because of what is known as "contact-induced throw," a friction effect that occurs when the cue ball hits the object ball and drags it along with it.

able to learn to play well enough to appreciate what pocket billiards has to offer unless you *begin by continually seeing what is not actually there.* Still, someone who gets stuck on the ghost ball is not going to go very far.

Different things are appropriate for different stages of development, and a wise person does not jumble these up. It does not follow that because what was necessary at the earlier stage was literally false, that it was *then* the wrong way to approach things. If we had been taught the literally true history of our country in middle school, there would be no chance for the development of the proper piety towards our heritage. But once we have this proper piety, we can usefully investigate the more nuanced, and sometimes shaming, truth about our heritage.

A methodological naturalist who cares about the phenomenon of religion will inquire into the moral and religious *cost* of getting stuck at a stage of religious development. He will resist the inference that because a supernaturalist narrative of salvation was once helpful, perhaps even required, in order to see certain things in this world, it must therefore be a true description of history and of the actual extent of this world. And he will characteristically suspect that too much reliance on *literal* supernatural means, means that carry with them psychological benefits extraneous to salvation, can fatally distort the understanding of what salvation is, and of what goodness requires of us.[6]

Of a course, a supernaturalist will insist that the supernatural apparatus of heaven is not at all like the ghost ball; it is not just something that it is helpful to focus on at a certain stage of spiritual development in order to see *this* world in an appropriate way. It is required to make moral sense of life, to answer the threat that death and the other large-scale defects present to the importance of goodness.

In this lecture and the next, I shall take very seriously a variety of forms of supernaturalism concerning the afterlife, and I shall argue that even if we grant their assumptions, a deep philosophical problem remains: On any tenable view of personal identity *we* can't get there—be it heaven, hell, purgatory, or the *limbus infantium*—from here. Then in the remaining lectures, I shall address the question of how a certain kind of naturalism can meet the threat that death and the other large-scale defects of human life present to our conception of the importance of goodness.

---

[6]These are central themes of *Saving God*.

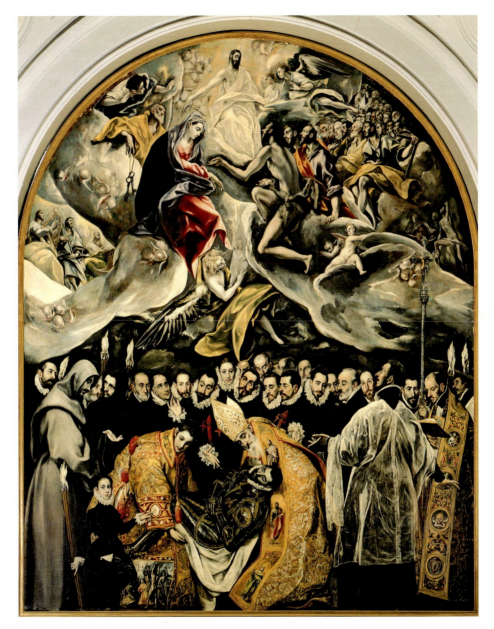

El Greco (Domenico Theotocopuli) (1541–1614), *The Entombment of Gonzalo Ruíz, Count of Orgaz, from a Legend of 1323*, 1586–88. Toledo, S.Tome, Spain/ Giraudon/The Bridgeman Art Library.

Detail, *The Entomb-
ment of Gonzalo Ruíz,
Count of Orgaz, from
a Legend of 1323.*

Titian
(Tiziano Vecellio)
(c.1488–1576),
*King Philip II of
Spain (1527–1598).*
Museo del Prado,
Madrid, Spain.
Photo: Erich
Lessing / Art
Resource,
New York.

When it comes to surviving death, there are a number of different forms of supernaturalism worthy of review.

Consider first the conception of the afterlife embodied in what is perhaps the greatest work on the theology of death, *The Entombment of Gonzalo Ruíz, Count of Orgaz.*

The story of the painting? It was completed by El Greco in 1586, and remains on the wall on the right as you enter the vestibule of the Church of Santo Tomé in Toledo. The chasubled figure on the extreme right of the painting is Andrés Núñez, the parish priest of Santo Tomé, who commissioned the painting to commemorate a miracle that supposedly took place in his church 263 years earlier, in 1323. In that year, a certain Don Gonzalo Ruíz, native of Toledo, señor of the nearby town of Orgaz, went to his eternal reward. The Don had been a pious man who, among other charitable acts, gave a considerable sum to the Augustinian order for the building of a church to honor St. Stephen. At his burial in the church of Santo Tomé, to the astonishment of the mourners, both St. Augustine and St. Stephen had the good grace to come down from heaven to officiate and convey the earthly remains of Ruíz into his tomb, while an angel ushered his soul, depicted just above the middle of the painting as a nebulous infant, up through the birth canal of heaven.

There Ruíz is awaited by the Virgin and St. Peter on the left; and on the right, pleading to our Lord on behalf of the soul of Ruíz, we have John the Baptist and, quite remarkably, Philip the Second of Spain.[7]

It is the upper half of the painting that is relevant to our argument. It represents, as I say, a theology of death, perhaps the theology of death that is best known in the West. In the birth canal of heaven we see, in the form of a nebulous infant, the soul of Ruíz, which is to be reembodied in a spiritual body and then judged for the life of Ruíz, with the prospect of joining the community of saints and angels in endless adoration prompted by the vision of God. The soul of Ruíz is, as we might put it, a seat of consciousness and the bearer of the personality of Ruíz; an immaterial something that carries the consciousness, identity, and moral quality of the man Ruíz; but this soul needs a body (be it material or

[7]Oddly enough, Philip was born almost two hundred years after the death of Ruíz and was still alive, though quite ill, in 1586, the date of the painting. So in any one of the twelve years until his actual death in 1598 Philip was in a position to visit this very painting and see himself in heaven. I do not know if he ever saw it.

spiritual) to sense, to communicate, and indeed even to encounter the face of God. So death is explicitly presented as a rebirth and reembodiment of the soul in another world. El Greco depicts surviving death as waking from a dark dream of moral confusion into a larger context of light, the context that makes moral sense of our earthly life. This larger context is already partly revealed to the faithful, who can hope for it while they are still locked inside the dream that is this life.

LOCKE AND THE *WISDOM OF SOLOMON*

Of course, we are all inheritors of the rhetoric of the Enlightenment, which tells us that the real dream is not in the bottom half of the painting but in the top half. It is the same rhetoric that tells us to grow up morally and learn to adhere to our principles in the absence of such supernatural support.

Except that, as a matter of fact, the Enlightenment (when properly charted) does not simply consist of thinkers like Spinoza and Hume; major Enlightenment figures, such as Locke and Kant, have no time for such rhetoric. As we noted, Kant argues that as rational beings we are *obliged* to hope for another life that makes moral sense of things. And Locke, who, like Kant, took the truths of morality to be accessible to reason, nonetheless insists that it is only divine judgment after death that makes morality a law we are truly obligated to follow. (This position was revived in the twentieth century by G.E.M. Anscombe, who famously asked in response to moral "oughts" and "musts," "Must I? And what if I don't?" to which she thought the only coherent answer was a description of the consequences of Divine justice.)[8]

Locke admits that reason can *derive* the principles of morality, but he claims that without the help of revelation, reason cannot adequately account for the force and importance of those principles. For this we need judgment after death, and Locke claims that Jesus has "Given us unques-

---

I can't help thinking that the fabulous coruscating armor of Ruíz looks as though it was copied from Titian's 1550 portrait of Philip the Second, a painting El Greco must have known from his apprenticeship in the workshop of Titian. This painting, reproduced in figure 3, now resides in the Prado. Doesn't the armor look the same?

Perhaps El Greco is not just carrying out his stated commission but also presenting his moribund king with a profound meditation on his forthcoming death.

[8]See G.E.M. Anscombe, "Modern Moral Philosophy," *Philosophy* 33 (1954).

tionable assurance and pledge of it, in his own resurrection and ascension into heaven." And then, most remarkably, Locke allows himself to scoff at Aristotle and the Stoics by waxing poetic on the fragile character of their mundane ideal of virtue. He writes that after the promise of resurrection and final judgment, the familiar praise of virtue by the ancient "heathens" pales by comparison with what we can now say of it.

> That [virtue] is the perfection and excellence of our nature; that *she herself* is her own reward, and will recommend our name to future ages, is not all that can now be said of her. It is not strange that the learned heathens satisfied not many with their airy commendations [of virtue].

For, unlike the learned heathens, we, "who possess the promise of the afterlife," are now able to see that virtue "wears a fairer crown." Virtue, Locke continues,

> *has another relish* and efficacy to persuade men, [namely] that if they live well now they will be happy hereafter.... This view of heaven and hell will cast a flight upon the short pleasures and pains of this present state, and give attractions and encouragements to virtue. . . Upon this foundation, and *upon this only*, morality stands firm and *may defy all competition.*[9] (my italics)

That is John Locke, the intellectual father of the American Republic! The ancient argument of the *Wisdom of Solomon* returns, but now as a triumphal blast.

LOCKE AND PERSONAL IDENTITY

Famously, we also find something else in Locke—namely an explicit philosophy of personal identity and accountability, in part tailored to allow for the possibility of judgment in another world. Indeed, it would not be too far from the mark to understand the philosophy of personal identity

---

[9]John Locke, *On the Reasonableness of Christianity as Delivered in the Scriptures* (Clarendon Press, 1999), edited with an introduction and notes by John C. Higgins-Biddle. It's a tough work to get through. In his essay in Leroy S. Rouner, ed., *If I Should Die* (Notre Dame University Press, 2001), Aaron Garrett discusses these and other passages by way of providing an intriguing narrative of the gradual mutation of the idea of immortality from the period of Scotus through to Locke.

as we now know it as an offshoot of the Christian, and in particular the Protestant, theology of death. Before Locke, Descartes, who at the very least was concerned to keep up the appearance of being a good Catholic, had written very proudly of his own achievements in the *Mediations*, and particularly of his arguments for the real distinction between mind and body, and the immateriality of the mind, on the ground that they opened the way for rational acceptance of Christian doctrine.

Locke seems more attuned than Descartes to actual Christian doctrine, at least as it is framed by Scripture. He knows that the essential doctrine of the New Testament is not the Platonic doctrine of the immateriality of the soul but of the resurrection of the dead, with subsequent judgment and assignment to heaven or to hell. And unlike the theology of death presented in *The Entombment*, the resurrection of the dead requires no mental or spiritual substance that at death might carry an individual's identity to heaven.

In Locke we get the first great meditation in the West on the nature of personal identity. This meditation is strongly conditioned by the Protestant theology of death, which at least in its earlier English form followed Martin Luther in excoriating the doctrine of the immateriality of the soul as an extraneous Platonic importation into true Christianity, indeed as a doctrine that obscured the radical promise of the New Testament. That promise was not a mere variant on the ancient theme of the soul's disposition after death; it was the promise to miraculously overcome the annihilation that is death by way of the General Resurrection. For Protestants like Locke, to dwell on the disposition of the soul in the period between individual death and final resurrection was in effect to invite the Trojan horse of Roman Catholicism back into the Reformed churches. For the inquiry as to the condition of the soul in the intervening period between death and Doomsday makes metaphysical room for purgatory as a place for the cleansing of the soul before the final judgment; this would justify the priestly craft of intercessory prayer for the sake of the dead, and also speak in favor of the very apparatus that Luther loathed and used as his lever for the Reformation—indulgences and masses for the dead. (You will remember what Sir Thomas More said of Luther: that he was a man who would rather see all the world lie in the fire of purgatory till Doomsday than have one penny given to a priest to pray for the dead.)

Luther himself favored a doctrine of soul-sleeping or "Psychopanny-chism" as it came to be called after Calvin attacked it, the doctrine that the soul is in a state of sleep or suspended metal life in the interregnum between death and the final judgment. Psychopannychism appears explicitly in Luther's *Exposition of Salomon's Book*, a commentary on Qo-heleth Luther wrote in 1532, and which appeared in English forty years later. There Luther cites such passages as "the dead know not anything; neither do they have a reward" (Eccl. 9:5) and "there is no work, nor device, nor knowledge, nor wisdom in the grave, where thou goest" (Eccl. 9:10). Thus, on the alleged authority of Solomon, Luther outlines his doctrine of soul-sleeping, obviously intended to secure Reformed Christianity against "the fiction of purgatory" and its concomitants of intercessory prayer and, of course, the indulgences he so much despised.[10]

The seventeenth-century English advocates of "Christian mortalism," most notably Richard Overton, John Milton, and Thomas Hobbes, out-did Luther in their attempt to insulate Reformed Christianity from the apparatus of intercessionary prayer and indulgencies. They claimed that the soul itself was *annihilated* at death; the promised resurrection was therefore the resurrection of both soul and body. During the interregnum, the dead simply did not exist, for their souls were *also* dead—a doctrine that came to be called "Thnetopsychism."

Overton's Thnetopsychism was set out in his tract *Man's Mortallite*, which appeared in 1644 with the following frontispiece:

Mans Mortallite, or a Treatise Wherin 'Tis Proved Both Theologically and Phylosophically, that the Whole Man (as a Rationall Creature) is a compound wholly Mortall, Contrary to That Common Distinction of Soule and Body; and That the Present Going of the Soul Into Heaven is a Mere Fiction; and That the Resurrection is the Beginning of Our Immortality, and Then Actual Condemnation, and Salvation, and Not Before. With All Doubts and

---

[10] In the 1970s, the Lutheran doctrine of soul-sleeping began to catch on among some Catholic theologians, most notably Karl Rahner. In the early 1980s, in one of his first official acts as the prefect of the Congregation of the Doctrine of the Faith, the then Joseph Cardinal Ratzinger officially condemned Psychopannychism, by the obvious Catholic argument that it made practical nonsense of both masses for the dead in purgatory and of prayers to dead saints for intercession. We can only be thankful that the Congregation of the Doctrine of the Faith did not go on to deploy the methods it had at its disposal in the days when it was known under its original, and more ominous, title.

Objections Answered, and Resolved, Both By Scripture and Reason; Discovering the Multitude of Blasphemies and Absurdities That Arise From the Fancy of the Soule. Also Divers Other Mysteries, as, of Heaven and Hell, Christs Humane Residence, the Extent of the Resurrection, the New Creation etc. Opened, and Presented to the Tryall of Better Arguments.[11]

Man's Mortallite is a barrage of unrelenting scorn directed at the idea of the soul's leaving the body at death, a proposition presented as the mere invention of Plato, confusedly mixed with true Christian doctrine, and in a way that obscures the radical promise of the resurrection. In defense of his anti-Platonic materialism, Overton appeals to the discoveries of the French physiologist Ambrose Paré to argue that men differ only in degree from the beasts, so that even reason depends on the proper functioning of the brain. It is in such contexts that materialism is first taken seriously in the English-speaking world, not only as a revival of ancient atomism but as an explicitly theological doctrine, whose purpose was in part to purge Christian belief of its Greek immaterialism and so to suppress any theological encouragement for the priestly craft of intercessory prayer and indulgences.

The same dynamic can be found in John Milton's *Christian Doctrine*, another spirited defense of Christian mortalism. Like Overton before him, Milton cites Christ's promise to the Good Thief as the major scriptural stumbling block for Christian mortalism:

Verily I say unto you, today you shall be with me in Paradise.

which unfortunately appears to entail that the Good Thief will exist in Paradise *before* the General Resurrection.[12] Luther would presumably have had the Good Thief's soul remain asleep in Paradise until Doomsday, but this does seem to invalidate Christ's promise, if not his reported words.[13] More to the point, no mortalist like Overton or Milton could

---

[11]As quoted in Norman Burns's brilliant history of the matter, *Christian Mortalism from Tyndale to Milton* (Harvard University Press, 1972).

[12]Burns (*Christian Mortalism*) has a nice discussion of Milton and Hobbes on these matters.

[13]Luther's soul-sleeping and his denial of individual judgment before the General Resurrection are obviously ill suited to handle the manifest content of the parable of Dives and Lazarus at Luke 16:19–34. This point applies a fortiori to those Christian mortalists who endorse Thnetopsychism. No fiddling with commas makes the obvious import of this parable go away.

tolerate a sleeping soul. So Milton suggests that the entailment is only apparent, and arises from an error in translation. We should, Milton says, move the comma so that Christ's promise reads:

Verily I say unto you *today*, you shall be with me in Paradise.

It is marvelous what can be revealed by attention to the syntax of sentences.

THE IRRELEVANCE OF THE SOUL?

Although Locke stands in the wake of the mortalist theological tradition, he finds independent philosophical reasons for not relying on immaterial souls to secure the possibility of resurrection. As carriers of our essential identities, souls would have to be substances, bearers of the acts and operations that make up our mental lives. But for Locke it is an open empirical question what actually lies at the base of our mental lives. He supposes that God is able to make matter that is "fitly disposed" come to think and experience, so there is at least the conceptual possibility that we only consist of material substances.

Moreover, it is Locke who initiates the method of imaginary cases in the philosophy of personal identity. (Ovid used similar cases, but to a different end.) By this method, Locke has us imagine someone surviving a succession of substitutions of his underlying spiritual substance. On the ground that such a person could still remember his earlier deeds, as it were "from the inside," Locke pronounces him the very same person, despite the imagined succession of underlying spiritual substances.

The description of the case is parasitic on Locke's definition of a person. By "person" Locke says he means "an intelligent thinking being that can know itself as itself, as the same thinking thing, in different times and places." Locke adds that "person" is a forensic concept; its primary use is to pick out something that is accountable for its past acts, and something that has a "concernment," as he calls it, a pattern of focused concern about its past and future. It is consciousness that, via memory and anticipation, extends this concernment outward from the present self. Accordingly, Locke believes that being the same person is not a matter of being the same animal, or the same immaterial substance or soul. It simply involves being the same *consciousness*. The great and reliable *sign* of being the same consciousness, and so the same person or self that existed at an earlier time, is memory of experiences had, and deeds done, at that earlier time.

Given this, a person is something that can be resurrected and then appear before the Divine judge, even if the person's bodily substance is destroyed by death, and even if his soul or immaterial substance is likewise destroyed by death. So Locke's view is consistent with, though it does not entail, Thnetopsychism.

At Book 2, Chapter 27, Section 28 of the *Essay Concerning Human Understanding*, Locke writes:

> And therefore, conformable to this, the apostle tells us, that, at the Great Day, when everyone shall "receive according to his doings, the secrets of all hearts shall be laid open." The sentence[s on the Great Day] shall be justified by the consciousness all persons shall have, that they themselves, in whatever bodies they appear, or what substances so ever that consciousness adheres to, are the same that committed those actions, and deserve that punishment for them.

Thus Locke elegantly evades the heated controversy that divided the English Christian mortalists from the followers of Luther: the controversy of whether the soul is destroyed by death or "sleeps inactive," as Luther had it, until the General Resurrection on the Great Day. Since for Locke, it is the person and not the soul whose survival matters, the heated issue on the postmortem disposition of the soul, be it to nonexistence, to sleep, or to purgatory, goes by the board.

In the same vein, in a well-known passage from Book IV, Chapter 2, Section 6 of the *Essay* Locke obliquely disparages those who, like Descartes, have expended some effort to defend the idea of souls or immaterial substances.

> All the great ends of Morality and Religion, are well enough secured without the philosophical Proofs of the Soul's Immateriality; since it is evident that He who, at first made us beings to subsist here as Sensible Intelligent Beings, and for several years continued us in such a state, can and will restore us to a like state of Sensibility in another World, and make us there capable to receive the Retribution he has designed to men, according to the doings in

this life. And therefore 'tis not a mighty necessity to determine one way or t'other, for or against the Immateriality of the Soul, as some overzealous have come foreward to make the World believe.

NEO-LOCKEANISM AND SURVIVAL

In so diverting our attention from the question of the persistence of either a bodily or spiritual *substance* to the question of the psychological connections that make for the same consciousness over time, Locke has bequeathed contemporary philosophy what is called "Neo-Lockeanism" or the "Wide Psychological View."[14] Twenty years ago, when I first turned to the topic of personal identity, Neo-Lockeanism was the dominant view, ably defended by Anthony Quinton, Sydney Shoemaker, and David Lewis.[15] Rightly or wrongly, they took Locke to be offering a clearly inadequate memory criterion for personal identity over time, and therefore sought to bolster Locke's position by adding other mental connec-

---

[14] *Psychological reductionism* is the view that truths about personal identity over time have as necessary and sufficient conditions statements about the holding of relations of mental continuity and connectedness. Connectedness involves the holding of direct psychological connections, such as the persistence of beliefs and desires, the connection between an intention and the later act in which the intention is carried out, and the connection between an experience and a memory of that experience. Connectedness can come in twice over in the statement of the conditions on personal identity. All psychological reductionists require that if two person stages are stages of the same person, then psychological continuity, the ancestral of strong or predominant psychological connectedness, holds between them. Some psychological reductionists also require that no two such stages be entirely unconnected psychologically. Neo-Lockeanism is sometimes called *wide* psychological reductionism because it has it that mental continuity and connectedness can secure personal identity even if the holding of these relations is not secured by its normal cause, the persistence of a particular human body or brain. For Neo-Lockeanism, any causal mechanism that operates so that these psychological relations hold will do. The identity over time of any particular human body or brain plays no strictly indispensable role in the identity of a particular person over time. Any particular human body or brain is just one causal means among others for the holding of the relations of psychological continuity and connectedness that constitute a particular person's survival. So the characteristic sign of Neo-Lockeanism is the consequence that a person would survive Teletransportation.

[15] See David Lewis, "Survival and Identity," in Amelie O. Rorty, ed., *The Identities of Persons* (University of California Press, 1976); Anthony Quinton, "The Soul," *Journal of Philosophy* 59 (1962): 393–409; and Sydney Shoemaker, with Richard Swinburne, *Personal Identity* (Blackwell, 1984). Shoemaker clearly had some sympathy for the view that bodily continuity is constitutive of personal identity when he wrote *Self-Knowledge and Self-Identity* (Cornell University Press, 1963), although he allowed that in exceptional cases the bodily criterion of personal identity could be overridden by the memory criterion. He decisively abandons the bodily criterion in "Persons and Their Pasts," *American Philosophical Quarterly* 7 (1970): 269–85.

tions such as the persistence of beliefs and desires, the tendency to carry out intentions just formed, the immediate carryover of character, and so on, so as to include all the direct mental links that are typically found from one moment to the next in a single conscious life. Neo-Lockeanism thus arrives at the position that a person at one time is identical with a later person just in case there is a chain of such direct mental links *uniquely connecting* the first mentioned person and the second. So according to Neo-Lockeanism you will exist at a later time just in case you have a unique, and sufficiently close, mental continuer at that time. (Lewis found an ingenious way to drop the requirement of uniqueness.)[16]

The term "Neo-Lockeanism" may partly rest on a confusion about just what Locke is up to in his "On Identity and Difference."[17] Nevertheless, it does secure the possibility that Locke cared most about. Given Neo-Lockeanism, you can come before the throne of the Divine judge on the Great Day, even if death annihilates your body *and your soul or spiritual substance*. All it takes is that there be another body, perhaps a spiritualized body created for the occasion, whose psychology is uniquely continuous with your premortem psychology. All it takes, in other words, is for your unique mental continuer to come before the throne of God.

There are popular ideas, spontaneously generated from our computer-dominated culture, which are actually just unwitting variants on Neo-Lockeanism. One is that a particular mind is like a detailed software program that can be implemented in various machines, so that one could get to the next world if God there provides a new body-like computer on which one's individual software can run again. Another is that a mind or soul is an information-bearing pattern instantiated in a brain and body, so that after a person's death, God will remember the person's "pattern" and will instantiate that pattern in a new brain and body at the resurrection. A sophisticated variant of this last view is used by John Polkinghorne to explain life after death.[18]

The arguments against Neo-Lockeanism set out below have been selected to also work, mutatis mutandis, against such mind-as-software and soul-as-pattern views.

[16]See Lewis, "Survival and Identity." This proposal is discussed in detail below.

[17]*Essay Concerning Human Understanding*, Book 2, Chapter 27, Section 9.

[18]John Polkinghorne, *The Faith of a Physicist: Reflections of a Bottom-Up Thinker* (Fortress Press, 1996), 163ff.

NEO-LOCKEANISM AND CHRISTIAN MORTALISM

In the spirit of Locke, we may now contrast the Platonized theology of death in *The Entombment of Gonzalo Ruíz*, a theology which assumes that the soul is an immaterial, independent substance, with what has now become the standard Protestant conception, a conception which places the emphasis not on the immateriality of the soul but on the resurrection of the dead person.

Given Neo-Lockeanism, the Protestant view may seem to allow for a satisfying compromise with a sensible materialism, as in the Christian mortalist tradition of Overton, Milton, and Hobbes. These early Christian mortalists emphasized the dependence of the mind or soul on the body. Yet they observed that in re-creating the body at the resurrection, God thereby re-creates the mind, and hence the whole person. So whereas the implied theology of *The Entombment* requires that the depicted mind or soul be a separable entity distinct from the brain and body of Gonzalo Ruíz, Protestant mortalism exhibits no such vulnerability to the scientific discovery of the dependence of the mind on its brain.

Moreover, the Protestant view avoids the philosophical question that faces the theology of death pictured in *the Entombment*. Why does the item depicted in the birth canal of heaven count as the very man Gonzalo Ruíz, that generous person who lived on earth, rather than just a spiritual remnant of that person? What stops us from correctly describing what is depicted as the fate of a spiritual remnant of Gonzalo, but not of Gonzalo himself? Yes, there are persons on the other side, but they (perhaps with the exception of the Virgin, who was raised bodily into heaven) are persons because they have been provided with spiritual bodies. How can something made up of a soul and a spiritual body be identical with something that was made up of that soul and a material body?

BYPASSING THE BODILY CRITERION

It is important that holding to the resurrection of the person while rejecting the immateriality of the soul does not depend on a conception that takes a person to be identical with his body and then supposes that resurrection would bring the very body of the deceased person *back* into existence.

That conception of resurrection might help itself to what philosophers call "the bodily criterion of personal identity." The bodily criterion has it that a person survives whenever and wherever his body does, for a person is identical with his body.[19] The bodily criterion may seem to suit exactly the needs of the mortalist theological tradition, which holds that the soul is destroyed along with the body at death. Mortalism would then require that the bodily criterion be augmented with the auxiliary assumption that a given body can exist *again* if the perimortem state of the body is re-created, reproducing its matter and organization just as it was at the moment before death. (God, we may suppose, then heals and invigorates the resurrected body in various ways.)

This version of mortalism may seem to stumble over the distinction between being copied and genuinely coming back into existence. Peter van Inwagen drives this distinction home with the example of a lost manuscript penned by Augustine. Suppose that long after the manuscript has been destroyed, the atoms of the manuscript magically coalesce to create a piece of paper that is qualitatively just like the original manuscript. Surely, van Inwagen says, the new manuscript is a magically produced *copy* of the original manuscript that was penned by Augustine. And where we have a copy, we have two things, not one thing coming back into existence after a period of nonexistence.[20]

However, upon reflection, van Inwagen's appeal to the intuition that the resultant manuscript is a copy may not settle the issue. It may only serve as an illustration of the ontological importance of the distinction between immediate parts, such as two halves of a manuscript, and remote parts like atoms. If the two separated parts of Augustine's manuscript were attached together that would be Augustine's manuscript. So

---

[19]David Wiggins endorses something like the bodily criterion when he writes in *Sameness and Substance* (Oxford University Press, 1980), "a person is any animal that is such by its kind to have the biological capacities to enjoy fully the psychological capacities enumerated" (176) and extracts this consequence: "There would be no one real essence of persons as such, but every person could still have the real essence of a certain kind of animal. Indirectly this would be the real essence in virtue of which he was a person" (172). Peter van Inwagen also claims that persons are organisms, a centerpiece of his *Material Beings* (Cornell University Press, 1987). A vivid defense of this view, and by implication the bodily criterion of personal identity, is found in Paul Snowdon, "Persons, Animals, and Ourselves," in Christopher Gill, ed., *The Person and the Human Mind* (Oxford University Press, 1990), and Eric Olson, *The Human Animal* (Oxford University Press, 1997).

[20]Peter van Inwagen, "The Possibility of Resurrection," *International Journal of Philosophy of Religion* 9 (1978), reprinted in Paul Edwards, ed., *Immortality* (Macmillan, 1992). Van Inwagen's views are discussed in detail in the addendum to this lecture.

also, if, in a stunning archaeological discovery, the original planks that made up the last form of the Ship of Theseus were actually found, the archaeologists could then *reassemble* the Ship of Theseus. The very ship that took its last sea journey centuries ago could then be shown in a museum.

Perhaps a practical anticipation of this point about reassembly from *immediate* parts is found in the Jewish, or more specifically Pharisaic, practice of double burial; the body is interred, and then after a period of decay the bones are dug up and placed in an ossuary, where they may survive indefinitely. That makes sense if the bones are thought to be the crucial immediate parts of the body, the parts essential, and with some added flesh sufficient, for the reconstruction of the original body.

So why can't God reconstruct a person's original body in steps, organic molecules from the body's perimortem atoms, cells from those organic molecules, organs from the cells, and then the original body again from its immediate parts, the organs?

The traditional answer involved the comical case of the cannibal who has lived on an exclusive diet of human flesh, a fancy deployed to make the point that the same remote parts might be taken up in the lives of a succession of distinct persons, each near his or her respective death. At the resurrection, because of the diets of such cannibals, there just will not be enough previously body-constituting matter to go around in the way required to re-create the perimortem bodies of all the dead.

To which the standard, if even more ludicrous, response was that thanks to an equitable distribution of perimortem atoms, the resurrected bodies of the cannibals and their luckless victims will be considerably smaller than they were at death.[21]

---

[21] As late as the seventeenth century, even distinguished members of the Royal Society were still agonizing about the cannibals. For example, Robert Boyle, in his essay, "Some Physico-Theological Considerations about the Possibility of the Resurrection," writes,

> When a man is once really dead, divers of the parts of his body will, according to the course of nature, resolve themselves into multitudes of steams that wander to and fro in the air; and the remaining parts, that are either liquid or soft, undergo so great a corruption and change, that it is not possible that so many scattered parts should be again brought together, and reunited after the same manner, wherein they existed in a human body whilst it was yet alive. And much more impossible it is to effect this reunion, if the body have been, as it often happens, devoured by wild beasts or fishes; since in this case, though the scattered parts of the cadaver might be recovered as particles of matter, yet already having passed into the substance of other animals, they are quite transmuted, as being informed by the new

The traditional invocation of the case of the resurrected cannibal was supposed to dramatize a point about the worrying competition on the Great Day for bodily parts had by more than one person at the moment of their respective deaths. How could both "perimortem" bodies be re-created from the same matter?

That kind of worry can be made vivid in a more exact, if less comical, way.

The Problem of Perimortem Duplicates

Consider two people, separated by two hundred years. Nonetheless, by the purest accident they turn out to be strict perimortem duplicates in the sense that at the moments of their respective deaths they have exactly the same bodily matter in the same bodily organization. After two hundred years of sweeping around the universe the matter that once made up one body at its point of death just happens to come to make up another, exactly similar, body at its point of death.

This, I am prepared to bet, will never happen. All I maintain is that such perimortem duplicates are what I shall call "per se possible," which is to say there is nothing in the essence of human bodies that precludes the possibility of perimortem duplicates.

How does the per se possibility of perimortem duplicates show that it is mistaken to appeal to the bodily criterion to secure the possibility of personal resurrection on the Great Day?

Well, if the bodily criterion is to underwrite the possibility of resurrection by reassembly then it must be wedded to some auxiliary principle that implies that *exact* reproduction of a perimortem bodily state brings a body back into existence. If less than exact reproduction will do it, then surely exact reproduction will do it.

So, here we get to the red meat, partly so called because it is not that easy to digest. Let us begin with a definition.

---

form of the beast or fish that devoured them and of which they now make a substantial part . . . And yet far more impossible will this reintegration be, if we put the case that the dead man was devoured by cannibals; for then, the same flesh belonging successively to two different persons, it is impossible that both should have it restored to them at once, or that any footsteps should remain of the relation it had to the first possessor.

Robert Boyle, *Selected Philosophical Papers of Robert Boyle,* ed. M. A. Stewart (Manchester University Press, 1979), 198.

A body *y* at *t* reproduces a body *x*'s perimortem state if and only if *y*'s matter and organic form at *t* is identical at every level of analysis (for example, atoms, organic molecules, cells, organelles, organ, body) with the matter and organic form of *x*'s perimortem state.

Then our auxiliary principle will be

Necessarily, if at some time *t* after the death of a body *x* a body *y* comes together out of simple elements in such a way as to reproduce *x*'s perimortem state then *y* is numerically the same body as *x*; that is, *y* is the very body *x* come back into existence.

The idea is that if the bodily criterion is to do effective eschatological duty, it must be the case that the exact reassembly on the Great Day of the bodily matter of a given perimortem body into the perimortem state of that body is none other than the re-creation of the very body that once died.

Now, any such principle, if true, will not be true simply as an accidental matter, a matter that could vary from one possibility to another. It must be true thanks to the nature of bodies. Accordingly, this auxiliary principle will be necessary if true.

But now, surely it is possible, if only in principle, that bodily matter be reorganized in a way that reproduced the perimortem state of a given person. This could be the act of a very powerful God with the capacity to draw together whatever matter he needs, and then organize it as he sees fit, or it could happen by the most unlikely accident; that is, its happening does not essentially depend on an act of God.

It seems to follow from this that the common perimortem state of *two* perimortem duplicates could be reproduced after their deaths. The one body that then results would be the body of *each* of the perimortem duplicates.

But recall the bodily criterion: Necessarily, a person survives where his body does, for a person is identical with his body. So long as we set aide a certain metaphysical conceit,[22] we are stuck with the absurd consequence that two distinct people have become identically one and the

---

[22] I have in mind a position on which the auxiliary principle is replaced by a principle governing when two non-identical body stages make up the same four-dimensional worm. Then we might say, in the fashion of David Lewis, that the two perimortem duplicates remain distinct *but become exactly coincident* in the afterlife. This idea is discussed in the section titled "Are We Worms?"

same. This yields a sheer contradiction given the necessity of distinctness, the principle that any two distinct things are necessary distinct and so could not ever become one and the same.

THE ARGUMENT ANATOMIZED*[23]

In summary form, we may set out the argument from perimortem duplicates as follows:

1. Necessarily, two distinct things cannot become identical with one. (Necessity of Distinctness)
2. Necessarily, if at some time t after the death of a body x a body y comes together out of simple elements in such a way as to reproduce x's perimortem state then y is numerically the same body as x; that is, y is the very body x come back into existence. (The Auxiliary Principle)
3. Necessarily, the re-creation of a person's body is the re-creation of that person. (The Bodily Criterion)
4. It is possible that there be two people who have the same perimortem bodily state and then that a body y comes together out of simple elements at some later time t in such a way as to reproduce that common perimortem state. (Assumption)
5. It is possible that two distinct people become identical with one person. (From 2, 3, and 4, contradicting 1.)

It is clear that the resultant absurdity—the implied contingency of numerical distinctness—should be blamed not on the bodily criterion but on the auxiliary principle that needs to be added to the bodily criterion in order to underwrite the possibility of personal resurrection. After all, we could drop the bodily criterion of personal identity and yet still get a violation of the necessity of identity at the level of bodies.

So those who simply advocate the bodily criterion of personal identity can insulate themselves from this argument by denying the auxiliary principle, say by denying that the body can have either an intermittent or a scattered existence, in the manner of a disassembled artifact. They

[23]From here on, when an asterisk is attached to the heading of a section, it is an indication that the section will be primarily of interest to philosophical specialists and may be skipped by the non-specialist reader without much loss.

could, for example, argue that the survival of a given body depends on the survival of the particular token dispositions to life functions that maintain that body. (Peter van Inwagen does just this.) When the body dies those particular token dispositions come to an end *forever*, even if the same type of dispositions are reproduced in a duplicate body reconstructed from the same matter. In this way a friend of the bodily criterion will be led to say that there is no possibility of re-creating a body after it has died and rotted away.[24]

To see that it is the auxiliary principle that is at fault consider this argument:

6. Necessarily, if at some later time *t* after the deaths of body *x* and a body *z*, a body *y* comes together out of simple elements in such a way as to reproduce both *x*'s perimortem state and *z*'s perimortem state then *y* is numerically the same body as *x* and numerically the same body as *z*; that is, *y* is the very body *x* come back into existence, and *y* is the very body *z* come back into existence. (A direct consequence of the auxiliary assumption)

7. Necessarily, if *y* is the very same body as *x*, and *y* is the very same body as *z* then *x* is the very same body as *z*. (An upshot of the logic of identity restricted to bodies)

So,

8. Necessarily, there are no distinct bodies *x* and *z* with the same perimortem state such that *y* comes together out of simple elements in such a way as to reproduce both *x*'s perimortem state and *z*'s perimortem state.

The conclusion, 8, is false. What 8 represents as impossible, or necessarily not so, is indeed incredibly unlikely, but not impossible. Because 7 is a matter of the logic of identity, the falsehood of 8 is to be blamed on 6, a direct consequence of the auxiliary principle. So, once again we see that the auxiliary principle is false.

But absent the auxiliary principle there is no getting bodies to the

---

[24] For direct difficulties with the bodily criterion of personal identity itself, and what is now called "Animalism," see my "My Body Is Not an Animal," in D. Zimmerman, ed., *Oxford Studies in Metaphysics*, vol. 4 (Oxford University Press, 2006).

afterlife by exact reassembly. And how could less than exact reassembly do the trick, if exact reassembly does not?

Bodies are stuck in this life, unless something very weird is happening at death.[25]

MUNDANE NECESSITY*

To respond that 8 is in fact *true*, because God would not allow perimortem duplicates to arise, is not to understand the full force of the problem of perimortem duplicates. Conceptually speaking, this response brings God in "too late." Although the idea that God comes in "too late" is a somewhat technical idea, it is a very useful idea, worthy of some discussion. After all, in the face of the old worry about the cannibals, someone might have just insisted that God actually monitors their diet, metabolism, and time of death, precisely to avoid messy complications on the Great Day. That response also brings in God too late. But what does "too late" mean when we are dealing with what is necessary and what is possible?

There thus remains a clear sense in which the logic of even the venerable argument from cannibals, an argument that has been around for much longer than a millennium, has not as yet been adequately clarified!

The whole issue turns on the kinds of necessity that might ground claims like

> 8. Necessarily, there are no distinct bodies x and z with the same perimortem state such that y comes together out of simple elements in such a way as to reproduce both x's perimortem state and z's perimortem state.

True, it is only possible *all things considered* that there be two people who are perimortem duplicates and who are followed by the relevant exact reassembly if it is not necessary that God prevents this from happening. A supernaturalist could then say that since persons are bodies that are only resurrectible by reassembly, God's essential justice requires that he prevent perimortem duplicates from existing, for if they existed then neither person could be resurrected and then face his or her just deserts.

---

[25]See the addendum to this lecture for an examination of the weird possibilities.

What is wrong with this kind of response to the argument against the auxiliary principle? In what sense does it enter the scene "too late"?

On its surface, the argument against the auxiliary principle seems to have the following form. If the auxiliary principle is true then 6 is true, and since 7 is a logical principle, and 6 and 7 entail 8, then 8 is true; but 8 is not true, so the auxiliary principle is false.

If that is all there is to the argument then the invocation of God's just will as the unexpected source of the truth of 8 would be responsive to the argument, and it would serve as a defense of the crucial auxiliary principle.

But there is more in the argument than that. The argument also shows that if the auxiliary principle is true then 8 is true in virtue of a *purely mundane necessity*, a necessity that holds thanks to the essences of the items (objects, events, times, properties, and relations) mentioned, described, or quantified over in 6 and 7. I say a "purely mundane necessity" because all those items are *mundane* items; that is, they include items like the relation of identity, the relation of reproduction of states, bodies, processes of reassembly, and perimortem states, but they do not include God or the operation of his just will.[26]

If that is right, then the invocation of God's just will as the unexpected source of the truth of 8 is *not* a relevant response to the argument.

Let us check to see that if premises 6 and 7 are true, then they are true thanks to mundane necessities, that is, necessities that hold in virtue of the essences of items other than God and his just will. Premise 7 is the easy one. It is merely a consequence of the principles of the symmetry and the transitivity of identity, restricted to bodies. These principles hold just in virtue of the nature of the relation of identity. It is not thanks to God's just will that if $y = x$ then $x = y$. It is not thanks to God's just will that if $x = y$ and $y = z$ then $x = z$. A will has no room to insert itself *here*.

Premise 6, the direct consequence of applying the auxiliary principle twice over, is true in virtue of a mundane necessity if the auxiliary principle is true in virtue of a mundane necessary. Let us now check the

---

[26]In writing of truths and necessities holding thanks to the essences of certain items and not others I am directly relying on Kit Fine's clarification and subsequent formalization of this crucial notion. See, for example, his "Senses of Essence," in Walter Sinnott-Armstrong, ed., *Modality, Morality, and Belief: Essays in Honour of Ruth Barcan Marcus* (Cambridge University Press, 1995), and "The Logic of Essence," *Journal of Philosophical Logic* 24 (1995).

auxiliary principle to see that if it is true then it is true in virtue of a mundane necessity.

> Necessarily, if at some time t after the death of a body x a body y comes together out of simple elements in such a way as to reproduce x's perimortem state then y is numerically the same body as x; that is, y is the very body x come back into existence.

If this auxiliary principle is true then it is true thanks to a necessity that holds in virtue of the essences of the items it mentions, describes, and quantifies over. These happen to be mundane items; that is, they include items like the relation of identity, the relation of reproduction of states, simple elements, bodies, processes of reassembly, and perimortem states. These items, whose essences are jointly sufficient to ground the truth of the auxiliary principle if it is true, do not include God nor the operation of his just will.[27]

So since the auxiliary principle entails 6, and 6 does not mention, describe, or quantify over items not mentioned, described, or quantified over in the auxiliary principle it follows that if the auxiliary principle is true, then 6 is true in virtue of a mundane necessity.

Since 6 and 7 entail 8, and 8 does not introduce new entities beyond those introduced in 6 and 7, it follows that 8 is true in virtue of a mundane necessity, a necessity that holds thanks to the essences of items like the relation of identity, the relation of replication, times, simple elements, bodies, processes of reassembly, and perimortem states.

So the deep form of the argument against the auxiliary principle is this. The principle entails 8*

> 8*. It is a mundane necessity that there are no distinct bodies x and z with the same perimortem state such that y comes together out of simple elements in such a way as to reproduce both x's perimortem state and z's perimortem state.

and 8* is false.

More explicitly elaborated, the argument is this. If the auxiliary principle is true then

---

[27]The thought that God's will enters in here to secure an identity that would not otherwise hold is a version of identity voluntarism, explicitly argued against in the section titled "Identity Voluntarism, the Last Temptation."

6*. It is a mundane necessity that if at some later time t after the deaths of body x and a body z, a body y comes together out of simple elements in such a way as to reproduce both x's perimortem state and z's perimortem state then y is numerically the same body as x and numerically the same body as z; that is, y is the very body x come back into existence, and y is the very body z come back into existence. (A direct consequence of the auxiliary assumption.)

But we also have

7*. It is a mundane necessity that if y is the very same body as x, and y is the very same body as z then x is the very same body as z. (An upshot of the logic of identity restricted to bodies.)

So,

8*. It is a mundane necessity that there are no distinct bodies x and z with the same perimortem state such that y comes together out of simple elements in such a way as to reproduce both x's perimortem state and z's perimortem state.

But, 8* is false, so the auxiliary principle is false.

Someone who says that *thanks to the essential justice of God* there cannot be perimortem duplicates has thereby offered no reason to doubt the falsity of 8*. Indeed, he may be thereby giving a kind of argument for the falsity of 8*, namely that there is no such mundane necessity; the only necessity in the vicinity is guaranteed only thanks to the just will of God.

All that follows from the objector's claim that *thanks to the essential justice of God* there cannot be perimortem duplicates is the claim that 8 is true.[28]

This means that God's just will does not eliminate the problem posed by perimortem duplicates. That problem shows that the auxiliary prin-

---

[28] Again, the idea of a necessity holding in virtue of the essences of some entities and not in virtue of the essences of other entities is an idea that Fine has done so much to make clear. Even if the essences of things derive from the essence of God, there are still some (necessary) truths that hold thanks to those derivative essences, such as the truth that I am necessarily self-identical. The specification of the truths that are grounded by those derivative essences will include many necessary truths. The subclass of these that makes no reference to God and his will are mundane necessities in my sense.

ciple is false. Without the auxiliary principle the bodily criterion does not underwrite the possibility of resurrection by reassembly.

In the same way, God's just will does not eliminate the problem posed by certain cannibal diets. That problem, properly worked up, could also be used to show that the auxiliary assumption is false.

"Christian Physicalism"

Does this failure of the bodily criterion to underwrite resurrection mean that there is no room for a Christian materialism, a view of resurrection which allows that the mind or soul is wholly dependent on the body, and so dies with the body?

Not yet, for it looks as though Neo-Lockeanism can come to the rescue! Neo-Lockeanism can make materialist sense of the resurrection while rejecting the bodily criterion of personal identity, and so allowing that one's postmortem heavenly body is not identical with one's perimortem body.

As it turns out, this is the very strategy pursued by the gifted theologian Nancey Murphy in her recent (2006) defense of Christian materialism, *Bodies and Souls, or Spirited Bodies*. She prefers to title her position "Christian physicalism" rather than "Christian materialism" on the plausible ground that "materialism" now connotes a godless worldview. Despite being a physicalist about persons *as they stand in the present dispensation*, Murphy anticipates her own resurrection in a new spiritual body, thanks to the fact that such a body could secure the memories, capacities, emotional orientation, and character that she takes to be the essential features of her person. (Following what she reads as a theme in Pauline theology, Murphy supposes that in the *Eschaton* there will be new body-constituting stuff governed by new laws of nature that work to secure a perfected alternative version of the present material world.)

She writes:

> I suggest that one's body provides the substrate for all the personal attributes discussed above: it is that which allows one to be recognized by others; that which bears one's memories, and whose capacities, emotional reactions and perceptions have been shaped by one's moral actions and experience. It is an empirical fact, in this

life, that these essential features are tied to a spatio-temporally continuous material object. Thus while spatio-temporal continuity is
a necessary part of the concept of a material object, I suggest it is
only a contingent part of commonly accepted concepts of the person. That is, all the personal characteristics as we know them in
this life are supported by bodily characteristics and capacities, and
these bodily capacities happen to belong to a spatio-temporally
continuous material object, but there is no reason *in principle* why
a body that is numerically distinct but similar in all relevant respects could not support the same personal characteristics.

This recognition allows us to avoid tortuous attempts, as in the
early church, to reconcile resurrection with material continuity.[29]

Our argument so far suggests that we should agree with Murphy, at
least to this extent: The prospects of Christian physicalism as a theologically coherent doctrine depend on the viability of Neo-Lockeanism.

We may illustrate the Neo-Lockean idea of resurrection on the Great
Day in this fashion: Think of the mind of God as including a vast store-
house of complete individual concepts of all of the dead, down to the last
details of their physical makeup. By re-creating that physical makeup, be
it out of matter or "spiritualized" matter, God may be making *a new
body*, but given Neo-Lockeanism he will also be resurrecting the *very
same person* who lived on earth. This is because the re-creation of the
very same kind of physical makeup, with or without any of the same
matter that inhabited the original body, will provide the dead person
with a unique psychological continuer. On the Neo-Lockean criterion of
personal identity, that unique psychological continuer will *be* the original person. Though bodies may be merely duplicated there, the afterlife
will not be a world of mere duplication of persons. Resurrection will be
the literal re-creation of a person.

To better understand that idea, consider an analogy that escapes

---

[29]Nancey Murphy, *Bodies and Souls, or Spirited Bodies* (Cambridge University Press, 2006), 141.
For some complaints that Murphy has not made her position on personal identity fully clear, in
effect that she sometimes seems to hover indecisively between the bodily and the psychological
criterion, see Lynne Rudder Baker's review in the online publication, *Notre Dame Philosophical
Reviews*. Myself, I think that Murphy's remarks about the early Church's struggle with issues of
material continuity (the cannibals and the like) make her position quite clear.

being blasphemous only by being farcical. I mean the analogy between the mind of God and a Teleporting machine. We are all familiar with the fantasy presented in *Star Trek* and the like. A human being gets into a machine that records all the information about the micro-details of his brain and body. The machine sends that information to a remote location, where a duplicate brain and body, exactly alike in all cellular and chemical detail, is created from ambient atoms. Once one understands how the machine is supposed to work, one can see that so long as the machine stores the relevant information, the creation of the new brain and body may be delayed, even unto the Great Day. And so the mind of God can play the role of the storage capacity of the machine; by drawing on this vast storage capacity at the Day of Judgment, God can create living bodies that duplicate the perimortem bodies of all the dead. A person can thus survive in the next world in a *different* body, so long as that body uniquely continues his psychological life, and so his consciousness.

What are we to say of this? Has the great Protestant theological ambition of expunging the Platonic and Aristotelian legacy from Christianity finally been achieved by Neo-Lockeanism?

There are various well-known objections to Neo-Lockeanism. Some say that the mentalistic criteria the Neo-Lockeans rely on are, like Locke's own criterion of experiential memory, fatally circular, in that they presuppose facts of personal identity. Then it is said that we can imagine a person's surviving a procedure resulting in total psychological discontinuity, and that there is no reason in the end to discredit this kind of imagining. Finally it is said that absent David Lewis's in the end implausible account of fission,[30] Neo-Lockeanism will violate the plausible principle that whether a person considered at one time is identical with a person considered at a later time depends entirely on the relationship between these persons, and not on anything else.

None of these objections, I believe, really gets to the core of the issue.

There is a much more systematic difficulty with Neo-Lockeanism, one that has yet to be appreciated. And on top of that, there is a further, purely moral, difficulty with the appeal to Neo-Lockeanism in order to underwrite the possibility of the resurrection.

[30] Lewis, "Survival and Identity."

How Do We Know *What* We Are?

However great the ambition of religious doctrine to foreclose on what a person is, that ambition is necessarily limited by our mundane, which is to say *this*-worldly, knowledge of what we are. That knowledge, though far from complete, emerges in the context of our mutual availability, one to another. Persons, human persons, are in some ways the things we know most about; for as long as humanity has existed we have been tracking each other, addressing each other, living with each other, caring for each other, and fighting each other. The framework that makes all this possible is a this-worldly mutual availability of persons, one to another; a framework that massively constrains the range of tenable answers to the question of what persons actually are and could be. So the view from this life, as it were the view from the lower half of El Greco's painting, determines in significant part *what it would be* for one of us to survive over time, and so what it would take for one of us to survive in any afterlife.

Therein lies the inevitable authority over the afterlife of a *Lebensphilosophie*, a philosophy from the side of this life, a philosophy of our concrete lived experience. It tells you what life is, and so what it would take to continue it.

Twenty years ago, in the essay "Human Beings" whose opening lines Alexander Nehamas quoted in his generous introduction, I appealed to one aspect of this mutual availability of persons in order to defend an answer to the question: What kind captures our essence and so determines our conditions of survival over time?[31] I relied on the easy and offhand ways in which we track each other in order to suggest that anything that deserves the name of a human being must be available in those ways. I suggested in passing that if we respected this simple way in which we are mutually available, then we can find a detailed metaphysical argument that shows why Neo-Lockeanism fails.

---

[31] Mark Johnston, "Human Beings," *Journal of Philosophy* 84 (1987), reprinted in M. Tooley, ed., *Metaphysics* (Garland Press, 1993), in J. Kim and E. Sosa, eds., *Metaphysics: An Anthology* (Basil Blackwell, 1999), and in *Postgraduate Foundation in Philosophy* (Open University Press, 2002). Alexander quoted the beginning: "Most of us hope for a kind of philosophy that is precise without desiccating its object, so that the results of a philosophical investigation might answer a question which was still worth asking."

In print and elsewhere, many have urged me to make explicit the argument to which I then referred.[32] So now, at last, I will make that argument explicit. The argument will go some way toward eliminating any remaining account of the resurrection that tries to make its peace with the enormous evidence of the dependence of the mind on the functioning of the brain.

Previously, when it came to philosophical theorizing about personal identity, the popular methodology—"the method of cases"—had been to collect "intuitions" about real and imaginary cases of personal survival and ceasing to be, and then bring those intuitions into some sort of reflective equilibrium that bore on the question of the necessary and sufficient conditions for an arbitrary person's survival, as it might be, same body, same soul, or same consciousness. Imagined cases were treated as more or less on a par with real cases; for the then natural idea was that we should not restrict our evidence base to the adventitious experiments of stepmotherly nature when we could also avail ourselves of the ingenious thought experiments found in science fiction and the philosophy journals.

Here, analytic philosophy found itself following Locke's own method. Indeed, Locke's own little circus of imaginary cases, including the Self-Conscious Little Finger, the Mayor with the Consciousness of Socrates, the Person with Distinct Personalities by Day and by Night, and, of course, the Famed Rational Parrot, still figured in the discussion.

SAVING COGNITIVE LABOR BY OFFLOADING

There are a number of reasons why the Lockean method of cases, with its implied parity of the real and the imaginary, should be rejected. First, the specific necessary conditions on our survival, conditions that are the upshot of our common essence, need not be available to armchair, or "a priori," reflection. It is after all a Lockean point, one suggested by Locke's own distinction between nominal and real essence, that our real essence cannot be discovered by attention to our concepts but only by empirical investigation into what is in fact the case. Second, in the massive core of

---

[32]See, e.g., David S. Oderburg, "Johnston on Human Beings," *Journal of Philosophy* 86 (1989), and Denis Robinson, "Human Animals, Human Beings, and Mentalistic Survival" in D. Zimmerman, ed., *Oxford Studies in Metaphysics*, vol. 4 (Oxford University Press, 2006).

cases of ordinary survival from day to day, many sources of evidence for personal survival, such as persistent bodily integrity and mental continuity, converge and agree, whereas the whole philosophical charm and supposed utility of the imagined cases in the literature on personal identity lie precisely in teasing these elements apart. The obvious question arises: Might we not have thereby *undermined* our ability to make good judgments about personal identity when considering these very cases?

There is a third point, which will loom large in what follows. When we take the trouble to look, we do not find much evidence that in tracking objects and persons through time we are actually deploying knowledge of *sufficient* conditions for cross-time identity. Instead, as a matter of empirical fact, it appears likely that nature saves us inferential labor by having us "offload" the question of sufficiency onto the objects and people themselves—if I may put it that way.

The idea of offloading can be expressed by means of a motto, "I don't know what the (non-trivial) sufficient conditions for identity over time are, but I do know a persisting object when I see one." Objects of various kinds are salient to us, they attract our attention, and we track them through space and time. Those objects either survive or fail to survive, as an objective matter of fact, determined by their respective natures. As long as they do not manifest changes we know to be destructive to things of their kind, we are ready to credit them as having survived, even if we remain properly agnostic about what their persistence actually consists in. So we should be prepared to discover that in tracking objects we are deploying knowledge of *some* necessary conditions for their survival over time—the thing can't explode into smithereens, for example—but not of any non-trivial sufficient condition. The objects just take care of themselves in this regard: they either persist or cease to be; to *witness* such outcomes we need not know any sufficient condition for their continued existence.

Accordingly, our perceptual system can save us inferential labor by exploiting an independently existing structure there in our environment. In disclosing persisting rather than merely momentary objects to us, our perceptual system allows us to offload what would otherwise be the cognitive task of stitching together momentary objects into persisting wholes by way of necessary and sufficient conditions for being included in the persisting whole.

We "offload" then onto a class of objects when our basic way of tracing or reidentifying them is *criterionless*, in the sense of not employing
sufficient conditions for cross-time identity so as to move from neutral
evidence to a conclusion concerning the identity over time or persistence of objects in the class. There is no such inference, explicit or implicit. After all, outside of detective cases, we seem uninterested in the
allegedly neutral evidence that would provide the minor premises for
such an inference to the conclusion that a person or an object is still in
existence. Instead, the persisting objects capture our attention at various
times and, crucially, *over* time; that is, they capture our attention *as* persisting objects, not as objects whose persistence has to be inferred by
way of a criterion of persistence.[33]

If we are "offloading" in the case of persons, it should be very bad
news for those philosophers who suppose that our intuitions about the
survival of people in imaginary cases are *manifestations* of an implicit
grasp of "genidentity" relations that would stitch together short-lived
entities like phases or temporal stages into significantly persisting wholes.
A genidentity relation is a necessary and sufficient condition for two
temporal stages (or phases, or temporal parts) to be stages of the same
persisting four-dimensional object. But as to the sufficient conditions,
they are precisely *what we do not need to know* when we are tracking
salient objects that are naturally individuated anyway.

Are we offloading in the case of personal identity? The relevant empirical facts revealed by psychology are both suggestive and complex.
The evidence from the study of object-perception suggests that we are
quite generally offloading, and that persons or human beings are not
exceptional "objects" in this respect. Human beings capture our attention at various times and *over* time, as when we see them moving or hear
them talking. Here, too, it seems that we perceive the motion of these
"objects" and hence their identity over time *directly*, that is, not *by* perceiving their varying positions and states at different times, and then
somehow inferring to facts of personal identity over time. (The motion
detection system and the place location system are, counterintuitively,
relatively independent psychological systems, as the waterfall illusion
and other motion/place illusions bring out.)

---

[33] This is related to the very surprising fact that we perceive the motion of objects, and hence their
identity over time, directly, that is, not *by* perceiving their varying positions at different times.

But some evidence from the study of the child's primitive theory of mind suggests that it may be more complicated than that. As well as off-loading onto human beings, we seem to have a habitual interest in the minds of animals quite generally, which is manifested in a primitive and developmentally early "dualism" of mind and body.[34]

So the upshot of empirical psychology might be that we are both offloading onto human beings, or perhaps human animals, *and* working with inchoate sufficient conditions for the persistence of their ostensible minds or souls or selves. If that is true then it would predict the central, and difficult to resolve, dispute found in the philosophy of personal identity, the dispute between those who argue that a human person is an animal and those who suppose that a human person would go where his or her mind goes.

THE OVERALL PLAN OF THE LECTURES

These various possibilities will be sorted out over the next few lectures. In this lecture and the next, I shall adopt the hypothesis that we track persons by offloading. In the third lecture, I shall take up the idea that we trace persons, or more exactly "selves," by means of an *evidential* criterion like this: numerically the same human body, therefore numerically the same mind; numerically the same mind, therefore numerically same person or, more exactly, numerically the same self.

The relevance of all this to the great mortalist attempt to make sense of the General Resurrection may be signposted in the following way, even if the signposts will not be fully understood yet.

As we have seen, the mortalist attempt cannot coherently rely on the bodily criterion of personal identity; instead it stands or falls with Neo-Lockeanism. Yet if we are tracing persons by offloading then what we are tracing cannot be things whose conditions of identity are given by the Neo-Lockean criterion. (This is the burden of the rest of this lecture and part of the next.) Alternatively, if we are tracing persons, or more exactly

[34]There is some empirical evidence that quite early on we employ a double-track approach to tracing animals and selves, evidence sometimes described as showing that young children are natural mind-body dualists. See J. Bering, "The Folk Psychology of Souls," *Behavioural and Brain Sciences* 29 (2006): 453–62, and J. Bering, C. Hernández-Blasi, and D. Bjorklund, "The Development of 'Afterlife' Beliefs in Religiously and Secularly Schooled Children," *British Journal of Developmental Psychology* 23 (2005): 587–607.

selves, by a criterion like numerically the same mind, therefore, numerically the same self, then the Neo-Lockean criterion fails as an account of our criterion of sameness of mind because it is too complicated a criterion for the youngest person-tracers and "I"-users to employ. "Same mind" can point to two different situations; it can amount either to same stream of consciousness or to same mental "bed" in which a stream of consciousness might flow. The Neo-Lockean account might be, or might be adapted into, a fair account of what it is to have the same stream of consciousness; but we are not employing that inevitably complex account when we trace ourselves or others. (This is argued for in the third lecture.)

The other possibility is that we are relying on a criterion of numerically same mind, numerically same self (or person), where sameness of mind is understood as sameness of consciousness in the sense of the persistence of the same mental "bed" in which a stream of consciousness flows. In that sense, numerical sameness of mind appears as a manifest fact in our own case, a fact we just take for granted; while in the case of others it is taken as a fact correlated with numerical sameness of body, where sameness of body in its turn is made available by offloading. Despite this general *correlation* of sameness of self and sameness of body, there remains the conceptual possibility of this self being resurrected with a numerically different body.

What rules that out? Have we not here found a way to make the afterlife conceptually available and, therefore, given the resources of supernaturalism, actually available, without reliance on the immaterial soul? Is this not, at last, a vindication of the great Protestant ambition to purge the promise of the resurrection of its Greek encrustations?

No, it is not. For it will transpire that insofar as numerical sameness of mind is manifest in our own case, it is the numerical sameness of a merely intentional object. And the persistence of something—"a self"— whose persistence depends on the persistence of a merely intentional object is not a rational object of concern.

That negative result, established in the third lecture, not only closes down the great Protestant ambition, it also entails that there is something confused about the very idea of *non-derivative* self-regarding reasons for action or preference. The apparent rational force of such *basic* "de se" considerations turns out to be founded on one or another metaphysical confusion. They can thus be seen to have no force. What is left are the reasons of universal impersonal concern, arguably the reasons valorized by the command of *agape*, or radical altruism. These can be applied, de se, to one's own case, for one is another as well, but there are no basic reasons that derive from one's own case as such.

That discovery about the structure of reason can be put together with an equally surprising claim about personal identity, a claim argued for in the fourth lecture. This is the claim that we are in a certain way Protean; that the concrete realization of our natures and thus of our conditions of our persistence over time are, in a certain way, determined by our pattern of future-directed concern. When this future-directed concern takes the form of *agape*, the only rational structure of concern given the incoherence of *basic* "de se" reasons, one's concrete realization allows for a variable and multiple constitution over time; one becomes one of those who is present wherever and whenever future persons are found. One quite literally lives on in the onward rush of humankind.

So, those who see through the self and adopt the outlook of *agape* will literally survive death. Of course, their individual personalities will not; but to them, lacking as they do any pure de se preference for their *own* individual personalities, this will be no great loss. The future will be full of individual personality and its flourishing. That at least is the hope and goal of those who share the outlook in question.

In the course of all this, several novel things will be demonstrated, but the thesis that we are Protean is not something that can be *demonstrated* in the course of half a lecture. I present it in the fourth lecture to make it come alive as a possibility, and I hope to defend it in more detail elsewhere. For those who find it too radical a thesis to be accepted on such an abbreviated accounting of the relevant considerations, let me offer the conditional, which is anyway interesting: If we are Protean then *agape* is identity-constituting in a way that makes for survival in the onward rush of humankind.

For those who reject the antecedent outright, there may still be something worthwhile on offer—a detailed account of the illusion of the self, of the consequent emptiness of non-derivative de se reasons, and of the irrationality of fearing one's own death, where this is felt and seen as something that goes beyond the thing that has happened billions of times, namely the closing down of the psychophysical life of a human being.

Put *surviving* death to one side for the moment. To the extent that understanding can shape feeling, and of course it is the presupposition of this kind of philosophy that sometimes and to some extent it does, these last considerations may help in *overcoming* death, that is, diminishing the threat of death to the one who is dying. (That is you, me, all of us.)

Overcoming death will be a matter of degree, and will correlate with the degree to which one has a good will, that is, to the degree that one lives in accord with the demands of *agape*. So here, too, the good stand to death in a different way from the bad. Of course, those who are already in this way good do not need the philosophy to help them. Philosophy is here defending the coherence of the ideal of goodness in the face of naturalism and the large-scale defects of human life. But philosophy may also undermine the alternatives to that ideal by demonstrating their irrationality.

It leaves the psychologically most impenetrable case: the death of the beloved other. Mourning is a process whose stages must be respected. It would be ham-fisted and obscene to try to interfere with the logic of mourning by prematurely appealing to the irrationality of purely de se attachment, the attachment not to the dead beloved as such, but to him or her as "*my* child" or "*my* lover."

The only hope is that with time the agony will pass and that the one who is left behind will be able to turn again toward reality and the real needs of others. By then, the moment when the appeal to the irrationality of purely de se attachment might have been relevant will have also passed.

Philosophy is very far from being everything, but that does not mean that it is nothing.

ENDURANCE, PERDURANCE, AND "THE SAME THING AGAIN"

Let us now return from this overview of the lectures to the argument at hand.

The hypothesis of this lecture and the next is then that our cognitive system "offloads." For the very simple purposes of tracking and recognition, we need not know, and do not know, sufficient conditions for identity over time. The developmental facts, for example, the very early age at which we begin to track objects and persons, seem to support this hypothesis.

Trying to make our implicit knowledge of sufficient conditions for identity explicit by examining our reactions to merely possible cases will be a particularly pointless task if the hypothesis of offloading is correct.

So far, that is just a point about method; but the point can also be parlayed into a substantive result about personal identity, namely that the Neo-Lockean account of survival is not an account of *our* survival. To put it simply, this is because if we are offloading then contrary to Locke's suggestion, we are in fact tracking substances, or more generally what I once called "enduring" things, and not the bundles of remembered acts and experiences that make up Lockean or Neo-Lockean persons.

There are at least *three* philosophical conceptions of substance. The most demanding incorporates the idea that a substance must be ontologically independent, so that no level of ontological analysis will properly treat it as some other item modified a certain way. Set that conception aside. The least demanding characterization of a substance is that a substance is a thing at the bottom of the hierarchy of predication; thus a substance is said to be "a bearer of properties that is not itself a property." That will seem insufficient to those who believe in events as well as substances, for events also seem to be at the bottom of the hierarchy of predication. I would say the same for species, understood as higher-order individuals. Species are not predicated; it is membership in a species that is predicated.

The third conception of substance augments this least demanding characterization by requiring that anything that deserves the name of "a substance" has, at each moment of its existence, a power of self-maintenance, development, and persistence (at least relative to its natural environment), which would have to be cited in any adequate account of what it is to be the substance in question. Something like this seems to be behind Aristotle's idea that "the individual man and horse" are among the paradigm sublunary substances. Consonant with the Aristotelian tradition, we may further require that the essence of a complex substance involves a form or principle of unity, a relation among its possibly varying parts which is such that if it holds at a given time then the substance exists at that time and has a power of self-maintenance, development, and persistence (at least relative to its natural environment).[35] In the case of a living thing, a paradigm substance in the sense under discussion, the form or principle of unity is *dynamic,* in that its holding of certain organic parts or cells may allow or require that the parts it holds vary over time—either by those very parts undergoing intrinsic change, or by their being replaced with parts of the same kind, or by their being shed without replacement. So in a living thing, the organic matter is unified into that living thing by a multitrack disposition to such life functions as ingestion, assimilation, excretion, growth, tissue healing, and so on and so forth. Whenever the living thing is present that multitrack disposition is present, and it is organizing some organic matter or other, related by a long series of matter exchanges to its original matter, so as to maintain a categorical basis for that very multitrack disposition. So we can say what it is to be a given living thing—we can in that sense capture the essence of the living thing—by saying that it is some appropriate sort of organic matter organized by a certain multitrack disposition, so as to maintain a categorical basis for that very disposition. This provides the content of the idea that a substance has a power of self-maintenance and hence persistence *in it*, at least relative to its natural environment.

On this conception of substance, it is also natural to require that anything that deserves the name of a substance persists by *enduring*, which is to say that it has all of its essence present at each time at which it is present.[36] So in the case of a living thing, at each time at which it is pres-

---

[35] For a more complete development of this view of a substance, see chapters 4 and 5 of my "Particulars and Persistence" (Ph.D. diss., Princeton University 1984), and my "Hylomorphism," *Journal of Philosophy* 103 (2006), where many issues from my thesis are taken up.

[36] This, and not the more familiar condition that an endurer be wholly present at each moment of its existence, is a better characterization of "endurance" that is then to be opposed to "perdurance," in the now familiar terminology first introduced in "Particulars and Persistence." Unfortunately, that work's gloss on endurance in terms of being wholly present, a gloss taken up by David Lewis in *On the Plurality of Worlds* (Oxford University Press, 1986), has now become standard. That should stop; for given this account of endurance, it is quite unclear how a variably constituted entity, one that is capable of gaining and losing parts, can even be a candidate to be an enduring entity. (Are all of the parts it has over time to be present at each time? Of course not! But then which parts are to be wholly present at each time?) Yet many enduring substances *are* variably constituted.

The reader familiar with perdurance and endurance will see in the text that follows the germ of an argument to the effect that endurers are perceptually easier to attend to and probably epistemologically more basic than correspondingly *long-lived* perdurers. (Short-lived perdurers, for example, short events like noises and flashes, may simply capture our attention, without the subvention of a grasp of genidentity conditions.)

ent, there is some appropriate sort of organic matter present, and its self-maintaining disposition is present. That is *all* of its essence, at least its intrinsic essence, namely its matter and form. (The question of essential origins will be discussed below.)

In respect of allowing for offloading, substances and other enduring things contrast with what I once called *perduring* things, which are not such that all of their essence is present at each time at which they are present. We do have to bring a criterion of identity or genidentity to bear in order to get a long-lived perduring thing determinately in mind, or so I shall argue.

This completes the conception of substance that is useful for present purposes; substances are in essence items that have in them a self-maintaining power of persistence, embodied in some matter sufficiently complex to sustain that power. A substance presents just such an essence at any time at which it exists. This manner of persisting is what enables us to offload onto substances. What is present at a time objectively determines *what it would be to have the same thing* at a later time.

In respect of their manner of persisting, substances are to be contrasted with what I will call "cross-time bundles" and "successions"; items that persist from one time to another by having distinct phases or distinct partial manifestations of their total reality present at the two times. We may think of a cross-time bundle in the following way. It is present at any time at which one of its phases or temporal parts is present, in the same way in which I am present wherever one of my material parts is present. The bundle's being present at a time consists in its phase or temporal part existing at that time, just as my being present where my foot is consists in my foot existing there. Any cross-time bundle that is a candidate for being one of us essentially persists; it could not be an instantaneous existent, like a sheer punctuate event.[37] So the candidate cross-time bundles consist of events and states that exist at different times, events and states tied together by a cross-time principle of unity. So if we restrict ourselves to the reality of such a bundle at a time, a phase of the bundle, we are not thereby capturing the essence of the bundle. What it is to be the bundle

---

Though we have stipulated that our second sense of substance requires that a substance be an endurer, it is arguable that not all endurers are substances. See the reply to Gilbert Harman in the question-and-answer section.

[37] For a defense of this claim, see the section titled "Are We Stages?"

involves something more than what is going on at the given time. It lies in the essence of such a cross-time bundle of phases that there should be more to it than what is present at an arbitrarily chosen time. The then present phase itself hardly constrains just which bundles include it. That depends on what has happened elsewhere and else-when, and on the available cross-time unity conditions or "genidentity relations" that can bundle phases together.

So I say that a cross-time bundle does not have all of its essence present at each time at which it is present, just as I do not have all my essence present at each *place* at which I am present. For example, not all of what is essential to me is present where my foot is. (In fact, none of what is essential to me is present where my foot is. I could lose my foot and still be me.) Not all that is essential to the history of New Jersey is present now. The cross-time bundle of states and events that is the history of New Jersey "perdures" through the times at which it has proper temporal parts, just as I could be said to perdure through those spatial regions where I have proper material parts.[38]

So cross-time bundles perdure through time. The same could be said of a succession of substances, say, the succession of my pets since I was three. That parade of favored animals is not such that its essence is present at each time at which it is present; at one time it was the essence of Whiskers that was present in the parade, now it is the essence of Jasper that is present in the parade. But the parade's essence is to be a parade of animals, not to be a cat or a dog.

---

[38]Perhaps we should not say that I exist in the region occupied by my foot. How can I exist in a region when my whole essence is not within that region? Likewise, in some moods, I feel we should not say that the cross-time bundle exists at each time at which it has a temporal part. For example, although this semester has temporal parts, and even instantaneous temporal parts, it seems wrong to say that this semester exists at this instant; only an instantaneous phase of the semester exists at this instant. I am in favor of shorter semesters, but it is not coherent to hope for an instantaneous semester. It lies in the essence of a semester to last more than an instant.

Maybe, at the end of the day, the thing to say is that there is actually no persistence by perduring, because any four-dimensional worm that takes up a significant period of time does not really *exist at* the various times at which it has temporal parts. For at none of those times does the whole essence of the four-dimensional worm exist, and how can a thing exist at a time at which its whole essence does not exist?

We already seem to take such a view of events. Events don't persist through time, they take up time. Is this connected with our reluctance to say that momentous events are now existing, as opposed to now *occurring*? Four-dimensionalism would then be seen not as an account of persisting objects but as a theory that replaces them with long events. As far as I can tell, Russell and Quine would have had little problem with this understanding of their views.

We can offload onto substances, for at any time at which they capture our attention all of their essence is present before us; at any such time the basis of their natural power to persist is present. Without taking any specific view of what that basis consists in, or even any specific view of the conditions under which it would persist, we can rely on there being such a basis. So even though we do not bring to bear any sufficient condition for the identity of a substance over time, when a substance does capture our attention, there is something in that substance at that time, namely its natural power to maintain itself in a certain way, which settles the question of *what it would be* for the thing that has captured our attention to persist.

Can we offload in this way onto cross-time bundles? Suppose that a phase of such a bundle now captures our attention. There is nothing in that phase which itself selects one cross-time bundle from a host of others as the bundle to which it belongs. There is an enormous variety of genidentity relations that could connect that bundle to this, that, or the other sort of phase in the future. There is an enormous variety of past and present things whose phases could be bundled together with any phase that is present to us at a given time.

Consider, for example, the very unfortunate recent event involving Governor Corzine's car crash. If you had witnessed that event you would have witnessed an event that was part of the history of New Jersey. But you could have only seen or witnessed it *as* an event in the history of New Jersey if you had some conception of what it would take for an event to be bundled into the history of New Jersey. After all, the very same event was also an event in the history of Corzine's administration, and in the history of the United States, and in the history of humanity, and in the history of high-speed crashes, and in the history of carelessness, and so on and so forth.

More restrictive genidentity relations determine shorter-lived bundles of events, and less restrictive genidentity relations determine longer-lived bundles of events. The present phase or event itself determines none of these bundles of events. So which bundle are we tracking, which has captured our attention? Absent our seeing the present phase or event *as* a phase of a bundle of a definite kind, there is no definite answer to that question. And if we are to see the present phase as a phase of a bundle of a certain kind, then we need to have some genidentity condition in mind.

On the bundle view of persons, the object of our attention when we glimpse a person is a phase and, by association, some bundle which contains that phase as its present part. But the phase radically underdetermines the content of, and hence the answer to, the question: What would it be for the bundle that is the object of attention to persist or fail to persist through time? There is no such thing as *the* bundle we are attending to; there are as many such bundles as there are genidentity conditions that apply to the phase. And as the example of Corzine's crash suggests, there are a huge number of those.

If in tracking objects and persons through time we were implicitly or explicitly deploying specific genidentity conditions, then this *would* determine a content for, and an answer to, the question: What would it be for the bundle to which I am now attending to persist or fail to persist? So, if we were deploying genidentity conditions to unite stages of cross-time bundles then the persons we have been tracking might turn out to be cross-time bundles of events or states. Likewise, if we were deploying genidentity conditions to unite substances into successions of substances like the succession of my pets, then the persons we have been tracking might turn out to be successions of substances. But the claim that we are implicitly or explicitly deploying specific genidentity conditions in tracking objects and persons through time is just the denial of the plausible hypothesis of offloading.

So, in tracking ourselves and each other, we have been tracking substances, not cross-time bundles or successions of substances.

The crucial remaining question concerns whether items deemed persons by the Neo-Lockean view can be understood as substances, or only as cross-time bundles or successions of substances. The Neo-Lockean view implies that we are the sorts of things that can survive bodily destruction and replacement. It also implies that we are the sorts of things that survive an interlude of *not existing*. After all, the passing of the signal from the Teletransportation booth to the supposed new destination of the original person takes a finite amount of time. During that time, the person who is supposed to survive the overall process has no bodily or psychological reality! Nor is he constituted by a signal, for the signal is not the sort of thing that could be psychologically (or physically) continuous with a human person. The supposed survivor does not exist during that period.

Here, then, is a pivotal consequence of Neo-Lockeanism: We can intermittently exist. This in itself is not an objection. Some things do intermittently exist. And if there is a general judgment on the Great Day, then absent souls or independent mental substances, the risen dead will have intermittently existed. But if we are serious about the Neo-Lockean account of the Great Day, we should investigate the sorts of things that can be intermittent and ask how it is that they can be so.

THE REAL PROBLEM WITH NEO-LOCKEANISM

I can find no incoherence in the idea of a simple particle "skipping" across time, that is, existing at two times without existing at any time between them. But clearly, on the Neo-Lockean view, or indeed on any plausible view, we are not to be analogized to simple particles.[39]

Complex events like processes, activities, and performances can also be intermittent. During the interlude between the first and second acts of a performance of *Tristan und Isolde*, the performance is not taking place. It has (mercifully, some will say) ceased for twenty minutes or so; it will begin again with the prelude to the second act.

Now, in the last raucous and disorienting moments of the performance of the first act, there is not something with all of its essence present that *is* the performance and incorporates the natural power to generate the prelude to the second act. That power lies in the conductor and the orchestra, who will play the music, and in the stage hands and the stage manager, who will see that the curtain opens, as the libretto requires, upon "a garden with tall trees in front of Isolde's apartment." The performance can be intermittent because these continuously existing items generate it. So, the performance is not a substance. It does not contain within itself, at each moment while it is going on, a power of self-maintenance, development, and persistence that would have to be cited in any adequate account of *what it is to be* that performance.

The performance should instead be modeled as a cross-time bundle of phases made up by events and states, phases united by a genidentity condition that might be something like: One phase is a phase of the same performance of *Tristan und Isolde* as a later phase if and only if they are

---

[39]See the remarks on Roderick Chisholm's view in lecture three.

in the ancestral of the relation of being the immediate next phase of a performance of *Tristan und Isolde;* where one phase is the immediate next phase of a performance of *Tristan und Isolde* if and only if the same company (of singers, musicians, and stage hands) produced both phases, and the later phase followed in sequence from the earlier in accord with the score, libretto, and stage instructions of the work *Tristan und Isolde.*

So there will be a non-trivial sufficient condition for the last phases of act one of a particular performance to be stages of the same performance of *Tristan und Isolde* as the first phases of the prelude to act two. And that condition will not require that the last phase of act one be anything like a substance, whose always present essence would involve a power of self-maintenance, development, and persistence that will itself under normal conditions bring about the first phases of act two.

We can distinguish two ways, among many, of attending to *what is going on* during a performance of *Tristan und Isolde.* One may simply be attending to the music, the singing, and the acting—simply drinking it in, however it happens to go. A child may do this at her first opera. Or one may also be attending to the particular performance and evaluating *it*, say by comparison with near ideal performances (such as the fabled June 1937 Covent Garden performances).

Notice that the second sort of audience member, but not the first, would have *made a mistake* if he sat down at the Met expecting the performance of an opera, and the conductor raced the orchestra through the prelude to the first act of *Tristan*, but only as the introduction to a lecture about the music of Wagner. For this listener would have heard the prelude *as* the opening of a performance of the opera; perhaps he then doubted whether the same frenetic tempo could be kept up throughout the whole performance.

If one's object of attention includes not just the music, the singing, and the acting but the unfolding performance of the opera, then one has to be seeing and hearing the phases of the opera *as* parts of a performance of an opera. And there is no way to do that without deploying knowledge of what a performance of an opera is. And that involves at least implicit knowledge of what is sufficient for one phase of such a performance to be a phase of the same performance as another phase.

I believe that what here applies to performances applies to cross-time bundles of phases in general. To trace such a bundle is to perceive phases in the bundle *as* parts of the same bundle. And that involves at least implicit knowledge of what is sufficient for one phase of such a bundle to be a phase of the same bundle as another phase.

The best explanation of what we are, consistent with the surprising claim that we can intermittently exist, is that we are either psychologically continuous cross-time bundles of events and states or potential successions of substances that exhibit those events and states. A succession of substances, like the succession of my pets since I was three, can also be gappy. There can be times when there is literally nothing to it, just like a Neo-Lockean person between his death and the Great Day. A complex self-maintaining substance, by contrast, cannot come back from the existential grave. It cannot have, as Locke put it, "two beginnings of existence." Even if one such substance causes an exactly similar substance to come into existence a few seconds after the first has ceased to be, what we have is one substance being replaced by another.

We argued earlier that in tracking ourselves and others through time, we are offloading; that is, we are relying on the ever-present power of self-maintenance, development, and persistence of salient substances, rather than deploying sufficient conditions for bundling phases together, to allow for a determinate fact about what it would be to have the same thing as the thing now present at some later time. At a very early developmental stage, we already seem to be tracking people, say, by the age of two, just to opt for a conservative estimate. It is plausible that we do not then have knowledge of such sufficient conditions.

We can now see why we might be led to reject the Neo-Lockean view of persons, that is, of *us*, on systematic grounds. To set out the promised argument:

1. When it comes to a cross-time bundle at a given time, what we can simply see at that time is only a present phase of that cross-time bundle. And when it comes to a (potential) succession of substances at a given time, what we can simply see at that time is the present "stand-in" substance.

2. We can only have a particular cross-time bundle as an object of visual attention and subsequent thought if we see a present phase *as* a phase of that cross-time bundle. And we can only have a particular (potential) succession of substances as an object of

visual attention and subsequent thought if we see a present
substance *as* a stand-in for that succession.

3. We can only see a present phase *as* a phase of a cross-time bundle
   and we can only see a present substance *as* the present stand-in of
   a (potential) succession of substances if we are employing a cross-
   time unity condition for the bundle or the succession, that is, if
   we are not offloading.
4. The Neo-Lockean treatment of persons counts them as either
   bundles or successions. (This is the best explanation of the fact
   that the treatment allows for the intermittent existence of something that is not a mere simple.)
5. But particular persons, and not just their present phases or
   present stand-ins, are objects of visual attention and thought.
   (Otherwise we could not see persons as persisting, and we could
   not have them in mind as the persisting objects they are. Our
   thoughts and judgments about personal identity would lack the
   content that they do in fact have.)
6. So if the Neo-Lockean treatment of personal identity is correct,
   then we are deploying a cross-time unity condition for the
   bundles or the successions that are persons; that is, we are not
   offloading.
7. We are offloading. (Hypothesis)
8. So, the Neo-Lockean treatment of personal identity is not correct.

THE MORAL PROBLEM WITH THE APPEAL TO NEO-LOCKEANISM

There is another problem with the appeal to Neo-Lockeanism in the
context of the afterlife. In that context, we are looking to Neo-Lockeanism
as an account of personal identity that could underwrite a system of
supernatural Divine justice, something that is in part a system of compensatory justice.

Now some who have a claim on supernatural Divine justice, if there
is such a thing, are not yet persons in the Lockean or Neo-Lockean sense
and may never come to be so, at least in this life. They are not thinking,
intelligent, or reflective beings that can "consider themselves as themselves at various times and places." They do not as yet have intentions.
They may have indeed have experiences, but memories of those experi-

ences are not yet being set down. The world may indeed present to them, but it only presents in ways that they are unable to distinguish from dreams or bodily sensations or fantasies, so that even talk of belief may be premature in their case. They are not persons in Locke's sense, and their nascent psychological life is quite minimal. Continuity of memory, intention, and belief—the crucial relations around which the Neo-Lockean account is built—just do not get a purchase in the case of these beings.

I am talking of course of midterm (and perhaps earlier) fetuses. You might try altering Neo-Lockeanism so that it allows for identity-making psychological continuity even when there is such minimal psychological life, but this would just bring out the sheer implausibility of supposing that the persistence of such a minimal psychology is what makes the fetus, or anything it naturally constitutes, the very same thing over time.

So, as others have noted, Neo-Lockeanism would be refuted, or at least badly embarrassed, as a theory of our identity over time if we were once midterm fetuses. But that is not the objection I wish to press here.

The relevant objection arises from the fact that many of these midterm fetuses die, and indeed some of them die by neglect or violence. They thereby suffer a great loss, the loss of a life that they otherwise would have had.

Now I can understand a naturalist supposing that there just is nothing to be done about this, besides taking legal measures against neglect and violence. But once we are taking seriously a system of supernatural Divine justice, in part a system of compensatory justice, there *is* something more to be done about this. A midterm fetus who is the victim of deadly violence, who dies by the hand of man rather than by the hand of God, deserves compensation, at least if it is morally considerable, at least if it has what philosophers call "a moral status."

Something else follows from supernaturalism, or at least from the forms of supernaturalism that are applicable here. Because a midterm fetus has the natural capacity for developing and then deepening its relation to God, it does have a moral status. This is, for example, part of the point of the theist's insistence that "a fetus is a person." This is not the obviously false claim that a fetus is a Lockean person, capable of conceiving of itself as itself at various times and places. It is the very discussible claim that a fetus, at some stage of its development, has the same moral status as a Lockean person.[40]

It would be very odd for a Judeo-Christian supernaturalist to back away from this claim. For if there is a God who cares about us then each midterm fetus does have the natural capacity to develop and thereby deepen its relation to God.

With this supernaturalism in place, consider an unjustly killed midterm fetus. (I offer no views on the conditions under which a fetus counts as unjustly killed; I just say it sometimes happens.) Such a fetus is certainly worthy of being resurrected in order to be given the chance of developing and deepening its relationship with God. It is, as is often said, an entirely innocent victim. One would be hard-pressed to find a better candidate for divinely instituted compensation in the afterlife. One wants to say: if compensation is not extended here, there is something deeply amiss with the whole economy of Divine justice by way of the afterlife. (Hence the old idea of the *limbus infantium*.)

But no application of the Neo-Lockean criterion can make the afterlife available for such midterm fetuses. And we have already seen that the bodily criterion cannot make the afterlife available either to fetuses or to those who develop from them.[41]

Are We Worms?*

Actually, we do have some unfinished business with the bodily criterion. The argument that it could not be consistently pressed into service to underwrite the resurrection depended, as you will remember, on setting aside what I called "a certain metaphysical conceit."

I meant an account of fusion proposed thirty years ago by David Lewis. Although Lewis developed this account by way of defending Neo-Lockeanism about personal identity, the account can be readily adapted to the bodily criterion of personal identity.

The presupposition of Lewis's account is that we persist by perduring,

[40]Typical is G.E.M. Anscombe's use of this idea of a person in her "Twenty Opinions Common among Anglo-American Philosophers," in Mary Geach and Luke Gormally, eds., *Faith in a Hard Ground* (Imprint Academic, 2007). Thanks to John Haldane for drawing my attention to this collection of essays.

[41]For more on Christian reliance on the bodily criterion and the like, see the addendum to this lecture.

specifically by consisting of different temporal parts at different times. Those temporal parts are bound to the times at which they occur. They exist only at those times. When temporal parts are not themselves built out of shorter-lived temporal parts they are instantaneous or arbitrarily short-lived, depending on the underlying structure of time.

On the standard version of this account of persistence, the account accepted by Bertrand Russell, W.V.O. Quine, and Lewis himself, a person is a four-dimensional "worm," that is, a cross-time mereological sum of momentary stages.

A "mereological" sum is a certain sort of whole, one that has the least demanding condition for its existence. A sum exists at a time just in case at least one of its parts exists at that time. Thus a worm, or mereological sum of momentary stages, exists whenever one of its stages exists.

So the idea is that persons are spread out over time in much the same way as they are spread out over space. Just as a person may be taken to have spatial parts in the various spatial regions he occupies, he is supposed to have temporal parts at the times or intervals that he occupies.

The trick is then to come up with a genidentity condition that determines when two person stages are part of the same person or four-dimensional sum of person stages. The bodily criterion and the Neo-Lockean criterion can each be reformulated as genidentity conditions, as accounts of when two person stages are stages of the same person.

Given this background, Lewis's idea about personal fusion can be presented in the following way. Suppose you wake up and find another person alongside you, a person who is connected to you at the hip. You and the other person remain distinct people, but you share a common spatial part, say, a part consisting of part of a hip bone and some surrounding flesh. You overlap spatially. This is a very unlikely occurrence, but it is in no way paradoxical. It is simply a matter of sharing spatial parts at certain times.

The paradox we blamed on the combination of the bodily criterion and the idea that a body can come back into existence by way of exact reassembly, the paradox of two things becoming one, can now be avoided given the persons as worms view.

For on the persons as worms view, the situation is this: Two spatio-temporal worms start out with distinct temporal parts and continue having distinct temporal parts through their earthly lifetimes. But each is such that their last earthly temporal part is genidentical to a person stage in the next world. This is a very, very unlikely occurrence, but it is in no way paradoxical. It is simply a matter of sharing temporal parts at certain postmortem times.

Two distinct persons (bodies) have not become one person (body) in the afterlife. That *would* be incoherent. Instead, what has happened is that two distinct persons (bodies) have become entirely coincident in the afterlife. In this life, these persons or bodies were made up of different temporal parts, whereas in the afterlife the two persons or bodies share exactly the same temporal parts.

Do we here have a way of using the bodily criterion to underwrite the possibility of resurrection by way of exact bodily reassembly?

No. There are three difficulties with this use of the four-dimensionalist account. The first has to do with the four-dimensionalist account of persons as such, while the second and third have to do with the application of that account to the particular view that persons are bodies or animals that can come back into existence after reassembly.

To begin on the first difficulty: Many philosophers pressed Lewis for an account of person stages, and he obligingly replied by saying that person stages were short-lived person-like things, things that were as person-like as they could be, consistent with their being so short-lived. Now a person stage is included in a person when that person is a maximal or most inclusive sum of those person stages interrelated with that stage by the relevant genidentity relation. Persons and person stages thus differ in their temporal length and in the properties that flow from that difference.

Now there is an enormous multitude of mereological sums of person stages intermediate in length between short-lived person stages and the maximal sums that are persons. Some of these intermediate sums are so long-lived that had things gone otherwise they would have made up a complete person. There is, for example, me for my first ten years, then me for my first ten years and one-tenth of a second, and so on and so forth.

These long-lived person-like things are, as it were, packed together in my life—not spatially packed, but packed along the dimension of time. It is important to note that they are not in any way defective entities on the four-dimensional view. They are all perfectly good mereological sums, no better and no worse as sums than the maximal sum that is the person I am. Most of them are physically and psychologically *more* unified than the persisting person they partially make up. And they are not ontologically derivative from persons, any more than the engine and the first three carriages are ontologically derivative from the whole train they partially make up. It is just that each fails to be a person only because of what happened *after* it ceased to be.

The trouble is that these long-lived person-like things are *sufficiently* person-like to deserve the special respect that we extend to persons. It would be arbitrary to deny them that respect because of what happened *after they ceased to exist*.

It is this that opens up a Pandora's box of difficulties.

For one thing, it makes practical nonsense of deliberation involving those future benefits that require sacrifices before they are achieved. As well as the one person deliberating (the *maximal* sum of physiologically continuous and connected person stages), there are a huge number of sums stacked within this maximal sum who are very person-like and whose interests deserve respect. But those interests radically conflict, for these person-like sums cease to be at different times. On Lewis's view, within the life of what we call a "single person" a huge number of very person-like things will undergo sacrifices whose positive fruits they can never enjoy.

For another thing, it raises apparently insurmountable difficulties for any account of the operation of Divine justice in the afterlife. Many fall into corruption after having lived relatively innocent and blameless lives. And that means that there have been huge numbers of very person-like things whose blameless existence is not recognized and rewarded in the afterlife.

Now let us turn to the two problems that attend the application of the four-dimensional account to the particular view that persons are bodies that can come back into existence after exact "reassembly."

The first such problem concerns the disjunctive and gerrymandered character of any genidentity condition that would fit with this proposed application of four-dimensionalism.

Once one goes four-dimensionalist about human bodies, one will need to articulate a genidentity condition, a necessary and sufficient condition for temporal parts being parts of the same four-dimensional human body. That is not easy to do while allowing for both the possibility of bodily re-creation from perimortem matter and the possibility of perimortem duplicates.

If, for example, the four-dimensionalist wants to allow for bodily resurrection on the Great Day, then he is looking at a commitment to a genidentity principle that admits intermittent bodily existence, that is, something along the following lines.

> If a bodily temporal part x at t consists of the very same matter formed in the same way as a bodily temporal part y at t^* then x is a temporal part of the very same four-dimensional body as y.

This does secure the possibility of the resurrection of the body, but it is inconsistent with the possibility of perimortem duplicate bodies. (Duplicate bodies are two bodies and not one body.) In effect, what we described as a case of perimortem duplication would be redescribed, utterly implausibly, as itself a case of *very brief* bodily resurrection.[42] All the ways of allowing for returning to existence by way of reassembly that block this implausible consequence seem to involve quite gerrymandered genidentity conditions.

When it comes to this life, our four-dimensionalist does best by mimicking the idea that a living body or animal exists at separate times only if its token dispositions to life functions persist from the one time to the other. But when it comes to the next life, he has to allow that reassembly is enough. That makes for a disjunctive and to that extent rather gerrymandered, or "unnatural," genidentity condition.

So what, you might say. This just comes with the territory if you are trying to make sense of bodily resurrection by reassembly. That is right, but this sort of gerrymandered genidentity condition leads to a serious—I think disabling—difficulty for the application of four-dimensionalism to the view that persons are essentially bodies that can be resurrected by reassembly.

Apart from some fine distinctions that need not detain us here, the bodily criterion is effectively the view that we are essentially animals, that is, things that survive if and only if the animal they are survives. Now, we do, I think, offload onto animals, and at a very early age. Ani-

---

[42]This point was made to me by Eden Lin. A further observation is that the principle counts strict reproduction of body states at any two times as a kind of bodily return or resurrection.

mals capture our attention; we see them running and ruminating, without our having in mind much of a criterion of what it would take for them to appear from moment to moment. They just, in fact, do appear from moment to moment, and we notice this. The four-dimensionalist, for what now should be familiar reasons, will find it hard to make sense of our easy, criterion-free access to persisting animals, at least given how he represents persisting animals. And this must count against his view of the things we call "human animals." For those things, along with everyday facts to the effect that they have just moved or, as it might be, stayed still, are readily accessible to us, without any knowledge of the genidentity criteria that distinctively pick out human animals. We just see human animals *as* moving or *as* being still, and this involves seeing them as persisting from moment to moment.

That whole extended pattern of "seeing as" would be explicable if what we encountered in a momentary encounter with a human animal was a thing that itself determined the relevant cross-time identity conditions for itself. But that is just what short-lived human animal stages do not themselves do. There is no uniquely natural way for them to be bundled together.

Suppose we now suspend that last claim and allow the four-dimensionalist about animals to say that there *is* a uniquely natural way for such stages to be knitted together into a persisting whole. We need not know what it is, but given a human animal stage, there is a uniquely natural genidentity relation that fixes one of, or at least a very limited range of, the otherwise huge multitude of persisting individuals as candidate items to which we could attend by way of attending to the momentary human animal stage.

In this way, the four-dimensionalist might be able to make sense of the fact that we offload onto persisting animals, human animals among them. We are able to have them, as it were, the four-dimensional "worms" themselves, as objects of attention and thought, even though we are perceptually presented with mere momentary stages of these worms.

It should now be quite clear, and this is the point of the foregoing, that the natural genidentity relation in question, the one that works as a default because of its naturalness, cannot be the disjunctive, gerrymandered relation. For the this-worldly disjunct, namely that two stages are stages of the same person only if there is a continuous body life that connects them, is far more natural than, and is less gerrymandered than, the disjunction of which it is a part.

This means that even if there are in fact resurrectible beings around us, we are not by default seeing or thinking of *them* when we see or think of human animals or human bodies. We are thinking of and seeing temporally more restricted beings, beings whose genidentity condition guarantees that bodily death is their eternal end. When we hope for postmortem existence for ourselves, the human animals or human bodies we supposedly are, that hope is empty.

I conclude, then, that the Lewis view of fusion cannot be satisfactorily employed to help the bodily criterion underwrite the possibility of resurrection by strict bodily reassembly.

The cannibals, or at least their more exacting descendants, the perimortem duplicates, still have the upper hand.

Are We Stages?*

Many have simply rejected David Lewis's account of fusion out of hand just *because* it allows for exact coincidence of objects. For example, in the case of interest we are supposed to have two people located in the very same body on the Great Day. And that in itself may seem odd or repugnant.

In "Constitution Is Not Identity" I noted that a four-dimensionalist could avoid admitting that objects can be in the same place at the same time by identifying objects not with worms but with instantaneous stages, and then saying that temporal predications of the form

Lumpl will F

are made true by facts like

Lumpl stands in the appropriate genidentity relation to a future stage that is F.[43]

---

[43] Mark Johnston, "Constitution Is Not Identity," *Mind* 101 (1992), reprinted in Michael Rae, ed., *Material Constitution* (Cornell University Press, 1995). See the discussion of the "third theory of temporal predication," described as the analog of David Lewis's theory of multiple counterpart relations (90–93).

Against the stage theory, I followed John Perry in arguing that objects persist, that is, exist at different and significantly separated times, and that while the longer-lived "continuants" built out of stages arguably do this, the instantaneous or near instantaneous stages do not. So the four-dimensional continuants built out of stages are better models for ordinary objects than are the stages themselves. I also suggested that the stages, if instantaneous, do not really *undergo* change. For something to undergo change *it* has to be there before and after the change, and to be there before and after *it* has to exist before and after. Again, the sums or four-dimensional continuants arguably satisfy this condition, but the instantaneous stages do not, except on a Pickwickian sense of "it."[44] So the attempt to resort to stages to avoid coincidence of objects at times seems at odds with the facts of persistence and change.

Someone might say that there are other senses of "change" and of "persistence" that can be defined. Such a person might respond to the worries just raised by suggesting that it is wrong to understand persistence as entailing existence at successive times, and just as wrong to understand undergoing change as entailing being around before and after the change.

In "All the World's a Stage" and elsewhere, Ted Sider defends the stage view on the ground that it avoids coincidence of objects. He writes,

A[n] objection is that on the stage view, nothing persists through time. If by "Ted persists through time" we mean "Ted exists at more than one time," then the stage view does indeed have this consequence. But in another sense of "persists through time," the stage view does not rule out persistence through time, for in virtue of its account of temporal predication, the stage view allows that I both exist now and *previously* existed in the past. Given that the stage view allows the latter kind of persistence, I think that the denial of the former sort is no great cost.[45]

---

[44]Dickens's character Mr. Samuel Pickwick allowed himself the privilege of using words in nonstandard senses.

[45]Ted Sider, "All the World's a Stage," *Australasian Journal of Philosophy* 74 (1996): 446. See also his *Four-Dimensionalism: An Ontology of Persistence and Time* (Oxford University Press, 2001). Stage theory is also defended in Katherine Hawley's *How Things Persist* (Oxford University Press, 2001) and by Achille Varsi in "Naming the Stages," *Dialectica* 57 (2003).

The suggestion is that to have previously existed is to be genidentical with a past stage, and to subsequently exist is to be genidentical with a future stage.

One might have thought, however, that the timeless proposition

Ted exists at more than one time

is obviously entailed by

Ted exists now and previously existed as well.

If that entailment holds then Ted cannot be identical with an instantaneous stage. Then the stage theory fails.

The stage theorist has something to say here. He can say that

Ted exists at more than one time

needs to be disambiguated. At least, there are two very different kinds of truthmakers for a claim like this. On one sense or reading of the sentence "Ted exists at more than one time" its truth is at odds with Ted being an instantaneous stage. But on *that* reading the sentence is not entailed by

Ted exists now and previously existed as well.

On the other sense or reading, the truth of the sentence "Ted exists at more than one time" is not at odds with Ted being instantaneous. On this reading the sentence is entailed by

Ted exists now and previously existed as well.

For in this second, less demanding sense, to say that Ted exists at more than one time is just to say that an instantaneous thing Ted is genidentical with some other instantaneous thing at another previous time.

Now if there are two senses of "existing at two times" then there are two senses of "existing at one time." That is, you can be said to exist at a time if you are an instantaneous thing and that time is your defining instant, *or* you can be said to exist at a time if you are an instantaneous thing whose defining instant is not that time and yet you have a representative or counterpart at that time, one related to you by an appropriate genidentity relation.

I take it that for many this will be the sticking point. They will say there is only one relevant way for an instantaneous stage to exist at a time. You can't get to exist at a time t if you are instantaneous and your defining instant is *another* time wholly distinct from t. Once that is settled, it is then of no help to add that *nonetheless* you have a representative or counterpart at time t, one related to you by an appropriate genidentity relation.

If that is right, then we must regard the stage theory as quite generally false, that is, false for tomatoes and sulfur atoms and rainbows as well as for persons.

I am not here asserting that the stage theory is false but only trying to identify the heart of the matter, namely that the stage theory needs to rely on what will seem to many to be a merely Pickwickian sense of "existing at t."

There is a closely related point, which can be put without relying on talk of "senses." The stage theory has a deeply disjunctive account of what it is to exist at a time. But existing at a time is too basic a phenomenon to allow only for such a deeply disjunctive account.[46]

A further question arises when it comes to the application of the stage theory to the particular case of persons. Does anything that is instantaneous deserve to be called a thing that can think, or a thing that can consider itself as itself, let alone at various times and places? The assignment of such capacities to such utterly punctuate entities is none too easy a thing to convincingly pull off. And the same goes for biological capacities, among them the disposition to various life functions that make something a living body. How can an instantaneous thing have a disposition to do something it is not presently doing? The best we can say is that an instantaneous thing gets credited by courtesy with the doings of some of the things that follow and precede it. But now consider those instantaneous stages that follow and precede my present stage. None of those actually completes a thought, for thought is not instantaneous. How is it then that *this* instantaneous stage gets to be able to think by courtesy of its relation to those unthinking things? The ability to think seems to be a disposition that is not able to be manifested either by an

[46]Why "deeply" disjunctive? Well, the stage theorist can note that a stage is trivially, as it were by stipulation, a temporal counterpart of itself, and he can then say in a non-disjunctive fashion that to exist at a time is to have a temporal counterpart at that time. But this superficially non-disjunctive account is still deeply disjunctive, for there are two very, very different ways of having a temporal counterpart at a time. One is by way of being *identical* with that counterpart, and the other is not.

instantaneous stage or by its instantaneous counterparts. A disposition that is not able to be manifested is a very odd creature, except when we are dealing with a case of a disposition being masked or suppressed, such as when a fragile glass is prevented from breaking when struck by having had a structure-supporting plastic mold placed inside it.[47] The case of instantaneous stages, none of which is around long enough to complete a thought, is not a case of a disposition being masked. It is then very unclear how such instantaneous stages could be said to be able to think, and hence be said to be persons.

I confess that I hate instantaneous stages, especially instantaneous person stages.[48] Instead, just to fix ideas, let us say that a person stage lasts a bit longer, say a second. Now there are 86,400 seconds in a day. That is a lot of persons, already too many, even without instantaneous stages. To put the point more exactly, there are many true statements like the following.

> Over the three days in November 1975 after the queen's representative dismissed Gough Whitlam as prime minister there were ten thousand different people protesting on the streets of Australia, and I was one of them.

The number was ten thousand, or thereabouts, and not anything like 3 (the number of days) times 86,400 (the number of seconds in a day) times 10,000, that is, more than two and one-half billion people. The total population of Australia in November 1975 was around 16 million people. (My memory is not all it should be, but I am pretty confident I would have remembered if two and a half billion people had come from overseas to join in the Australian protests.)

That kind of objection has been accepted by the stage theorists. They say that when we take a large historical perspective we refer to the worms and not the stages as the "persons." For example, in defending the stage view, Ted Sider writes,

> In response I propose a partial retreat. The stage view should be restricted to the claim that *typical* references to persons are to person stages. But, in certain circumstances, such as when we take the

---

[47] For an extended discussion of masking, see my "How to Speak of the Colors," *Philosophical Studies* 86 (1992), reprinted in A. Byrne and D. Hilbert, eds., *The Philosophy of Color* (MIT Press, 1997).

[48] Of course, without instantaneous or arbitrarily short-lived stages the whole theory of persisting by perduring breaks down. If a stage *endures* for a second, or even a microsecond, then the game can quickly be seen to be up.

timeless perspective, reference is to worms rather than stages. When discussing the cases of counting roads above, I suggested that we sometimes use "road" to refer to extended roads and sometimes to road segments, depending on our interests. In typical cases of discussing persons, our interests are in stages.... But in extreme cases, such as that of timeless counting, these interests shift.[49]

However, the remark about the protests after Gough Whitlam's dismissal drives home another point, not wholly accommodated by this concession about "extreme cases." In many contexts the pronoun "I" cannot be construed as referring to a stage. Of course, there was during those dark days of November 1975 a person stage that came to be in the genidentity relation to me now. In fact, there were at least a quarter of a million such stages back then. But none of those is included in the reference of "them" in the remark about the protests. For ten thousand was the number of them, and if one of the quarter million of my second-long person stages falls within the reference of "them" then on what grounds are the rest of the quarter million excluded?

The same point applies to other forms of reference to people, as with proper names, and numerically quantified phrases. Kosmos Tsokas was one of the ten thousand as well. Kosmos was one of *five children*, all utterly brilliant in their own way. Unfortunately, Kosmos then joined the Spartacist League of Australia, which on the day he joined had *four members*. And so on. One quickly begins to wonder whether these sorts of counterexamples are rare or "extreme" cases.

In any event, we need not tally up numbers of cases, for the stage theorist who engages in a "partial retreat" is already allowing that there are two legitimate forms of talk of "people" and two legitimate associated forms of temporal predication. The worm theorist says there is just one of each. Whenever the stage theorist sees advantages over the worm theorist, say in the counting of people in Lewis-style fission or fusion, the worm theorist can reply:

Look, you admit my way of talking is legitimate, indeed you admit that it has to be used in certain circumstances, and you say that on my way of talking certain puzzles arise. Are these not then puzzles for you as well? For your way of talking includes mine, along with

[49]Sider, "All the World's a Stage," 448.

your novel proposal that there is another legitimate way of talking.
You can't then comfortably say that my way of talking about the
very cases you cite as favoring your account is just false of those
cases, can you? All you are doing is describing those cases in one
of the two forms of description you have been forced to recognize
as legitimate. How do you yourself handle the consequences of my
legitimate description?

In response to this sort of difficulty, Sider writes,

This admission [the partial retreat] might be thought to undermine my arguments for the stage view. Those arguments depended
on the claim that the ordinary material objects over which we
quantify never coincide, but now I admit that in some contexts we
quantify over spacetime worms, which do sometimes coincide.
However, I don't need the premise that there is *no* sense in which
material objects coincide; it is enough that there is some legitimate
sense in which, e.g., the coin is numerically identical to the lump
of copper, for I can claim that our anti-coincidence intuitions are
based on this sense.[50]

So the stage theory is really misnamed. At least in Sider's hands, it is
the theory that "person" has different legitimate senses, and that on one
of these senses both "persons are stages" and "persons never coincide"
are true. On the other sense of "person" both "persons are worms" and
"persons can coincide" are true.

This, of course, means that there are also two senses of "was F" and of
"will be F" and of each of their cognates. One sense will be given by the
theory of temporal predication that fits stages and the other sense will be
given by the theory of temporal predication that fits worms. A worm was
F at *t* if and only if the worm had an F-ish temporal part at *t*. A stage was
F at *t* if and only if it is genidentical with an F-ish stage at *t*. Or to use
Sider's preferred terminology, a stage was F at *t* if and only if it had at *t*
an F-ish stage that was its temporal counterpart at *t*.

Let us leave this multiplication of "senses" alone for now. For the
really urgent question is whether the stage theory can be a better "retro-
cessionaire" than the worm theory proved to be. Can the stage theory be

[50]Ibid.

used to shore up the appeal to the bodily criterion for the purpose of underwriting the idea of resurrection by bodily reassembly? Can the stage theory here adequately underwrite the underwriter?

If worms made up of person stages are among the things that are legitimately described as "those persons" then they, presumably, are deserving of Divine justice in the next life. So, when it comes to "underwriting the underwriter," what is misleadingly called "the stage theory" will have all the liabilities of worm theory. For once it has allowed itself the partial retreat, the stage theory agrees that worms made up of person stages are among the things that it is legitimate to describe as "those persons."

The stage theory may bring some special liabilities of its own, thanks to its distinctive claim that stages are also among the things that deserve the description "those persons." For even the most corrupt of we worms (if I may put it that way) have had utterly innocent moments, and some of us have had utterly innocent childhoods.

Imagine a stage person Punctilious, who is before us now, and is entirely innocent and has had an utterly blameless history. Under a scheme of Divine justice, Punctilious, the stage that is before us, is in the following *very dangerous* situation. If, years after the stage Punctilious has had its defining moment something is done by *another* stage, then Punctilious will be damned. If, for example, ten years from now there is some other stage who commits an unforgivable sin and this stage is an appropriate temporal counterpart of Punctilious, then Punctilious will have an even later temporal counterpart who is damned, that is, at the very least, denied the benefits of the Divine presence. Given the theory of temporal predication that is appropriate for stages, it follows that if Punctilious has a future temporal counterpart who is damned then Punctilious will be damned.

You might well think that Punctilious now has no real complaint against Divine justice, at least if he understands what is involved in "his" upcoming damnation. For Punctilious *qua stage* never suffers the condition of being damned. But if you are prepared to save Divine justice in that way, then you are undermining its claim to be justice in the contrast cases, such as that of a person who remains good throughout his entire life on earth. Despite this heroic history, the relevant perimortem stage person never *qua stage* enjoys the benefits of the Divine presence.

Further to the issue of whether the stage theory can help underwrite the view of resurrection by bodily reassembly, we should note that the stage theory is built around talk of "temporal counterparts," that is, stages that stand in a relevant genidentity relation to a given stage. Now consider the combination of the theory that persons are identical with bodies (and are essentially so) with the claim that a body can come back into existence if it is exactly reassembled. A stage view of persons that implements this combination will need to rely on a disjunctive genidentity relation, something pretty messy along the lines of the following.

> A later stage is genidentical with an earlier stage just in case *either* it evolves out of the present stage thanks to the continuation of bodily life *or* it is the strict reproduction of an earlier stage that is not followed by later stages that evolve out of it thanks to the continuation of bodily life.

Something like this is required if one is to allow resurrection by reassembly but not implausibly imply that strict stage reproduction across living persons would be itself resurrection. To avoid the further consequence that the case of perimortem duplication is itself resurrection takes a further clause, but what we have is already messy enough.

The thing to see is that we are offloading, at least onto human bodies. They, and their actions and passions, capture our attention, and so we predicate things of them. We do all this at an impressively early age, when we have no such genidentity criterion in mind, either at the level of explicit or implicit "sub-personal" formulation. After all, bodily resurrection *by way of bodily reassembly* after death is a topic that comes up relatively late in humanity's day, whether we are considering human phylogeny, human history, or human ontogeny. It would be bizarre then to suppose that our evolved and relatively hardwired sub-personal psychology already includes a genidentity condition that is specially trimmed and tailored to allow for resurrection by bodily reassembly.

A supernaturalist could say that God has planted the messy genidentity condition in our mind precisely so that we, from early on, can see and think about the resurrectible human bodies around us, and not merely about other unresurrectible things that are temporally truncated variants of the resurrectible human bodies. Why, then, do we not have a flash of recognition, an "aha" experience, when the "messy" genidentity condition is explicitly formulated?

Nor could we get such a genidentity condition in mind by a route often relied on by those who follow David Lewis. Lewis argued that we need something novel if we are to patch up the failures of those reductive accounts of intentionality that make use of causation and descriptive satisfaction. Lewis's proposed patch for such reductive accounts of intentionality is sometimes called "reference magnetism," that is, a mysterious automatic defaulting on our part to thinking about the most natural thing in the vicinity.[51]

Even granting all this, there is no gain to be had here. For the first disjunct of our disjunctive genidentity condition is *more* natural than the whole condition itself. Reference magnetism would therefore predict that the genidentity condition for human bodies that we have in mind by default, and so can use to predicate things of the first human animals we grow up with, is *not* the disjunctive genidentity condition required for resurrection by reassembly. Reference magnetism would predict that the "messy" disjunctive genidentity condition is beaten out by its more natural first disjunct, the one that governs our life on earth.

The upshot would be that the human bodies or human animals we have been attending to from our earliest days are subject to a genidentity condition that *precludes* resurrection by reassembly.

I conclude, then, that the stage-variant of the Lewis view of fusion is not to be relied on to avoid the conflict between the possibility of perimortem duplicates and the version of the bodily criterion that allows for resurrection by strict reassembly. It is *at least* as badly adapted to this end as the worm-variant of the Lewis view.

When joined with our previous results this means that the problem of perimortem duplicates shows that the bodily criterion is not effective in underwriting the possibility of resurrection.

It is beginning to look as if we can know by empirically informed reason that if we are particular bodies or particular human animals, and essentially so, then there is no resurrection by reassembly.[52]

The cannibals, or at least their more exacting descendants the peri-

---

[51] Why "mysterious?" Well, as everyone admits, we obviously do think and talk about "unnatural things." So just how "strong" is the reference-magnetic force, how do we measure it, and what predictions does the strength of the force make when it comes to just what is required to pry us from the natural defaults that are the alleged reference magnets? Please don't just describe the cases, then describe the desired results, and then say that the force is strong enough to get the desired results.

[52] For more on this claim, see the addendum to this lecture.

mortem duplicates, have indeed gobbled up the possibility of resurrection by bodily reassembly.

The Unhelpfulness of Reference Magnetism*

Return for a moment to our main argument against Neo-Lockeanism, namely that since we are not using a criterion for bundling shorter-lived things into persisting persons Neo-Lockeanism leaves us without a way to get to see the persons around us *as* persisting persons, rather than *as* their shorter-lived stages or "stand-ins." And yet, without relying on a criterion, we are indeed seeing and thinking of the persons around us *as* persisting persons.

It should now be clear why the appeal to reference magnetism, that is, to the supposed automatic defaulting on our part to thinking about the most natural persisting thing in the vicinity of person stages or stand-ins, will not be of help in responding to this argument against Neo-Lockeanism.

Suppose you were to express Neo-Lockeanism in explicitly four-dimensionalist terms, complete with a genidentity condition that counted two person stages as stages of the same four-dimensional person just when they were related by psychological continuity, the ancestral of the direct relation of psychological connectedness. Should we suppose that we get such worms in mind as objects of visual attention and subsequent thought by default, because they are the most natural persisting things in the vicinity of the person stages that we are simply seeing at any given time?

No, we should not. For consider the direct relation of psychological connectedness, the relation whose ancestral is psychological continuity, the proposed genidentity condition that is to knit stages together into a four-dimensional whole that is to count as a persisting person. Psychological connectedness holds between successive stages when the later stage has the psychological profile that it does in large part *causally* because of the psychological profile of the earlier stage. Now there are two relevant ways in which this kind of causal explanatory dependence can come to hold. It can hold in virtue of the normal, everyday kind of underlying cause, namely the operation of a single brain. Or it can hold in virtue of very abnormal causes, such as the operation of a Teletransporter, or God's creation on the Great Day of a new brain to match an old brain that has died long before. Now consider these two forms of psychological connectedness, normal psychological connectedness (due to normal brain operation) and psychological connectedness*, the form of psychological connectedness that holds either when normal psychological connectedness holds, or when a Teletransportation machine operates, or when it is the Great Day. Normal psychological connectedness is obviously a much more natural relation, a less gerrymandered relation, than psychological connectedness*, which involves a disjunction of this first sort of causal relation and several other quite different sorts of determinate causal relations, one of which will only happen the Great Day.

It follows that the ancestral of the relation of psychological connectedness is also a more natural genidentity condition than the ancestral of the relation of psychological connectedness*. If there were automatic defaulting on our part to thinking about the more natural persisting person-like thing in the vicinity then when it comes to the genidentity condition for personal identity, the ancestral of the relation of psychological connectedness* would be systematically beaten out by the ancestral of the relation of psychological connectedness. So if we get from simply seeing a person stage to seeing it as a stage of a persisting person thanks to the default mechanism that associates a more rather than less natural genidentity condition with the person stage, then the persisting beings around us that we first regard as persons—our parents, our siblings, our playmates, ourselves—will actually be counterexamples to Neo-Lockeanism! They will not be capable of surviving Teletransportation, nor will they come back on the Great Day, even if God creates for each of them his or her own unique mental continuer. For normal psychological connectedness does not hold across such brain-destroying events as Teletransportation and bodily corruption.

The combination of four-dimensionalism with reference magnetism is at odds with Neo-Lockeanism. Of course, you might say that all that has been shown is we can't get persisting Neo-Lockean persons in mind by default. But the argument was that a constraint on truly deserving the description "persisting person" is being the sort of thing that can be by default an object of visual attention and subsequent thought. For, we do not get persisting persons "in mind," we do not have them as objects of visual attention and subsequent thought, thanks to our bringing to bear on the shorter-lived items we experience a metaphysical criterion of personal identity.

ONLY SOULS CAN SAVE US

Given the defects of both the bodily criterion and Neo-Lockeanism as ways of underwriting the possibility of entry into the afterlife, our intermediate conclusion should be this: Christian eschatology does stand or fall with the legacy of Plato, namely the immaterial soul, which could carry the identity of the deceased to the Last Judgment. The removal of the Platonic and Aristotelian legacy from Christianity, one of the defining ambitions of Protestant theology from Martin Luther to thinkers as various as Rudolf Bultman, Karl Barth, Emil Brunner, Paul Tillich, and Oscar Cullman, looks to be an operation the patient cannot survive. The availability of the afterlife, and hence the coherence of any appeal to the afterlife to meet the threat of death to the importance of goodness—all this depends essentially on the immateriality of the soul.

This happens, by the way, to be the traditional Catholic teaching, and it is also accepted by some contemporary Protestant philosophers such as Alvin Plantinga and Dean Zimmerman.[53] But, as we shall see in the next lecture, the demonstration of the dependence of supernaturalist Christianity on the immaterial soul is something of a Pyrrhic victory for the traditional Catholic point of view.

QUESTIONS AND REPLIES[54]

Just what is involved in your hypothesis that we offload questions of identity over time onto the things themselves, or more particularly the substances themselves? How would you defend that hypothesis?[55]

Let me then say a little more about offloading, and what I take to be the evidence for it. The first part of the hypothesis of offloading is that in

---

[53]See, e.g., their respective contributions to Peter van Inwagen and Dean Zimmerman, eds., *Persons: Human and Divine* (Oxford University Press, 2006).

[54]In what follows here, and after the text of each of the other lectures, the questions that appear were asked by people who attended or read the lectures. I have noted who pressed the question, when the person was known to me. I hope that I have given the questions their proper force and emphasis; if and where I have failed to do this I apologize to the relevant questioner.

Some of the answers are the answers I *should have* given, or they fill out in more detail the answers I did give. I have omitted the questions that sought clarifications of points when those clarifications were contained in the long text from which the lectures were sampled. It is that text that is here presented in an updated and revised form.

[55]Anthony Appiah.

tracing ourselves and other people, in the easy and offhand ways we do, we are not employing metaphysically sufficient conditions for personal identity.

Now I take it that we are attending to persons *as such* at a very early age; they are among the most salient objects of attention, and we seem predisposed to be interested in them and to get them to take an interest in us.[56] So if we were employing sufficient conditions for personal identity, we must have them from very early on. This is not impossible, but it does not fit well with many empirical results, such as those mentioned in the lecture. There are also the empirical results produced by the study of categorization.

A familiar theme from the cognitive science literature on categorization is this: Where the K (e.g., the tiger, the human being, the frog) is a kind, categorization of individuals at a time as Ks (tigers, human beings, frogs) is not based on exploiting sufficient conditions for being a K; it is based on the actually reliable evidential signs Ks do in fact exhibit. In our cognitive apparatus, these signs, indicia, and symptoms may be organized around a prototype of a K, around similarity to paradigm Ks, or, perhaps more interestingly, around strong evidential criteria for being a K. Here the relevant notion of being a strong evidential criterion for being a K entails that recognizing that the criterion is satisfied gives you a high level of surety that it is a K that you are dealing with. This last, of course, allows for the possibility of error; you may only be dealing with a very convincing counterfeit, or a non-K presenting in an illusory way, or you may be hallucinating. Still, in the absence of defeating evidence against its being a K, you still have a right to a high level of surety as to its being a K.

If categorization of individuals *at a time* is not based on sufficient conditions for being a K, then it is correspondingly plausible that reidentification of individual Ks over time, that is, the tracing of individual Ks through time and change, is not based on sufficient conditions for being the very same K over time.[57]

---

[56] As to how early we are aware of persons as such, there is recent evidence that as early as fifteen months infants are surprised by intentional action that does not fit the perceived reality of the situation. See Kristine Onishi, Renee Beillargeon, and Alan Leslie, "15-Month-Old Infants Detect Violations in Pretend Scenarios," *Acta Psychologica* 81 (2007), which vindicates a crucial empirical prediction of the seminal work of Alan Leslie on pretense.

[57] That is further confirmed by certain cases of "kind misidentification," such as the "Capgras

This is one part of the hypothesis of offloading. Along a certain dimension, we are doing less cognitive work than was supposed by philosophers in the analytic tradition when they used our reactions to real and imaginary cases to try to articulate the metaphysically necessary and sufficient conditions for personal identity through time.

The ideology behind this method of cases and the associated supposition that we must be employing sufficient conditions did have a sensible motivation. If all we are presented with are momentary slices of objects, artifacts, and persons, then doesn't it surely fall to us to knit together momentary things encountered at different times so as to then have definite *persisting* items as topics of our thought and talk?

There is something to the conditional. But the second and crucial part of the hypothesis of offloading is that we are not just presented with momentary items and left to knit them together to make this or that kind of persisting thing.

Here the ontology of substance figures in an important fashion. A substance, in the sense that is relevant here, is something whose present manifestation determines what it would be to have that very same thing again. In this way, a substance differs from a cross-time bundle of stages or events, and from a mere succession of different substances. In dealing with those sorts of things we need to put in the cognitive labor of bringing to bear a specific condition for what it would be to have the very same thing again.

So the hypothesis of offloading has three parts: first, in tracing ourselves and other people we are not employing sufficient conditions; second, that nevertheless our thoughts and judgments involve definite persisting items, and so can be true or false of those items; and third, that this is possible because those items are substances in the sense emphasized. That is, a momentary appearance of a substance is the appearance of something that contains within itself something that determines what it would be to have the very same item again.

---

person" case discussed below in reply to Nicholas Stang. In this example, even though the observer was working with a sufficient condition for being the same "Capgras person," the observer nonetheless had, as the object of his thought and talk, the actual individual human being. That is how the observer came to make a mistake about the persistence of the human being before him. The best explanation of this phenomenon is that a particular person had captured the observer's attention, both at a time and over time, independently of any metaphysically necessary and sufficient condition for the continued existence of persons over time that the observer might have employed.

This is how we can get by without the cognitive labor of employing sufficient conditions to bind together things encountered at different times. It is not left to us to always set down what makes for sameness; we can offload that issue onto the substances themselves.

Why not think that we employ sufficient conditions sub-personally?[58]

Of course, it might be that somehow our cognitive systems trace persons, artifacts, and material objects over time by using kind-relative sufficient conditions for identity over time. This might happen, as you say, "sub-personally," that is, not in a way that would show up as conscious knowledge of sufficient conditions.

The first question is why the sub-personal system's capacity to trace should be organized around sufficient conditions rather than reliable evidential signs of having one and the same thing over time. (Recall the comparison with classification under kinds, which seems to be mediated sub-personally.) The second question is whether we already have evidence against sub-personally employed sufficient conditions for identity over time. Focus, as we were doing, on the identity of persons over time. If the sub-personal system is employing sufficient conditions for personal identity over time, then it ought to be possible to clearly articulate its implicit principle, say by the method of cases. We produce cases both real and imaginary. Competing accounts of the sufficient conditions implicitly followed by the sub-personal system are then evaluated in accord with how well they jibe with intuitions wrung from these cases. As I argued in the essay "Human Beings," by way of developing a related point first made by Bernard Williams in "The Self and the Future,"[59] when we do this we fall into a certain kind of systematic disarray. The method of cases seems in some contexts to favor the bodily criterion, in others the Neo-Lockean criterion, and in still other contexts we can be induced to react as if we were tracing "bare loci" of consciousness that can survive any amount of bodily and psychological discontinuity. The best explanation of this seems to be that we (or our sub-personal systems) are operating with evidential criteria or de facto reliable signs of personal identity and not with sufficient conditions. In the imaginary cases that produce real conundrums as to the facts of personal identity, the reliable signs,

[58]Ron Mallon.
[59]Bernard Williams, "The Self and the Future," *Philosophical Review* 79 (1970).

the merely evidential factors, such as bodily continuity and psychological continuity, which ordinarily go together, are teased apart. That is why we boggle, or react as if we were employing inconsistent sets of metaphysically sufficient conditions.

So if we take the relevant sub-personal hypothesis seriously, and test it by trying to articulate its principles, we find that a better explanation is that we, or the relevant sub-personal systems, are relying on evidential criteria, not metaphysically sufficient conditions for identity.

Why can't we be offloading onto spiritual substances that are attached to bodies?[60]

Well, I have been ignoring spiritual substances for now in order to concentrate on prospects for the afterlife allowed by the bodily criterion and by the Neo-Lockean criterion. So the real answer to your question will come in lecture two, where I shall argue that there aren't such spiritual or non-material substances there to be traced. But for now, let me admit that there is one way to observe bodily behavior and trace a substance associated with, but not constituted by, the body in question.

Take an analogy: Suppose you live in a marina, where you can watch boats go out to sea. You have a friend who never lets anyone else use his boat, and who goes out regularly just before sunset. So then, given those auxiliary hypotheses, by watching your friend's boat sail out through the channel you can trace his movement as well, even if he is not visible to you.

My point is that our ordinary tracing of other people over time is not in fact like this. We count it the same person very easily, on the basis of signs like physical similarity and some evidence of sameness of character. If we are using auxiliary hypotheses, these are not auxiliary hypotheses connecting a soul or spiritual substance attached to the body whose bodily activity we are observing. If anything, the relevant auxiliary hypotheses connect minds or selves with bodies, and we shall have to see just what minds or selves in the relevant sense are.

Couldn't your strictures on offloading be met by a self-maintaining process as well as by a substance in your sense? And why not conceive of one's mind or consciousness as a self-maintaining process?[61]

---

[60] Adam Elga.
[61] Gilbert Harman.

Often when we talk about a self-maintaining process, like the water cycle for example, we are really talking of a larger substantial whole, like the earth, maintaining a certain consistent operation over time. That is how I think of an individual mind, as really a complex mode of functioning sustained by its associated brain, body, and environment. In saying this I am not endorsing a functionalist analysis of mental states as such, but simply saying that minds are not substantial, and not self-maintaining processes, at least insofar as I have a grip on that idea.

Couldn't the cross-time sum theorist, in effect the temporal stage theorist, model your idea of offloading onto substances, say, by treating the sums of stages that are stages of substances as more natural units, and hence as more "eligible" as David Lewis would have put it, to be objects of attention and thought?[62]

Though it is widely relied upon as the only thing that could make a naturalistic reduction of intentionality work, there are grave difficulties with Lewis's idea of "reference magnetism," the idea that the more natural units are thereby more eligible as referents, that is, as objects of our attention and thought. In the hard cases, you have to let the facts of reference determine what is natural; you can't antecedently predict the facts of reference from an intuitive conception of what is more or less natural. For that reason I think that the relevant modeling by means of reference magnetism won't work. That was the point of asking, "Just how strong is this magnetic force?"

To take an illustrative example, imagine you are aberrant in your view of others and of yourself. You suppose that you have the same person before you if and only if you have the same consciousness before you. You also suppose that a consciousness cannot survive deep sleep, sleep in which consciousness is interrupted. In your view, what happens when consciousness returns after unconsciousness is that a numerically different consciousness and hence a numerically different person comes into existence. Naturally, you have become addicted to coffee, amphetamines, and nicotine; indeed, you will take anything that promises to keep you awake or at least keep you continuously dreaming throughout the night.

So in this case you are actually working with an explicit criterion of personal identity over time, necessary and sufficient conditions for being

[62]Nicholas Stang.

the same person. As one criterion among others it will provide a way of bundling together momentary person stages, restrictions of persons to times, into cross-time persisting wholes.

Despite your aberrant views about the shortness of life, you do have one remaining friend, whom you also take to be a continuously conscious person, that is, one who will cease to exist upon becoming unconscious. Naturally, you try to addict him to coffee, amphetamines, and nicotine, indeed, to anything that promises to keep him awake or at least continuously dreaming throughout the night.

One night, your friend eventually falls into a deep, dreamless sleep. Your cerebro-scope detects the sad fact that all his conscious functioning has ceased. You mourn the death of your friend. When his body wakes up, and the person there still claims to be your friend, you look mournfully at him and nod your head. Even given this very plausible simulacrum of your friend, somehow things are not the same.

Now, suppose, as we do suppose (and later I will ask why), that in actual fact your friend, like each person around you, does survive through periods of unconsciousness. You are thus deeply mistaken about the identity conditions of the people around you, so much so that you are in danger of being diagnosed with Capgras syndrome, the delusion that one or more of your close associates have been replaced by duplicates.

There are two ontological accounts of just what your mistake amounts to. The first account is given by the theorist who supposes that persons persist by perduring. That is, when a person persists through time, that is, exists at successive times, this is because (1) he exhibits at each period of time a short-lived entity exactly co-incident with that period of time, and (2) these short-lived entities—person stages—are *properly* bundled together by a certain criterion, one that is less demanding than the criterion you have been employing. You are wrong because you are using the *wrong method* of bundling arbitrarily short-lived person stages into a persisting person.

The second account of what your mistake consists in is given by the theorist who supposes that in tracking persons you are offloading onto substances that essentially are all there at each moment of their existence, in the sense that they exhibit their essence at each moment of their existence. In the case of your friend, one of these substances captured your attention, and *you* simply held a false theory of the things it could survive.

So far the two theories seem to be on a par. But here is another thing that it would be better to explain rather than simply explain away. In the case of your friend there was no persisting person-like thing whose persistence conditions you were actually right about.

The second theorist can readily explain this; persons are substances, and the only relevant substance (as opposed to the mere qua-object, your friend qua conscious) in the closest vicinity of your friend was a substance whose persistence conditions went far beyond those allowed by your criteria.

However, the first theorist regards persons as cross-time sums of person stages united by a certain genidentity condition, a certain criterion, or set of necessary and sufficient conditions for being in the sum in question. But in the closest vicinity of your friend there are many, many cross-time sums of person stages united by some genidentity criterion or other. Indeed in the vicinity of your friend there is a cross-time sum of person stages united by a genidentity condition that precisely corresponds to your criterion. That will be the sum of person stages united by the condition that they be causally connected in the right way *and exhibit uninterrupted consciousness*. Call this sum a "Capgras person."

Now there are three observations to be made. The first is that the theorist who supposes that persons are cross-time sums must count you as having been right about the persistence conditions of this person-like thing, the Capgras person. The second observation is that the persistence conditions of a Capgras person seem *more* natural in a certain way. The intermittent existence of consciousness is actually quite a surprise. (Descartes, for example, supposed that we must be continuously conscious even in deep sleep.) Abstracting away from it, and allowing that you have the same person even so, may capture our actual view of persons; but this does seem to be replacing a more natural, and more united, cross-time sum with a less natural, and less united, cross-time sum.

The third observation is the most telling, and is best left as a question. How, on the view that persons are cross-time sums, can we reconstruct the facts (1) that you had a certain persisting thing in mind, namely your friend, and (2) that you were wrong about *his* persistence conditions? Given the criterion of persistence you were actually employing, why doesn't the Capgras person turn out to be your object of thought and attention? After all, on the view in question, all we are presented with at a given time is a person stage; the persisting person comes into view as a topic for thought and talk only thanks to the application of a given genidentity condition to this stage. And there is nothing defective about your criterion as one genidentity condition among others.

The theorist who supposes that your friend is a substance, a self-maintaining entity that has all its essence present at any time at which it exists, can say that there is not in the nearest vicinity of your friend any substance with the persistence conditions of a Capgras person. Given that when it comes to identity over time it is substances that primarily capture our attention, it is your friend and not any other person-like thing that primarily captured your attention. That is how you got to be wrong about *him*.

Can we nonetheless make the cross-time bundle theory generate the same result? Here is where you might try to appeal to David Lewis's theory of reference magnetism, namely the theory that the more unified or "natural" cross-time bundles are the ones that are more eligible to be the default objects of awareness thought and talk. You would then have to add the claim that maximal sums of stages that are the momentary manifestations of what we have been calling self-maintainers are *more natural* than the less inclusive sums that admit only the momentary manifestations of self-maintainers that are united by continuous consciousness.

But this second claim seems false. Exhibiting continuous consciousness is a very unifying or "natural-making" feature for a cross-time sum to have. Lewis's view actually pushes you toward denying that you were wrong about your friend. To that extent it is at odds with the natural description of the case.

Substances do not capture our attention because they are more natural than all the qua-objects that come from restricting them; your friend qua continuously conscious may be more united across time, and so a more natural cross-time unit, than your friend. Nonetheless, it is your friend who captured your attention.

Don't you elsewhere suppose that substances could be spatially co-incident or entirely overlapping for certain periods of time? Wouldn't that interfere with offloading, by making it fail due to lack of uniqueness?[63]

---

[63]Edin Lin.

Yes, it would, if it happened at all regularly. But the cases of co-incidence of *substances* that I have described are especially contrived for the sake of showing that this is a bare possibility. Those cases do not show that in the ordinary run of things co-incidence of substances is a common occurrence. Evolution has us exploit the ordinary run of things, so substances turn out to be default objects of attention over time because attending to them requires less cognitive labor.

In the end, however, do you suppose that when it comes to personal identity we are simply offloading?[64]

No, that is just one part of a destructive dilemma against the Neo-Lockean. We are either offloading or we are attempting to trace embodied selves, that is, selves embodied by human beings or perhaps human animals. The Neo-Lockean describes something that we cannot offload onto, and something that is also a bad candidate to be a self.

My own view is that we are attempting to trace embodied selves by offloading onto the human animals that embody them. We use a simple auxiliary hypothesis: by and large, same human animal, same self embodied by that animal. We also get persuaded by neurophysiology that the mere persistence of a brain can secure the persistence of the same self. So we end up thinking that same brain, same self. That is why we think we go where our brain goes. We are tracing embodied selves, and we take it to be the case that those selves would continue on if their associated brains were kept alive and functioning.

Why can't the Neo-Lockean split the difference and describe his theory this way: we manage to track persons by offloading onto a substance, namely a human animal, whose persistence is a reliable guide to the persistence of the person as understood by the Neo-Lockean account?[65]

Yes. Something like that is just what I anticipate. But notice that the persistence of a human animal is a reliable guide to many things which are not Neo-Lockean persons. For example, the persistence of a human animal is a reliable guide to the persistence of the organism that constitutes him, to the persistence of his brain, and to the persistence of his individual personality. But none of these is a person on the Neo-Lockean view.

[64]Carla Merino-Rajme.
[65]John Haven Spencer.

So the Neo-Lockean who employs your suggestion must say something like this: we manage to track persons by offloading onto a substance, namely a human animal, whose persistence we *take to be* a reliable guide to the persistence of the person as understood by the Neo-Lockean account.

This involves attributing to us, as trackers of persons, a *complex* auxiliary hypothesis, namely something like: For the most part, whenever a normal human animal persists, its persistence secures the continued existence of a cross-time bundle of mental events and states united by patterns of psychological continuity and connectedness. There are various problems with this. But the most telling is that the auxiliary hypothesis involves concepts that need not be possessed by all those who are able to track persons. As will be shown in lecture three, psychological continuity and the exact overall constraint of connectedness are quite delicate notions, formulated late in the philosophical day. Yet infants are tracking persons in their first year or so, and children become "I"-users at two and three.

If we are working with an auxiliary hypothesis, as I think we may be, it must be a simpler hypothesis available to be formulated out of ideas more obviously available to the developing child, say, for example, the idea of his mind as a mental place where thoughts and experiences happen—the mind as an arena, as it were. Early on one takes oneself to be an embodied mind and one tracks others as embodied minds by working with the auxiliary hypothesis that if you have the same human animal you have the same mind, and hence the same embodied mind.

As we shall see, the Neo-Lockean account is not an account of a mind in this sense.

ADDENDUM: FROM CORPSE SNATCHING TO IDENTITY VOLUNTARISM

It is very striking feature of the contemporary theological scene that a number of leading Christian philosophers actually take the position that we are animals or that we are identical with our bodies, and so are prepared to face head-on the old worries for the view that our resurrection requires bodily identity, that is, the posthumous existence of *numerically the same* body that once lived on earth.

There are many purely theological questions that arise for these Christian thinkers who take us to *be* our bodies and treat those bodies as *mere organisms*, as having always a merely organic principle of development and continued life. For one example, does this not imply Traducianism, the doctrine that the intellectual and spiritual side of human beings is a product of their natural development as organisms, a doctrine that Aquinas plainly condemns as heresy? And for another, how does the view that we are identical with our merely organic bodies fit with Paul's view that we are resurrected in incorruptible spiritual bodies?

The crucial text here is 1 Corinthians 15:29–55, one of the most influential pieces of writing in the entire history of the West. It is worth quoting in full in order to get a feel for the heavy burden it places on any scripturally guided Christian who supposes that before and after death we have a merely organic principle of continued life, that is, a principle of continued life that could simply be extrapolated from the continuity of organic life leading up to death. Paul writes,

> But someone will say, "How are the dead raised up? And with what body do they come?" Foolish one, what you sow is not made alive unless it dies. And what you sow, you do not sow that body that shall be, but mere grain—perhaps wheat or some other grain. But God gives it a body as He pleases, and to each seed its own body.
>
> All flesh is not the same flesh, but there is one kind of flesh of men, another flesh of animals, another of fish, and another of birds. There are also celestial bodies and terrestrial bodies; but the glory of the celestial is one, and the glory of the terrestrial is another. There is one glory of the sun, another glory of the moon, and another glory of the stars; for one star differs from another star in glory.
>
> So also is the resurrection of the dead. The body is sown in corruption, it is raised in incorruption. It is sown in dishonor, it is raised in glory. It is sown in weakness, it is raised in power. It is sown a natural body, it is raised a spiritual body. There is a natural body, and there is a spiritual body. And so it is written, "The first man Adam became a living being." The last Adam became a life-giving spirit.
>
> However, the spiritual is not first, but the natural, and afterward the spiritual. The first man was of the earth, made of dust; the

second Man is the Lord from heaven. As was the man of dust, so also are those who are made of dust; and as is the heavenly Man, so also are those who are heavenly. And as we have borne the image of the man of dust, we shall also bear the image of the heavenly Man.

Now this I say, brethren, that flesh and blood cannot inherit the kingdom of God; nor does corruption inherit incorruption. Behold, I tell you a mystery: We shall not all sleep, but we shall all be changed—in a moment, in the twinkling of an eye, at the last trumpet. For the trumpet will sound, and the dead will be raised incorruptible, and we also shall be changed. For this corruptible must put on incorruption, and this mortal must put on immortality. So when this corruptible has put on incorruption, and this mortal has put on immortality, then shall be brought to pass the saying that is written: "Death is swallowed up in victory. Death, where is thy sting?"

There is an enormous amount going on in these passages, but so much seems clear: our resurrected bodies will be spiritual bodies, bodies in some way animated by the spirit of God. This, it seems, requires that they will be made of a very different kind of flesh or body-constituting material, material that is not "mere flesh and blood" but a kind of flesh that is incorruptible. The great mystery is that this glorious transformation will not simply happen to the resurrected dead; those still alive on the Great Day will also be "changed" in this way, and changed suddenly, in the twinkling of an eye. Of course, this cannot mean that they are replaced by new and better persons. They will *undergo* this miraculous change.

The anticipated change is something utterly unprecedented relative to anything that ordinarily happens in premortem bodily life, so we can be pretty sure that we will not capture the import of Paul's doctrine of the resurrection of the body if we think of our resurrected bodies as merely organic, as the sorts of things that continue to exist thanks only to operation of those life functions evident in our premortem existence. To give one interpretation of Paul's view of the resurrection in anachronistic—but at least approximately accurate—ontological terms: the essence of a *resurrectible* body is Janus-faced, its principle of unity, the condition that has to hold among the body's constituents for those constituents to make up that very body, has two radically different forms of manifestation. How this really differs from there being two related bodies, a premortem and a post-resurrection body, is a very good question (which I will discuss in the third lecture.) Yet it seems that Paul is in general committed to the idea of the revivification of the very *person* that died. And he has no truck with the persistence of an immortal soul, which is incorruptible by its nature and not thanks to God's miraculous gift. So what else will secure personal identity across the resurrection but the identity of a body?[66]

The gospels are more unequivocal than Paul in their commitment to the revivification of dead *bodies*, for this is the obvious reading of those passages in the gospels in which various distinguished persons are brought back to life.

But let us put these matters aside for now.

Of course, there is no question that Christian orthodoxy requires that one believe in bodily resurrection, *even if* one does not take oneself to be identical with a body (as, for example, Aquinas did not). If bodily resurrection entails the posthumous existence of numerically the same body that lived on earth (as some take Paul to deny), then the Christian philosophers I have in mind will have done all small "o" orthodox Christians a service by explaining how bodily resurrection is possible.

Have they done this?

Can one get to the next world by having one's merely organic body, numerically the same body that died, resurrected?

Corpse Snatching

Peter van Inwagen has been the most influential of the contemporary Christian philosophers who approach the resurrection with the conviction that a human person is identical with his body. Though I believe it can be shown that a person is not identical with his body, it seems clear that van Inwagen has drawn the right consequence from the view that

---

[66]In lecture three we shall consider another answer to this question, one not ruled out by Paul's remarks, for he really only insists that *persons* be revivified.

For a detailed and authoritative account of the Pauline doctrine of resurrection, see Murray J. Harris, "Resurrection and Immortality in the Pauline Corpus," in Richard H. Longenecker, ed., *Life in the Face of Death: The Resurrection Message of the New Testament* (William B. Eerdmans, 1998). Harris emphasizes that Pauline resurrection is at the same time revivification ("resuscitation," as he puts it), transformation, and exultation.

we are identical with our bodies, understood as mere organisms. Our resurrection is then only possible if God does something very weird, or something *unthinkable*, in one or another of the senses of that word.

Other Christian philosophers have tried to avoid this consequence of the view that human persons are identical with their bodies. But I believe that they have failed for reasons I will set out below.

Van Inwagen is rightly interested in *what it takes* for numerically the same organism to survive and hence exist at earlier and later times. He writes,

> The atoms of which I am composed occupy at each instant have the positions they do because of the operations of certain processes within me (those processes that taken collectively, constitute my being alive.) Even when I become a corpse, provided I decay slowly and am not say cremated, the atoms that will compose me occupy the positions relative to one that they do occupy largely because of the processes that used to go on within me: or this will be the case at least for a short period. Thus a former corpse in which the processes of life have been "started up again" may well be the very man who was once before alive, provided the processes of dissolution did not progress too far while he was a corpse.[67]

The (quite plausible) picture seems to be this. To have the very man that was alive, and hence on van Inwagen's view the very body that once was alive, come back to life requires that the same life processes that went on in the living body be "started up again," and this in its turn requires the continuous persistence of some organic basis that allows for such processes, even if it is not actively subserving such processes.

Van Inwagen uses the phrase "a short period." What exactly is the physiological and metaphysical significance of that? When it comes to bodily death, a distinction is commonly made between somatic death, the death of the organism as a whole, and cell death. Somatic death is a global physiological phenomenon; the signs of somatic death are the cessation of heartbeat, breathing, movement, and brain activity. Cell death is a smaller-scale biochemical process in which various cells in

---

[67] Van Inwagen, "The Possibility of Resurrection," 119.

various organs lose the capacity to subserve life functions, that is, those processes that "taken collectively" constituted the body's being alive. Cell death sets in some time after somatic death. That is why the organs of the dead can be usefully transplanted into the living if those organs are recovered quickly enough. Cell death in these organs has not progressed to the point where the organs have lost the capacity to subserve various life functions. As it happens, cell death sets in at different times for different types of cells. Left to themselves, brain cells may survive for about ten minutes after somatic death, while those of the heart can survive for about twenty minutes, and those of the liver for about thirty to forty minutes. (Some estimates of these average times are more liberal, others more conservative.) Freezing of the cells can prolong their "life," that is, their capacity to once again subserve life functions. So the slippery slope from science to science fiction encourages some people to invest in the idea of living again after having been cryonically preserved at somatic death.

Algor mortis, the loss of heat from the body, begins almost immediately after somatic death. Rigor mortis, the stiffening of the musculature after death, begins from five to ten hours after bodily death. By the onset of rigor mortis there has been massive cell death. Practically none of the cells in the major organs is then capable of subserving the processes that kept the person alive. In rigor mortis and thereafter the body exhibits an eerie "stone-cold" feel. The dissolution of the natural bases of the processes that constituted the life of the body is now pretty much complete.

Let us, as a matter of stipulation, say that a "stone-cold body" is one in which there has been a dissolution of the natural bases of the processes that once constituted the life of the body. Once a corpse is "stone-cold" in this sense, there is, it is natural to suppose, no bringing the very body that died back to life by revivifying the corpse. Even if the atoms of the corpse were *miraculously* arranged into the *living* perimortem state of the body of which the corpse is the remnant, this would not be the original body coming back to life. Why? Because the new life processes would not be the reactivation of the particular life of the original body. The atoms that make up the body will have the positions that they do *because of the miraculous intervention* and not because of the operation of the particular natural processes that were the life of the body.

In conformity with this, van Inwagen writes,

Thus if God collects the atoms that used to constitute the man and "reassembles" them, they will occupy the positions relative to one another because of God's miracle and not because of the operation of the natural processes that, taken collectively, were the life of the man.[68]

And so, van Inwagen concludes that God's reassembly of a body's peri-mortem atoms would not *re*vivify that body, and so would not bring that very body back to life.

We can draw a further consequence. Once a corpse is stone-cold, not even God can make the living body that had the corpse as its remnant come back to life. For this would not be the restarting of the life of the body, it would be God breathing new life into the corpse; that is, making it come to live again out of a miraculous creation in it of a natural basis for various life functions. A fortiori, if the corpse is destroyed by fire or explosion, or is rotted away, then God cannot bring the very body that died back to life. For the particular processes which collectively consti-tuted that body's life, individuated as they are by their particular natural organic basis, cannot be started up again once that basis has ceased to be. Van Inwagen's insight is that unless a particular body is brought back to *its* life, that very body cannot exist again.

Yet, by hypothesis, we are identical to our bodies. So isn't our resur-rection ruled out? Not utterly strictly, not with logical certainty, observes van Inwagen. For example, it might be that God has all the time been snatching our corpses before they become stone-cold and storing them somewhere, so that they can later be retrieved and revived at on the Great Day! Or he might simply be doing this with our brains and hearts and other vital organs!

How is that human beings have not noticed this ubiquitous corpse or organ snatching, given our close attention to the dead? Well, says van Inwagen, God could have been replacing corpses or their crucial organs with corpse or organ simulacra, in ways we are unable to notice!

That, of course, is possible in the broadest, most unconstrained sense. This just illustrates the mighty scope of what is possible in the broadest, most unconstrained, sense. It also shows how far that sense of what is possible is from what we are engaging with when we ordinarily think

[68] Ibid.

about what *might* happen. As William Hasker points out, this logical possibility is one in which God, in preparation for the Great Day, is operating like the manager of a secret, but vast, cryonics unit.[69]

Commenting on van Inwagen's proposal, Dean Zimmerman writes,

> But the Christian materialist would surely do well to look for a better story than this. I once helped a friend with some of the more laborious steps in the process of taking a human corpse apart. The friend was not a mobster, but a student of anatomy. Saddled with a lazy lab partner, she recruited my wife and me to assist. Opening a human skull and finding a dead brain is sort of like opening the ground and finding a dinosaur skeleton. Of course it is in some sense possible that God takes our brains when we die and replaces them with stuff that looks for all the world like dead brains, just as it is possible that God created the world 6000 years ago and put dinosaur bones in the ground to test our faith in a slavishly literal reading of Genesis. But neither is particularly satisfying as a picture of how God actually does business.[70]

Both pictures are unsatisfying; each makes God seem like a deceiving trickster.

Perhaps we can intensify our sense of this in the following way. Suppose we now try to empirically confirm the van Inwagen suggestion by means of radioactive marking of a significant number of the particles that make up a dying person's body. The prediction would be that because at each person's death his body is snatched and a simulacrum of his corpse, made of different particles, is placed in the bed or on the battlefield, there will be a sudden disappearance of the radiation associated with the markers.

Now I suppose that this is not what we would in fact observe. After all, people *have* died with radioactive dye in their vital organs, and yet no such vanishing of the radioactive materials has been observed at their death, or soon thereafter. Otherwise, we would have already had startling

---

[69]William Hasker, *The Emergent Self* (Cornell University Press, 2001), 223. In this well-argued book, Hasker briefly mentions the life of the phoenix as emblematic of resurrection, something I take up in lecture five.

[70]Dean Zimmerman, "The Compatibility of Materialism and Survival: 'The Falling Elevator' Model," *Faith and Philosophy* 16 (1999): 197.

announcements to the effect that something remarkable is happening at some deaths, something that cries out to be explained.

Presumably, the thing to say is that God is of course an infallibly effective trickster, ready not only to cover his trail but to cover up the cover-up as well. So he switches the radioactive markers across to the newly minted corpse. Still, just *why* he takes the trouble to do this remains something of a puzzle.

And perhaps an even more worthy puzzle, even a serious question, is this: Why are we allowing ourselves *especially labile* epistemic standards in this kind of case?

ZIMMERMAN'S WAY OUT*

Zimmerman proposes another way in which bodily resurrection might be made compatible with van Inwagen's plausible strictures on the continued existence of bodies. He works up to this proposal by having us consider two cases.

Here is Zimmerman's first case.

> Suppose my body were to undergo an extraordinary and discontinuous case of fission: every particle in my body at a certain time t is immanent-causally connected with two resulting particle-stages after that time. The two sets of resulting particles appear at some later time t^* in disjoint spatial regions, and each is arranged just as the set of "parent" particles that produced it; what's more, they are so arranged because the original particles were so arranged—for each particle produces its "offspring" at precisely the same distances and directions as every other particle, insuring duplication of my body's overall structure. My body, in this case, replicates itself over a temporal gap.[71]

This is fission not only of particles but of the body they made up. Zimmerman takes the standard view that if fission results in two (or more) equally good continuers, the original ceases to exist. So there is no help or hope for us yet; bodily fission would just be a bizarre way in which one's original body comes to an end. This leads Zimmerman to present

[71]Ibid., 206.

a second, related case, a case in which the original body survives thanks to a globally "unequal" fission, a fission that results in a live body and a dead body.

> Suppose that the same sort of fissioning of each particle occurs, but that only one set constitutes at t^* a living human body structured just like mine; the other set appears at t^* as an unstructured pile of dead matter. Perhaps many of the particles failed to "send" one set of "offspring" to the right place, so that the particles that appear on one side are not arranged just like the original set of particles. Then, thanks to the failure of one body to "take," my life is continued by the successful candidate that appears after a temporal interval.[72]

This bifurcation of the particles that make me up provides a model of how God might "resurrect" my very body. Just before my body completely loses its living form, God causes each particle in my body to divide—or at least to be "immanent-causally" responsible for two resulting "particle stages." Zimmerman is here thinking of a particle stage as a short-lived particle-like thing, and a particle as a cross-time sum of such stages, where each link between stages consists of one stage causing the next in the way that is characteristic of persistence. Hence his talk of "immanent" causation, the sort of causation immanent to, and characteristic of, a persisting thing.

To grasp Zimmerman's model for bodily resurrection, consider the two resulting particle stages caused to be by a specific particle stage that inhabited my body before death. One of the resulting particle stages is right where the old one was, that is, it is part of my dead body here on earth. The other is either part of my living body in heaven now (for immediate resurrectionists) or, thanks to forward time travel, part of my living body somewhere in the far future (specifically at the Great Day). Indeed half of all the particles or "particle stages" produced by the divine bifurcation now make up my corpse here on earth, while the other half make up my living, and indeed never dead, body in heaven or in the future, at the Great Day!

Here is the crucial difference with Zimmerman's first case of equal

---

[72] Ibid.

fission: in this second case the dead aggregate of particle-stages on earth that are immanent-causally connected with my dying body do not participate in a life. So there is no danger of my "fissioning out of existence" due to my earthly corpse and my live body turning out to be equally good competitors to be me. My corpse, left here on earth, is not even a *candidate* for being me, since it does not participate in a life. My body, the best, indeed the only, candidate to be me, lives on in heaven, or in the future. This means that the dead body, the corpse, was never me.

So *this* is where we have arrived? Immediately before the death of every human being who has ever appeared to have died, something quite magical happened, the same sort of magical thing every time. In each and every case, as the point of death appears to approach, God has caused the particles that make up the living person's body to "slough off" exactly duplicating particles into a dead organic receptacle, which we call "a corpse." God then whisks away the still living body, and the loved ones and the mourners are left with the corpse that God has just made.

This entails the remarkable thesis that no human body has ever actually died, and on the hypothesis that human persons are identical with their bodies, that no human person has ever actually died. People simply disappear and are replaced by corpses that God miraculously generates to cover things up. There is no bodily death at all. Bodily death is a grand illusion.

A number of things could be said here. First, on Zimmerman's proposal God still seems to be in the business of snatching *bodies*. True, he has not sunk to the level of a *corpse* snatcher. Instead he snatches *live* bodies and covers up by leaving behind matching corpses that he has just made. It is thus unclear why the call to realism that Zimmerman issued to van Inwagen does not echo back, in something like the following way.

> Of course, it is in some sense possible that God takes our bodies to heaven *before* we die and replaces them with things just made to look for all the world like the complete remains of a person who has just died, thereby producing the illusion of a death for the loved ones watching at the deathbed, just as it is possible that God created the world six thousand years ago and put dinosaur bones in the ground to test our faith in a slavishly literal reading of Gen-

esis. But neither is particularly satisfying as a picture of how God actually does business.

That is, God remains a deceiving trickster on this view.[73]

A second point concerns whether Zimmerman's proposal actually does satisfy van Inwagen's strictures on bodily identity, or a natural elaboration of them. Consider the ongoing life of the body that God whisks away. That body's life involves a divinely initiated fission of particles, and then the incorporation of half the fission products into the life of the body. Thus the "postmortem" bodily states of the supposedly surviving body have not themselves evolved out of earlier body states *simply in accord with* those processes that make up the life of the organism. Those states occur in part "because of God's miracle" and not wholly because of "the operation of the natural processes that, taken collectively, were the life of the man," as van Inwagen phrases it.

Third, it is worth asking how any of this stands to Christianity, at least anything remotely like scriptural Christianity. For one thing, Paul should not have said that the wages of sin is death. Instead, the wages of sin is being secretly whisked away. Death is an illusion on the view under discussion. And if Christ's death and resurrection is to be the model for our own, then presumably his human body did not die on the cross either. This is not exactly the heresy of Docetism, the belief that the apparent death of Christ's physical body was an illusion *because* Christ was a pure spirit that could not physically die, but it is a kind of materialist counterpart of Docetism. We might call it "Deceitism" to mark the difference, and the similarity. Deceitism, like Docetism, seems at odds with the manifest content of the New Testament.

Let us take up these last two issues in reverse order.

Is *This* Christianity?

No doubt the metaphysics of body snatching is good clean fun, at least up to a point. But what does it have to do with Christianity?

When it comes to preserving the central details of Christian eschatology, in particular the claim that our bodies will be miraculously raised

---

[73] As a tu quoque to Zimmerman, this is not inaccurate or unjust, but it is in a certain way *unfair*, for he was simply trying to help out the adherents of body resurrection.

from the dead, the Zimmerman proposal seems quite heterodox. Our bodies are not *raised* from the dead on the Great Day, for our bodies never actually die!

Further to this point of heterodoxy, Lazarus of Bethany, so the Gospel of John tells us, was raised from the dead after four days, certainly long enough for his body to have become stone-cold. Can we believe that it was really the *undead body* of Lazarus that lay in the tomb for four days? Then it can only be a source of some embarrassment that according to John what came out of the tomb was wrapped in burial clothes. And what or who came out likely smelled very bad, as the ever practical Martha warns Jesus at John 11:39. Are these not meant to be the indisputable signs of death and of physical corruption?

Then there are those, for some reason often forgotten, "holy ones," who were raised from their tombs after Christ's death on the cross, as described in Matthew 27:52–53.

> The tombs broke open and the bodies of many holy ones who had died were raised to life. They came forth from their tombs, and after Jesus' resurrection they went into Jerusalem and appeared to many people.

But surely many of these holy people were dead for many years, yet they *came from* their tombs. Are we then to believe either that they were buried alive for many years or that a switcheroo—a quick substitution of their real bodies for the buried remains—took place before they *came from* their tombs?

And what about *the* resurrection? Christ's dead body was taken down from the cross, sealed in the tomb, and raised to life on the third day. Which body? Was it the never dead body or the dead body created to replace it?

In raising that question, we need not assume that Christian materialists also have to be complete materialists about the *person* who is Christ. It is just that on any orthodox view Christ's *body* is a human body, governed by whatever metaphysical necessities govern human bodies.

Zimmerman himself emphasizes this point. He himself, at the end of the day, is a dualist about human beings and is simply making a handsome offer to those who need to explain how a materialist might admit the possibility of our resurrection. Nonetheless, he quite rightly points out that even Christian dualists should have an interest in understanding how the body can be resurrected. Zimmerman writes,

> Although I tell the story under the supposition of materialism, its relevance for Christian dualists should be clear. According to venerable theological traditions, Christ, like all of us, was a spirit united to a normal human body. After his body was killed, he (i.e., his spirit, since his body was still in the tomb) descended into hell to "preach to the spirits in prison" and "lead forth captives." On "the third day," his body was raised to life again—that very same body that lay in the tomb was reanimated by his spirit and subtly transformed. Identity of the dying and resurrected body is necessary to make sense of the empty tomb. And if Christ's death and resurrection provide the model for our own, it would be a great theological advantage to be able to say that we, too, get numerically the same body back—transformed and improved, no doubt, but not a body newly cut from wholly different cloth. The Christian dualist moved by these theological considerations can put the theory that follows into service as an account of one way in which our resurrected bodies could be the same as the bodies we had in this life, in much the same sense in which Christ's resurrected body was the same as the one laid in the tomb.[74]

Yet it seems that Zimmerman's promise to allow for the resurrection of Christ's body, while granting with van Inwagen that stone-cold bodies cannot be resurrected, remains unfulfilled. Even if Christ had an always living body of the sort that Zimmerman describes, this would not comfortably fit with the description of Christ's bodily resurrection in the gospels. The extra body is no help at all. In fact it is a hindrance.

For neither Christ's never dead body (if such exists) nor his corpse, which over three days presumably became stone-cold, individually satisfies the three conditions imposed by the gospels, namely

> It was dead when *it* was taken down from the cross.
> *It* was sealed up in the tomb.
> On the third day *it* was raised to life.

[74]Dean Zimmerman, "Materialism and Survival," in Eleanor Stump and Michael Murray, eds., *Philosophy of Religion: The Big Questions* (Blackwell, 1999), 381.

At least this is so if we follow van Inwagen and Zimmerman and insist that it is metaphysically impossible for a stone-cold body to be resurrected or raised again to its life. And, to put it mildly, it would *not be good* to redescribe the miraculous reviving of the dead bodies of Lazarus, the holy ones, and Jesus as a sort of Divine parlor trick, a sleight of hand in which corpses, which have been in the grave, are swapped sight unseen with living bodies that have never died.

The fact is that the manifest import of the gospels is that *stone-cold* bodies—the four-day-old stinking corpse of Lazarus, the long dead bodies of the "holy ones," the body of Christ dead for three "days"—*are* being resurrected by miraculous revivification. These "impossible" miracles are in part supposed to testify to the special status of Jesus and his promise of resurrection.

So much, then, for the attempt to square the Christian scriptures with the claim that each of us is identical to some body understood as a mere organism.

As noted earlier, I believe that van Inwagen has given the right account of the cross-time unity conditions of a *merely organic* body, and I believe that he is quite right that short of *something like* corpse snatching and miraculous prevention of the onset of the stone-cold state in the snatched corpse there is no chance of a *merely* organic body coming back to life.

Still, a Christian who gives significant weight to the manifest content of the New Testament *might* admit that van Inwagen has the right account of the cross-time unity of mere organisms but hold that revelation implies that our bodies were never the mere organisms that van Inwagen describes, but rather things that differ from them in a subtle way, a way only made evident at the resurrection.

In doing this, a Christian who gives significant weight to the manifest content of the New Testament need not follow the strained interpretation of Paul, which has him insisting that our post-resurrection bodies, because they are "spiritual" bodies, are somehow made of spiritual matter. (What, after all, is "spiritual matter"?) For such a Christian, there remains the possibility that our bodies are always made of matter but nonetheless have a cross-time unity condition that allows for survival either if there is a continuous life function or if there is Divine reassembly out of perimortem organic matter. And if such a Christian also gives weight to the fixations of the Church fathers he or she might see in the attempts of the likes of Origen and Augustine to meet the objection from cannibalism—an objection that *only* arises on the reassembly model of resurrection—a further sign that our bodes are not the *mere* organisms that van Inwagen correctly anatomizes.[75]

As it were, the best interpretation both of Paul's account of the resurrection and of the manifest content of the resurrections of various persons in the gospels is that our bodies *already are* the sort of things that can be revivified by Divine intervention.

All that, however, simply concerns what is orthodox and what is heterodox, and there is something to the view that what is called orthodoxy is just a motley bunch of heterodoxies that have caught on.

There is a further problem that puts both corpse and body snatching at odds not with orthodoxy per se but with God's mercy and goodness. This is the problem of the warm corpse, if I may be so indelicate as to put it that way. By inspection, we know that there are warm corpses, corpses that are not "stone-cold" in the special sense introduced earlier. There have probably been billions of warm corpses. Some of them are the "products" of untimely accidental death and would be capable of long and rich lives if they were revived, or better, "enlivened," since on the view in question, they never were alive. On the van Inwagen view of bodily identity it follows that there have been large numbers of such corpses that could be enlivened by God but have not been.

Of course, both Zimmerman and van Inwagen are led to claim that these corpses have recently come into existence and are therefore not the persons who died. But consider these warm corpses as they are in themselves. We find ourselves harvesting viable organs from many of them. Many of them could be enlivened, if miraculous intervention came quickly enough! If those corpses were enlivened then a person would come into existence for the first time. It thus seems callous not to enliven a warm

---

[75] In the eleventh century, Anselm of Laon proposed that the objection from cannibals fails because digestion is not the uptake of matter into the body! Digestion warms the body on analogy with the way that burning wood heats a room, but just as the wood that has been burned does not fill the room, the digested matter adds nothing to the body. Once again, a form of "Deceitism" could come to the rescue. Maybe Anselm was right after all; maybe God just makes it *look* as if the matter is taken into the body. I mean, where do you actually stop?

For a discussion of the scholarly basis for the attribution to Anselm of the thesis that digestion does not result in assimilation, see Caroline Walker Bynum, *The Resurrection of the Body in Western Christianity, 200–1336* (Columbia University Press, 1995), 127–28.

corpse if you can; it seems at least as bad as not reviving a revivable mid-term fetus that has been somatically dead for a short while, no?

Why does God leave all these warm corpses around to grow cold and rot? Is it just because he cannot have us know of his miraculous interventions at or around death? Is it that belief in the supernatural *must* be left as a difficult epistemic achievement? Why, then, does God tip his hand to the putative witnesses of the miraculous interventions having to do with the deaths of Lazarus of Bethany, the holy ones, and Jesus himself?

THE METAPHYSICAL OBJECTION*

There are two ways of developing a Zimmerman-like picture of what is called "death," depending on how we construe the "fission" of the particles that make up a body. On one understanding, which may be Zimmerman's, this really is equal fission for each *particle*. An advocate of this view will be naturally led to say that strictly each particle ceases to be, and two new particles replace it.[76] Then we have something unprecedented in the bodily life of an individual, a massive and miraculous influx of new matter. The van Inwagen–style principle of unity of natural bodily life does not hold across the massive and miraculous influx.[77]

The other version is this. Nothing in any way out of the ordinary happens to the particles that make up a living person's body at or around his death; everything proceeds naturally, but there is a miraculous side-causation that leads to the coming into being of new bodily matter, which makes up a corpse. God then whisks away the body that has not died, leaving the newly created corpse behind.[78] (By the way, doesn't van Inwagen still need something like this to handle the case of people blown to smithereens in explosions? Or does God kill them just before the explosion and whisk away their corpse before it can be blown to bits, so

---

[76] An alternative is the "Lewis view" of fission, according to which equal fission is consistent with identity because it simply shows that the number of particles was the same before and after fission, thanks to pre-fission collocation of particles. The upshot of the Lewis view in this case is that there have been two wholly coincident bodies all along, finally distinguished by perimortem fission. One dies, the other never does. Again, on this adaptation of the Lewis view there is no literal resurrection. There is just a preternatural perimortem sleight of hand.

[77] David Hershenov offers some different but related objections to this idea in "Van Inwagen, Zimmerman and the Materialist Concept of the Resurrection," *Religious Studies* 38 (2002).

[78] This may be the version of Zimmerman's proposal that Kevin Corcoran is depicting in one of his diagrams in the helpful essay, "Physical Persons and Post-Mortem Survival without Temporal Gaps," in his edited volume, *Soul, Body, and Survival* (Cornell University Press, 2001).

that no one who dies *in* an obliterating explosion dies *from* the obliterating explosion?)

Once we get to this particular point, we may as well allow that God just makes the dummy corpse come into being. Why does it have to be causally related in any way to the original body? After all, the corpse is now just a stand-in for the purposes of a Divine sleight of hand. What is now doing the work of making the view that we are identical with bodies consistent with something misleadingly called "the resurrection" is the startling claim that we never actually die.

Unfortunately, we do die, or, as a substance dualist would put it, our bodies do die. And Christianity, true or false, is not inter alia a description of a preternatural perimortem parlor game built around the illusion of bodily death; it is a religion that presents itself as the crucial response to the undeniable fact of bodily death.

REVELATION AND THE NATURE OF BODIES

Now consider a Christian "materialist" who *does* give significant weight to the manifest content of the Christian scriptures. Perhaps he or she bristles at talk of body snatching and corpse swapping. But more important, he or she will see that according to the gospels stone-cold bodies—the four-day-old stinking corpse of Lazarus, the long dead bodies of the "holy ones," the body of Christ dead for three "days"—are being resurrected by miraculous bodily revivification.

As already noted, such a person can admit that van Inwagen has the right account of the cross-time unity of *mere* organisms. However, he or she will then take it that Christian revelation suggests that our bodies were never the mere organisms with which van Inwagen concerns himself. Yes, our bodies are made wholly of organic matter, but our bodies have a cross-time unity condition that allows for their survival either if there is continuous organic basis for the very same life functions or if there is Divine revivification of perimortem organic matter.

Here, with this version of Christian "materialism," we revert to the main line of the first lecture. Now the decisive problem with bodily resurrection is the possibility of strict perimortem duplicates, call them "Ed" and "Fred." Ed's and Fred's deaths are separated by two hundred years. Yet, thanks to a cosmic coincidence, at the times of their deaths they are made of the very same matter in the very same arrangement. If each is identical with his body, how is God to resurrect Ed *and* Fred when the condition that makes for the very same body is the very same for both? Two bodies can never become identical with one.

THE BONE KNOWN AS *LUZ*

One way to highlight the possibility of perimortem duplicates is to investigate the sort of thing that would have to be upheld in order to rule the possibility out. Someone might take the position that each complex body has a special simple particle that individuates it. So Ed's body has its own simple identity-maker, a particle we could call e. When e is present in a body then that body is Ed's body and no body in which it is absent can be Ed's body. If each body has its own unique identity-maker, there is then no possibility of there being *two* bodies that are strict perimortem duplicates.

The only problem is that it seems entirely arbitrary to privilege a specific particle in this way. None of the particles or simples that now make me up is such that the transference of that particle or simple out of my body would make what is left cease to be me.

Compare the rabbinical idea of the *luz*, an indestructible bone found in the spine, which will be that from which the dead body is resurrected. This, too, is an idea of a physical "identity-maker" but one that is complex rather than simple.[79]

---

[79]See Edward Reichman and Fred Rosner's excellent essay, "The Bone Called 'Luz,'" *Journal of the History of Medicine and Allied Sciences* 51 (1996). Though they quote the report of Bauhinus that the *luz* was first described by the Rabbi Uschaia, around 210 C.E., in his *Glossa Magna in Pentateuchum*, Reichman and Rosner write that the first definitive reference to the *luz* is in the Midrash at Ecclesiastes Rabbah 12:5.

> Rabbi Levi says it refers to the nut *(luz)* of the spinal column. Hadrian, may his bones be crushed, asked Rabbi Joshua ben Hananiah: whence will man sprout in the Hereafter? He replied: from the nut *(luz)* of the spinal column. He said to him: prove it to me. He had one brought; he placed it in water but it did not dissolve, he put it in fire, but it was not burnt, he put it in a mill but it was not ground. He placed it on an anvil and struck it with a hammer; the anvil split and the hammer was broken but all this had no effect on the *luz*.

Though some take the view that the *luz* is located at top of the spine where the knot of the tefillin sits, Reichman and Rosner show that the exact location of the *luz* bone remains a moot point. Scholars in the Middle Ages who accepted the indestructibility of the *luz* offer conflicting accounts of its identity. It is the last vertebra of the spinal column, or it is the coccyx, or it is the twelfth dorsal vertebra, or it is one of the wormian bones in the skull, or it is one of the sesamoid bones of the left big toe. Or perhaps Samuel Butler, in his poem *Hudibras*, had it right when he identified the *luz* with the Os sacrum.

If each body had its own *luz* then strict perimortem *duplication* would be impossible. Instead, the case imagined would be a case of temporary resurrection. But all bones are destructible, and furthermore the transplanting of any bone would be like the transplanting of a kidney, in that it would not carry the identity of a person across with it. So there is no *luz*; we are living in a *luzless* world.

The idea of a *luz* may seem utterly quaint to modern sensibilities, but unless there is a *luz* or something like a *luz,* the very idea of same-body resurrection founders. For the re-creation of a body has to consist in something that makes it that same body again, and unless there is a *luz,* or something like a *luz,* then bodily assembly need not be uniquely related to just one body that has died. But two or more bodies cannot become identical to one.

In fact, the idea of the *luz* has a metaphysical descendant in the idea that there can be a bare difference of identity between bodies, something in virtue of which some future body could be *this very* body, something that does not itself *wholly* consist in more particular facts such as that they have the very same matter, arranged in the very same way.

If that were true then we could allow perimortem duplicates and make sense of God's raising *one* of them rather than the *other*.

Resurrection by Replay from Origins*

Many philosophers have been persuaded by the argument of Saul Kripke to the effect that something about the material origins of a material thing enters into the essence of that thing. Put at its simplest, the argument was that if a material thing could have had two different but compossible (possible when taken together) origins then we could patch together a possible world in which that material thing comes into being at two distinct places, and so begins its existence wholly present in two places at once. Since this does not seem possible, we should look for an exclusionary genesis for each material thing, an origin such that it and it alone is sufficient for the coming into being of the material thing in question. So, anyway, the argument goes.

At the end of their scholarly investigation, Reichman and Rosner wisely conclude, "Despite its religious significance, however, it is quite evident from the above sources that the location of this *elusive* bone remains obscure, even to this day. Clarification of this latter issue may have to wait until the very time of the resurrection" (65; my italics).

When it comes to human bodies, two accounts of their exclusionary geneses suggest themselves. On the one account, a particular human body can only come from the particular gametes, the particular sperm and egg, from which it actually came. But one's gametes do not in fact provide fully individuating origins. There is the process of identical twinning, where two bodies come from the very same zygote, and hence from the very same fertilized egg, and hence from the same gametes. So in seeking an exclusionary genesis, we should look to a point in embryonic development when twinning is no longer possible, a point at which the embryo has reached sufficient complexity for it to be true that any natural development of the embryo can result in one and only one body. On this second account, a particular human body could not have but come from the particular advanced embryo from which it actually developed.

Suppose, then, just to clarify the argument to follow, we adopt the view that if Ed is to come into being in any possible situation then in that situation he develops from the particular advanced embryo E that he actually develops from, and if Fred is to come into being in any possible situation then in that situation he develops from the particular advanced embryo F that he actually develops from. The identity of E enters into the correct account what it is to be Ed, and the identity of F enters into the correct account of what it is to be Fred.

Here, the idea of original material origins is a sort of historical counterpart of the idea of the *luz*. My body's true *luz* is not a bone but a particular embryo that entered essentially into the earliest history or immediate prehistory of my body. Without that embryo coming into being, my body, *this very body*, cannot come into being, and if that embryo comes into being in some possible situation and develops into a body then my body comes into being in that situation.

Now I have heard the suggestion that since this is so, God can resurrect a body, and resurrect it at the appropriate healthy and vital age, by re-creating the embryo from which that body developed and then replaying that embryo's original development up to say the age of thirty-one, all done, of course, at miraculous speed.

Is that why one's life "rushes before one" at death?

But what exactly is involved in this *re-creation* of an embryo? Does it not simply reproduce the problem of *re-creation* of the body? If one is identical to one's body then, if one is to be resurrected, numerically the same token body needs to be resurrected. Paralleling the problem of strict perimortem duplicates we also have a problem of strict original duplicates, or strict clones. Late in the eighteenth century Edwina comes from an embryo E*. Late in the twentieth century Fredericka comes from an embryo F*. As it turns out, E* and F* are strict duplicates, they consist of the very same material simples in the very same organic arrangement. (Historical research reveals that environmental influences aside, Edwina and Fredericka were remarkably alike. They were, after all, accidental but strict clones!)

Still, F* is not E* come back into existence, for F* and E* are in their turn individuated as numerically distinct embryos by their numerical distinct origins. Ultimately, as Aristotle appears to suggest in the *Physics*, the individuation of complex material things will turn on the independent unrepeatability, and hence token individuality, of the events that are their comings into being.[80]

On the Great Day, prior to a miraculous fast-forwarding, God can clearly create an embryo that is a strict clone or duplicate of both E* and F*. What he cannot do is make it *one of* E* or F*. He has nothing like a *luz* to draw upon, no further individuating ingredient that would make the embryo he creates be E* (or be F*) come back into existence. And sheer logic blocks the thought that it is both E* and F* come back again. Two distinct embryos cannot become identical with one embryo. So neither E* nor F* can come back again!

Suppose we change our example slightly and junk the fantasy of post-resurrection fast-forwarding. Let us suppose that Edwina and Fredericka are both fetuses that die at the twenty-second week, due to chromosomal abnormalities. (And suppose that they are strict peri-mortem duplicates.) A natural, many would say irresistible, Christian thought is that Edwina and Fredericka are "persons," not of course in Locke's sense of intelligent reflective beings that can think of themselves as themselves at various times and places, but in the sense that guarantees that they are worthy of being resurrected, in order to be given the chance of develop-

[80] See *Physics* 228a3ff. This leads us to one of the deepest questions: whence the unrepeatability of such events? We can make that question come alive by exploring the consequences of natural thoughts like this: Couldn't a token unrepeatable collision have happened slightly earlier or later? Now take a symmetrical double collision within the "grace period": what makes it the case that the double collision is two distinct collisions rather than the same collision happening twice over? You could write a book on the origin of unrepeatability and not waste your time.

ing and deepening their relation to God.[81] God can clearly create a fetus that is a strict clone or duplicate of both Edwina and Fredericka. What he cannot do is make it *one of* Edwina or Fredericka. He has nothing like a *luz* to draw on, no further individuating ingredient that would make the third fetus be Edwina, or as it might be Fredericka, come back again. And sheer logic blocks the thought that it is both Edwina and Fredericka come back again. So neither Edwina nor Fredericka can come back again. But Edwina and Fredericka are persons, not of course in the Lockean sense but in the sense that matters to resurrection for the sake of justice.

Here, as with the appeal to Neo-Lockeanism, the whole economy of bodily resurrection as a system of Divine justice breaks down. One wants to say: If it can't work here, in the case of *the utterly innocent*, it can't work anywhere.

You might try reverting to the suggestions of van Inwagen and Zimmerman to deal with this kind of this case, but I find it impossible to dwell on the unseemly obstetrics that would have to be involved.

In any event, the reader will not be surprised to hear that there remains some unused weaponry in the onto-theological armamentarium that *might* be pressed into service on behalf of the body resurrection understood as involving identically the same body.

Identity Mysticism*

One temptation for a Christian who believes that we are identical with our bodies is to say that God can just intend to resurrect Edwina's body rather than Fredericka's body, even though at their respective deaths they are utterly the same in constitution and structure, and even though God's resurrecting Edwina involves the very same arrangement of the very same matter as would be involved in God's resurrecting Fredericka.[82]

On this view it is God's intention that makes all the difference, and he can just intend to resurrect Edwina's body rather than Fredericka's body. God can have such pure identity-discerning intentions, and can presumably carry them out, if and only if the possibilities in question are

---

[81]Recall G.E.M. Anscombe's use of this idea of a person in her "Twenty Opinions."

[82]"Identity Mysticism" is Dean Zimmerman's nice term for this kind of position. He provides his own argument against identity mysticism in his intricate essay, "Criteria of Identity and the 'Identity Mystics,'" *Erkenntnis* 48 (1998).

really distinct. The view that the possibilities are really distinct is some-times called "bare haecceitism" (from the Latin "haec," meaning *this*) about human bodies, the view that bodies can be simply numerically different, and *not* thanks to any difference in their matter, that matter's history, and how it is arranged.

So God just intends to bring back *this* body, that is, Edwina's body.

How, then, does *Fredericka's* body get to be resurrected? I suppose that the Christian materialist could exploit a variation of an idea from Augustine and say that when Edwina has lived after her resurrection for long enough to expel the matter common to both at their respective deaths, God collects that matter and arranges it appropriately as he wills the resurrection of Fredericka.

In fact, the Christian materialist armed with bare haecceitism about bodies might be emboldened to go further. He might say that the nu-merical difference between Edwina's body and Fredericka's body does not consist in anything *else* being thus and so. Hence God is not even constrained to reassemble perimortem matter or any large sampling of it into a form that is like the form of the perimortem body that is to be resurrected. Armed with bare haecceitism, the Christian materialist might say that perimortem matter and its arrangement is irrelevant to the res-urrection of bodies. All God needs to do is resurrect Edwina, that is, make it the case that Edwina's body comes back, and then make it the case that Fredericka's body comes back.

A certain question is now worth pressing. Why, in doing that, does God need *to any extent* copy how those bodies were at death? In resur-recting Mother Teresa, say, the important property to make something have again is just the property of being Mother Teresa's body. Now if something's having that property does not consist in anything else hav-ing some other property or properties, then the more particular facts about the form and constitution of her body, that is, facts about how matter is arranged, will be irrelevant to her resurrection. Call this the emboldened view.

The emboldened view makes it seem that God could resurrect the very body of Mother Teresa and yet have that very body consist at her resurrection of just the matter that made up Bismarck at the time of his death, arranged in just the way that it was in Bismarck's body at the time of his death. (And vice versa for the resurrected body of Bismarck.)

Something has gone wrong here. God could not do that, and not just because it would be an insult to the sensibilities of Mother Teresa and those who love her.

The source of the error in the emboldened view seems to be that "consists in" is used in two different ways. In the first use, the use that amounts to meaning *wholly consists in,* if some fact consists in other facts, if the fact of identity-preserving resurrection consists in facts about the arrangement of particles, and the identity of the particles involved, and perhaps their historical succession from a certain quantity of original matter, then those more particular facts are themselves sufficient for the constituted fact. The bare haecceitist about bodies must deny that the fact of it being numerically the same body *wholly consists in* such facts. But he need not take the emboldened view, the view that it has nothing to do with such facts, that it does not even *partly consist in* such facts. He can say that after all the bodies in question have a certain essence as bodies, and this essence, this *what it is to be a body,* requires the holding of facts that rule out the switching of the character, size, and composition of Mother Teresa's resurrected body to that of Bismarck's perimortem body.[83]

Thus the friend of bare haecceitistic differences between bodies need not, and should not, adopt the emboldened view. He should allow that there are certain general necessary conditions on the persistence of bodies, but insist that these are not sufficient for the persistence of this or that specific body. There can still be a brute difference between God's resurrecting Edwina's body and God's resurrecting Fredericka's body.

In two important essays on bodily resurrection, Trenton Merricks has argued that these apparently contrasting possibilities really are distinct, even though we are dealing with the identity of mere bodies, that is, with matter arranged in a certain way.[84]

[83]Compare two uses of the idea of the *luz,* the physical identity-maker for a body. On one, the emboldened use of the idea, the existence of the *luz* is in itself sufficient for the existence of its original body, so that my *luz* could be surrounded by a bodily form entirely unrelated to my present bodily form. On the other, saner use of the idea of the *luz,* the existence of my *luz* is necessary for the existence of my body, but other things can be necessary as well, e.g., a certain bodily form.

[84]See his "How to Live Forever without Saving Your Soul: Physicalism and Immortality," in Kevin Corcoran, ed., *Soul, Body, and Survival* (Cornell University Press, 2001), and "The Resurrection of the Body," in Thomas P. Flint and Michael C. Rea, eds., *The Oxford Handbook of Philosophical Theology* (Oxford University Press, 2009). Merricks denigrates sheer reliance on modal intuitions delivered out of the blue, and here I would agree with him. Modal intuitions, intuitions about what is

But are there really two possibilities—the resurrection of the body that is Edwina versus the resurrection of the body that is Fredericka—here?

Many philosophers would admit that there can be purely haecceitistic differences at the level of simples, that is, entities that are not compounds of other entities. Suppose we have two simple particles, call them "Sam" and "Pam."[85] Then, these philosophers would say, there really are distinct possibilities that simply turn on the numerical difference between Sam and Pam, for example, two really distinct possibilities of the following sort. In the first possible scenario, Sam spends all of its existence within the Milky Way carving out a total spatiotemporal position S, and Pam spends all of its existence outside the Milky Way carving out a total spatiotemporal position P. In the second possible scenario it is Pam that carves out S, and Sam that carves out P. We may never have any specific evidence that could support our distinguishing in practice between these two possibilities, but we could have global evidence for a particle theory that admitted such possibilities as distinct in its calculations of the probabilities of certain aggregate outcomes.[86]

Suppose, then, that one admits purely haecceitistic differences between simple particles. The thing to see is that there remains no basis for allowing *further* purely haecceitistic differences among the sets or sums or complexes or wholes made out of them. That is what undermines bare haecceitism about bodies.

Here is something that even God cannot intend: that *first*, the set of a and b should come into existence, *and next*, that another numerically distinct set whose only members are a and b should come into existence.

---

possible and what is not, should be tested against more comprehensive accounts of the essences of things. On the other hand, in the first essay, Merricks himself gives an argument for bare haecceitistic differences between bodies based on a very general modal "assumption" about what can be held fixed when we suppose that a sub-region of a given possible world exhausts the whole reality of another possible world. Anyone who doubted that there could be further haecceitistic differences between complexes like bodies can find good and independent reasons to reject the assumption. Here again, the way to resolve this dispute about modality is to examine what a human body *essentially* is.

[85] That this is just the wrong way to think of particles is a thesis of my colleague Shamik Dasgupta, who sees the whole drift of modern physics as involving a rejection of merely haecceitistic differences between particles. Be that as it may; the argument here is that even if one admits purely haecceitistic differences between particles there is no basis for allowing *further* purely haecceitistic differences among the sets or sums or wholes or complexes made out of them.

[86] See the discussion of point particle collision in my "Is There a Problem about Persistence?" *Proceedings of the Aristotelian Society* 88 (1987), reprinted in S. Haslanger, ed., *Persistence: Contemporary Readings* (MIT Press, 2006).

This is not some limitation on God's power. There is no such double possibility. This is because all it takes for an individual set to exist is for its members to exist.

Here is something else that even God cannot intend: that *first*, the mereological sum of a and b should come into existence, *and next*, that another numerically distinct sum whose only parts are a and b should come into existence. This is not some limitation on God's power. There is no such double possibility. The sequence described is impossible, because all it takes for a sum to exist is for its parts to exist. So also, there is no possibility in which it is *this* sum rather than *that* sum that is brought back into existence.

In conversation, Judy Thompson once introduced me to a certain kind of whole, the "all-sum." The all-sum of Anthony and Cleopatra has the same constituents as the mereological sum of Anthony and Cleopatra, but its principle of unity or continued existence, the descriptive condition that these constituents have to satisfy for the all-sum to exist and continue to exist, is different from the descriptive condition these constituents have to satisfy for the mereological sum to exist. Whereas the mereological sum only requires for its existence at a given time that either Anthony or Cleopatra exist at that time, the all-sum requires that *both* exist at that time.

Here is still a third thing that even God cannot intend. He cannot intend that an all-sum of Anthony and Cleopatra should come into existence, *and also* that another numerically distinct all-sum of Anthony and Cleopatra should come into existence. This is not some limitation on God's power. There is no such double possibility. This is because all it takes for an all-sum to exist at *t* is for its members to coexist at *t*.

Suppose, however, that a living body is a whole but not a mereological sum, nor even an all-sum. This is plausible, because for a living body to exist its varying constituents have to satisfy a more complex and demanding descriptive condition than existence or coexistence.[87] How, then, do the prospects of bodily resurrection look? Could God simply intend to resurrect *this* body rather than *that* body, and so bring back Edwina rather than Fredericka, even though in their last manifestations the two wholes consisted of the very same parts in the very same arrangement?

---

[87] For more on the status of this kind of consideration, see my "Hylomorphism."

Is there room for further haecceitistic differences between bodies once we see that bodies are not mere sums of their constituents? I shall argue that the *mere complexity* of the descriptive condition associated with the whole that is a human body does not essentially alter the situation.

Just as you have only "one shot" at generating an all-sum at t from Anthony and Cleopatra by having them satisfy the descriptive condition that gives the principle of unity for the all-sum, namely that both Anthony and Cleopatra exist at t, you have only one shot at generating a persisting human body from aggregates of perimortem and postmortem particles by having them satisfy the descriptive condition for being particles of the very same body.

This argument will become clearer when we offer some candidates for the descriptive condition in question. But even if I am wrong about the *specific* features of this condition, the general point will still apply.

A body has fundamental organic constituents, but what it is for the body to exist is not simply for these constituents to exist. They could exist and be scattered over the universe. More is required, for example, that the fundamental organic constituents be taken up in a life, or more specifically that they be organized in such a way to sustain a disposition to various life functions (e.g., ingestion, assimilation, excretion), which disposition sustains its own organic basis by way of such functions. Here the details do not matter that much. The general form of what is required for the existence of a particular body at a given time is that some organic matter satisfies some biological condition C at that time, where C may be partly organizational and partly historical. The historical aspect of the condition C may involve the requirement that the matter presently organized in a certain way came to be in that organization by way of the continuous operation of life functions first based in some original organic matter, say that of a specific embryo.

As already noted, C is the kind of condition that rules out God's reviving a stone-cold body. So for the sake of exploring the possibility of resurrection, we shall take it that revelation implies that human bodies are not mere organisms.

It is then natural to think that the crucial condition, call it C*, the satisfaction of which makes for the persistence of a particular human body, can be satisfied between death and resurrection if the body's perimortem matter comes to be organized in just the way it was around death.

A particular body is then to be thought of as a certain kind of non-mereological whole, that is, it is a whole whose principle of unity, whose principle of existence and continued existence, involves more than the mere existence and continued existence of its parts. A body persists, that is, exists at two different times, because there is some matter at the earlier time and some matter at the later time that together satisfy the condition C^*.

Consider, then, the adult perimortem duplicates, Ed and Fred, who are separated by two centuries. By hypothesis, they are identical with their bodies. By further hypothesis, God is capable of satisfying the existence condition C^* for some body by reassembling its matter in its perimortem state. Can he then first re-create Ed and then, after a long period of matter exchange, re-create Fred?

No, there is no room for *first* re-creating Ed. Given what a body is being taken to be, the only bases for a numerical difference between two bodies at a given time is a difference in their matter, or in that matter's historical connection to the original matter of the body, or in that matter's arrangement at that time. Any appeal to a historical connection, one way or another, would be arbitrary here. To say of a single postmortem body state, one which strictly duplicates both the perimortem state of Ed and of Fred, that it stands in a special relation to Ed's perimortem state, and hence to Ed's origins, would be arbitrary. Mutatis mutandis for Fred's perimortem state and origins.

In the case at hand, the only bases for the numerical difference between its being Ed's body and not Fred's body that is re-created first on the Great Day is a difference in their matter or in that matter's arrangement at that time. But by hypotheses those bases are not present. For what God produces on the Great Day will be matter and an arrangement of that matter that stands in just the same relations to Ed's perimortem body as it does to Fred's perimortem body.

Supposing that there are further bare haecceitistic differences between bodies is no more plausible than supposing that there are further bare haecceitistic differences between sets with the same members or between mereological sums with the same parts or between all-sums with the same parts.

It lies in the essence of a body to be a certain sort of variably constituted whole made of particles. You make such a whole exist or exist again by having various particles at various times satisfy the descriptive condition characteristic of the sort of whole in question. Whatever that condition is, there is only "one shot" at making various collections of particles at various times satisfy it. A perimortem collection of particles and a collection of particles conjured together at the resurrection cannot satisfy the descriptive condition *twice over*. And it would be utterly arbitrary to call the one pattern of satisfaction of this descriptive condition by the two collections of particles Ed's life as opposed to Fred's life, or vice versa. How, then, does *either* Ed *or* Fred come back?

A Reply and a Response*

There is a reply to this argument that is worth considering. The argument depends on thinking of the relevant cross-time unity conditions C or C* (or whatever) as purely descriptive, that is, as not themselves invoking haecceities like being and continuing to be Ed or being and continuing to be Fred. Only then can the invidious comparisons with sums and all-sums be made.

But here, it might be said, the argument just begs the question against the position it addresses. Suppose Fred comes into existence in 1985. Fred is identical with a body. What cross-time unity condition is required for Fred's body to continue to exist? That, the bare haecceitist about bodies will say, has a trivial, and only a trivial, answer. It is that Ed's body continues to exist. In saying this one need not adopt the emboldened view. There are indeed necessary conditions on the continuation of Fred's body, conditions that arise from what it is to be a body, say, those conditions articulated by van Inwagen or those built into condition C*. But there is no capturing a sufficient condition short of requiring that it be Fred's body that continues to exist. Nothing *else* is in itself sufficient for this.[88]

It is important to see where this idea leads. Consider Fred on his twenty-first birthday. Consider how his body is on that day, and suppose that the descriptive condition built into van Inwagen's account for what it is for a body to persist holds between that bodily state and a bodily state exhibited by a person a year later. That is,

---

[88]Compare Trenton Merricks, "There Are No Criteria of Identity Over Time," *Noûs* 32 (1998).

1. There has been a continuous exchange of matter that led from the one body state to the other.
2. This exchange was directed by the operation of certain individual dispositions to various life functions characteristic of the kind of body in question.
3. Those individual dispositions were themselves preserved throughout; thanks to the kind of matter exchange in question, the variably constituted organic basis for those very dispositions continuously persisted.
4. (You may provide some further descriptive condition or conditions you deem necessary.)

Isn't it obvious that there is some way of completing this list of purely descriptive conditions such that it will no longer be an open issue whether Fred's body has survived until his twenty-second birthday? Even with just 1–3 satisfied, I am inclined to think that it then just follows from the stipulated facts of the case that Fred's body has lived another year.

For the reply on behalf of the bare haecceitist to be cogent it must not follow.

Suppose that it does not follow. Then despite all this dynamic continuity Fred's body could have ceased to exist and, totally imperceptibly, another body that looks for all the world like Fred's would have come into existence during that year!

But as a claim about *bodies* that seems wrong. It involves a mistake about what is metaphysically possible. New *bodies* cannot come into existence when an earlier body and a later body stand to each other in this kind of normal dynamic continuity. That is just not a way for a new *body* to come into existence and an old body to cease to be. Given that it is *bodies* we are dealing with, what is here jointly necessary for the persistence of a body—the satisfaction of purely descriptive conditions that address themselves to life processes and bodily parts and the like—is also sufficient for the persistence of a body.

Otherwise, how could we ever know that the so-called victims of Capgras syndrome—those who suffer from the conviction that their friends have been replaced by duplicates—have really gotten it wrong? Why is eyewitness testimony, or indeed constant surveillance, at all probative when it comes to the persistence of bodies? Don't say on behalf of the bare haecceitist about bodies that (for the most part) this undetectable replacement never happens. Given bare haecceitism about bodies, how could we possibly know about the rate of replacement? Don't say on behalf of the bare haecceitist about bodies that the underlying dynamic continuity makes it more probable that a single body has survived. Given bare haecceitism about bodies, it is hard to see why the more probable situation is the one in which bodies survive from one moment to the next.

This is not to claim that there are never facts we cannot in principle know. Instead, the claim is that bare haecceitism about bodies radically severs the connection between the facts of bodily persistence and our actual knowledge of those facts.

Identity Voluntarism, the Last Temptation

The onto-theological armamentarium is still not entirely exhausted. Those who are familiar with it might try to defend the same-body view of resurrection by invoking two doctrines that Jonathan Edwards (1703–58), America's most distinguished theologian, and the third president of what was then known as the College of New Jersey, famously used to defend the imputation to each of us of the guilt for Adam's sin.

First, Edwards holds that we have no natural capacity to continue to exist. It is to God that we owe our persistence through time.

> God's preserving created things in being is perfectly equivalent to a continued creation, or to his creating those things out of nothing at each moment of their existence. If the continued existence of created things be wholly dependent on God's preservation, then those things would drop into nothing, upon the ceasing of the present moment, without a new exertion of the divine power to cause them to exist in the following moment.[89]

To this Edwards adds that it is entirely up to God how to constitute a persisting person out of such momentary stages.

> [P]ersonal identity, and so the derivation of the pollution of guilt of past sins in the same person depends on an arbitrary divine con-

---

[89] Jonathan Edwards, *Original Sin* (Yale University Press, 1970), 401.

stitution.... And with respect to the identity of created substance itself, in the different moments of its duration, I think, we shall greatly mistake, if we imagine it to be like that absolute independent identity of the first being, whereby "he is the same yesterday, today, and forever." Nay, on the contrary, it may be demonstrated, that even this oneness of created substance, existing at different times, is a merely dependent identity; dependent on the pleasure and sovereign constitution of him who worketh all in all.[90]

So Edwards concludes that if God wants to treat us as responsible for the sin of Adam, this is perfectly coherent. The imputation of the guilt of Adam's sin to us just requires that each of us is "one with" Adam according to "the pleasure and sovereign constitution of him who worketh all in all."

Even though Edwards himself was working with a broadly Lockean understanding of personal identity as requiring sameness of consciousness, the relevance of these doctrines to the project of making materialist sense of the resurrection should be immediately evident.

In the spirit of Edwards, a Christian who believes he is identical with his body might say something like the following.

I am identical with this body, but the persistence conditions of this body are not those described by materialist philosophers. A body persists through an extended period of time or across a time gap just in case God wills that it so persists. Likewise, the resurrection conditions of this body are just that God will that it exist *again*. As it happens, in this life God wills the persistence of someone's body whenever the continuity of life criterion is met. In the next life (so at least it seems if we bring philosophy and revelation into harmony) he wills that a dead body exist again when the reassembly from the perimortem matter criterion is met. There *may be* a special case, namely when we have perimortem duplicates. Then God wills the re-creation of the body of the earlier of the duplicates, and has the re-created body quickly expel its matter in exchange for new matter. Then he wills the re-creation of the later of the duplicate bodies.

Or perhaps God is more liberal than this. Perhaps for the next life of a body to begin he does not require reassembly of perimor-

---

[90] Ibid., 478.

tem matter. He requires that there be *a* body somehow representative of the body that died, and he then wills that the body that died come back into existence by way of the existence of the representative body.

If bodies endure these thoughts are not helpful. For we will have an enduring premortem body and an enduring postmortem body that are either numerically one and the same body or numerically two bodies. God does not have the option of making two bod*ies* identical, or making one body two. There is no such option to be had. The logic of identity leaves no such option. There is no room for a will, even an omnipotent will, to insert itself here.

Suppose, however, that we follow Edwards and deny that "created substances" like bodies endure, as he seems to be doing when he writes,

> And with respect to the identity of created substance itself, in the different moments of its duration, I think, we shall greatly mistake, if we imagine it to be like that absolute independent identity of the first being, whereby "he is the same yesterday, today, and forever."

Here Edwards seems to be endorsing something like the view that "created substances" persist by perduring, that is, by having distinct momentary stages at the various times at which they exist. So, once again, we are to think of a body as a cross-temporal sum of momentary body stages united by a certain genidentity condition, that is, a condition that bundles together those momentary stages into a persisting whole. Now the *standard* philosophical conception of the genidentity condition for bodies is something like the continuity of life condition, or perhaps some mix of the continuity of life condition with the material reassembly condition. But on the proposal at hand, these conditions are at best coextensive with the real genidentity condition for bodies, namely the condition that God wills that these body stages and only these body stages make up a body!

All our problems are now solved thanks to God's "sovereign constitution" of four-dimensional bodies, and hence of persons.

Except that we have now severed both the resurrection and the life of the world to come from any real conception of justice.

When did I first firmly place my foot on the road to perdition? I believe it may have been at the age of eleven when, after having been a good altar boy for so long, I made the familiar discovery that by mixing candle wax with the incense and burning charcoal in the thurible, I could smoke up Father Curran's mass. Now, if the fact that I was the boy who put the candle wax in the thurible is a fact independent of the will of another, then I am sorry for this act, and I am (within reason) prepared to take my lumps for it in the afterlife. But if I am told that the fact that I was that boy holds just in virtue of "arbitrary divine constitution," that is, just in virtue of God's deciding to bundle together the stages of the mischievous boy with the rest of the stages of my life, then I am taken aback. The fact that it was *I* who did it is now being claimed to consist in a fact about God's arbitrary and sovereign will. How then can I justly be asked to take my lumps for the acts of that mischievous boy? God has, as it were, just *foisted* those acts on me; so also for "my" good acts.

More generally, then, given this kind of identity voluntarism, the afterlife will be a system of hellish injustice, as much in heaven as in hell. Here I take myself to be recovering a long familiar theological objection against arbitrary imputation, indeed the objection put so well by Jonathan Edwards's nemesis John Taylor.[91] Taylor wrote the following against the Reformed version of the doctrine of the universal imputation of Adam's guilt.

> But that any man, without my knowledge or consent, should so represent me, that when he is guilty I am to be reputed guilty, and when he transgresses I shall be accountable and punishable for his transgression, and thereby subjected to the wrath and curse of God, nay further that his wickedness shall give me a sinful nature... surely anyone who dares use his understanding, must clearly see this is unreasonable, and altogether inconsistent with the truth and goodness of God.[92]

[91] Against Taylor, Edwards writes,

According to my observation, no one book has done so much towards rooting out of these western parts of New England, the principles and scheme of religion maintained by our pious and excellent forefathers, the divines and Christians who first settled this country, and alienating the minds of many from what I think are evidently some of the main doctrines of the gospel, as that which Dr. Taylor has published against the doctrine of original sin. (Ibid., 102)

[92] John Taylor, *The Scripture-Doctrine of Original Sin, Proposed to Free and Candid Examination* (M. Waugh, 1767), 108–9. For contemporary discussions of these issues, see John Kearney, "Jona-

A Body Can't Get There from Here

This has been a brief review of the ingenious body-swapping suggestions of van Inwagen and Zimmerman, of resurrection by replay from origins, of the bare haecceitism of Merricks, and of an identity voluntarism in some ways reminiscent of the views of Jonathan Edwards. These were different ways in which contemporary Christian materialism might try to avoid the problem of perimortem duplicates.

Upon examination, each suggestion appears to be unsatisfactory. Moreover, the identification of a person with a purely organic body seems at odds with the manifest content of the New Testament.

---

than Edwards and the Imputation of Adam's Sin," *Princeton Theological Review* 8 (2001), and the essays by Oliver Crisp and Paul Helm in Crisp and Helm, eds., *Jonathan Edwards: Philosophical Theologian* (Ashgate Press, 2003).

Chapter Two

The Impossibility of My Own Death

The last lecture converged on certain Protestant theological attempts to bridge the gap between earthly life and the afterlife, without recourse to an immaterial soul that could continue after the death of its brain and body. These were attempts to make sense of the resurrection without drawing on the legacy of Plato, illustrated by *The Entombment of Gonzalo Ruíz, Count of Orgaz*, with its depiction of Gonzalo's immaterial soul carrying his identity to heaven.

The Entombment is Platonized Christianity of just the sort firmly rejected as unscriptural by Protestant thinkers as various as Rudolf Bultman, Karl Barth, Emil Brunner, Paul Tillich, and Oscar Cullman. In this vein, Emil Brunner writes,

> Our death will be the dying of the whole man and not merely of the body. The whole man must pass through an experience of annihilation which affects the whole man, since the whole man is a sinner.[1]

Here Brunner takes himself to be elaborating the thanatology of Paul's epistles. The whole man, body and soul, has sinned. The annihilation inherent in death is the wages of sin, so the whole man, soul included, must be annihilated by death.

In his mortalist treatise, *Immortality of the Soul or Resurrection of the Dead?* Oscar Cullman sets out the same doctrine of Hellenist pollution of the radical message of the New Testament faith in the general resurrection.

> If we want to understand the Christian faith in the Resurrection, we must completely disregard the Greek thought that ... the death

[1]Emil Brunner, *Man in Revolt: A Christian Anthropology*, trans. Olive Wyon (Lutterworth Press, 1939), 475–76.

of the body would not be in any sense a destruction of the true life [of the soul]. For Christian (and Jewish) thinking the death of the body is *also* destruction of God-created life. No distinction is made: even the life of our body is true life; death is the destruction of *all* life created by God. Therefore it is death and not the body which must be conquered by the Resurrection.[2]

Unfortunately, neither Brunner nor Cullman offers any details as to what it would take for the whole man to literally *pass through* the annihilation of death. What could possibly make it the case that the whole man, himself, the very one who lived and breathed on this earth, and whose body and soul were annihilated by death, could *come before* the Divine judge?

As mortalists, Brunner and Cullman might have consistently appealed either to the bodily criterion of personal identity or to Neo-Lockeanism. But in the last lecture, we found that the bodily criterion cannot be used to plausibly underwrite the resurrection. And we saw that Neo-Lockeanism does not give the criterion for *our* survival.

Thus it emerges that Christian eschatology, its account of the last things, and in particular the disposition of the dead, stands or falls with the Platonic legacy of the immaterial soul, which could carry the identity of the deceased to the Last Judgment. The removal of the Platonic and Aristotelian legacy from Christianity, one of the defining ambitions of Protestant theology since Martin Luther, looks to be an operation the patient cannot survive. The availability of the afterlife, and hence the coherence of the appeal to the afterlife to meet the threat of death to the importance of goodness—all this now seems to require the immateriality of the soul.

THE FAITH-THREATENING CHARACTER OF CREEDAL RELIGION

Here we have something of a paradox, which arises in one form or another in each of the creedal religions. You might call it *the faith-threatening character of religious doctrine*. Independently of our religious beliefs, or of whether we have any religious beliefs, we are all required to have faith in the importance of goodness, even in the face of death. But since there

[2]Oscar Cullman, *Immortality of the Soul or Resurrection of the Dead?* (Macmillan, 1958), 17.

is no sin in being cautious on the epistemic front, so long as it is not a form of distrust in life, we are not required to accept any doctrine with highly debatable, even dodgy, philosophical or empirical implications. The distinctive claims about the structure of reality made by the creedal religions are just of this sort, and the immateriality of the soul is a paradigm case. By making such distinctive claims and representing them as conditions of faith, such religions move illegitimately beyond faith; they make faith hostage to empirical (and philosophical) fortune, and in that sense they place a lodestone around the neck of the faithful, especially those with a genuine intellectual curiosity. That is why dogmatically creedal religions sometimes look like schools that expel their best pupils, as Voltaire once put it. And that is why some of us admire the central figure in *The Gospel of Thomas*; whoever he is, he seems to background religious doctrine *in order to* foreground faith.[3]

There is a blatant example of the faith-threatening character of religious doctrine in Paul's first letter to the Christian community at Corinth. As Paul puts it in his characteristically hectoring way, if there is no resurrection of the body then there is no point to faith, hope, or charity; the lives of the faithful have been wasted. Most strikingly, he writes,

> If the dead are not raised: "Let us eat and drink, for tomorrow we die." (1 Cor. 13:32)

It is a reprise of the familiar argument from Qoheleth and the *Wisdom of Solomon*, now refigured in the earliest writings of what came to be the Christian tradition. I hope that among my readers there will be those who regard Paul's remarks here as deeply false to the religious— and indeed even to the Jewish and Christian—point of view. After all, Paul's Pharisaic doctrine of the resurrection of the dead, a doctrine, it seems, which emerged in a faction of Judaism partly as a psychological compensation for the experience of tragic destruction and loss at the hands of Nebuchadnezzar, is a metaphysical doctrine.[4] (The same could be said for its close cousin, Apocalypticism, the doctrine that the end of

---

[3]A similar view is expressed by Elaine Pagels in her *Beyond Belief: The Secret Gospel of Thomas* (Random House, 2004).

[4]On the relations between Apocalypticism, the Pharisaic doctrine of the resurrection of the dead, the destruction of the temple, the Babylonian exile, and the fate of the martyrs in the Maccabean war, see Alan F. Segal's magisterial work, *Life after Death: The History of the Afterlife in Western Religion* (Doubleday, 2004).

this world is nigh.) Why should the this-worldly afterlife, which Paul describes himself as already living when he writes,

I have been crucified with Christ, and it is no longer I who live, but Christ lives in me; and the life which I now live in the flesh I live by faith in the Son of God, who loved me and delivered Himself up for me. (Gal. 2:19–20)

be thought dependent for its ethical and salvific coherence on certain metaphysical doctrines that arose under highly disorienting historical circumstances, doctrines to the effect that the end is *nigh* and that the dead will *soon* be raised? Because of the faithlessness that confounds salvation with concrete vindication and ultimate compensation?

The question of what a religion would look like that was not in this way faithless is a large one, best left for another occasion.[5] Here the task is to explain how the intellectually curious could still keep faith in the importance of goodness even in the face of death, and perhaps in the face of the other large-scale structural defects of human life—arbitrary suffering, disease, disabling poverty, and the decay of aging—defects religious doctrine attempts to palliate.

Since the explanation of how we can consistently keep faith in the importance of goodness in the face of death will be a philosophical one it will be debatable, though not, I hope, too dodgy. It is important that the proffered philosophical explanation is not taken as a dogmatic secular substitute for an otherworldly religious creed. (And it should go without saying that the philosophical explanation of consistency need not have been anticipated by those who do in fact keep faith in the importance of goodness.) The philosophical explanation in question, like all such explanations that are of any interest, is fallible, which is to say it could be wrong. It is not presented as something that must be true if faith in the importance of goodness is warranted. It represents how someone with a certain cultural, religious, and intellectual formation thinks about the question of death and finds that death, so far from threatening the importance of goodness, helps us see what kind of goodness overcomes death.

That is not, of course, an expression of relativism about the truth of the matter; it is just a fallibilist's worry as to whether his formation has been adequate to disclose the non-relative truth of the matter.

[5] For the beginnings of such an account, see my *Saving God*.

One thing more: In describing how a good person may overcome death, and perhaps also survive death, it is not my purpose to explain away the manifest tragedy (for both the living and the deceased) of certain deaths. And here what I have to say may seem profoundly inferior to the consolations of the afterlife, in particular the consolation of seeing your loved ones again. That is an intended result. What I have to say is not intended to diminish the tragedy and horror of the world, as it were to somehow remove the loss of a beloved one or outweigh the anguish of natural animal suffering. In my view there is something both childish and obscene, and I would add irreligious, about the attempt to put an otherworldly frame around such things so they seem not to be the tragedies or the horrors that they manifestly are. Sometimes things are so horrible and tragic that nothing that subsequently happens can diminish the tragedy or the horror; anyone who tells you otherwise is just making it up or relying on someone else who just made it up.

Our question is not: Is there an acceptable naturalistic surrogate that would do all of the work of the idea of the afterlife? I take it that the answer to this question is known. However, it remains true that some of the work of the idea of the afterlife is bad work, with bad effects in this life, while some of it, like the attempt to address the threat that death poses to the importance of goodness, is worthwhile. Our purpose here is to see whether there is a naturalistic account of how it is that death does not threaten the importance of goodness. And the interest of this may lie mainly in what it shows about our nature and the nature of goodness.

WHAT DO WE KNOW OF THE SOUL?

To require commitment to the dogma of the immateriality of the soul, as a condition of faith in the importance of goodness, is faithless in the present sense because the question of the immateriality of the soul is a notoriously dodgy empirical and philosophical matter. The empirical facts, I take it, are these. As we know more and more about the brain, even the highest mental functions seem to have definite brain functions as their condition sine qua non. The intriguing specificity of cognitive loss, depending often on the precise location and extent of this or that brain lesion, continually confirms that brain function cannot be overridden as a source of mental capacity. Even in cases of recovery from the specific cognitive losses produced by local brain damage, there is, significantly, no reported phenomenology of memories of an intact thinking soul being "locked inside" an inept, because damaged, brain and body. The thoughts and mental capacities were just not there, it seems. Yet an immaterial bearer of these mental capacities and thoughts need not be damaged just because the brain is damaged.

To develop this line of thought just a little, consider trepanation, one of the oldest surgical procedures, in which holes are made in the skull and through the durus, the tissue surrounding the brain, in order to drain a stroke-induced hematoma that has been putting pressure on the brain, thereby often causing unconsciousness, or at least all the bodily signs of unconsciousness. (The pharaoh Ptolemy VI seems to have died in 145 BC either from the effects of trepanning or from the stroke that prompted it.)

Many victims of unconsciousness caused by a subdural hematoma now recover full consciousness as a result of successful trepanning, or "craniotomy" as it is now called.

Why, then, are there no reports of the phenomenology of "being locked in" when the victim "wakes up" after craniotomy?

Contrast the genuine cases of being mentally "locked in" thanks to almost complete bodily paralysis. Such reports arise because in such cases the higher centers of the brain remain intact. But on the substantial dualist conception even these higher centers are mere instruments by which thoughts have their effects. There are, as it were, still "higher" centers, located in the soul or independent spiritual substance that drives the brain, centers that brain damage would leave intact.

Yet temporary brain damage leading to unconsciousness is not phenomenologically like bodily paralysis, as substantial dualism would predict, given natural auxiliary assumptions.

This kind of point goes beyond the mere correlations revealed by lesion study and by MRIs. In the face of all the bodily signs of unconsciousness found in severe cases of subdural hematoma, the natural dualist expectation would be that if and when the pressure on the brain was relieved and the patient awoke, he or she would report having been "locked in" to a bodily prison. This is just what we do not find.

(I do not say that there are no auxiliary hypotheses that would make the facts concerning the phenomenology of recovery from subdural hematoma *consistent* with dualism. I just say that I expect any genuine substance dualist to be surprised and slightly dismayed by such facts.)

If a lecture like this was taking place a hundred years ago, the next topic would be the material corralled, generated, and meticulously examined by the then famed Society for Psychical Research. Established in London in 1882 to scientifically examine the purported evidence generated by telekinesis, telepathy, mesmerism, trances, ghostly apparitions, possession, and the various phenomena associated with séances, the society had the famous philosopher Henry Sidgwick as its first president, and its subsequent presidents included William James, Henri Bergson, C. D. Broad, and H. H. Price.

That last name is of particular interest, for Henri Haberley Price, now known for his important work in the philosophy of perception, was the don who supervised David Malet Armstrong in Oxford in the 1950s. A decade later, Armstrong would go on to advance the mind-brain identity theory as the best empirical hypothesis on offer. Knowing Armstrong's cast of mind, he would have been very eager to present any real evidence to the contrary, and he cannot have been ignorant of his supervisor's knowledge of, and deep connection with, psychical research.

In fact, the history of the society's "discoveries" has been one of recurrent promise followed by anticlimactic deflation. It is very telling that neither Sidgwick, James, Bergson, Broad, nor Price succeeded in bringing before the world any evidence from psychical research that was significant enough to resist or in any way hinder the rise of materialism in twentieth-century philosophy. It is certainly not that they lacked the rhetorical and augmentative abilities required to effectively present the evidence.

As most reliable reviews of that evidence find, it is mostly weak and inconclusive. Then there is the sort of thing that invariably turns up when a given domain is subjected to intense scrutiny, the *purely puzzling*, which leads nowhere experimentally or theoretically. A similar pattern is exhibited by the contemporary counterpart of the old psychical research, the investigation into "near death" experiences, which is discussed below.

On this side of the ledger then, it therefore seems that it was Simmias and not Socrates who held the correct position in Plato's *Phaedo*.[6] Simmias, you will remember, objected against Socrates that since the mind stood to the body as the harmonious sound of a lyre stood to that lyre,

---

[6]See *Phaedo* in Plato, *Complete Works*.

the mind could no more survive the destruction of the body than the sound of a lyre could survive the destruction of that instrument. And Simmias seems vindicated; for the evidence from neurophysiology suggests that the mind is just the mode of functioning of the brain and nervous system.

On the other side of the ledger, there are the startling reports, more or less spontaneously produced in roughly 10 to 15 percent of resuscitated cardiac arrest cases, of what are now called "out-of-body" experiences. The experiences, which seem to their subjects to be happening during a period that coincides with the clinical death of their own bodies, involve such things as the sense of leaving one's body and of looking down at the medical personnel pumping one's chest in their attempts at resuscitation. As the experience develops, one seems to be traveling through a tunnel to a bliss-inducing white light. As one moves in the light, dead relatives, and even old pets, are encountered, and in some cases one is presented with a review of one's life. This, of course, would represent the beginning of an empirical vindication of the very theology of death implied by *The Entombment of Gonzalo Ruíz*!

Indeed, even agnostics and atheists are susceptible to out-of-body experiences. Most notably, the well-known empiricist and agnostic A. J. Ayer had an apparently postmortem out-of-body experience, with two results. First, his firmly negative attitudes on the question of life after death softened, and second, as Dee Wells (who managed to be both Ayer's second and fourth wife) put it: "Freddie was a much nicer man after he came back from the dead." Not surprising, really, since by Freddie's own account the light that he experienced was not white and calming; it was red and threatening.[7] And we all know what that portends!

Here is what I take to be least controversial in this controversial area. There is a genuine phenomenon that goes under the name of the "out-of-body experience." However, in investigating this phenomenon, one does not find *robust* evidence of distinctive knowledge of the external world that could only be gleaned from the ostensible vantage points of the disembodied subject. If one has left one's body and is looking down upon it, then one could be expected to take in facts about, say, the emergency room that are not available to the normal viewers, there on the

<hr />

[7] A. J. Ayer's own account of the experience appeared as "What I Saw When I Was Dead," *National Review*, October 14, 1988.

floor. Experiments have indeed been proposed, even partly performed, but what we do not have is a decisive case that clearly passes the obvious test. I have in mind a cartoon that effectively presents the obvious test: We see an emergency room in which a cardiac arrest patient is being resuscitated by doctors. Mounted high up on the back wall of the emergency room is a sign whose message is visible *only* from near the ceiling of the room.

What if such obvious tests were frequently passed by the resuscitated patients—what if they reported reading such signs as "You're Dead!" "Eat at Joes!" "Medicare Won't Be Covering This!" or whatever happens to be displayed at the moment of their deaths. And suppose we could rule out collusion and suggestion? What then?

We should have to think again about the empirical viability of locating our mental lives in independent substances, substances whose men-

If you can read this...

tal functioning can outlive the functioning of their associated brains. This serves to highlight what should be anyway be obvious, namely that the immateriality of the soul is an empirical question.[8]

ABSENCE OF EVIDENCE

So the existence of the soul and consequently the nature of personal identity are empirical questions, to be settled by our total evidence, including such putative evidence as the reports of postmortem observations from the ceilings of operating theaters. If the reports included revelations only accessible from the ceiling, then we would have to think again, either about the soul or about the possibility of remote viewing.

In fact, however, the revelations from the ceiling, and similarly elevated positions, have not been readily forthcoming.[9] Furthermore, there is considerable evidence of cultural variation in the content of out-of-body experiences; in Japan, for example, the journey to the next life bypasses the tunnel and the white light. Instead, after you leave your body, you walk through a charming garden where a boat awaits to take you out to the open sea. Of course, no one should lay down limits a priori on the means of transportation that heaven might use; but the methods used to convey us to eternity do seem suspiciously tailored to our cultural expectations.

Then there are the facts about horse tranquillizer, or ketamine, the drug known on the streets as Special K. Special K systematically induces out-of-body experiences *in the living*, along with the tunnel, the light,

[8]In his "Mental Events," Donald Davidson famously attempts to rule out a priori any dualism of mental and physical events. See *Essays on Actions and Events* (Oxford University Press, 1980). For resistance to this whole approach, see my "Why Having a Mind Matters," in Ernest LePore and Brian McLaughlin, eds., *Actions and Events: Perspectives on the Philosophy of Donald Davidson* (Blackwell, 1985).

[9]Notwithstanding the anecdotal report of a resuscitated patient apparently recalling a green sneaker that did indeed happen to be on a landing two floors up from the emergency room in which his "dead" body lay. Here again, we encounter the purely puzzling, which invariably appears when we intensely scrutinize a given domain. Compare the undeniable fact, captured on the Zapruder film, that on a clear sunny day in Dallas, Texas, a spectator watching the presidential motorcade go by opened up a black umbrella a split second before John F. Kennedy was shot in the back by Oswald. The man with the umbrella, a certain Louis Steven Witt, was later interviewed by the Warren Commission and explained that his opening the black umbrella was meant as protest against Kennedy's policies. Here we have an example of the purely puzzling, a very suggestive happening, which in the end points nowhere. Such events may be all around us, there to be discovered by a certain kind of intensive examination, which fortunately we are almost never ready to carry out.

and the view from the ceiling. Devotees of Special K are often reported as being viscerally convinced, by their experiences, of what we philosophers would call substance dualism, in particular its natural implication that the soul can leave the body behind.

I think it would be better to concentrate on the arguments rather than on the deliverances of drug-induced states. So, while the victim of Special K poisoning is "out of his body" he is also manifestly in it, drooling, vomiting, and mumbling inarticulately, as the minders of such victims often report. The poisoned body is still animated and capable of carrying on conversations *based on the scene in front of its eyes*. How is that possible if the soul has left it, in order to explore how things look from up there on the ceiling?

THE SOBERING VERDICT

That is the briefest overview of how the evidences presently stand with respect to souls or independent immaterial substances that would be the unambiguous carriers of our respective identities. In the post-resuscitation reports, we have an absence of adequate evidence for such souls or independent immaterial substances. And in the case of brain damage and its impact on even the highest mental functions, we have close to adequate evidence for the absence of souls or independent immaterial substances. The best hypothesis is that an individual mind is no more than a mode of functioning of its brain.

So all paths to the other world now seemed blocked, either by the nature of personal identity or by the absence of immaterial substances. There is no way to get there from here, which suggests that we are not talking about a genuine destination.

That is how I would put it, but only so long as we exclude the purported evidence provided by the revelations particular to this or that religion. To decisively rule out spiritual substances would take much more than these brief observations, especially so if we admit as evidence the creedal claims of this or that supernaturalist religion understood as forms of revelation about the actual facts of the matter. Revelation *could* in principle disclose the facts of the matter about the soul and the afterlife. It is just that the actual histories of the supernaturalist religions make their metaphysical claims about the afterlife look like bad embodiments of their more genuine salvific visions. That, for example, is manifestly the case with Apocalypticism, the doctrine that the end of the world and the final judgment are *at hand*. No one who has looked at the history of *that* claim should now regard it as something on which genuine faith depends. Every time the bet has been made, it has been a losing bet. The faith that was thereby dashed was to that extent not real faith. Here then is a case where what was taken as a revelation, a disclosure of the actual truth of the matter, was manifestly not. And in point of historical fact, it may be no easy thing to decouple the origins of the doctrine of Apocalypticism from the origins of the doctrine of personal resurrection.

So let us tentatively proceed with what is suggested by the unaugmented empirical facts, the facts that are there without adding purported revelations to one side of the ledger. Then the conclusion that is invariably drawn is what we might call *the sobering verdict*, namely that death is THE END, total annihilation, the collapse of presence, the severance of life with others.

As it happens, I do not believe that the sobering verdict actually follows.

My argument will be—and, of course, this must at first blush appear deeply paradoxical—that the very nonexistence of the soul opens up the possibility of a kind of survival of death, one that does not depend on Neo-Lockeanism or on the bodily criterion. Moreover, this form of survival is secured by the very kind of self-transformation urged by the best forms of Judaism and Christianity. And the form of survival in question in no way depends on either the superstitious or, more broadly, the supernaturalist elements in those religions.

All that will become clearer in lectures four and five. Our present task is to understand just what the sobering verdict has been thought to involve by those who accept it and so have no hope for an afterlife.

THE ONE AT THE CENTER

In *The View from Nowhere*, Thomas Nagel writes that when you really appreciate what is involved in your death, it is as if you are *already* dead.

Perhaps I know something of what he means. One's own consciousness, the arena of presence and action in which and out of which each one of us lives our lives, presents itself as a fundamental context for the worldly happenings that make up the details of one's life. So long as we are alive, we ourselves are always around; every time we wake up in a chair or in bed, there we are, coeval with the appearance and reappearance of the world. And so we operate as if the world just wouldn't be the world unless we were here, as it were, at the center of it. This is the sense in which our everyday experience of life prevents us from understanding the fact of our mortality. By all ordinary standards of knowledge, we know that we are mortal, we know that we are just one of the others, all of whom go down to their deaths, but we can't really believe it. Phenomenologically speaking, it seems as if we are the fountainhead of the very reality we inhabit.

One sort of terror at the looming end of presence consists in the revelation that one's centrality in one's own arena of presence and action is *utterly misleading*. When it comes to the details of the world, to how things really go, each of us is utterly peripheral. Or worse, from the side of the world, the very contrast between being central and being peripheral makes no sense. The position one prizes most, of being at the center of *this*—one's own—arena of presence, as I shall call it, is not, and never has been, *a position in the world*. The world has no such center. The world, as Nagel put it, is centerless.

There are occasions, other than in the face of death, on which the uncanny centerless character of the world can rush in. Recall the opening passage from Vladimir Nabokov's autobiographical memoir *Speak, Memory*.

> Although the two are identical twins, man, as a rule, views the prenatal abyss with more calm than the one he is heading for (at some forty-five hundred heartbeats an hour). I know, however, of a young chronophobiac who experienced something like panic when looking for the first time at homemade movies that had been taken a few weeks before his birth. He saw a world that was practically unchanged—the same house, the same people—and then realized that he did not exist there at all and that nobody mourned his absence. He caught a glimpse of his mother waving from an upstairs window, and that unfamiliar gesture disturbed him, as if it were some mysterious farewell. But what particularly frightened

him was the sight of a brand-new baby carriage standing there on the porch, with the smug, encroaching air of a coffin; even that was empty, as if, in the reverse course of events, his very bones had disintegrated.[10]

The chronophobiac's panic is directed at the utterly unnecessary character of his own existence, as shown by the antecedent completeness of the family scene. So also when we imagine the world healing seamlessly around our deaths, we see how unnecessary we are to a world that was always centerless.

But why did we think otherwise? Why do we take ourselves to be the fountainhead of the very reality we inhabit? I believe it is because of the fundamental structure of self-consciousness. In describing that structure, I shall be forced to use the first person, but corresponding thoughts apply in your own case.

THE ARENA

The most immediate way in which I am given to myself is as the one at the center of this arena of presence and action. Let me say more about what I mean by this term of art "arena of presence and action." The modes of presentation of the items in my perceptual field are *perspectival*, that is, they present items to a particular viewing position, or more generally to a particular point from which someone might sense the surrounding environment. The implied position at which those modes of presentation seem to converge is the position of my head and body. To that same implied position, a bodily field, as it were a three-dimensional volume of bodily sensation, also presents. And that implied position is also one from which certain acts, presented as willed, emanate. Furthermore, it is the position where mental acts seem to be available for higher-order awareness. And when mental "images" and sounds are generated by imagination in a space detached from their respective fields—as when I imagine the Hindenburg bursting into flames or rehearse a tune "in my head"— those imaginings appear at the center, in my mind's eye or ear as it were.

This whole centered pattern, existing at a particular time, and perhaps over time, I call *an arena of presence and action*. There is one such

[10]Vladimir Nabokov, *Speak, Memory* (Everyman Library, 1990), 9.

arena here, and I assume you can truly make a corresponding remark about your own case. The extent of that arena includes all the items that are in principle open to introspection in the broad sense. This includes the deliverances of proprioception and the immediate knowledge of which intentional acts you are currently performing or trying to perform. Think of the arena as a sort of virtual frame or "container" that includes all this; it is if you like the mind considered as a sort of place, the mental "bed" in which the stream of consciousness flows.

So given in my total experience now is an apparent arena that, as it were, bounds my thought and experience and makes it seem like a unified whole. And this bound or arena is structured around another apparent item, the implied position to which external items and mental events present. Even though there is no such center in the external or mental world, the contents of the arena are given as structured around this center.

Again, I assume, it is like this in your own case as well. Each one of us finds him or herself at the center of an arena of presence and action.

Heidegger plausibly held that the basic form of engaged human activity is *Being There*, in the midst of things. But for the individualized human subject, the one who is aware of his own life and death as his own, the basic form of life is *Being Here*, at the virtual center. (These are two characteristic moments or aspects of human life; a philosophy is one-sided if it includes one at the expense of the other.)

Some immediately grasp the ideas of the arena and of the center; others find them opaque.[11] So let us make another pass at these ideas.

In my occurrent mental acts, my mental goings on, I am now accessing a host of modes of presentation of external items, and modes of presentation of bodily sensory conditions, and modes of presentation of the possible states of affairs that are the objects of my thoughts, and modes of presentation of activities under my voluntary control. Those occurrent mental acts *are* just the accessing of these respective modes of presentation. This host of accessed modes of presentation forms an appar-

[11]J. J. Valberg, following Zeno Vendler and Thomas Nagel, offers the most detailed and insightful account of the centered nature of the phenomenology of self-consciousness that I have found in the analytic tradition. Though, as will be evident below, I have learned much from Valberg's impressive work, we are fundamentally at odds on a pivotal point, in many ways the central structuring point of his wonderful book *Dream, Death and the Self* (Princeton University Press, 2007).

ent unity or whole. When I turn my attention to myself and my "inner" condition, I encounter my occurrent mental acts as lying within such a whole. This, their forming an apparent unity or whole, *is* the appearance of the arena, the arena's presence in my mental life as (at least) an intentional object. In using the technical term "intentional object," I mean only to register that the arena *may* have no existence apart from the mental acts in which it presents or appears. It is not an "object" in the sense of a salient compact thing, nor is it an experienced bright line; it is just the unity that appears when I turn my attention to myself and my "inner" condition.

Consider how things seem in "inner" mantric meditation. One is given a mantra to repeat over and over, an inner word or phrase to gently return to when one's mind fills with other thoughts. The mental word is mildly charming, and for considerable stretches it can simply be what fills one's consciousness. (One is, say, in a silent room with one's eyes closed in a condition of complete relaxation in which bodily sensational experience is at a minimum. All effort is renounced.) Nonetheless the word presents as being "here." I mean first that it seems contained in a quasi-space that includes all the potential objects of "introspection" or higher-order awareness of one's own mental goings on. When thoughts intrude, they seem to intrude "into" this quasi-space. Second, one is oneself presented as intimately related to this quasi-space, it is one's own, one is at the center of it. THERE, very close, is the mantra or word, and HERE, closer than any mere object of attention could get, one is.

The point of mantric meditation, described in merely psychological terms, is for the mantra first to be the only occupant (apart from oneself) of this quasi-space or arena and then, crucially, to fade away. We can now redescribe the oft-repeated claim that when the mantra finally drops away without the return of thought one experiences a "centerless" form of consciousness in which the sense of self temporarily disappears. The quasi-space, the arena, remains, but because there is no thought or sensation or intention in that space, there is nothing with respect to which one can locate a center, the locus at which one finds oneself. Because there is nothing close, the closest thing does not appear. But once a thought intrudes into the empty arena the closest thing, the center, reappears and I am able to pick myself out as the one located at it.

LICHTENBERG VINDICATED*

Recognizing the arena and the center helps diagnose just what is wrong and what is right in G. C. Lichtenberg's famous objection to Descartes' reliance on the *Cogito*. Descartes reasons from the fact that he is thinking to the fact that he exists. Lichtenberg observed that Descartes' starting point looks over-described, at least given Descartes' scrupulous methodological skepticism, that is, his commitment to accept only what is rationally forced on him, and so not open to doubt. Descartes, Lichtenberg suggests, should have simply begun with the observation that thinking is going on. In fact, however, whenever there is thinking going on there is more that is directly phenomenologically evident. There is an arena in which the thinking is taking place, and that arena is centered, and the thinking is occurring at the center.

The real question that bedevils Descartes' use of the *Cogito* to establish with indubitable certainty that he exists is whether one is rationally compelled to believe just on the basis of introspection *that there is someone or something at the center.* There appears to be a human being here, but that is not indubitable in Descartes' special sense.

The idea of centered arenas provides the material to respond to Bernard Williams's well-known argument against G. C. Lichtenberg, namely that we have to provide the resources for the distinction between thinking going on and thinking going on in some sense *here*, and Lichtenberg's ownerless description of experience does not provide those resources.[12] The idea of centered arenas provides for this without entailing that there is anyone at the center. Perhaps the best summary of the situation is that while Lichtenberg found less than was indubitably available, Descartes found more, and so *did* over-describe his starting point in describing it as "Cogito."

ON DISCOVERING THAT "YOU" DON'T EXIST*

Is it really dubitable that there is someone here at the center, and so conceivable that no one has the property of being me? I believe that it could be made plausible within this arena of presence that there is no one at the center of this arena of presence.

[12] Bernard Williams, *Descartes: The Project of Pure Inquiry* (Humanities Press, 1978), 95–101.

First it would have to be made plausible within this arena of presence that the visual, bodily sensational, and proprioceptive deliverances as of a human being here were all hallucinatory, as they might be if I were in fact a brain in a vat. That is certainly conceivable. Testimony to the effect that these are all hallucinations could print out in bright red letters along the bottom half of THIS visual field. At first there would be no reason to take the printout as anything more than a symptom of mental illness. But then the printout begins to make precise predictions of bizarre changes that are about to happen in this visual field, predictions such as "That apparent laptop will now apparently turn into an apparent chicken" and lo, the laptop turns into a chicken. If this happens with absolute consistency and regularity, the source of the testimony may acquire considerable credibility. (Don't ask "Credible to *whom*?" That simply presupposes that there cannot be justified or well-reasoned beliefs occurring at the center without anyone being at the center.)

Now the apparent testifier takes a new and more worrying tack. He prints out sentences in THIS visual field that express the following propositions. *We members of an incredibly advanced civilization have discovered precise psychophysical correlations that enable us to create physical realizers of arenas of presence and to fill those arenas with hallucinations of people at them. But it is not that these physical realizers are persons, who could then be candidates to be the ones really at the respective centers that they create. For one thing the realizers themselves never will appear at any of the respective phenomenological centers defined by the arenas of presence; though the realizers cause arenas of presence they never are at the phenomenological centers defined by the arenas of presence. For another, despite our vast psychophysical knowledge, we have never been able to achieve the goal of one realizer/one arena of presence. What we know of psychophysics tells us that our realizers always realize arenas of presence in batches of seven. We can find no way of parsing out subparts of the realizers to overcome this difficulty, and our best psychophysics strongly suggests that this problem cannot be overcome. So there is not even a physical system that is especially causally responsible for any one of the seven separated arenas of presence in which these words are now appearing.*

To the extent that those propositions became plausible at this arena of presence, it would be plausible that there is no one, no person, occupying this arena of presence. It would be plausible that there is no one to pick out as "I, myself" even though this arena of presence is filled with thought and bodily sensational and ostensible perceptual experience.

That is how Descartes might have found his own existence to be dubitable; how he might have imagined a scenario that was thoroughly consistent with the deliverances of perception and thought, narrowly considered, and yet was a scenario in which he did not exist.

What this shows, of course, is the emptiness of Descartes' method of doubt. Not even the Cogito survives as something indubitable. It also shows that the source of our knowledge of our own existence is not merely introspective awareness of an arena and its contents considered as merely inner items; for the knowledge that we exist depends on taking the deliverances of (bodily sensational and visual) perception, in particular the perception of a human being at the relevant center, at face value.

ON BEING ME

So it is the property of being at the center of this arena of presence that is the property of being me in the most intimate and important sense. It is because the human being Johnston is at the center of this arena of presence that he *is* me. I wake up, in bed or in a chair, and there is Johnston occupying the central phenomenological position. If it had turned out that it was someone else here at the center of this arena of presence, say, Mother Teresa, or Locke's Rational Parrot, or the Prince of Darkness, then I would have been that woman, or that parrot, or that fallen angel. But time after time, without exception, when I wake up, or when I come to self-consciousness out of absorption in the flow of life, it has just been Johnston HERE at the center. That is why I have grown so attached to him, despite his many obvious limitations. He's me. Given all the other options that being me appears to leaves open, I am happy enough to settle for Johnston. (Would I dare put my hand in the bag of snakes *again*?)

But now, when I reflect on my own death, I don't just think of the demise of the human being Johnston, but of the obliteration of the very thing that made him me—this arena of presence and action that "happens" to have Johnston at its center. More than this, in anticipating my own death and the way that the world will then close seamlessly around my absence, I discover that the supposedly central phenomenological position is not underwritten by the world. There never was a center but only the appearance of one. In thus seeing what will be involved in my death, the very idea of being me can seem to be some kind of illusion, or more exactly the product of a kind of continuous hallucination whose intentional objects, this arena and its center, were *mere* intentional objects, answering to nothing in the world.

This is worse than simply *anticipating* nothingness; I HAVE ALWAYS ALREADY BEEN A THING DEFINED RELATIVE TO A MERE APPEARANCE. Vertigo? Terror? Angst? All these seem less than what is called for.

CALM DOWN!

There is a streak in analytic philosophy that wants to treat this sort of thing as a simple confusion. So in the Blue Book, Wittgenstein says,

> The idea that the real "I" lives within the body is a product of an illusion produced by the peculiar grammar of "I."[13]

And P. F. Strawson, particularly in his reply to J. L. Mackie on the transcendental self, bases his rejection of talk of the self on the simple semantic analysis of the first-person pronoun as an indexical, according to which the semantic rule for "I" is that an occurrence of "I" in an utterance denotes the person or human being who made the utterance.[14] Because "I" is governed by this semantic rule, one can use it to pick out a human being, even while one is ignorant of who that human being is. So any identity statement like "I am Johnston" will be a posteriori, that is, knowable only on the basis of an external identification of the human being one in fact is. The a posteriori character of such statements creates the illusion that they are genuinely contingent, and that illusion allows us to attempt certain feats of auto-alienation, which falsely separate our supposed selves from the human beings with which we are *necessarily* identical. That is the official doctrine.

Could it possibly be that simple? Could it be, as Wittgenstein and P. F. Strawson suggest, that the idea of the self is just an artifact of misunder-

---

[13] Ludwig Wittgenstein, *The Blue and Brown Books* (Basil Blackwell, 1987), 60.
[14] See Strawson's reply to J. L. Mackie's "The Transcendental 'I,'" in Zak van Straaten, ed., *Philosophical Subjects: Essays Presented to P. F. Strawson* (Oxford, 1980).

standing the peculiar grammar of "I"? Could we have just been mistaking a reflexive mode of presentation associated with the first-person pronoun for a subject or an innermost self or an *ownmost* identity, an illusory something that is then dramatically cast as the real subject of death, the thing whose ceasing to be is close to unimaginable, but once imagined utterly terrifying?

I believe that it is the Strawsonian position that is the product of an illusion, namely the illusion that the content of the essentially subjective thoughts naturally expressed by certain uses of "I" can be fully explained by the simple semantic rule governing the first-person pronoun.[15]

Mere Facts of Identity

For one thing, to treat all uses of "I" in this way threatens to make *superficial* nonsense of our special concern for ourselves, the concern that manifests itself in one's everyday egocentrism and in one's unique fear of one's death.

So, sitting in a booth in the Triumph Brewery I overhear some thugs in the next booth planning to beat someone up. As a public-spirited citizen, I am appalled. But then I overhear them use my name and realize that they are planning to beat *me* up. My attitude changes, now that I know it's *me*. My special concern for myself has been activated. Not *me*, I think, as if that would somehow be worse than having someone or other beaten up. (Luck, someone once said, is when the other chap gets the bullet.)

That is rather egocentric, I freely admit. But this kind of everyday egocentrism is perfectly intelligible; we mostly organize our lives around it, and so it is treated as a reasonable default starting point in practical deliberation. In ordinary decent people, such everyday egocentrism does not so much disappear; it remains at the core of a pattern of concern C. D. Broad once called "self-referential altruism," an expanded circle of special concern for oneself, one's friends, one's familiars, one's family, and perhaps one's tribe or nation. And in decent people, this whole pat-

---

[15] At the end of the day, after an enormous amount of revisionary work, we may be led to the view that there is nothing better for an occurrence of "I" to refer to than the person who uttered it. But this is best understood as a reconstruction of our practice, after a surprising discovery of the failure of "I" to refer to something like a self.

tern of self-referential concern is itself partly offset by the impersonal concern that things go well for others, whoever they are. Still, egocentrism remains, and it remains a mutually intelligible starting point in reasoning about what to do when the interests of others are not much at risk. The thing that would really need explanation is someone who did not react in this kind of way, someone who treated himself as just another, one whose needs and interests happened to be immediately present, but which thereby had no special practical weight as sources of reasons to act and prefer.

But all the thugs actually announced was their intent to beat up *Johnston*. It is because I know that I am Johnston that my special self-concern was not only activated but justified.

How exactly does that work on the official semantic doctrine? The indexical "I" as used by me simply serves to pick out Johnston; it does not introduce any other ingredient of reality besides Johnston as a topic of thought or talk. The fact that I am Johnston is just an identity fact. It is the fact that Johnston is Johnston. How could that fact possibly *justify* any pattern of concern? Johnston is Johnston, Mother Teresa is Mother Teresa, the Prince of Darkness is the Prince of Darkness. So what? These identity facts are all on a par, and they mean little or nothing to me. Of course, on the official doctrine, I stand in a particular way to one of these identity facts. I am able to represent the identity fact that Johnston is Johnston by way of the sentence "I am Johnston." For in my mouth "I" denotes Johnston. But so what?

Here and throughout when I talk of facts I mean not true truthbearers, or true propositions, but rather ingredients of reality that make propositions true or false. I am not assuming some picture of propositions on which the (true) proposition that I am Johnston is the (true) proposition that Johnston is Johnston. I am concerned with facts as truthmakers, the things that make true propositions true. On the official view of "I," my being Johnston and Johnston's being Johnston are the very same fact, the very same truthmaker. But that seems wrong, whatever view of the propositions expressed by "I am Johnston" and "Johnston is Johnston" we take.

The official view says that I have available a mode of presentation of the identity fact that Johnston is Johnston which others do not have available to them. If I add to the factual content of the thugs' conversation the fact that Johnston is Johnston, then I am still left pretty cold. As a public-spirited citizen I am appalled, of course, but my special concern for myself is not engaged. But when I add the fact that I am Johnston, I really get warmed up.

Yet, on the official doctrine the fact that Johnston is Johnston is the fact that I am Johnston.

The whole structure of my intelligibly egocentric self-concern now looks like it depends on my confusing a difference in the mode of presentation of a fact for a difference in the fact presented. That's bizarre. I seem to be like the drunk who thinks that the lampposts get bigger as he moves toward them and shrink in size as he moves away. He thereby mistakes a difference in the modes of presentation of the lampposts for a difference in the facts about the lampposts. But he does this only when he is drunk; whereas on the official doctrine, we are doing something like that whenever our special self-concern is engaged.

That's a bizarre interpretation of the human condition! It would be better to find something other than a fact of mere identity associated with the "I"-thoughts that ground our special concern.

Feats of Auto-Alienation

Taken as a thesis about what is *conveyed* by all uses of "I" and its cognates, the official doctrine is anyway rather forced. Many uses of "I" are not *blank* indexical uses, uses whose communicative function is just to introduce the speaker or writer as a topic of thought and talk. There appear to be uses of "I" where a certain interesting subjective property is being introduced as a topic of thought and talk.

I am told that some girls want (or wanted) to *be* Ms. Britney Spears, and not just have her talent, her wealth, her feckless lifestyle, and her looks. I imagine there are also some fanatical Britney Spears imitators on the model of those imitating Elvis Presley. But the girls who want to *be* Britney would not be satisfied with being one of those Britney imitators, nor even with being a better version of one of those. They do not just want to exemplify the Britney type. They want, I suppose, to live Britney's actual bodily and mental life from the inside.

Compare the movie *Being John Malkovitch*, where the depiction of living Malkovitch's mental and body life is given in terms of the still inadequate metaphor of being a homunculus inside Malkovitch's head. That won't quite do either. The girls who want to be Britney do not thereby want to occupy a position inside her head. What, then, is it, exactly, that these girls want? One such girl might fantasize waking up one morning to find only Britney there (at the center of the girl's own arena of presence and action). She expresses the content of her fantasy as "I am Britney." Must this be just the thin indexical thought, which automatically makes the content of the fantasy necessarily false *and* very difficult to conceive? If so, what is the content of the vivid desire to which the fantasy answers?

For a second consideration, what are we to make of certain feats of auto-alienation on the part of those who obviously know who they are? Here is perhaps one of the most famous of such feats, taken from Jorge Luis Borges' short story "Borges and I."

> The other one, the one called Borges, is the one things happen to. I walk through the streets of Buenos Aires and stop for a moment, perhaps mechanically now, to look at the arch of an entrance hall and the grillwork on the gate; I know of Borges from the mail and see his name on a list of professors or in a biographical dictionary. I like hourglasses, maps, eighteenth-century typography, the taste of coffee and the prose of Stevenson; he shares these preferences, but in a vain way that turns them into the attributes of an actor. It would be an exaggeration to say that ours is a hostile relationship; I live, let myself go on living, so that Borges may contrive his literature, and this literature justifies me. It is no effort for me to confess that he has achieved some valid pages, but those pages cannot save me, perhaps because what is good belongs to no one, not even to him, but rather to the language and to tradition.... Years ago I tried to free myself from him and went from the mythologies of the suburbs to the games with time and infinity, but those games belong to Borges now and I shall have to imagine other things. Thus my life is a flight and I lose everything and everything belongs to oblivion, or to him. I do not know which of us has written this page.[16]

[16]Jorge Luis Borges, *Labyrinths: Selected Stories and Other Writings* (New Directions, 1964), 246–47.

What is Borges here trying to convey with his use of "I"? Certainly the character and content of what he is conveying are not fully captured by the simple semantical rule for the first-person pronoun and the necessary truth that Borges is Borges.

Or consider a third case, an elaboration of a nice example of J. J. Valberg's. Suppose a friend, Sally Smith, tells me that in her dream last night her father, Mr. Smith, asked her to marry him. Having read a little too much Freud, I've become jaded by this sort of thing. I think, "Well, yes, another predictable Freudian conceit slipping into our dream lives. When will all this stuff about the Electra Complex finally fade away?" But then Sally adds: "But the funny thing is, in that dream I *was* my father." Now I perk up; this is something new.

I can understand Sally's claim that in her dream she was her father. She means something like this: the human being who occupied the central phenomenological position in her dream, the one to whom events in the dream were presented, the one who apparently initiated action from this center, was her father, Mr. Smith. Sally was just another human being appearing in the dream. Sally was not occupying the position at the phenomenological center of her dream.

Sally was the dreamer of her dream, no doubt about that. But this is compatible with the central phenomenological position in her dream being occupied by another human being, or by a rational parrot, or by an angel. (All of this, of course, is how things might go, according to the dream.) And so it is compatible with the human being, Sally Smith, turning up in the dream and addressing the person at the center of her dream. And so it is compatible with Sally being proposed to by the one who is at the center of her dream—as it turns out, by her father. (An outbreak in her dream of anxious self-concern would properly focus on her father.)

It is a contingent claim, and one that is not always true, that in my dreams I am the human being Johnston. In some of my dreams, I am Hannibal. The contingency of the claim cannot be explained by treating the use of "I" that figures in the claim as an indexical use. For I am not at all trying to convey that, in some of my dreams, Johnston is Hannibal. I don't have any idea of what that could possibly come to. (A strange hybrid, perhaps? But that was not the content of my dream.) So we must understand the claim as having a different structure.

The interesting thought I express by "In my dreams, I am the human being Hannibal" comes to something like this: In my dreams, the person who occupies the apparent center of the arena of presence and action in which the dream develops, the one to whom the dream events are presented, is the human being Hannibal. But then the thought I express by "In my waking life, I am the human being Johnston" should come to something structurally similar: In my waking life, the person who occupies the apparent center of this arena of presence and action, the one to whom these mental and bodily events are presented, the one who is the initiator of these actions, is the human being Johnston.[17]

For this reason, and reasons like this, we might distinguish *purely* indexical uses of "I," which, for example, occur when you are introducing yourself, from truly subjective uses of "I" where the intent is, *in effect, or can be reconstructed as,* the intent to pick out the one at the center of an immediately available arena of presence and action.

The purely indexical thought that I am Johnston is obviously necessarily true (if, as the standard doctrine supposes, "I" in my thought picks out Johnston). Nonetheless, it can appear contingent that it is Johnston who lies at the center of this arena of presence and action. I believe that is really a version of Locke's insight: He is the first to develop in detail the idea that it is contingent that a given substance, as he puts it, "adheres" to a given consciousness. And that idea may be usefully elaborated in terms of the notion of an arena of presence and action. I can be struck, when I wake up in a chair, at the apparent contingency of the fact that it is Johnston, or even Johnston's soul, here again at the center of this arena of presence. As Borges suggests, it can come to seem a rather tedious imposition: Why does he, or that, always have to be hanging around?

Am I Now Contingently Johnston?*

Of course it is *apparently* contingent that water is H_2O, even though upon philosophical reflection we can come to see that it is necessary that water is H_2O. (A doctrine I accept, even though I take the truth "Water

---

[17] I don't mean "is semantically equivalent to" by "comes to," as lecture three will illustrate. Valberg makes a structurally similar point about this kind of example, but he appeals to his notion of a horizon rather than to the arena. For a comparison and contrast of our respective views, see the addendum to this lecture.

is H$_2$O" to express a claim of material constitution rather than an identity claim.)[18] It was of course Saul Kripke, in his groundbreaking lectures in this very series, who taught us how to discredit the apparent contingency of such claims. In *Naming and Necessity*, Kripke explained that when one conjures in imagination a seeming situation in which water turns out to be, say, H$_2$O$_4$, one is not really presenting to oneself the genuine possibility of *water* turning out to be H$_2$O$_4$.[19] One is merely presenting to oneself in imagination a phenomenological-cum-evidential copy or counterpart of water, that is, something that looks, feels, and acts like water even though it is not water precisely because it has a different chemical constitution. So the apparent contingency of water being H$_2$O is compatible with the necessity of water being H$_2$O.

Isn't it like this with the apparent contingency of Johnston being the one at the center of this arena of presence and action? Why shouldn't that apparently contingent claim be nonetheless necessary?

For one thing, there is a snag that disables the version of Kripke's deflationary explanation of the appearance of contingency that would be required in this instance. Let us try out the deflationary explanation and see where it fails.

I look down and, lo and behold, there is a beak sticking out in the middle of my visual field. I cock my head and see the plumage of a parrot covering me. I shiver in fear, and my wings go up. When I thus seem to myself to be imagining a rational parrot being here at the center of this arena of presence, and therefore conclude that it is contingent that Johnston occupies that center, the required deflationary explanation would have it that I am not really presenting to myself the possibility that *this* arena of presence and action has something other than Johnston at its center. All I am doing is presenting to myself a phenomenological-cum-evidential counterpart of this arena of presence and action, that is, a numerically *distinct* arena of presence, one that turns out to have a parrot at its center.

Here is the snag. Anything that is *now* given to me phenomenologically and evidentially just as this arena of presence and action is given to me now *is* this arena of presence and action. In that respect "this arena of presence and action" is more like "pain" than "water." For anything

[18]See Mark Johnston, "Manifest Kinds," *Journal of Philosophy* 94 (1997): 564–83.
[19]Saul Kripke, *Naming and Necessity* (Harvard University Press, 1980).

that is phenomenologically just like pain *is* pain, as Kripke himself emphasized. And anything that is given to me now that is phenomenologically just like my mind is my mind.

Suppose that I have been in a drug-induced sleep, during which someone actually dressed me up as a parrot, complete with a beak and movable wings. I now wake up, and in my slightly stilted way I think, "Oh, no, the one at the center of this arena of presence and action is... A PARROT." What I've supposed is false, but it seems *possible*; my immediate thought about myself was far from incoherent. The crucial question is this: Let me enter into this scenario, consider it actual *and actually taking place now*, and consider the phenomenological context of the demonstrative act by which I pick out this arena of presence and action; is there really a epistemic possibility of another distinct arena of presence and action being given then to me in that very way? No, any arena that could be given to me now in this very way would be this very arena of presence and action. There is no question of the possibility of *another* arena of presence and action—one that is not my own—now being given to me in just the way that this arena of presence and action is now given to me.

For recall how the notion of an arena of presence was introduced. We observed that the modes of presentation of the items in one's perceptual field are perspectival; that is, they present items to a particular viewing position or, more generally, to a particular place at a particular time, a place and time from which someone might sense the surrounding environment. The implied position at which those modes of presentation seem to converge is the position of one's head and body. To that same implied position, a bodily field, as it were a quasi-three-dimensional volume of bodily sensation, also presents. And that implied position is also one from which certain acts, presented as willed, emanate. Furthermore, it is the position where mental acts seem available for higher-order awareness. We called such a centered pattern of presence and action, existing at a particular time, and perhaps over time, *an arena of presence and action*. There is one given to me now, which I may demonstrate as this arena of presence and action. What makes it this very arena of presence and action is the convergent phenomenological pattern that constitutes it.

Clearly, then, anything that could be given to me *now* in just the same phenomenological and evidential way as this arena of presence and action would be this arena of presence and action.[20]

The conclusion is not that it is finally established that it is contingent that Johnston is the one at the center of this arena of presence, but only that a Kripke-style diagnosis will not work to explain away that apparent contingency.

However the issue of contingency or necessity might end up, we already have enough to cement the distinction between the merely indexical remark that I am Johnston, a remark I might make at a party or a reunion, and the truly subjective thought that Johnston is me, the one at the center of this arena of presence and action.

In addition, it seems clear that the subjective use of "I" and its cognates is the philosophically interesting use. For example, the narrative "I" or "ego" of Descartes' *Meditations* mostly involves not the indexical use but the truly subjective use. When Descartes uses first-person imaginings to argue that he is not essentially a body or to suggest that he is not essentially the human being Descartes, he is not making a mistake that could be corrected by the observation that the first-person pronoun is an indexical term, any use of which rigidly denotes whatever it denoted on the occasion of that use. He is observing that a certain mind or consciousness, or, as we now might put it, a certain arena of presence and action, which he can directly pick out, seems detachable from any body and hence from any human being. And in the spirit of Locke we might add, contra Descartes' intent, from any soul as well.

Something I (Almost) Always Know*

How do I know that certain "I"-thoughts are my thoughts? That may sound like the oddest of questions, but such knowledge is an achievement, which, however easily attained in ordinary life, can be denied me in special circumstances. After all, schizophrenics sometimes report first-person thought insertion, as when they feel that the devil or some

---

[20]Notice something that will turn out to be crucial in what follows. In making these claims I am not asserting claims of diachronic identity, or identity over time, for this arena of presence and action. My own view is that such claims are in themselves radically indeterminate. The issue is instead whether anything that could be given to me *now* in just the same phenomenological and evidential way as this arena of presence and action could be anything other than this arena of presence and action.

other tempter has inserted his "I"-thoughts into their heads. The queer thing about the thought-insertion experience is that certain "I"-thoughts are phenomenologically displaced; they seem not to fit "here"—at this center, as I might put it—and so are not really my thoughts.[21] But this makes it look as if the subjective, immediate sense of mineness, by which I know that even the "I"-thoughts that passively occur to me are indeed my thoughts, goes by way of locating them as occurring at this center. (The passivity of some of my "I"-thoughts is at odds with the idea that they count as mine because of a veridical sense of agency I have with respect to them. I seem to have no such sense of agency when the thought that I have left the gas on *hits me with a jolt*.)

It is natural to pair this observation with an unnoticed difficulty for the frequently made semantic claim to the effect that

A token of the word "I" refers to the one who tokened it.

It is not that this claim is obviously false, but it is in a certain way mysterious. For "tokened" is here a philosopher's term of art intended to cover writing, uttering, or thinking the token in question. And this is a motley group of acts. Writing or uttering a token "I"-sentence requires that you caused it to exist and, indeed, knowingly did so. But it is much less clear that this is required when it comes to thinking a token "I"-thought. Imagine that just as bodily sensations can be produced by direct stimulation of the brain, certain forms of "I"-thought can also be so produced. So suppose a neurophysiologist in this way directly causes in me the thought, "I will win the Battle of Waterloo." He has knowingly

[21]This way of thinking of thought insertion goes with the idea that the two cardinal symptoms of schizophrenia, namely auditory hallucination ("hearing voices") and reports of awareness of other people's thoughts inserted into the one's own mind, are perhaps dual expressions of a unitary phenomenon. The voices that schizophrenics hear are more like imagined voices than heard voices, particularly with respect to their poverty of sensory quality, but unlike ordinary non-pathological auditory imagery they are not experienced as issuing from HERE, the center. The thoughts reported as inserted seem to their subjects as neither wholly HERE nor wholly THERE. Close enough to HERE would make them seem to be thoughts rather than heard voices, but the residual displacement from HERE undermines the sense of ownership. That is a hypothesis that fits with some of the reported phenomenology of schizophrenia and begins to account for the puzzling availability of the conviction, "I am *having* a thought that is not mine."

For the view that auditory hallucinations and thoughts experienced as inserted are on a continuum, see E. Bleuler, *Dementia Praecox or the Group of Schizophrenias*, trans. J. Zinkin (International Universities Press, 1950), and the excellent overview of the whole issue given by P. Langland-Hassan in "Fractured Phenomenologies: Thought Insertion, Inner Speech, and the Puzzle of Extraneity," *Mind and Language* 23 (2008): 369–401.

caused this token of "I" to exist. It is not produced by any agency of mine. Now consider the claim that this "I"-thought nonetheless is my "I"-thought and refers to me. That does not look to be a *semantically* incoherent claim. In fact, I am inclined to accept it. If that is not a semantically incoherent claim and the tokening account of "I" is to remain in place as a semantic thesis, then "tokening" an "I"-thought must be understood to be quite different from "tokening" an "I"-sentence. It must not be understood to require that the tokener causes the thought to exist, and knowingly so.

What, then, does it require? What is it to token an "I"-thought? Perhaps only this: the "I"-thought has to occur at the relevant center of an arena of presence and action. This is, after all, all I immediately know about my passive "I"-thoughts, the ones that just occur to me. And yet I thereby know that they are mine and refer to me.

So far, I have intended to leave open the exact role of a descriptive conception like "the one at the center of this arena" in guiding "I"-use. The descriptive conception, which the description makes explicit, could function as a reference-fixing description for "I," which competent users can call to mind in using "I." Or it could function as the incommunicable sense of "I." Or it could function as the implicitly grasped unity condition for the denotation of "I." In the next lecture I shall try to make sense of this third proposal.

WHAT IS DEATH?

This completes our brief and necessarily compressed case for the conclusion that there are uses of "I" and its cognates whose cognitive content is best captured by way of a certain demonstrative description "the one at the center of this arena" than by the resources of the thin indexical account.

Having distinguished two uses of "I" and its cognates in thought, a use whose content is captured by the thin indexical account and the other whose content is better captured by a demonstrative description, we can now associate two different ideas with the phrase "my death." The human being Johnston, whom I can pick out with the indexical "I," will wither and die; his psychophysical life will be no more. But that is the sort of thing that has happened *billions* of times. Johnston's death is special to ME only because he is ME, not in the trivial indexical sense but in the sense that he lies at the center of this arena of presence and action. It is my taking Johnston to have that property that explains my special solicitude for him, and his future, as opposed to that of Mother Teresa or some parrot.

Consider: If I forgot that I was Johnston, I might then learn of his amnesiac condition, feel sorry for the poor chap, and send him a check to help him out. That would not be egoism but a kind of altruism. When I do not take Johnston to be the one here at this center, my acts toward him cannot be guided by direct self-interest.

What is it about being at the center of an arena that makes so much practical difference? Here again I ask you to consider your centered phenomenology and notice a profound asymmetry of apparent value given in your arena. THERE is the world or at least ostensible occupants of the world; these present as appealing or repellent or in between, as, say, desirable to "degree zero." But HERE there is something primitively presented in a way we might describe as "to be protected" or even "to be prized." Particularly during occasions of threat or conflict or frustration or competition the arena is affectively charged, and asymmetrically so: then what is special and especially worthy of protection is what is HERE. THERE is a sphere of action whose fruits can benefit what is HERE, and a sphere of potential harms to what is HERE.

In saying this I am not so much trying to capture thoughts we go on to have about ourselves and the world but simply trying to articulate a pre-verbal structure of affect that comes with the arena.[22]

This, we might suppose, is not a bad way to organize the consciousness of an animal with our kind of evolutionary history. There is considerable survival value in developing a form of consciousness that is primitively mobilized to favor what it finds at the center as opposed to what is THERE.

Perhaps this pre-verbal asymmetry of evaluative affect is at the base of our more sophisticated disposition to seek premium treatment for ourselves. That might partly explain why each of us is naturally disposed to be a secret (or not so secret) enemy of impersonal morality, as Kant observed in articulating his famous doctrine of radical evil. Kant's

---

[22] For more on this idea of a pre-verbal structure of affect, see Mark Johnston, "The Authority of Affect," *Philosophy and Phenomenological Research* 61, no. 4 (2001): 181–214.

doctrine that we are radically evil is not the doctrine that we are bad to the bone, bad through and through; it is the manifestly true claim that there is something at the root of human nature that disposes each one of us to favor himself or herself over the others. The present proposal is that this is something in the very structure of our consciousness, a profound asymmetry of evaluational affect, which privileges what is HERE over those things THERE.

That is why thinking of Johnston as me, as the one at the center of this arena, makes him appear privileged, even if he is actually just one human being among all the others. Here two things line up: the incommunicable way each one has of thinking of himself, and the appearance of distinctive worth that naturally drives special self-concern. We could secure the first without the second, as with the proposal that the cognitive content of "I"-thought involves the incommunicable sense of the direct demonstrative description "the thinker of this very thought." But here the content of the description does nothing to explain why it seems coherent to privilege the thing that satisfies it. (Why are THESE thoughts so great? What is so great about thinking them?)

On the back of our account of "I"-thought we can thus elaborate a distinction between biological death and subjective death. In my case this distinction would amount to the distinction between the death of Johnston and the end of this arena of presence, and hence of the very property of being me, the property whose possession by Johnston made him worthy of my self-concern.[23]

I (and here I use the mere indexical), that is, the human being Johnston, will die. A particular human being, one of the teeming horde, the one who has just used the first-person pronoun to pick himself out, will die. His mental and bodily life will cease to exist. When I think of this outcome in that way, my special concern for myself need not be engaged. The shutting down of the mental and bodily life of a human being has happened billions of times before, and it will continue to happen, as part of the natural life of our species. Biological death, the death of the human being I pick out by the first-person pronoun, is thus not even a prima

---

[23] Perhaps this distinction has some affinity with Martin Heidegger's distinction between my death and my *ownmost* death. See his *Being and Time*, trans. John Macquarie and E. S. Robinson (Harper and Row, 1962), 279ff. In any case, in what follows, I shall appropriate Heidegger's term for my subjective death.

facie object of the intense self-concern that the threat of death provokes. But in thus holding Johnston at such a distance, I am forgetting something. That human being is ME, the one at the center of this arena of presence and action. When that human being dies this arena of presence and action will come to an end. That is my subjective death, my *ownmost* death, and it does jog my intense self-concern. My *ownmost* death is terrifying; it is the end of this arena of presence and action, and *thus the end of the frame in which the fundamental distinction of value, the distinction between the value of what is HERE and of what is THERE, appears.*

This is why it appears, *madly I know, but nonetheless it does so appear,* that a world in which no one is ME is in a certain way defective: the very frame in which the fundamental distinction of value appears is missing from such a world.

And yet I find nothing obviously defective in the myriad possible worlds and actual times that are without Johnston.

JOHNSTON'S DEATH AND MY DEATH

It seems that Johnston's death and my ownmost or subjective death can come apart in imagination. If I imagine myself as the central protagonist in a scene like that depicted in *The Entombment*, I find it natural to describe it as the death of Johnston but not of his soul, and so not of me. Johnston is not a soul, he is a human being.

As I might put it, I was first constituted by Johnston and then came to be constituted by his soul. But then I can imagine my soul dying, and then there would be no arena of presence around to make anything *count* as me. It is this last thing that really terrifies me. This suggests that it is only insofar as I see Johnston's death as my ownmost death—the end of this arena of presence and hence of the property of being me—that Johnston's death terrifies me.

I find I can significantly diminish my fear of Johnston's death by certain thoughts like these: Johnston will soon be old and increasingly a burden to himself and others; it then won't be such a bad thing for him to pass away and make room for others, and it will be a good thing for this to happen before he is subjected to the indignity that comes with the massive medicalization of the end of life. What there is to fear in Johnston's death is just that he will not receive the grace of a timely and relatively

painless death. Grant him that and there is little to fear on his behalf;
certainly nothing to be terrified at. This, I presume, is how my friends,
though I hope not my closest friends, would think about my death. (Like
you, I hope those closest to me will share something of my delusion of
my own importance.)

None of that works when I think of this arena of presence coming to
an end. Something visceral, something else entirely, is engaged. Stoicism
works for Johnston, but not for me.

Perhaps each one of us can imagine his or her own funeral, with the
dead body in the coffin being lowered into the hole in the ground. At the
wake, one's house is filled with people, but all of them are the others. The
mourners are sad, and perhaps it is sad, but it is not THE TERRIFYING
END. It is the sort of thing that invariably happens. But in imagining
such things we are feigning a visual perspective, indeed a visual field,
and a more inclusive arena, in which such events are taking place. So
such imaginings need not threaten the standing implicit sense of there
still being an arena that is one's own, which has oneself at the center. So
when people say that death itself, mere nonexistence, is not such a big
deal, I wonder whether they have really have subjective death, rather
than mere biological death, in view.

In defending the Epicurean doctrine that death should be nothing to
us, Lucretius offers an argument from the symmetry of prenatal and
postmortem nonexistence. Surely both conditions are equal in value, yet
we regard the first as of no account. So, Lucretius concludes, we should
regard our postmortem nonexistence as of no account. The general Lu-
cretian claim of symmetry has struck many as wrong since untimely
death shuts down something, namely a functioning individual personality, which once under way seems to call out for more life. And in the case
of a timely death, old age and illness has already done the destructive
work we rightly fear in fearing untimely death.

Lucretius seems to miss something else, which suggests that subjective death never came into view for him. He regards coming into being
as merely a natural biological event amounting to the assembling of
atoms in a certain form. He does not register the uncanny quality of
"subjective" birth. In my own case I might describe the uncanny quality
of subjective birth in this way. (You can do a similar thing in your case.)
For eons of time everything existed without this arena of presence exist-

ing, and THEN sometime in Melbourne, Australia, in the twentieth century, THIS arena of presence came to be. How could the frame that marks the fundamental distinction of value, the evaluative distinction between what is HERE and what is THERE, have come into existence so late in the day? (Recall Nabokov's chronophobiac looking at the home movie made weeks before he was born.)

If there is any symmetry here it may be this: perhaps it is only those who are capable of appreciating the uncanny quality of their own subjective birth who can fully grasp the apparent loss involved in subjective death.[24]

WHAT REALLY MATTERS IN SURVIVAL?

Nothing in the capacity of "I"-thought to motivate our special self-concern depends essentially on the fact, if it is a fact, that a token occurrence of "I" denotes in every possible situation(in which the whole token utterance can be evaluated for truth or falsity) the person who actually tokened the word.

It is thinking of the human being I am as the one at the center of this arena of presence and action that gets me going for him. There is nothing in the semantics of "the one at the center" that makes it something which denotes in every possible situation the very thing it actually denotes. It is not, as we say, a "rigid designator." As far as having a vehicle to express our special concern for ourselves goes, we could have done as well with "I#," a term of art introduced just to abbreviate the demonstrative description "the one at the center of [this] arena of presence and action." "I#" is thus a non-rigid designator, one whose meaning allows that it pick out different persons in different possible scenarios.

We are now in a position to see how using "I#" might illuminate a crucial practical distinction.

Suppose I# anticipate my body ending up in a persistent vegetative state, a state in which my body has undergone brain death. Will the person Johnston exist then? The answer is probably yes; one possibility for

---

[24]For more on the uncanny nature of birth and death, see Thomas Nagel's chapter, "Birth, Death and the Meaning of Life," in *The View from Nowhere* (Oxford University Press, 1996). Caspar Hare in *On Myself and Other Less Important Subjects* (Princeton University Press, 2009), while giving expression to a very sophisticated form of solipsism, describes his own subjective birth as an uncanny and unbelievable event.

a human being (or for a human animal) is that he ends up in the tragic condition of brain death. But now, I# might wonder whether I# will exist then. There are two distinct contents that can be associated with this concern.

Will the one now at the center of this arena of presence and action *then* exist?

Will there be *someone* at the center of this arena *then*?

The situation where the one presently at this center, namely Johnston, is then a brain-dead human being so that there is, then, no relevant arena, no center, and so no one at it, does not get Me# going in the special way about Johnston. I# might have some residual attachment to him, as I# might to a friend I# lost touch with long ago. But my attitude toward him is not one of self-concern.

Once we distinguish these two questions about some future time,

Will the one now at the center of this arena of presence and action now be flourishing then?

Will the one who is *then* at the center of this arena be flourishing then?

it is clear that the second question is the more pressing from the present self-interested point of view. Just allow the conceptual possibility of another human being coming to occupy the center of this arena *then*, and he, that other human being, will be the one to whom I# will extend my special future-directed concern. For he will then be ME#.

Self Identity versus Personal Identity

Here, then, is the important practical point that the semantic rigidity of "I" (plus the assumption that the indexical picks out a person) serves to mask, and which the use of "I#" or the description it abbreviates makes evident. Self identity, the identity that guarantees the continuation of one's immediately available arena of presence over time, is more basic in its importance than personal identity, the identity over time of the public person who happens now to be at the center of one's arena of presence. When they are *imagined* to come apart, self-concern follows the lineaments of self identity, not personal identity!

This point, it seems to me, must completely alter one's view of the terrain known as the topic of personal identity. When I fear my death in the vivid first-personal way that makes me enter into what that death really involves, what I fear is that at some point in the future no one will have the property of being me. No one will be at the center of this arena of presence and action, for this arena will be no more.

Johnston does not explicitly enter into that fear. And that remains so, even if, as a matter of a posteriori fact, this center could only continue if Johnston's brain were kept alive and functioning.

My sheer desire to survive may *feed* a desire that Johnston survive, but it is not itself a desire that Johnston survive. It is the desire that there will continue to be someone with the property of being me (in the subjective, and not the thin, indexical sense).

Unsurprisingly, almost all of the philosophy of personal identity has configured itself around these questions:

What is the nature of persons? Are persons bodies, animals, souls, or mind-body composites of some sort?

What are the metaphysical conditions of personal identity over time?

In caring about survival, is it rational to care non-derivatively about personal identity as opposed to the "more particular" bodily and psychological connections that in ordinary cases correlate with personal identity?

Once personal identity and self identity are distinguished, it becomes clear that if we are to address the question of what it is rational to care about in caring about survival our topic should be self identity and not personal identity. The topic of personal identity is organized around a blind spot, for the central importance of self identity has been obscured by the way the topic is framed.[25]

Along with many others, Derek Parfit and I have been involved in a debate, on and off over twenty years, as to whether it is personal identity

[25] A point also made by Valberg.

or the associated physical and psychological continuities that are of non-derivative importance when it comes to caring about survival or continued existence. On the present view, we may all have been wrong. On this view, it is self identity that is of non-derivative importance; personal identity gets to count because it makes for self identity. There are conceivable situations, as when I wake up as a rational parrot, where the human being Johnston is no more, and I survive. And contrary to some of Locke's passages in the *Essay*, this is not a case where a single *person* is first a human being and then a parrot. It is a case in which I, this self, am first constituted by a human being and then a parrot.

So it is being me, being the one at the center of this arena of presence, that seems to really count.

Here is the first of the promised major surprises. There may never have been such a property, or at least not one that would allow for the thought of my *prospective* subjective death. My prospective ownmost death is impossible, or more exactly, it is not a possibility that has been provided for.

I don't mean to offer that as any sort of consolation; on the contrary, the idea that there is nothing real to being *you*, when properly grasped, is even more terrifying than death. Each human being would be a victim of a continuous hallucination, but a hallucination on the subject end of experience, the hallucination of the center. Selves would be essentially defined relative to merely virtual items; as it were, things dreamt by the objects of experience, virtual items at which perspectival modes of presentation of those objects appear to converge.

A Merely Intentional Object

Reflection on my death and on the way the world will close seamlessly around my disappearance shows that reality itself is not centered. Still, I might try to save MYSELF—save the very idea of myself, and save the possibility of my ownmost death, by thinking of myself as the one at the virtual or *apparent* center of this arena of presence. The center is a merely intentional object and not a feature of objective reality made manifest in our experience.

There is no problem in principle in picking oneself out by way of a description involving reference to a merely intentional object. Macbeth

could have picked himself out as "the one who is enjoying THIS" referring to his hallucinated dagger. So what is the problem with thinking of
myself as the one at the virtual or *apparent* center of this arena of presence?

The problem is that the arena is also a merely intentional object, and
the identity of merely intentional objects is not an objective matter, and
so not an important matter.

As we shall see, this means that there remains something deeply problematic about the very thought of *this same arena existing later*, and with
similar notions such as "this same consciousness existing later," "this
same self existing later," and "this same subject existing later."

The sortals or kind characterizations "arena of presence and action,"
"consciousness," "subject," "self"—these are all *pseudo*-substance sortals.
That is, despite appearances, mastery of these notions does not confer on
us knowledge of what it would be to have the same arena, or consciousness, or self *again* at some later time. These notions do not provide a
basis for distinguishing one person from another, until and unless they
are wedded in thought to some genuine substance sortal that would indeed apply to its examples essentially and so at all times at which they
exist, as it might be a substance sortal such as "Individual Human Soul."
We shall have occasion to come back to this crucial point, but we need a
bit of a breather before we approach the argument that makes the point
come alive.

PRESENCE AND THE SELF

Let's turn for a moment to a related question. Is presence fundamentally
presence to a mental something, a mental self or subject of experience,
the essential *mental third term* of any mental act, something besides the
object of the act and the manner of presentation of the object? Does every
mental act involve *an object* presenting in a certain way *to a subject*?

Try as I might, I just do not find the third term of my mental acts. I
do find objects presenting in this or that way, and in the perceptual case,
at least, these modes of presentation have an interesting property: they
are perspectival. That is, they disclose how objects appear from a particular point in space. From here, I am able to access how the lectern
looks from here, how you, the audience, appear from here, and how this

body here feels. These modes of presentation converge on the position occupied by the human being with whom I am so terribly familiar. I find him, that is, Johnston, here at this position, but I do not find a substantial mental self or subject of experience here. In this respect I seem to resemble David Hume, who famously wrote,

> There are some philosophers, who imagine we are every moment intimately conscious of what we call our SELF; that we feel its existence and its continuance in existence; and are certain, beyond the evidence of a demonstration, both of its perfect identity and simplicity. To attempt a farther proof of this were to weaken its evidence; since no proof can be deriv'd from any fact, of which we are so intimately conscious; nor is there any thing, of which we can be certain, if we doubt of this.
>
> For my part, when I enter most intimately into what I call *myself*, I always stumble on some particular perception or other, of heat or cold, light or shade, love or hatred, pain or pleasure. I never can catch *myself* at any time without a perception, and never can observe any thing but the perception.... If any one, upon serious and unprejudic'd reflection thinks he has a different notion of *himself*, I must confess I can reason no longer with him. All I can allow him is, that he may be in the right as well as I, and that we are essentially different in this particular. He may, perhaps, perceive something simple and continu'd, which he calls *himself*; tho' I am certain there is no such principle in me.[26]

Of course, I do not deny that these mental acts I am pleased to call mine have a certain impressive feature when considered collectively. They cohere, they are integrated, they follow one from another, and, most important, they are available to be made the topics of higher-order reflective acts, which would in their turn also be integrated into the flow of my mental acts. Thanks to this integration, and availability for further reflection, certain mental acts, as it turns out precisely those that depend for their occurrence on the functioning of Johnston's brain, feel cozy, familiar, MINE. Those mental acts being MINE—that fact may just consist in their sharing this property of relative integration and availability for reflection.

---

[26] David Hume, "Of Personal Identity," *A Treatise of Human Nature* (Clarendon, 1888), 252.

The felt "mineness" of my mental acts is not itself the awareness of a common intrinsic constituent of those acts, as it were, the mental self or ego at the subject pole. It is a feeling of fit; a sense that these present mental acts cohere with a dominant stream of mental life. This feeling of fit is a grace of fortune, secured by the functioning of our brains.

We now know that the feeling of fit can break down even though thought and experience continue. This happens, for example, in Cotard's syndrome, where the patient's very sense of selfhood breaks down. Patients with Cotard's syndrome just come right out and honestly deny that they exist. When you try to explain *Cogito ergo sum* to them, they either dismiss it as a mere trick, or they deny that there is anyone thinking their thoughts or speaking their words. One patient with Cotard's syndrome turned up unannounced at funeral parlors, asking to be buried.[27]

What is wrong with a victim of Cotard's is not that he can no longer find in introspection a mental third term, a persisting mental self at the subject pole of each of his mental acts. Hume could not find such a thing, but he did not have Cotard's syndrome; Hume was not denying that he existed or asking that he be buried because he no longer existed. The mental acts of a victim of Cotard's syndrome are not integrated or smoothly available for further reflection. There is no longer the kind of experiential fit that makes for the sensed "mineness" of experience. The arena and its center are not in view.

Compare the remark of Kant about the breakdown of the so-called unity of apperception, the remark in the second edition of *The Critique of Pure Reason* at B134.

> Only because I comprehend their manifold in a consciousness do I call them all together *my* presentations, for otherwise I would have as multicolored and diverse a self as I have presentations of which I am conscious.

The fact of certain mental acts being mine does not appear to consist in those mental acts sharing a common third term, a substantial self or subject of experience that is most fundamentally ME. For I can find

[27] See J. Pearn and C. Gardner Thorpe, "Jules Cotard (1840–1889): His Life and the Unique Syndrome Which Bears His Name," *Neurology* 58 (2002), and A. W. Young and K. M. Leafhead, "Betwixt Life and Death: Case Studies of the Cotard Delusion," in P. W. Halligan and J. C. Marshall, eds., *Method in Madness: Case Studies in Cognitive Neuropsychiatry* (Psychology Press, 1996).

them to be mine without finding the third term. That, I believe, is the sort of discovery that Hume is reporting in his famous account of the deliverances of his introspective acts. Experiences, or mental acts quite generally, come in integrated bundles and are available to be topics of higher-order mental acts, which if they occurred would likewise be integrated into a larger, more inclusive bundle. But these mental acts are not owned by a mental self. There is no mental third term in the structure of the mental act. There is just the structure of objects presenting, and a mental act is an occurrence in which part of this structure is accessed, thanks to the operations of the brain and nervous system of some human being.

The Impossibility of My Ownmost Death

Given this "no-ownership" view of mental acts, the occurrences that make up our mental lives, is there then any residual sense to be made of one's ownmost death, the death that REALLY matters?

We introduced a term of art "arena of presence and action" to pick out something we were supposing is enjoyed by all conscious beings. I then proposed that whatever natural kind of thing I might discover myself to be, I antecedently have a way of picking myself out as the person at the center of this arena of presence. I then look down to see who that is, and I find that it is not a rational parrot, and it is not Mother Teresa; it is Johnston. That is what Johnston's being me amounts to; it is his being at the center of this arena of presence. And that is why it makes sense for me to care about Johnston's death in the special way that each one of us cares about his or her own death. Facing a situation I believe to be one in which Johnston continues on without the continuation of this arena of presence, Johnston immediately loses his appeal, at least as the object of my special solicitude.

But what is it for someone to *continue* to be at the center of this arena of presence? Perhaps the most surprising hypothesis I have to offer is that there is no good answer to this question, no answer that could bear the weight our future-directed self-concern. Even though our mental life is coherent enough to make for apparently central phenomenological positions, allowing us to formulate a relevant idea of being ourselves *at given times*, there is nonetheless something fundamentally defective about our *prospective* subjective way of thinking of ourselves, the one that figures in the thought of our ownmost death.

The subjective or "inner-directed" ways of thinking of ourselves—as THIS *consciousness*, THIS mental *self or mental substance*, the one at the center of THIS arena *of presence and action*—all involve what I will call "busted" substance sortals. Because of the way in which they are busted, they can only provide for ways of picking ourselves out *at a time* and not *over time*. But the thought of my ownmost death is the thought of this arena of presence having a future that terminates at some point. That is the very kind of thought that may now lack determinate content.[28]

Let me explain.

Offloading Again

In the first lecture we considered the hypothesis that our basic way of tracking or reidentifying each other from the external perspective provided by observation is *criterionless*, in the sense that in so doing we are not employing sufficient conditions for cross-time identity to move from neutral evidence to a conclusion concerning identity. What we see, when we watch each other over time already, as it were, begs the question of identity, so there is no place for criteria that would combine with neutral visual evidence to yield a conclusion about identity. Visually tracking each other without reliance on such criteria is made possible by the fact that we can offload the question of sufficient conditions onto the very human beings or human animals we are tracking. They are substances; at any time at which they present they include a power of self-maintenance and persistence that defines what they each essentially are, say, some flesh and bones kept alive by a disposition to various functions, a disposition realized in the flesh and bones themselves. (Substitute here your favorite up-to-date account of the matter of the body and the powers of self-maintenance realized in it.) Just *when* such a realized power of self-maintenance would cease to be, and when it would continue on, are objective facts that determine the facts of a particular person's identity over time. Given that, all we need do is have some person attract our

---

[28]What is the connection between a consciousness, an arena of presence, and a self? In the next lecture, I identify an arena with a consciousness (in contradistinction to a stream of consciousness), and I explain selves in terms of arenas.

attention, and then the object of our attention will itself determine what sorts of things it would survive and fail to survive.

This works *because* we are here dealing with a substance in the sense of an item that has its essence present at each time at which it is present. It is because we are dealing with such a thing that we are not faced with the task of having to bring to bear on some present manifestation a conception of necessary and sufficient conditions for the persistence of something there manifested in order to make it determinate *what it would be* for the very same thing to be manifested again. The nature of the substance that has attracted our attention already settles this. So our observational tracing of ourselves and others can be criterionless because we are thereby tracing substances and not, say, cross-time bundles of events and states that do not include an active principle which itself determines what it would be to have the very same bundle again.

The main issue here concerns the question of how the thought that one might encounter the *same thing again* gets a determinate content. What is it to have the same thing again, the same thing as is now present here in my visual field or in my inner life? What would it be for some later manifestation to be a manifestation of the same thing again?

There are two models of how such questions might acquire a determinate answer. We might provide the content. That is, given a present manifestation we might have in mind necessary and sufficient conditions for the same thing to be manifest again. Or the world might provide the content. The object of our attention might be a substance, or more generally an endurer, in the sense introduced last time. If it is, then its present manifestation includes a power of self-maintenance and persistence that itself determines what it would be to have that same thing again. In such a case, we are spared the cognitive labor of having to bring to bear any criterion of sameness, any set of necessary and sufficient conditions that would connect this present manifestation to the right future manifestations. The determinacy of the issue of sameness is settled by the objects of our attention themselves, if those objects are substances.

The general point at work here is that criterionless tracing is viable, that is, has determinate success and failure conditions, only when there is some substance (or more generally some endurer) being traced.

Now, our most basic "inner-directed" tracing of ourselves is also criterionless. In looking into my mental life and finding that I am here as I was a moment ago, I am not deploying necessary and sufficient conditions to bundle together events and states at one time with events and states at another. In effect, I am offloading onto a supposed something manifest in my inner experience.

One sign that I am offloading comes from reflection on what it would take, without offloading, to make the question of my persistence a salient question with a determinate answer. So suppose that in reidentifying myself over time I was employing a criterion, in the sense of necessary and sufficient conditions for being the very same person. Then my experiential life would be like this: I would be presented with some evidence about the condition of my inner life. I would apply the criterion and see that it is satisfied by the available evidence. And then I would conclude that I had persisted through time.

To make things a little more concrete, suppose I was employing a Lockean memory criterion of my identity over time. Then the relevant evidence would be my remembering someone experiencing some past event "from the inside," as it were. I would apply the memory criterion and conclude that it was I who existed then. That is how my experiential life would be if I were employing such a criterion of identity or numerical sameness.

That is *not* how my experiential life actually is. For if it were that way, then the following would be a position I might find myself in from time to time. I reason from my memory of a past experience and the memory criterion to it having been me who had the experience. Then I am given overwhelming evidence that I couldn't have had the experience. So I retract the claim of identity. However, I could still be left with the evidence that *someone* had the experience.

That is not how it actually goes. Suppose you seem to remember seeing *The Entombment of Gonzalo Ruíz, Count of Orgaz* being touched up in the Church of Santo Tomé in Toledo, Spain. You apply the memory criterion and conclude that *you, yourself*, were once in Toledo. But suppose that in fact you have never left the United States, and you come to be persuaded of this. You withdraw the identity claim. And you also immediately junk the putative evidence of memory. You do not hold onto evidence to the effect that someone saw the painting being touched up.

Why is that? It is because the evidence of memory was not neutral evidence that only yielded a conclusion of identity when wedded to a criterion of identity. Your memory already "begged the question" of identity. It presented *you* as having been in Toledo. That is why, if you come to believe that you were never in Toledo, the memory gets junked as a source of evidence.

Most of our inner reflective judgments about our own persistence are like that. We are not applying a criterion to some neutral evidence. The evidence is already fully committed on the question of identity. Our own apparent persistence is just given to us. It seems that we trace ourselves through time without a criterion.

An Inner Substance?

Here is another fact, one dramatized by Descartes. I can look into my mental life and seem to find the same subject or self or consciousness or arena of presence *without taking myself to be any externally demonstrable kind of substance, be it a human being, or a rational parrot, or an angel, or whatever.* In looking into myself over time, and tracing myself from the first-person point of view, I seem to know that I am the same, without having tracked the persistence of the same human being, or parrot, or angel. In my first-personal experience of myself over time I am offloading, or I am attempting to offload, but I am not offloading onto any externally demonstrable kind of substance.

One sign that in tracing myself as "I" I am not offloading onto anything like a human being is given by certain subjectively coherent descriptions of how my experience might go. After a very late night, I wake up at noon in a hotel room. Something is very wrong, something is missing from the middle of my visual field, something I notice only when it is gone... my nose is no longer down there. I try to raise my hand and feel for my nose, but... nothing happens. With mounting desperation, I turn my attention toward the mirror opposite my bed and... there is no human being in the bed. My body has disappeared on me.

In this, as I say, subjectively coherent anticipation of how my experience might go, I trace my self through the mounting desperation, but not by tracing some body or human being. My surprise is that there is no longer any human being HERE, but it is still, it seems, MY surprise. In tracing myself through this experience I am not offloading onto any externally demonstrable substance.

The familiar Cartesian idea can now be reconstructed in our terms. It is the idea that I therefore must then be offloading onto an internally demonstrable substance, a *mental* substance, and so I must *be* a mental substance. Sortals like "consciousness," "self," "ongoing arena of presence," "thinking thing"—these are just ways of picking out the kind of mental substance I am. They are substance sortals, and they pick out some kind of mental substance or soul with its own inbuilt persistence conditions.

This is the conception that is busted, and busted by the actual facts of the matter. We may distinguish two broad varieties of mental substance. There are *independent* mental substances of the sort that could carry your identity on after your death. As emphasized earlier, the empirical evidence, having to do with the radical dependence of one's mental functioning on the functioning of one's brain, counts against there being any such independent mental substances in the vicinity of our mental lives. We can also conceive of *dependent* mental substances, which are wholly dependent for their existence and operation on their associated brains.

We may also go on to distinguish two kinds of dependent mental substances. The first would just be a substance in the sense of being a bearer of predicates. Thus we sometimes hear minds spoken of as if they were the primary bearers of mental predicates. This is not only semantically jarring, since it seems to be persons who see, feel, plan, decide, and so on, not their minds; it is also explanatorily idle, since everything that can be explained by assigning one's mental functioning to a mind can be more directly explained by understanding that mental functioning as a form of brain functioning and assigning that mental functioning to the person whose brain it is. In any case, this first kind of mental substance is not relevant to the argument at hand; being only a bearer of predicates, it need not endure, and so it need not be even a candidate target of offloading.

Let us then consider a dependent mental substance in the sense of a mental endurer, something that presents a self-maintaining essence at each time at which it exists, a mental thing that maintains itself by its dispositions grounded in its mental structure. This would be the kind of thing that one could have successfully offloaded onto when tracing oneself over time. Unfortunately, the same evidence that testifies to the radical dependence of mental functioning on the brain suggests that there are no discrete emergent minds with their own self-maintaining mental structures. The maintenance of mind is the maintenance of mental functioning, and mental functioning seems to be the upshot of brain functioning, thanks to lawlike connections between brain events and mental events. From the side of neuroscience, neuropathology, and even cognitive science, there is no explanatory push to postulate an emergent and *self-maintaining* mental substance.

If that is right, then at least when it comes to our subjective mental identities over time—the supposed identities of THIS self, THIS consciousness, THIS arena of presence of action—we have not actually latched onto anything that would make for a determinate answer to the question of when we would have the same self, the same consciousness, or the same arena of presence persisting over time.

That was the motivation for introducing the term of art "arena of presence and action." I believe it is a term you have made some sense of, enough to see that it applies to your mental life at any given time. But tell me this: Under what conditions does the very same arena of presence and action continue on? You have no idea, and neither do I.

Return for a moment to Cotard's syndrome. Whereas as the victim of Cotard's syndrome was not in a position to formulate a determinate thought of subjective "mineness" at a time, we are not in a position to formulate a determinate thought of continued subjective "mineness" over time.

You could put it this way: We all suffer from a cross-temporal version of predicament of a Cotard's patient, a predicament for which there is no treatment, even in principle. As we have argued, this is because, in being criterionless, our inner-directed tracing of ourselves presupposed that we were mental substances of some sort or other. But the empirical facts suggest that there are no mental substances in the vicinity.

A FALSE PRESUPPOSITION OF "MY OWNMOST DEATH"

At each conscious moment of his life, any given human being is at the center of some arena of presence and action or other. At any such time he can enjoy the thought: "The one located at the center of this arena of presence and action—who is that, I wonder?" In this way, *at each time* there can be a determinate content to questions like "Who am I?" "Who has the property of being me?" "Who is at the center of the relevant arena of presence?" Yet, for all that, there need be no determinate content to the prospective subjective question, the question of whether such and such a human being in the future *will* be me. For that requires that there be determinate facts concerning the identity and difference of arenas of presence over time.

Suppose someone asks, "The mental shutdown involved in dreamless sleep is unlike anything I go through during the day. I wonder if this very arena of presence and action will survive tonight's dreamless sleep." He has not thereby asked a question with a determinate answer. The putative substance sortal "arena of presence and action," like "consciousness" or "self," is a *busted* substance sortal; busted, I take it, by the empirical fact that there are no mental substances. So these sortals fail to implicate any determinate conditions of success or failure when it comes to such things as believing that I, the same consciousness, or self, or occupant of the central position in the same arena of presence, will be around in any anticipated future.

Here, finally, all room for the thought of my *ownmost death*—the end of this very arena of presence and action—has disappeared.

The Retreat to the Human Being

There is an obvious response to the absence of mental substances; we can try to externalize our inner-directed self-identifications. Instead of intending to pick out a mental something by "self" or "consciousness" or "arena of presence and action" we can aim to pick out the human being who is the site of this consciousness, who is located at the central phenomenological position.

Our inner-directed reidentifications may have failed us, but we can trace whatever *external* substances are "here" at a given time. Human beings are "here" at the various apparent centers that reveal themselves to acts of introspection, and human beings are substances and so can be traced by offloading. Those substances can be picked out by indexical uses of "I."

Now one thought about death does come back. The thought about death that comes back is just the indexically mediated thought about a particular human being's death. I, the human being Johnston, which has just picked itself out by way of the first-person pronoun, will cease to be. Even so, that need not engage my special self-concern. The end of this human being will be my death, but not my *ownmost* death.

Here we have made a discovery of some importance, namely that there is nothing that adequately plays two roles: the role of carrying one's determinate identity, and the role of independently justifying a certain temporally extended pattern of special self-concern, which manifests itself in one's everyday egocentrism and in one's special fear of one's own(most) death.

The Irrelevance of Substantial Selves

Elsewhere, and long ago, I introduced the notion of a superlative substantial self, something defined to be that which not only carries our determinate identity but is also an independent justifier of our egocentric concern.[29] That is, a superlative self is something that would justify the special and urgent concern each of us has for our own future survival, and its persistence would determine what our survival consists in. So long as my self, my mental substance, survives, I survive, and when it ceases to be I cease to be. But this mental substance is not just an invariable concomitant of my survival; it is what makes it especially rational for me to care about my survival in the edgy protective way that I do. It not only justifies that concern, but it calls out for or *demands* that concern.

How can the persistence of a substance, be it mental or physical or whatever, present this kind of objective demand, and so justify the responses that it demands? That seems to me to be one of the deepest problems about personal identity.

Recall the distinctive content of the demand: that a person care about himself in a certain favored way, the way that makes it seem rational to seek premium treatment for himself, beyond what is owed to an arbitrarily chosen other. Suppose I do have just such a superlative mental substance. Presumably you are also graced with one. That one justifies your special concern for yourself; but it does not justify my adopting that kind of concern for you. For imagine that I replicated your egocentric

---

[29]Mark Johnston, "Human Interests without Superlative Selves," in J. Dancy, ed., *Reading Parfit* (Basil Blackwell, 1996), reprinted in R. Martin and J. Barresi, eds., *Personal Identity* (Basil Blackwell, 2002).

concern for yourself. I adopt a corresponding concern for you. Then I would need to become an unwelcome meddler in your life; I would then reasonably want to consult with you about your pursuit of your self-interest, since it is your superlative self that I now care so much about. In caring so much about your self, I would be so much worse than a clingy lover.

Crucially, whatever your superlative self might demand from you in the way of egocentric concern, it makes no such demands of me. It is to the demands of *my* superlative self that I must look in organizing my basic concerns. When you think about it, this is very odd. Your superlative self may not be accessible to me in the way that my superlative self is accessible to me, but it is supposed to be no less objective than mine. How is it, then, that *it* makes a demand that only *you* are called to meet? (Of course it is *your* self, but that supposed fact and its justificatory role are just what we are trying to understand.)

The crucial idea of a superlative self as the ground of an objective and *yet utterly and essentially privatized* demand for certain responses—those associated with egocentric concern—is difficult to make coherent.

Thus it seems that adding superlative selves to the world, one for each person, does not help explain, or provide a prima facie justification for, egocentric concern. At best, it would put us all on a par metaphysically; each one of us is worth caring about to the same degree because each has a superlative self. That does nothing to explain or even begin to justify our sense that our own selves are, as it were, entitled to premium treatment, beyond what is owed to another. Yet providing a prima facie justification for precisely this excess of self-concern was half of the defining role of a superlative self.

This objection to superlative selves may now seem more important than the argy-bargy about out-of-body experiences versus the effects of horse tranquilizer. That was a debate about the *existence* of any independent mental substance that could play the role of a soul or superlative self. But it now seems as if the addition of superlative selves to the world—be they independent of, emergent from, or dependent on brain functioning—would not make *any* difference so far as justifying the excess of self-concern, the concern that goes far beyond what one is owed as an arbitrarily chosen other.

Every person may be taken to have superlative mental substances at the base of their conscious life, substances that make their existence an all-or-nothing matter, never a matter of degree and never a conventional matter. Then as one person among others, one also has a superlative self. But this doesn't help at all in justifying the most obvious fact of one's mental life—one's tendency to give oneself *premium treatment* (if the effects on the others are not too egregious). What would be needed to justify *that* would be to suppose that reality is so conformed that only you are graced with a superlative self. But the intelligibility of giving oneself premium treatment is general and "allocentric"; each of us finds it intelligible that *all* of us have a tendency to do this. It is the default we all work with; someone who treats himself as just one of the others would be the case that needed a special explanation.

So superlative substantial selves seem to have been a bad idea from the very beginning; they could not, even in principle, justify the kind of asymmetry that is constitutive of egocentric concern.

On Having No Self

We are thus left with a vision of the world under the aspect of *Ego Absconditus*. There is not the kind of metaphysical justifier that would independently determine which parts of nature ought to be the foci of our respective patterns of self-concern.

Given that, it is hard to account for *the significance* of the objective facts of personal identity, for example, facts involving the persistence of this or that human being. There are a variety of relations of persistence in terms of which we might have organized our special self-concern; we might have found ourselves caring about shorter- or longer-lived things than human beings. What would have made those patterns of self-concern simply mistaken, as opposed to merely inconvenient, or difficult to organize a culture around? There seems to be no good answer to this question in the absence of appropriately placed superlative selves, independent justifiers of our self-concern that might have inhabited the mental lives of *human beings* but not of any longer-lived thing that includes a human being.

So not only are the subjective conceptions of ourselves as persisting consciousnesses, or as persisting selves, or as occupants of persisting arenas of presence, all busted, but it also seems that the special significance of the persistence of human beings has evaporated. Why should I care, in the special egocentric way, about the persistence of a *human being* into an imagined future, if there is no sense to be made of the thought that this human being will then still be ME, in the sense that matters, the subjective sense? (This question is taken up again in lectures three and four.)

Perhaps the key to deathlessness is the realization that YOU, in the relevant sense, could not possibly be real—or anyway, not *real enough* to justify a certain temporally extended pattern of self-concern, which manifests itself in your everyday egocentrism and in your special fear of your own(most) death.

Summary of an Argument

Here, then, by way of summary, is a sketch of the main line of argument.

1. It is my ownmost or "subjective" death that especially engages my concern.
2. In doing that, it crucially involves the thought that this self, or this consciousness, or this arena of presence and action will persist for a while and then cease to be.
3. In tracing myself as such a thing I am offloading, or I am attempting to offload, but I am not offloading onto any external substance, such as a human animal or human being.
4. If I am offloading onto anything, it will be onto a mental substance that is this self or this consciousness or this arena of presence.
5. But since there are no such substances as this self, or this consciousness, or this arena of presence and action, we cannot offload onto them.
6. So, I have not succeeded in offloading when tracing myself from the inside.
7. So, the thoughts that appear to concern my ownmost death lack determinate content.

Our conclusion should then be that one's ownmost death is impossible, because radically undefined. The absence of mental substances not only eliminates the basis for hope in an afterlife, it also eliminates the death we feared most. Properly thought through, the rejection of the soul goes hand in hand with the rejection of the self, at least if the self is thought of as the independent justifier of that special self-concern our evolutionary history has implanted in us.

As yet, however, these conclusions are to be understood as conditioned by the same proviso entered at the end of lecture one, a proviso to be lifted only in the next lecture. In tracing ourselves from the inside, there may be some way, other than offloading onto a substance, in which our cognitive system can save itself from excessive cognitive labor, and perhaps this other way allows us to make sense of the self, the thing whose continued existence over time is intimately bound up with the continued existence of a given arena of presence.

QUESTIONS AND REPLIES

Isn't the distinction between your death and your ownmost death robust anyway, that is, no matter how the metaphysics of the self turns out, for is it not just given to you by the distinction between the de re directed toward yourself and the genuinely de se? Surely that semantic distinction is good anyway.[30]

Yes, there is nothing wrong with that distinction. But I want to make a further distinction between two sorts of de se thought, a merely indexical thought directed to the person or human being that I am, and a truly subjective thought, as it were directed to the self that I am. It is the second kind of thought that appears to ground special, or non-derivative, self-concern and appears to reach out to my subjective death. But this appearance is illusory. The first kind of thought is still useful in applying perfectly impersonal considerations to my own case. But it will not provide a coherent basis for the sense that one deserves premium treatment.

One point that seems to have gotten lost in the discussion is that for many old people death is a release; for many people it is not death but the dying that is horrible.[31]

Of course, that is so, and it is part of why the hospice movement is so important. But as a matter of fact, the hospice movement is, among other

[30] Philip Pettit.
[31] Michael Smith.

things, concerned with allaying *the fear* of the dying, and that fear is complex. The fear of the lugubrious accompaniments of death, that is, pain, loss of one's capacities, incoherence, radical dependence on others, and so on so forth—all that is only part of the fear of death. Another part is the fear of the end, nothingness, annihilation, or perhaps the opposite fear of "the undiscovered country from which no traveler returns." And here philosophy can clarify the object of the fear, ask whether it exists, and to same extent allay the fear.

Moreover, as we shall see, a transformed understanding of what you are may also radically affect the quality of your dying.

There is still another point in the question. There are at least two large-scale defects associated with death. To properly locate them we need to make a distinction between a premature death and a belated death, a death that comes too early in that it cuts off life before the decay of aging and/or sickness has practically undermined that life, and a death that comes too late precisely because that life has been already undermined by the decay of aging and/or sickness. Premature death, because it cuts us off from further life that would be good for us, and because it does this in a way that is indifferent to the moral quality of our lives, presents a threat to the importance of goodness. However, when death is belated, and so eventually comes as a release, it is the corrosive aging or sickness that then presents a threat to the importance of goodness. The same with a death that is utterly timely, neither premature nor belated; here, too, it is the decay unto death that is the relevant defective part of the human condition.

ADDENDUM: THE ARENA, THE HORIZON,
AND THE LIMITS OF THE WORLD*

An arena can be mistaken for other quasi-containers, openings, or fields, fields that "contain" smaller and larger ensembles than any arena. An arena is a mental quasi-place, a field of psychological fields. There is a way of clearing your mind and relaxing your body so that your mental goings on consist of awareness of the sensations within your bodily field. Your bodily field is an intentional object, a quasi-three-dimensional volume, which contains the ongoing play of bodily sensations and bodily feelings. But your arena includes your bodily field and more. For example, it includes your visual field, understood not as the objective sector of visible things before your eyes but as a field in which illusions and after-images and hallucinations occur "alongside" the perspectival presentations of visible items in the objective sector of reality that is before your eyes. Your visual field, so understood, is a very odd sort of container; it includes both after-images and visible items in the objective sector before your eyes, and it has them in quasi-spatial relations. Your after-image may appear "on" the wall, and then it "moves" across your visual field and thus appears "closer" to different external objects as it moves. (That is a remarkable, though utterly ordinary, fact.) Unlike the objective sector, the visual field is a mere intentional object. That is why there is no answer to the question about what is in the other side of it. Compare Macbeth's dagger, or any other generic object of hallucination. There is no answer to the question of what their backs look like.

The arena is the all-inclusive psychological field. Its constituent psychological fields do not simply concatenate to form the arena; they are organized around a phenomenological center, a sort of virtual limit where perspectival modes of presentation converge.

The empirical facts drawn from neuropathology suggest the arena and the center are graces of neurological fortune. If the implied position to which items in your visual field present radically came apart from the implied position to which your bodily field presents, and apart from the apparent position from which actions presented as willed emanate, then your very sense of self would be fragmented. This fragmentation of fields may be part of what is happening with those unfortunate patients who suffer from Cotard's syndrome, the syndrome whose defining feature is the lack of the conviction that one exists.

The arena, the all-inclusive psychological field, must also be distinguished from utterly comprehensive fields, items such as what Wittgenstein referred to as the world, the totality of facts.

The world, so understood, is obviously not a psychological item, whose existence is a grace of neurophysiological fortune. Moreover, the world is presumably equally available to all as an object of thought—we inhabit the world on equal terms, no one has special access to it, so no one could pick himself out as the one of the center or limit of it. There is one world and there are many arenas of presence.

Yet strikingly, at the end of the *Tractatus*, in some of his most difficult work, having to do with the allegedly deep but unsayable insight in solipsism, Wittgenstein writes,

> Where in the world is a metaphysical subject to be found? You will say that this is exactly like the case of the eye and the visual field. But really you do not see the eye. And nothing in the visual field allows you to infer that it is seen by an eye. (*Tractatus*, 5.633)

And further

> Thus there really is a sense in which philosophy can talk about the self in a non-psychological way. What brings the self into philosophy is the fact that "the world is my world." The philosophical self is not the human being, not the human body, or the human soul, with which psychology deals, but rather the metaphysical subject, the limit of the world, not a thing in it. (*Tractatus*, 5.641)

Whatever "the world is my world" means or tries to mean, it cannot guarantee that Wittgenstein can *literally succeed* in picking the metaphysical subject he is associated with out as "*the one* at the center of, or at the limit of, the world" as *the one* that stands in that proprietary relation to the common world. Wittgenstein's remarks, cast in the first person, like Descartes' remarks in the first person—*Cogito ergo sum*—have an essentially "allocentric" quality. They are meant to be understood as the sort of thing that *others, such as the reader,* can also think about themselves. They are not meant to convey something about the special and exclusionary standing of the man Wittgenstein.

Given the construal of the world as the totality of facts, we might say that the *mistake* in solipsism is to confuse one's own arena of presence with the limits of the world. Just as the eye is at the "center"—the virtual limit of convergence of the perspectival modes of presentation that now make up my visual field—I am at the center of the virtual limit of convergence of the perspectival modes of presentation that now make up my total conscious field. But I am not at the center or the limit of the world. The world, or some part of it, appears to me—and so is *mine* to directly demonstrate—thanks to the appearances in the arena, but the world that appears is not that apparent thing within which it, the world, appears. The same could be said of you and your arena. So the world is both mine and yours (to directly demonstrate).

If my left eye were a reflective being that could be aware of its own seeing, and of its own visual field, it would fall into a counterpart of the error in solipsism if it took that visual field to be the boundary of the whole of the reality that is capable of being seen. My eye would then think: this visual field, the one that has me at its center or limit, is the boundary of the visible itself. My eye has here made a mistake, but is it a *deep* mistake?

In a masterful recent work, J. J. Valberg tries to bring into view what he calls "the horizon," which he takes to be crucial to the full phenomenological account of self-consciousness. The horizon is a bound or quasi-container of all the world, the infinity of space and time. By paradoxically *endorsing* a certain kind of solipsism, Valberg wants to explain philosophically interesting uses of "I" in terms of demonstrative descriptions like "the one at the center of THIS horizon." Being at the center of THIS horizon is, on Valberg's view, the property of being me.

By way of summarizing his extraordinary book, Valberg writes,

We are, each of us—it seems—at the center of a horizon *that not only contains the world and the infinity of space and time* but impossibly both includes and is co-ordinate with all other horizons, a horizon, that is, whose ceasing to be entails a NOTHINGNESS that is both absolute and, impossibly, separately faced by all of us (the solipsistic puzzle of death); a horizon that despite being outside of time, will, impossibly cease to be (the temporal puzzle of death); a horizon that despite being, since it is outside time, outside the range of causation, is, impossibly, causally maintained in existence by the activity of my brain (the puzzle of the causation of consciousness); a horizon that, despite being necessarily unified, could, given its causal dependence on the bit of matter that is my brain, be caused, impossibly to double (the puzzle of division); a horizon from within which, despite the direct availability of the world and the past, things are as they are because, impossibly, of what is going on right now in my brain (the puzzles of experience and memory).[32]

Now the first thing to note is that the puzzles Valberg mentions are also straight paradoxes, in that they can be formulated so that they entail

---

[32] Valberg, *Dream, Death and the Self*, 482. My italics.

contradictions. Why, then, should we not take the puzzles as proofs that the notion of a horizon is itself under impossible strain, that it is an incoherent notion that could not apply to anything at all? If so, then "the one at the center of THIS horizon" is a rotten definite description—it picks out nothing. A fortiori, it cannot be used to explain how philosophically interesting uses of "I" get their reference.

This is much too quick a way with Valberg's intriguing, dense, and intricate book. Perhaps Valberg's own work has in effect shown that the horizon is a merely intentional object! (I am reluctant to attribute this explicit aim to him, however.) Merely intentional objects can be incoherent or contradictory in their description, and yet they can be the objects of hallucination, hope, worship, and fantasy. And merely intentional objects can be demonstrated. Could it be that my basic way of picking myself out is in terms of a contradictory intentional object, to which I alone have access?

Yes, it *could*. The real problem is that Valberg's account of the horizon makes it seem like the wrong sort of object to play that role.

For one thing, as Valberg admits, there is no stable way to assign content to a horizon in accord with his strictures. I am, I am told, at the center of a horizon that contains the world and the infinity of space and time. And you are, too. But it is not that the horizon is multicentered. Your horizon is different from mine, though co-ordinate with it. So far we seem to be on a par. Yet my death is the end of THE horizon, and that is an absolute NOTHINGNESS. As it were, after my death PRESENCE comes to an end, not just HERE but everywhere. For my horizon is, as Valberg puts it, "preeminent"—it includes your horizon and all the other horizons. That is why my death is, as Valberg puts it, THE DEATH.

Yet these remarks are also intended to be "allocentric," that is, the *sort* of remarks that everyone can make from their own point of view. So your horizon is also preeminent—it includes your and all the other horizons. But now there is no stable way to assign contents to horizons, to say in any consistent way just what a given horizon includes.

"So what? It was already admitted that merely intentional objects might be contradictory objects. This is just another contradiction." Yes, so it is.

But let us now ask this: why suppose that this very complex kind of contradictory object must be mentioned in an adequate account of the phenomenology of any form of self-consciousness that supports "I"-thought?

After a session of mantric meditation, "I"-thoughts return, there is once again the sense of being at the center, and I pick myself out as the one at that center. The center of what? Well, from the phenomenological point of view, it seems gratuitous to suppose that it is the all-inclusive horizon that presents to me. It seems to be something much more modest, something that simply presents as conferring a unity on my thoughts, my acts, and the contents of my bodily and sensory fields—an arena, and not a horizon, as I would put it. I find myself at the center of THIS arena of presence, *not* THIS all-inclusive horizon.

As Valberg develops his account of the horizon, it appears more and more as a highly theorized object, one that comes into view by way of an elegant philosophical interpretation of what threatens to cease to be with one's death. Yet, self-consciousness is compatible with being completely oblivious to the fact of one's death. It often happens that a child has been an "I"-user for several years before he learns that he will die. The horizon that is disclosed by philosophical reflection on death is not obviously an object of the phenomenology of the ordinary self-consciousness that supports "I"-thought.

Further to this point, it is unclear to me how appeal to the horizon, something that contains the infinity of space and time, could explain the content of "I"-thoughts in dreams. I am able to enjoy "I"-thoughts in dreams, as when I dream that I am flying, and find myself startled by the apparent fact that I am in the air without any visible means of support. Do I in my dream have access to the all-inclusive horizon or to something much more limited, namely an arena of presence in which my dream unfolds?

Valberg himself makes a brilliant distinction between the trivial and false hypothesis that I am now dreaming, and the tantalizing and open hypothesis that all THIS is a dream, the hypothesis that he calls the Dream Hypothesis. About the Dream Hypothesis Valberg says,

> The hypothesis that THIS is a dream is the hypothesis that I might emerge from THIS into a wider horizon, that there is a horizon that might displace THIS in the way that THIS displaced my dream of the other night, and from whose perspective the one at the cen-

ter might regard THIS, the horizon of which I (JV) am at the center, in the way that I (JV) now regard the dream of the other night. The wider horizon, that into which I would emerge, would have its own world, and infinity of space and time, a world, etc., internal to it in the way that what I call "the world" and its infinity of space and time is internal to THIS. Such is the meaning of the [Dream Hypothesis].

On the hypothesis that THIS is reality (not a dream), there is no wider horizon, no horizon into which I might emerge into the way I emerged into this from my dream the other night; no horizon then that might displace this in the radical way that this displaced the dream. If THIS is reality it is a horizon wider-than-which does not exist. It is the widest horizon of all. Its world (we could say) is the widest world, its infinity of space and time the widest infinity, etc.[33]

But now there seems to be a tension between these remarks and Valberg's account of "I"-thought. Suppose that I am first dreaming and enjoying "I"-thoughts in my dream. And suppose I wake up, and the Dream Hypothesis is false. I wake up to reality. I wake up, then, into the widest horizon from a more limited horizon, the horizon of my dream. *Still, that earlier, limited, horizon must have sufficed for the formulation of "I"-thoughts in my dream. And that limited horizon, as it were, the frame of my dream, seems nothing more than an arena of presence.*

Why, then, is anything *more* required when I wake up and enjoy further "I"-thoughts? After I wake up there is still an arena of presence here. How is it that in formulating my waking "I"-thoughts I need to have recourse to a much more complex and inclusive intentional object than I had recourse to in my dream?

What happens when I am dreaming, and then wake up? While I am dreaming my arena of presence is filled with dream images, bodily sensations, feelings, emotions, memories, and thoughts but *little* in the way of veridical perceptions of the external world. (While dreaming I might hear real voices and dream around them, as it were.) When I awake, a host of veridical perceptions of the external world flood in. So my arena

[33] Ibid., 57.

of presence is a field of fluctuating and disparate presentations; it can include presentations that are dream images and hallucinations along with presentations that are essentially presentations of external objects. When I awake, presentations of the latter sort flood in. But that is no evidence that a different frame for my conscious life has come into view.

When I awake and recall that *I was dreaming that I was flying*, an apparently common frame grounds these "I"-uses. That apparent common frame is an arena that with my awaking has apparently come to include a host of veridical presentations.

I have dwelled on Valberg's ingenious and hard-won ideas not only because of their great intrinsic interest but because he has, in my view, come closer than anyone before him in correctly characterizing the content of "I"-thought as thought about the one at a given center. But it is not the center of a horizon, let alone the center of the preeminent horizon. It is the center of an immediately available arena of presence, a field made up of sensory, bodily, and mental fields. This will be crucial in what follows.

Chapter Three

From *Anatta* to *Agape*

Philosophers have distinguished mere "de re" thought about oneself—thought that *happens to be* about oneself, as when Muhammad Ali in the last stages of mental decay and forgetfulness takes a wholly impersonal interest in the career of a fighter called "Cassius Clay," no longer realizing that this man is he—from true "de se" thought about oneself, thought that involves the recognition of who one in fact is, thought about oneself *as oneself*, thought characteristically captured by identifications involving the first-person pronoun and its cognates. What Ali has forgotten is the de se truth that he would express by saying, "I am Cassius Clay."

It has been widely noted that de se thought is rationally motivating in certain characteristic ways. John Perry gave the example of shopping in the supermarket, happening upon a looping line of sugar, and concluding that someone has a sugar bag with a hole in it in his cart. Then comes the essentially de se or first-personal realization "It's the bag in *my* cart," and this leads to, and rationally motivates, the action of Perry's turning his attention to his cart and the sugar bag in it and then attending to the cleaning up of the mess.

Thus de se thought is a way of registering one's actual objective situation as it appears from one's own present point of view. Having done this, one can then appreciate the reasons that apply to one as a person in that situation and act accordingly. So in Perry's case, there is an impersonal reason we might capture by saying, "Everyone has reason to see to it that the mess he makes in public places is cleaned up." When Perry discovers that the mess is *his* mess, he also discovers that this reason applies to him, and he cleans up the mess, or sees to it that it is cleaned up.

Parts of this lecture were given to the Humanities Council at Princeton.

BASIC DE SE REASONS

So far we have only described *derivative* de se reasons for action. The whole of the apparent force of the de se reason which Perry would formulate by thinking "It is *my* mess, so *I* should see that it is cleaned up" is just the apparent force of an impersonal reason as it applies to Perry's own case.

However, to the extent that we demand or expect or rejoice in premium treatment for ourselves, to that extent we are operating as if there were also non-derivative or *basic* de se reasons. Our everyday egocentrism is distinctively marked off in this way. It is not experienced as having its source in the application of general impersonal principles of preference and action to one's own case; it is the felt expression of the apparent *specialness* of one's own case.

So when I find out that I have won the lottery, I also thereby find out that someone has won the lottery, but my attitude to my winning the lottery is very different from my attitude to the winning of the lottery by an arbitrary other. I do not merely think that the significant fiduciary duty of having so much money has just fallen upon me, so that I better get about using the money wisely and justly. I am *elated* that I have won the lottery, and an ever-growing shopping list fills my mind.

Here we are near to the explanation of why various moral traditions have looked askance at gambling in its various forms. That has always seemed to me to be a little overdone, for often gambling is a kind of sporting play, as with a flutter or a put-up-or-shut-up bet. Neither side is harmed in a way that they are not fully ready to accept for the sake of other ends that they value more than the potential harm of losing the bet. However, when it not just a form of sporting play, gambling is invariably a zero-sum (or worse than zero-sum) matter. I win at the significant expense of the others. *That* kind of gambling is essentially a form of training in egocentrism.

In mass lotteries, the method of shaving (tickets cost very little) and aggregating of funds may offer huge winnings while avoiding the imposition of significant loss, but the elation that lottery winners feel is often the elation of the successful gambler, the one who has won out over the others. Elation involves a very strong affirmation of the event that is its cause and object. When I am elated at my winning the lottery I strongly affirm *my* wining the lottery, to the exclusion of *others* winning it. I look anxiously to see if my winnings might be carved up by others who also have winning tickets. Who would suggest that I am here merely applying a pattern of impersonal reason to my own case?

In the same vein, recall what I overheard in the booth at Triumph Brewery. I first overheard the thugs in the next booth planning to beat someone up. As a public-spirited citizen, I was appalled. But once I heard them use my name and so realized that they were planning to beat *me* up, my attitude changed. Knowing that it was *me* they were planning to beat up, activated my special concern for myself. Not *me*, I thought, as if that would be somehow worse than having someone or other beaten up.

Again, this kind of everyday egocentrism is perfectly intelligible; we mostly organize our lives around it, and so it is treated as a reasonable default starting point in practical deliberation. As noted in the last lecture, in ordinary decent people, such everyday egocentrism does not so much disappear; it remains at the core of a pattern of bias C. D. Broad once called "self-referential" an expanded circle of special concern for oneself, one's friends, one's familiars, one's family, and perhaps one's tribe or nation.

These concerns are also essentially de se in form. My attachment to my family, my friends and my familiars cannot be adequately reconstructed as attachments to Johnston's family, friends, and familiars. For unless I know that *I* am Johnston or that they are *my* family, friends, and familiars, those attachments will seem to me be a odd form of other-regarding devotion, just as if I were to find myself suddenly devoted to Mother Teresa's family.

In part these self-referential attachments and the concerns they prompt register what is, from an objective point of view, *anyway* owed to family members, friends and others. Yet who amongst us can say that in giving expression to this wider pattern of self-referential concern he or she has just been applying the reasonable impersonal principles of family life, friendship and loyalty to his or her own case? No, the realization that it is *my* friend who drowned, or that it is *my* child who is in danger, *seems* to register something more than the impersonal reasons which govern friendship and family devotion. It is not at all like the case where I discover that I have made a mess.

When one knows that one has made a mess, one does *what is to be done*. But in these other cases, one's finger is often on the scales. It seems as if one is here partly responding to basic de se considerations, non-derivative reasons to act and prefer that essentially concern oneself and one's own. Otherwise whence the demand for the premium for oneself and one's own?

Nowhere is this more evident than when one anticipates one's own death. My subjective death seems to me more ominous than the death of an arbitrary other, and here I seem to be responding to something about the situation I anticipate, something that is real, and reason-giving. But clearly the putative reason in question is not to be captured by a derivation from the impersonal reasons available to all, for those reasons are impotent to capture what is especially bad about *my* subjective death. Here, as with other self-referential concerns, it can seem as if one is responding to basic de se considerations, reasons to act and prefer that non-derivatively concern oneself and one's own.

But are there basic de se reasons of this sort? This is the question that this lecture will address. Along the way it will emerge that there is no persisting self worth caring about, and that this undermines the thought that our ordinary egocentrism is in fact a response to basic de se reasons.

"I"-THOUGHT

In the last lecture, we distinguished two uses of first-person pronouns: a straightforward indexical use that refers simply to the human being that one is, a use characteristic of self-introductions and the like, and a truly subjective use where an interesting subjective property, the property of being at the center of a given arena, is in play.

The thesis was that this interesting subjective property, roughly the property of appearing at the center of THIS arena of presence, is the property of being me. Each of us in our own case can formulate the corresponding thought about the corresponding subjective property.

This claim about the nature of the property of being me need not be understood as a semantic thesis, as a thesis to the effect that the sense or meaning of "I" is given by the description "the one at the center of THIS arena" as if "I" were equivalent to the "I#" of lecture two.

Instead, we could allow that semantically "I" is indeed an indexical, and yet also allow that in *some of its uses* this indexical picks out not the person who tokened it but a self that is constituted by that person, where a self is something whose nature is to be explained in terms of the subjective property just described.

If that is so then there may be two different forms of "I"-thought. One involves a straightforward indexical use of "I" in order to register facts about the situation of a certain person or human being. The other involves a truly subjective use of the first-person and its cognates, a use mediated by thinking of oneself as some person or other qua at the center of an immediately given arena or consciousness.

One of these forms of thought goes with the relation of personal identity and hence with the person that one is, and the other goes with self identity and hence with the self that one is. If we are to understand our place in the world, in particular the prima facie appeal of the demand for the premium in the case of ourselves and our own, it is important to understand the status of this second form of "I"-thought.

NOT AMBIGUITY BUT SYNECDOCHE*

Philosophers are rightly leery of postulating lexical semantic ambiguities, at least where they are not almost immediately obvious. How, then, could some uses of "I" refer to a person and others refer to a self? There is certainly no felt *lexical* ambiguity in the use of "I." (Contrast "pen.")

What we are dealing with here is a limit case of synecdoche, generally understood as a substitution either of a part for whole, as when we say "they counted heads," or whole for part, as when we say "California is engulfed in flames." The limit case of this part/whole referential shift that is synecdoche is a case that may pass relatively unnoticed. It occurs where the parts exhaust the whole but are nonetheless not the whole.

So, for example, there are very good arguments that (liquid) water is not identical with H_2O, for if it were then ice would be identical with H_2O by parity of any argumentative consideration you might think up; and ice is not identical to water. Pure water and pure ice are wholly constituted by H_2O; they are not identical with it. However, even knowing that, I can say to someone at the gym, "Can I have some of your H_2O?" If he pulled out some ice I had not yet seen and offered it to me, he would not be responsive to my request. Similarly there are uses of "water" where the referent is the constituting stuff (as it turns out, H_2O) rather than the liquid it constitutes, as when I say, "As I predicted, the dogs' water is now frozen."

I believe that something like this is going on with self and person. This self is not identical with Johnston, but it is now wholly constituted by him. Sometimes my use of "I" or one of its cognates is best understood as picking out Johnston, as when I suppose that even in a world in which the human being Johnston is in a persistent vegetative state I would *thereby* still exist. Sometimes my use of "I" or one of its cognates is best understood as picking out this self, as when I suppose that I might have existed as someone else in a world in which Johnston never came into existence.

What could possibly push us to this position? And what would the self in question be? And, to connect to the main theme of the lectures, do such selves have any actual prospect of resurrection or reincarnation?

Two Kinds of Rigidity

In the last lecture I claimed that a certain feature which "I" is taken to have by almost all philosophers of language, namely its so-called "semantic rigidity," obscures a crucial distinction in the philosophy of self-consciousness: the distinction between personal identity and self identity. That was oversimplified in one respect; what obscures the crucial distinction is a combination of the doctrine that "I" is semantically rigid with the view that a use of "I" denotes the *person* who used it. Let me say a little more about this issue.

In the 1980 preface to his famous lectures in the series that became the Hempel Lectures, Saul Kripke proposed that what he there calls the de jure or semantic rigidity of a designator "D" turns on the question of whether it is *semantically* coherent to suppose that D might not have been D. So, we can make sense of the thought that

The author of *Koba the Dread* might not have been identical to the author of *Koba the Dread*

say, by considering a possible situation in which Martin Amis abandoned the project very early on. This shows that "The author of *Koba the Dread*" is in Kripke's terms not a semantically rigid designator; that is, it does not pick out the same item in every conceivable situation in which

it is understood as bearing its actual meaning. But there is no corresponding room to move with the sentence,

Martin Amis might not have been identical to Martin Amis.[1]

Ordinary proper names, such as the name "Martin Amis," Kripke famously proposed, are semantically rigid designators; they pick out the
same item in every conceivable situation in which they bear their actual
(and disambiguated) meaning.[2]

What about "I" and its cognates? Can we get anywhere with the idea
that I might not have been me? Many philosophers would say not. I myself, having a less secure grip on my own identity, am not so sure. (I often
feel I am not myself, but that hardly seems relevant.) But let us go with
informed common opinion here and treat "I" as rigid.

But now it seems that we have an immediate tension. The name "Johns-
ton" (when appropriately disambiguated) rigidly denotes this person here.
So, also, the designator "I" when it occurs in my mouth or in the sentences
I produce rigidly denotes this person here, namely Johnston.

So, on the standard account, given my knowledge that I am Johnston
it should be semantically incoherent—incoherent given a full understanding of the semantics of the expressions—for me to suppose that

I might not have been identical to Johnston.

But it does not seem to be semantically incoherent to suppose this,
and things like this. I can imagine being FDR, and then being killed in a
global catastrophe that destroys all human life, so that Johnston never
comes into existence. It seems that in imagining that, what I have imagined is a scenario in which I exist and Johnston does not, and so I have

---

[1] There is a use of "Martin Amis" to pick out a certain literary figure who the person Martin Amis
became. In this sense, Martin Amis (the person) might never have become Martin Amis (the figure)—a point made by Nick Stang. But this does not threaten the rigidity of "Martin Amis," for the
thesis of rigidity is a thesis of rigidity relative to a full disambiguation of the name. Still, and here is
the interest of Stang's point, we might think of the figure Martin Amis as a certain kind of qua object, namely Amis qua literary figure, an object distinct from but wholly constituted by the person
Amis.

[2] See the preface to Kripke, *Naming and Necessity*. There is a choice about how to implement the
idea of the rigidity of the name "Martin Amis" with respect to situations in which Amis does not
exist. We can say that the name still denotes Amis in such circumstances—after all, "Amis does not
exist" is true of those circumstances—or we can restrict the notion of the rigidity of a designator so
that it only requires unvarying designation in all situations in which it designates anything.

imagined a situation in which I am not identical to Johnston. And recall "Borges and I," Sally Smith's dream, and the girl who wanted to *be* Britney Spears.

It is worth entering a caution here. I am not assuming that imagination is an invariably reliable guide to real or "metaphysical" possibility. I am not in these remarks supposing that there is a real possibility in which I am FDR. That would be to naively rely on the method of imaginary cases. However, even though these sorts of imaginings may not be reliable guides to metaphysical possibility, they are not ruled out merely by the semantics of "I" and its cognates. That observation will be driving what follows.

When philosophers talk of rigid designation, they often gloss over Kripke's important distinction between de jure rigidity and de facto rigidity, that is, rigidity that is secured merely by the semantics of the designator, and rigidity secured by the semantics plus the metaphysical facts of the matter. So, to take Kripke's own example, the designator "the square root of 25" is not de jure rigid, even though it is de facto rigid. That is, even though we cannot get anywhere with the thought that

The square root of 25 might not have been the square root of 25

this is because we are taking it that as a matter of fact the truths of arithmetic are necessarily true, so that there is nothing but the number 5 for "the square root of 25" to denote in any situation in which it has its standard meaning. But imagine a philosopher influenced by W.V.O. Quine, who famously argued, after John Stuart Mill, that arithmetic is an empirical matter. The philosopher then makes an inferential step that was once highly favored: he persuades himself that since the truths of arithmetic are empirical, they are contingent. So, he finds himself in a position to get somewhere with the thought that the square root of 25 might have been other than it is. (What else could it have been? Well, he answers, maybe 5.000000000000001, and then goes on to talk about his theory of the symbiotic relationship between mathematics and physical theory.)

This is utterly odd, of course. As we now would now put it, in large part thanks to Kripke, in thinking that the empirical must be contingent, the philosopher has too simple a picture of the relation between epistemic and metaphysical modalities. But despite his confusion about the metaphysical status of arithmetic, he remains competent with the expression "the square root of 25." He *expresses* part of his utterly odd view about the numbers by using that expression with its standard meaning.

But on the standard view in semantics the name "Johnston" and the designator "I" are not merely de facto rigid, they are de jure rigid. That means that even without relying on any metaphysical fact (except perhaps the fact that one thing could not come to be numerically identical with another distinct thing) to block my imagination, I should not be able to get anywhere with the thought that

I might not have been (identical to) Johnston.

But I can get somewhere with this thought. I wake up, I look down, and there is Spinoza. More than that, the mind that surrounds me is the mind of Spinoza, fussing about proofs *more geometico*, imagining new techniques of lens grinding, and musing on Leibnitz's uncomprehending summary of the first chapter of my *Ethics*. It is February 7, 1676, and although I am distracted by these thoughts I am penning a letter to my admirer Oldenberg. As I finish the letter, a comet hits the earth, mankind is wiped out, and Johnston never comes into existence. (By the way, are we really doing enough about these comets?)

Here I have imagined being Spinoza in a situation in which Johnston does not exist. It would utterly distort what I have imagined to insist that I have really imagined Johnston being Spinoza. In fact, I don't have any idea of how to do that.

Here, then, is the paradox of auto-alienation.

1. While knowing that I am Johnston, I can, without semantic incoherence and without ignoring the structure of the fact that I am Johnston, imagine myself existing without Johnston existing.
2. As a semantic matter, both "I" and "Johnston" rigidly denote what they denote.
3. The fact that I am Johnston is a fact of identity, namely this fact: I = Johnston.

This is not a general paradox that arises simply in virtue of having two (or more) semantically rigid designators for the same person. Knowing that Cicero is Tully, I cannot, without semantic incoherence or without ignoring the structure of the fact that Cicero is Tully, imagine Cicero existing without Tully existing. (I can, of course, imagine Cicero never coming to be called "Tully," but that is something else entirely.)

What, then, do we have to say about the nature of self-consciousness and self-reference to avoid the paradox?

THREE RESPONSES TO THE PARADOX OF AUTO-ALIENATION

There are three responses that merit consideration. Discredit the apparent *semantic* coherence of such feats of auto-alienation, thereby denying 1. Allow, after all, that there are semantically non-rigid uses of "I," thereby denying 2. Or allow that "I" in my mouth, at least sometimes, does not rigidly designate the person Johnston but rigidly designates something that stands in some substantive relation to him; as it might be, this self, thereby denying 3.

How exactly is the first option supposed to work? I am pretty sure I am not fudging on the meaning of "I" when I engage in a feat of auto-alienation. At worst, I am using "I" coherently to suggest or make a false claim about what is possible.

And here is something that supports the third option over the second: In imagining being FDR or Spinoza, I seem to imagine that I am someone other than Johnston, but I do not seem to be imagining a situation in which "I am I" is false. Yes, I can be said to have imagined being someone other than myself, but the truth in this is just that I have imagined that I am Spinoza or FDR or the like. If that is right, the semantic rigidity of "I" is not in the end threatened by such feats of auto-alienation.[3] What is threatened is the idea that "I" denotes the likes of Johnston, FDR, or Spinoza rather than items associated with them.

What are these items? Well, if anything, they would be selves. But it is one thing to just say that those items are "selves," another to find a conception of a self that could be psychologically available to be the referent of one's earliest "I"-thoughts.

The suggestion that "I" instead picks out a self is a common one, embodied in the very term "the Ego," but the suggestion is usually paired with the idea that a self is, as Galen Strawson puts it in his fertile paper "The Self"—"something less than the whole human being"—as it might

---

[3]This remains true on the account below, which recognizes two uses of "I." "I" remains rigid in each of its uses, so any given use either rigidly refers to a person or rigidly refers to a self. When, in describing a dream in which I was Hannibal, I say, "I was not myself last night," the first use of "I" rigidly refers to this self and the second rigidly refers to Johnston.

be a mental substance or mental core of a self-conscious life, the true or primary subject of thought, something that inhabits a human being.[4]

We have found reason to doubt that there are such selves; and there is a further reason for doubting that a use of "I" denotes a self in *this* sense. Just suppose that there are no such selves. Still, "I" seems to remain a denoting term; for example, "I am Johnston" still seems to be true in the conceivable scenario in which there are no such selves. Likewise, David Hume looked into himself and found no self, in what is in effect Galen Strawson's sense. Yet Hume successfully uses "I" and its cognates throughout his very repudiation of such a self. This suggests that the successful use of "I" carries no such metaphysical commitment to a self in Galen Strawson's sense.

All we had better rely on for uses of "I" to denote, it seems, are arenas of presence with human or other self-conscious beings at their centers. If we are to resort to selves as the references of various uses of "I," then we should employ no more than these materials to explain the nature of selves.

So, absent persisting mental particulars that lie at the heart of our mental lives, what could a self, understood as the denotation of "I," be?

Drawing on our earlier notion of an arena of presence, a self could be something whose cross-time unity condition was that all the entities that successively constituted it were successively at the center of a given persisting arena of presence. A self, in this sense, need not have anything but biological parts making it up over its lifetime. It need not be, at any time, made up of something less, or more, than the human being.

Let me explain.

An Available Self

When it comes to the constitution of objects, or items quite generally considered, philosophers are more and more sorting themselves into three camps. Since this is philosophy, the first camp wonders what the

---

[4]See Galen Strawson, "The Self," in J. Barresi and R. Martin, eds., *Personal Identity* (Blackwell, 2003). In *The View from Nowhere*, Thomas Nagel parses "I am Thomas Nagel" as something like "This objective self occupies the perspective of Thomas Nagel." In a lecture appearing on YouTube, a lecture given in 2006, Saul Kripke seems to endorse the view that "I" denotes a self or ego; but he resolutely withholds anything more on what a self is and how it could get to be semantically associated with the use of "I."

other two camps are up to, what they mean, whether they are involved in a real dispute, that sort of thing. The second camp says that the relation of constitution never holds, so that contrary to appearances there are no composite objects. The third camp says constitution is ubiquitous and occurs whenever some items stand in an appropriate unity condition, a whole-making relation, where the whole that is made has the related items as its parts. This camp remains divided about what the whole-making relations are. Some say whole-making requires no more than that the parts in question exist, others say they must be taken up into a life, and still others allow that the holding of a wide range of relations can make for wholes whose parts are just those items that stand in the relations in question.

This last view treats wholes or complex items as ten-a-penny, that is, both very easy to obtain and in a certain way ontologically trashy, which is to say that they are certainly not primary phenomena or basic items. This is the ontological view I shall assume for present purposes, but let me say a little to motivate it.[5]

When certain items come to stand in certain relations, such as being glued together, being coupled with each other, or being bonded to each other, there then comes to be some *further* item that has those original items as parts. That is presumably how we have such complex items as trains, molecules, and model airplanes. Just why are those relations and their ilk "whole-generators," while other relations such as *being six feet from* seem impotent when it comes to the production of wholes? Whence this invidious ontological distinction? The science of matter doesn't even consider the invidious distinction as an object of explanation, it simply takes it for granted, and instead explores the forces that hold apparently complex items together. So what does explain the invidious ontological distinction?[6]

[5] See my "Constitution Is Not Identity," "Is There a Problem about Persistence?" and "Hylomorphism" for anticipations of what follows. An important influence on the view that follows is Kit Fine's "Things and Their Parts," *Midwest Studies in Philosophy* 23 (1999). The idea of the real definition of objects is in part inspired by Fine's "Essence and Modality," *Philosophical Perspectives* 8 (1994). Hylomorphism is defended in detail by Kathrin Koslicki in *The Structure of Objects* (Oxford University Press, 2008). All that is strictly needed for the development of the relevant idea of the self is the notion of a qua object, which is given an appropriately generalized form in Fine's "Things and Their Parts."

[6] A question pursued in fascinating detail by Peter van Inwagen in his *Material Beings*, where he

Of any item in any category, be it a state, event, activity, material object, artifact, organism, person, quantity of stuff, property, fact, proposition, kind, group, set, or mereological sum, we may inquire whether it is simple or complex, in the sense of having parts. Of anything that has parts we may inquire as to what principle unifies those parts into the whole that is the complex item. The principle had better not be *merely* another part, for the question would remain: Consider that part along with the other parts; what relation is such that its holding of *all* these parts gives us the whole? And that would be the principle we really seek.

So glue may hold together parts of a model airplane; but glue is another part, and it counts as a part along with the wings, the tail, and the fuselage because of a pattern of bonding holding among it and the other parts. This pattern of bonding is not another part but rather a way of realizing a principle of unity, a relation that must hold among the parts if they are to be parts of the model airplane. Roughly, they are to *hang together in the modeled shape of an airplane in such a way as to resist separation in the face of the range of forces to which we usually subject such models*. (Here, as below, I italicize the relational predicate that expresses the principle of unity.)

Consider a particular train, that is, an engine and some carriages coupled together, with the engine coupled into a position from which it can pull or drive the train. What it is for a particular train to be is for *enough of* those carriages *and* the engine *to be so coupled*. This complex quantified relation that holds of the engine and the carriages is the principle of unity of the train. There is no need to think of that relation as in any way part of the train. Yet it has to be mentioned in specifying what it is for that train to be.

We may make a distinction between a complex item's parts, its principle of unity, and its origin. All three factors may enter into the account of what it is for a specific item to be, the account of the essence of the item. For now, we shall prescind from origins and concentrate on parts and principles.

A principle of unity for a given item is a relation holding of some

---

ends up adopting the striking view that only when simples enter into a life do they constitute something.

other items, such that (origins aside) what it is for the given item to exist is for the relation to hold among those items. Each genuine kind of complex item will have associated with it a characteristic principle of unity; for arguably, it is sameness in principle of unity and kinds of parts that in turn qualifies the members of a given kind to be included in the complex whole that is the kind.

A statement of the genuine parts and principle of unity of an item (at a given level of composition) takes the following canonical form.

> *What it is for*... (the item is specified here)... *to be is for*... (some parts are specified here)... *to have the property or stand in the relation*... (the principle of unity is specified here).

As in: *What it is for* this hydrochloric acid molecule *to be is for* this positive hydrogen ion and this negative chlorine ion *to* be bonded together.

Or in: *What it is for* this particular train *to be is for* the engine and enough of the carriages *to* be coupled together, with the engine coupled into a position from which it can pull or drive the carriages. (Allowing enough of the carriages, and not requiring all of them, is to allow that the particular train in question can have a varying constitution over time and across possible scenarios.)

The idea that each complex item will have some such canonical statement true of it might be fairly called "Hylomorphism." For it is the idea that each complex item admits of a real definition, or statement of its essence, in terms of its matter, understood as parts or components, and its form, understood as a principle of unity. When an item's parts are themselves complex, they in their turn will have their own principles of unity (forms) and genuine parts (matter), and so on and so forth, either ad infinitum, or terminating in indefinables or "simples." That is the familiar layering of hylomorphic structure, beginning with the immediate parts of a whole and continuing through the more and more remote parts of that whole.

For any complex item that persists over time, the relevant principle of unity will impose not only synchronic constraints but also diachronic constraints; it will not only constrain how the parts of the item have to stand at a given time, it will also constrain how successive realizations of the item over time have to stand to one another for the item in question to persist. So, for a complex item that persists in a manner that allows for loss, exchange, or rearrangement of at least some of its parts, the principle of unity will specify how much and what kind of change in material parts secures the continued existence of the item.

IDENTITY IS ALWAYS "STRICT"

In *The Analogy of Religion*, Bishop Butler famously distinguished between "strict" identity and identity in the "loose and popular sense." His example of the latter relation involves a tree that has stood in the woods for fifty years but now shares no part with the original stripling. Nonetheless, Butler says that they are one and the same "as to all the uses of property and common life" even though they are not strictly identical.[7]

Here Butler seems to be confounding variable constitution over time with the failure of strict identity over time. A variably constituted thing can be strictly one and the same over time. So it is with the tree: it is one and the same tree even if its matter has been exchanged over time. The tree, like all such living things, simply has a dynamic principle of unity. What is to be that very tree over time *requires* that its matter be exchanged with its environment.

A related point is that a multiply constituted thing can be identically one and the same, despite having many distinct examples at different times, and at the same time. It is one and the same species, the Tiger, which moved from northern Asia to Bengal, even though it did that thanks to various distinct tigers making only parts of that journey. This is not "loose and popular identity" whatever *that* might turn out to be. Identity, the simplest relationship between a thing and itself, comes in just one form.

Roderick Chisholm once made a threefold distinction between simples, items that were essentially unchanging in their parts and in the arrangement of those parts, and what he called *entia successiva*, entities variably constituted over time.[8] Trees and the Tiger are examples of *entia successiva*, but if we are not to recapitulate something like Butler's confused idea of "loose and popular identity" then we must distinguish

[7]Joseph Butler, "Of Personal Identity," in Samuel Halifax, ed., *The Analogy of Religion* (Oxford University Press, 1849), 305.
[8]Roderick Chisholm, *Person and Object* (Open Court, 1976).

them from the succession of collections of items that constitute them. The constituting collections are not in any sense identical, but the constituted items are identically one and the same through time.

One might be prompted by Chisholm's approach to think of the self as a simple, but there are grave problems in plausibly associating a simple with a complex brain or body or psychology so as to make it the self of that brain or body or psychology.[9] Could a self then have parts (physical or spiritual) that could not, in principle, change, develop, or be shed? That, too, is a difficult conception to make out. How, for example, would a change in fundamental moral dispositions, as when an innocent soul is corrupted, be modeled on this picture of the self? The remaining possibility is that a self is a certain sort of *ens successivum*, one with a special kind of cross-time unity condition, one that invokes the very items, namely an arena of presence and its center, awareness of which makes us capable of "I"-thought.

That is the conception of the self that I wish to set out. So, I can pick out the self that is mine in the following canonical hylomorphic fashion: the self that I am is constituted by a potential succession of persons united by the following cross-time unity condition—that they be successively at the center of this arena of presence. And you can pick out your own self in the analogous way.

Chisholm would have rejected this account of the self out of hand, for he had the intuitions that he was strictly identical over time and that no *ens successivum* was strictly identical over time. But the latter "intuition" just looks like a version of Butler's mistake. A tree and the Tiger are "strictly identical" over time, unless we unjustly weigh down that notion with the further requirement of invariability of constituents or parts.

"I*" Denotes a Self

Now that we have introduced the idea of a self, something with a subjective form or principle of unity and something that, at least conceivably, can be constituted by different persons at different times, we may stipulate the following semantic rule.

---

[9]One of the most telling difficulties is the "causal pairing problem" raised in its modern form by Jaegwon Kim. The best discussion of this problem known to me is in Hong Yu Wong's very careful essay "Cartesian Psychophysics," in van Inwagen and Zimmerman, eds., *Persons*.

"I*" rigidly denotes the self that "tokened" it.

The thesis that "I" in some of its uses functions like "I*" is distinct from the suggestion that "I" has uses in which it functions like the demonstrative containing description "The actual one now at the center of this arena of presence." On that view "I" denotes a person, not a self. On the present view, to use "I" meaningfully over time you would have to be able to trace a self, and in doing that you would have to use something like this criterion: SAME ARENA OF PRESENCE, SAME SELF.

However—and here is a crucial observation—in tracing selves in that way, you would not have to take any specific metaphysical view on what the *constituents* of selves will turn out to be; they could turn out to be mental substances, or special mental parts of our mental life, "something less than the whole human being," or human beings, or rational parrots. To trace according to the criterion—SAME ARENA OF PRESENCE, SAME SELF—is to have the general concept of the self; it is not to thereby endorse any specific conception of the constituents that make up selves.

I have heard the remark that from a serious philosophical view, Jorge Luis Borges' feat of auto-alienation in "Borges and I" comes to no more than an elegant play on words, a bagatelle that could not be consistently rendered. As such, it could not be used to put any pressure on the standard account of "I" as a designator that always picks out persons or human beings. But this seems utterly wrong. The story could be recast as "Borges and I*." It would read like this:

> The other one, the one called Borges, is the one things happen to. I* walk through the streets of Buenos Aires and stop for a moment, perhaps mechanically now, to look at the arch of an entrance hall and the grillwork on the gate; I* know of Borges from the mail and see his name on a list of professors or in a biographical dictionary. I* like hourglasses, maps, eighteenth-century typography, the taste of coffee and the prose of Stevenson; Borges shares these preferences, but in a vain way that turns them into the attributes of an actor. It would be an exaggeration to say that ours is a hostile relationship; I* live, let myself go on living, so that Borges may contrive his literature, and this literature justifies me*.

Thus rendered, the very intent of the story is to highlight the distinction between a self and the person who constitutes that self. Borges' self has developed a somewhat strained relation with *his* person*, Borges! (And isn't that something of a condition on ordinary decency?) So also, the girl who wanted to be Britney did have a coherent desire, a desire whose content she could have expressed by "It will soon be the case that the person who constitutes me* is Britney." If that were to happen, she would have what she wanted. So also, when I have the sort of dream that I am inclined to report by saying, "In my dream I was Hannibal," I am dreaming that another person, namely Hannibal, has come to constitute me*.

Return to the practical puzzle that arises for the standard semantic account of "I." The fact that Johnston is Johnston is no more important to me than the fact that Mother Teresa is Mother Teresa; both are mere identity facts. But the fact that I* am Johnston is very important to me. It is not an identity fact. It is the fact that this self is presently constituted by Johnston. Johnston presently has the property of being me. As noted earlier, this property, the property of being at the center of this arena of presence and action, is a property we can understand as appropriately focusing and mobilizing a human animal's self-protectiveness. It is because Johnston has this property that my* self-concern flows to Johnston.

Have We Built Too Much into "I"-Use?

Kant famously remarked that "I" is the most impoverished of representations, and offered in the Paralogisms a corresponding diagnosis of the Cartesian mistake of supposing that "I" denotes a non-physical substance.

> I think myself on behalf of a possible experience, at the same time abstracting from all actual experience, and I conclude therefrom that I can be conscious of my existence even apart from experience and its empirical conditions. In so doing I am confusing a possible abstraction from my empirically determined existence with the supposed consciousness of a possible separate existence of my thinking self, and I thus come to believe that I have knowledge that what is substantial in me is the transcendental subject. (*First Critique* B427)

Kant's idea might be put this way, if we allow ourselves more than a pinch of anachronism. One need not know very much at all to pick oneself out as "I," and so we can easily be misled into reifying our unspecific conception of ourselves as "I" into the idea of a thing, the self, that can undergo any amount of psychological or physical discontinuity, a transcendental or spiritual subject, as it were.[10]

There is something in this idea of the unspecific nature of the content of "I," but it is compatible with thinking that "I"-use has some determinate conceptual and psychological requirements.

One thing to note is that I can get further imagining that I am Spinoza than I can get with imagining that I am a carbon atom or a set. In these cases, we are dealing with things that seem to be essentially mindless. Accordingly, there is no way of attaching an arena or a center to the item in question, so that there is nothing that would count as my finding an atom or a set here at the center of this arena.

This suggests that some of my uses of "I" are drawing on an awareness of something like what Kant called the unity of apperception, the experience of one's present mental life as a whole, as an arena or "consciousness" if you will, in which mental events are occurring. At least Kant thought so when he wrote, "Only because I comprehend their manifold in a consciousness do I call them all together *my* presentations, for otherwise I would have as multicolored and diverse a self as I have presentations of which I am conscious" (*First Critique* B134).

What we were calling an arena, or, as Kant puts it, a "consciousness," is the apparent whole that one experiences when one experiences the unity of apperception or more generally the unity of consciousness. But the experience of that unity is a grace of fortune; it can break down, and it may break down in a way that disables "I"-use.

Imagine a human being whose visual field appeared centered on a position disjoint from his body field, whose proprioceptive sense of where action was issuing from defined still another location, and whose auditory field was displaced outside his head, so that the auditory location "here" with respect to which sounds are located was not even apparently where his body was. Such a human being may have no sense of these various fields being unified in an arena or consciousness with himself at the phenomenological center. Applied to such a case, Kant's thesis seems to entail, plausibly, that such a human being would not be capable of coherent "I"-use.

---

[10]See the discussion of the "bare locus" view in my "Human Beings."

Earlier we were inclined to see a possible empirical confirmation of this idea of experienced mental unity as a condition of coherent "I"-use in the syndrome characteristic of Cotard's patients. They are characteristically unable to use "I" in the normal way, even to the point of questioning whether they exist. And they seem to exhibit the very fragmentation of "fields" described above. Is it because they have no experience of a centered arena, the integrated experience of the various fields around an implied position, that they cannot pick themselves out as "I," as at the center of an immediately demonstrable arena or "consciousness"?

The Concept of the Self versus the Metaphysics of the Self

The present concept of the self, tailored as it is to make conceptual sense of feats of auto-alienation and the like, is the concept of a potentially variably constituted entity, an entity potentially consisting of many human beings, indeed potentially consisting of many self-conscious beings of different kinds, who are united into a single persisting thing—the self in question—by being successively at the center of a given persisting arena of presence and action. Now it might be that the *conceptual* possibility of the variability of my constitution as across many self-conscious beings is not a real possibility thanks to a certain metaphysical fact, for example, that only this brain or a significant portion of it could sustain *this arena* of presence and action. Then this self, my self, is always and necessarily constituted by a body that houses my brain or, in special cases, by that brain alone.

Is it not this way of thinking of the brain as a sort of chariot of the self that undergirds the intuition that in brain transplantation you would go where your brain goes? This does not show that you are identical with a brain, only that you are a self carried across by that brain.

The Proviso: An Alternative to Offloading

We may now explain the proviso entered at the end of both lectures one and two. From quite early on we have *not, or not just*, been offloading onto persons understood as substances, we have been tracing selves, our own and others', by means of a cross-time unity condition that appears to be *directly* available to us in our own case, namely the condition of being and continuing to be at the center of an arena.[11]

One appealing developmental hypothesis is that there is in fact no time at which the problem of other minds—and this might be adapted for the problem of other selves—could actually arise in any *serious* way. We never have to rely on what has been stigmatized as the worst form of inductive argument, the so-called analogical argument *from* the one observed correlation where bodily behavior is expressive of mental events in an "inner" arena *to* the existence of many unobserved correlations of bodily behavior with mental events in an "inner" arena. For, on the relevant developmental hypothesis we don't actually encounter *ourselves* as having a mind until we see ourselves as one of these minds whose outer behavior is experienced as expressive of events in their inner arena (or something like that). That is, we acquire the concept of *a* mind, and only then can we conceive of ourselves as a mind. If this is right then perhaps we also acquire the concept of *a* self and then conceive of ourselves as one of those. So although the self as we are now understanding it is a potentially successive entity, and so an entity onto which we cannot offload, we still are, quite early on, in a position to attend to selves because of an inchoate understanding of what we are attending to as united over time by being at the center of *that* arena of presence, that is, the one whose occurrent mental events are expressed in *that* behavior.

TRACING SELVES VERSUS TRACING NEO-LOCKEAN PERSONS

Contrast this view with the Neo-Lockean view rejected in lecture one. Recall that Neo-Lockeanism holds that truths about personal identity have as their necessary and sufficient conditions the holding of relations of mental *continuity* and *connectedness*. In its turn, connectedness involves the holding of direct psychological connections, such as the persistence of beliefs and desires, the connection between an intention and the later act in which the intention is carried out, and the connection between an experience and a memory of that experience. In emphasizing these other mental connections the Neo-Lockeans thought of themselves as improving on what they took to be Locke's purely memory-based criterion.

[11]Consider the empirical evidence cited earlier, in particular the work of Bering, "The Folk Psychology of Souls."

The Neo-Lockeans required that if person x and person y are to be the same person, then psychological continuity, the ancestral of psychological connectedness, holds between them. By thus building a chain with the direct psychological connections as links, and only requiring that if x and y are the same person then some chain of such links must connect x and y, the Neo-Lockeans avoided the kind of objection leveled at Locke's own account, which (allegedly) relies simply on memory of past experiences. Building a metaphysical criterion of personal identity just on such a direct mental connection, as Locke is often supposed to have done, leads to intransitivities that are incompatible with the very concept of identity. For the old general may remember his days as a lieutenant, and the lieutenant may have remembered his days as a boy, while the old general remembers nothing of his days as a boy. If memory is necessary and sufficient for identity, the general is identical with the lieutenant, and the lieutenant is identical with the boy, but the general is not identical to the boy. An absurd result, and one to be blamed on any criterion that generates it.

David Lewis, among others, noticed an awkward side effect of using the method of chaining, or taking the ancestral of the relation of direct psychological connectedness, so as to meet this old objection from intransitivity. You can get from any psychological condition to any other psychological condition by such a chain, if it is long enough. So mere psychological continuity, the ancestral or chained relation built up from psychological connectedness, seems insufficient for personal identity, at least if we are thinking of personal identity as in some way constrained by psychological sameness. A corresponding point arises with physical continuity; you can describe a long but physically *continuous* process by which a human corpse reduces to a few cells. (Imagine the corpse shedding one cell at a time.) It would be absurd to say that the corpse is then identical to the collection of the few cells. We need some overarching constraint that limits the amount and kind of physical change the corpse can be taken to undergo.

Likewise, Lewis reasoned, we need some overarching constraint that limits the amount of psychological change a person can undergo.[12] So Lewis thought that a sufficiently long-lived and continuously developing "Methuselah," as he put it, might include many Neo-Lockean persons within his lifetime.

---

[12]Lewis, "Survival and Identity."

Of course, in retrospect, the choice of just which overarching constraint to impose can seem arbitrary. Given the basic orientation of Neo-Lockeanism, with its focus on mental continuation, why not simply recognize within such a long-lived and continuously developing entity more and less psychologically compact persons?

That is not intended as an objection, so much as part of a reminder about just how complex any *extensionally adequate* Neo-Lockean criterion would have to be. The Neo-Lockean criterion was formulated very late in the philosophical day, and is far from obvious. Locke himself, to take one notable example, supposedly got the criterion wrong! It is correspondingly implausible that it is this criterion that the young child is bringing to bear, either personally or sub-personally, in tracking itself and others over time.

The cognitive system, we argued, likes to avoid unnecessary labor. One way to do this is to offload onto substances. Another might be to trace ourselves and others as entities whose cross-time unity condition involves an item whose present manifestation just settles what it would be to have the same thing again, independently of any criterion we might bring to bear. And that is just how an arena, a mind, or a consciousness appears, as a thing whose present manifestation just settles what it would be to have it continue to exist.

The difference in cognitive labor as between tracing Neo-Lockean bundles and tracing selves is due to the fact that although the self is not a substance, it can be specified in terms of a unity condition that involves an item—an arena of presence or a consciousness—that *seems* to settle its own conditions of identity over time in just the way that a substance does. If we do not need to bring to bear unity conditions to unite temporal slices of an arena of presence into a persisting arena of presence, then without relying on detailed psychological unity conditions we can get a self in mind as the entity constituted by the things that successively occupy the center of a persisting arena of presence.

Do We Trace Selves or Trace Persons?

The question of when and whether we are tracing selves or tracing persons by offloading onto substances is an empirical one, and yet it is a very difficult question to operationalize in a child experimental or observational setting. Outside of such settings, there are things that provide some prima facie evidence that we have come to trace selves and not just persons. There is, for example, the widespread Christian belief that one could first be a living human being, and *then* a spiritual substance or soul, and *then* perhaps a quasi-human being with a resurrected "spiritual" body, so that one is successively constituted over time by things in very different categories. The apparent coherence of this belief may be the mere effect of inculcation, but here is something that points to it being more than that. Even those of us who believe this could *not be so* find the corresponding thought about a spider becoming a spiritual substance and then having a resurrected spiritual body very much harder to have. We are, I take it, offloading when we visually track spiders. We do not trace spiders in terms of something "inner" that their outer behavior expresses; we are just tracing the animals that spiders essentially are. (Is that why some people find it easy to squash them?)

The idea that we have come to trace selves rather than persons also fits better with the fact of the widespread belief in reincarnation, which is also found, surprisingly enough, in the very Buddhist tradition that holds to *anatta,* the doctrine that there is no permanent persisting self, so that if anything deserves the name of a self it is at most an *ens successivum*. What is supposed to reincarnate looks less like a person and more like something that is constituted by different persons in its different incarnations.

The details of Christian, Hindu, and Buddhist belief aside, the hypothesis that we are tracing selves by bringing to bear a salient subjective unity condition, rather than tracking persons by offloading onto the most salient substance in their vicinity, may make better sense of the way in which humanity has been easily haunted both by thoughts of an afterlife in which we come to be things in a very different category from human beings and by thoughts of "coming back as another person."

RESURRECTION AGAIN

In thus providing for a self, and arguing that it is the self and not the person who is the proper object of self-concern, have we not then finally provided the very thing that would serve the great ambition of Protestant theology from Milton to Cullman, namely the removal of the Platonic foul spot from the otherwise beautiful promise of the resurrection?

Once again I shall illustrate the point in my own case, inviting you to do the same in your case. This self (the self that thus presents to me now) could first be constituted by the human being Johnston; that human being is throughout this life the one at the center of this arena of presence. When that human being dies this arena of presence would come to an end, so that "the whole man is obliterated by death." But then—and here is perhaps our best understanding of the beautiful promise of the resurrection—on the Great Day, God could re-create this very arena of presence with a spiritualized variant of Johnston at its center. *I* would then have come back, and then...

In this way our theologians could forgo *both* the Neo-Lockean and bodily criteria of personal identity in favor of an appropriate criterion of *self* identity!

A Comparison with Thomas

Our thoughts about a hylomorphic self may put us in a position to resolve a longstanding conundrum left over from the best-known Catholic theology of death. Thomas Aquinas, you will remember, was a hylomorphist, and so offered a metaphysical analysis of the human being in terms of matter and form. Thomas explicitly rejects the idea that he is identical with a mind or soul with the cry "Ego non est anima"; he regards the soul as the substantial (or essential) form of the body. Yet, in conformity with Catholic teaching, Thomas also holds that we exist during the interregnum between death and the final judgment. But if the body is no more, and the soul is just the substantial form of the *body*, its principle of life and self-maintenance, and I am the hylomorphic entity that is some biological matter so formed, then after death there is nothing of me left!

I have heard some Thomists hint, somewhat darkly, that God miraculously keeps one's soul or substantial form in existence after one's death by providing it with some other kind of matter, perhaps a spiritualized analog of biological matter. But on simple hylomorphic grounds this must mean that one's substantial form was never *merely* a principle of organization of biological matter; it must have always contained within it the possibility of organizing different kinds of embodiments, as it were a human being or human animal and then, a partly miraculous variant on a human being, into a single persisting whole.

Of course, it would be anachronistic to import our post-Cartesian thoughts about the self into the text of Aquinas. But the problem that he leaves us with, namely how to think hylomorphically about something that is at one time constituted by a human being and then by a variant made up of spiritual matter, may appear to be solved by thinking of the one who exists during the interregnum as the *self* of the deceased rather than the deceased human being.[13]

SELF AS DETERMINED BY CONSCIOUSNESS, BUT THE BED NOT THE STREAM

At various points, I have expressed some slight unease with the Neo-Lockean interpretation of Locke. To put it all too simply, where Locke speaks of consciousness, the Neo-Lockeans characteristically interpret this as always referring to the stream of consciousness, the kind of item whose persistence through time is best captured by something like their criterion of mental continuity. But suppose that Locke, in speaking of consciousness, sometimes had in mind something closer to the bed in which the stream of consciousness flows, something akin to an arena of presence. Then certain passages in Locke could be read as prefiguring our hylomorphic account of the self. Is the following such a passage?

> [P]ersonal identity consists ... not in the identity of substance, but, as I have said, in the identity of consciousness, wherein if Socrates and the present Mayor of Queensborough agree, they are the same person.[14]

Here I think that Locke is *not* supposing that there is some tortuous pattern of psychological continuity that connects the stream of consciousness of Socrates with that of the Mayor of Queensborough. His position is therefore not captured, and then improved upon, by Neo-Lockeanism. In speaking of Socrates and the Mayor of Queensborough

[13]There is another kind of anachronism here, for I am following the maxim that we should try to save something in traditional hylomorphism by substituting wherever we can talk of principles of unity in my sense for the traditional talk of substantial forms. This captures at most one strand in the hylomorphic tradition. Still, for all that, there is the historical tradition, and there are the philosophical insights and problems it leaves behind. The proposal is just to deploy the present account of hylomorphism to deal with one such problem, not to provide an interpretation of Aquinas.

[14]*Essay*, Book 2, Chapter XXVII.

as having the same consciousness, Locke may well be speaking of the bed and not the stream; in our terms, of the arena and not what passes through it.

Locke's very forgivable error is to move smoothly between same person and same self, as when he observes, "PERSON, as I take it, is the name for this self," as if same person and same human being came to very different things. For us, I would argue, the person is a human being, and Socrates and the Mayor of Queensborough are manifestly different human beings, even though it is conceivable that there is a self that is constituted by both, as in the fantasy of reincarnation.

In any case Locke seems concerned to bring out, correctly, that self identity is determined by same consciousness, particularly in section 19 of "Identity and Diversity."

> SELF is that conscious thinking thing,—whatever substance made up of, (whether spiritual or material, simple or compounded, it matters not)—which is sensible or conscious of pleasure and pain, capable of happiness or misery, and so is concerned for itself, as far as that consciousness extends. Thus every one finds that, whilst comprehended under that consciousness, the little finger is as much a part of himself as what is most so. Upon separation of this little finger, should this consciousness go along with the little finger, and leave the rest of the body, it is evident the little finger would be the person, the same person; and self then would have nothing to do with the rest of the body. As in this case it is the consciousness that goes along with the substance, when one part is separate from another, which makes the same person, and constitutes this inseparable self: so it is in reference to substances remote in time. That with which the consciousness of this present thinking thing can join itself, makes the same person, and is one self with it, and with nothing else; and so attributes to itself, and owns all the actions of that thing, as its own, as far as that consciousness reaches, and no further; as every one who reflects will perceive.

Once again I am tempted to think that Locke is *not* supposing that it is because of the holding of some pattern of psychological continuity that the man and the little finger could be supposed to share a consciousness. He is just stipulating that they do share a consciousness, and claiming that they would then each constitute the same self. Although there are some passages in Locke that support the standard interpretation of him as offering an inadequate memory criterion for personal identity, the better Locke, if not the predominant Locke, seems to be offering a same-consciousness criterion for the persistence of selves.

DIVINE JUSTICE AND THE SELF

Is a hylomorphic self—a variably constituted entity with an arena- or a consciousness-based principle of unity—a fitting subject for divine reward and retribution? Locke emphasizes what he calls the "forensic" nature of personal identity, the way in which the lineaments of personal identity make it legitimate to hold people responsible for the deeds *they* committed, and the way in which the lineaments of personal identity determine what patterns of property ownership and other rights are even prima facie legitimate.

So just to take up responsibility, it is a conceptual point that punishing someone for a crime he did not commit is a manifest injustice. Now a single self is, at least conceptually speaking, open to being constituted by various people or people-like things, as it might be a human being, a brain, or a spiritualized variant of a human being. Letting "I*" and its cognates denote a self and "I" and its cognates denote a person, which of these two claims captures the conceptual point about responsibility?

> Punishing someone* for a crime he* did not commit is a manifest injustice.

> Punishing some person for a crime he (that person) did not commit is a manifest injustice.

If it is just the latter claim, so that as a conceptual matter responsibility is tied to personal identity, then the resurrection of the self will be of no help at all in laying the foundation for Divine justice. On the other hand, it cannot be that as a conceptual matter any conceivable connection of self identity is enough to ground cross-temporal responsibility. It is conceivable that I* wake and find myself* to be constituted by a rational, that is, self-conscious, parrot. Part of the conception involves my dispositional and occurrent psychology radically changing to that of a parrot, albeit a rational, self-conscious parrot. In the situation so conceived, it would be absurd to punish the parrot for the wrongs I* have committed while being constituted by Johnston, and not just because parrots are rather stuck in their ways. It would be absurdly *unjust* to punish the parrot.

This seems to be because, in the imagined situation, although the parrot is me*, his psychology is not in any way a descendent of Johnston's.

Perhaps we can hear an echo of the same point even if we restrict ourselves to cases of personal identity. There does seem to be something less than coherent in the thought that justice demands that we punish a person in the later stages of Alzheimer's disease or profound psychosis for something that very person did when he was younger and mentally intact. These brief reflections suggest that the lineaments of responsibility are not the lineaments of mere personal identity or mere self identity. They require something more, namely that the object of punishment must exhibit a reasonable degree of psychological connection with the perpetrator of the crime. Justice requires that we have the same "individual personality," the same self or person still exhibiting a reasonable degree of psychological connection with the perpetrator of the crime.

My conjecture is that personal responsibility follows the lineaments of individual personalities. *If* that is right then the resurrection of selves could in principle lay the ground for Divine justice. For the resurrected person at the very minimum has a reasonable degree of psychological connection with the deceased person whose merit and fault he is supposed to inherit.

Many will say that all this is pointless onto-theology, for there is no God, and so no one ready to re-create an arena of presence after the demise of the brain that supported it. But remember our aim here is not to deny that there is a God, or use that as a premise in an argument against the afterlife, but to show that even if God exists there is a problem in principle with the idea of the afterlife as a destination we (or we*) could hope to reach.

The "Constitution View"

The idea that we can be resurrected by having our selves resurrected is in a certain way akin to a suggestion made by Lynne Rudder Baker, although she talks instead of persons and first-person perspectives.

Impressed by Pauline texts like

Now this I say, brethren, that flesh and blood cannot inherit the kingdom of God; nor does corruption inherit incorruption. (1 Cor. 15:50)

Baker plausibly takes the promised change from a perishable or corruptible body to an imperishable or incorruptible body to be a *substantial* change, that is, a change that a particular body does not survive. So she supposes that God does not resurrect a person by re-creating numerically the same body that she had here on earth, but by re-creating the person, where a person is essentially tied to what Baker calls a "first-person point of view." She writes,

> Now let me turn to the constitution view, according to which sameness of pre- and post-mortem person is sameness of first-person perspective. In the first place, the constitution view avoids some of the pitfalls of the other candidates for a metaphysics of resurrection. Since human persons are essentially embodied, the constitution view avoids the problem of individuating disembodied souls—a problem that afflicts Thomism. Since a person's identity depends on her first-person perspective, the constitution view avoids the problem of the numerical identity of corruptible and incorruptible bodies—a problem that afflicts both animalism and Thomism.

Still, as Baker herself writes, the constitution view is not home free.

> What is needed is a criterion for sameness of first-person perspective over time. In virtue of what does a resurrected person have the same first-person perspective as a certain earthly person who was born in, say, 1800? In my opinion, there is no informative non-circular answer to the question: "In virtue of what do person P at t and person $P\#$ at t^* have the same first-person perspective over time?" It is just a primitive, unanalysable fact that some future person is I; but there is a fact of the matter nonetheless.[15]

Peter van Inwagen objects that this is not at all helpful. In response to Baker, he has this to say.

[15]Lynne Rudder Baker, "Persons and the Metaphysics of Resurrection," *Religious Studies* 43 (2007): 345.

But what is it for x and y to have the same first-person perspective? Baker insists that no criterion of sameness of first-person perspective is possible, and that it would be a mistake to demand one. Perhaps that is so, but I am not asking for a criterion—whatever that means—but for a definition. I am asking what the words "x and y have the same first-person perspective" *mean*. Baker makes it plain that, in her view, the familiar distinction between descriptive and numerical identity applies to first-person perspectives. My *Doppelgänger* on Twin Earth and I have minds with identical content at each moment and can therefore be said to have *descriptively* identical first-person perspectives. But we have *numerically distinct* first-person perspectives because, if for no other reason, our first-person perspectives are "directed at" different human bodies....

But what is the numerical identity of first-person perspectives? "Well, you understand what it is for x and y to have first-person perspectives, and you understand numerical identity, so you must understand the sentence 'the first-person perspective of x is identical with the first-person perspective of y.'" To paraphrase Wittgenstein, you understand "it's five o'clock" and you understand the adverbial phrase "on the sun," so you must understand "It's five o'clock on the sun." No, my antecedent understanding of "first-person perspective" and "is identical with" are not sufficient for my understanding "the first-person perspective of x is identical with the first-person perspective of y." I need some sort of definition, some explicit statement of meaning. And, unfortunately, the only definition I can think of (Baker gives none, and would probably not agree with me that one was needed) is this: The first-person perspective of x is identical with the first-person perspective of y is by definition the same as x has a first-person perspective and y has a first-person perspective and x is identical with y.

But if this is what identity of first-person perspectives *means*, then it's hard to see how being told that God can make a post-resurrection person *me* by giving that person a first-person perspective numerically identical with mine explains anything—for an essential part of giving a person a first-person perspective identical with mine is to make that person identical with me. And how

God might do *that* is just what identity of first-person perspectives was supposed to help us to understand.[16]

However, Baker does tell us quite a bit about the nature of a first-person perspective. First she characterizes perspectives quite generally.

Experience is perspectival. For example, the dog digs there (in the garden) rather than here (by the house), because she saw you bury the bone there in the garden and she wants it. A conscious being has a certain perspective on its surroundings with itself as "origin." If the dog could speak, she might say: "There's a bone buried over there, and I want it."[17]

On Baker's view the dog has a perspective, but not a first-person perspective. The dog, though conscious, is not self-conscious.

To be self-conscious, a being must not only have a perspective, but also must realize that she has a perspective. To be self-conscious, a being must not only be able consciously to experience things, but must also realize that she experiences things. Merely to have a perspective, or to be a subject of experience, is not enough. One must be able to recognize that one is a subject of experience; one must be able to think of oneself as oneself. One must be able to think of one's thoughts as one's own, and to have immediate access to her thoughts in that she can know without evidence that she is entertaining a thought that so-and-so.

Baker then goes on to connect having a first-person perspective with "I"-thought.

The first-person perspective opens up a distinction between thinking of myself as myself, on the one hand, and thinking of myself as Lynne Baker, or as the person who is writing this paper, on the other. The first-person perspective is the ability to consider oneself as oneself in this way. This is the basis of all forms of self-consciousness.[18]

---

[16]Peter Van Inwagen, "'I Look for the Resurrection of the Dead and the Life of the World to Come,'" a manuscript posted on http://philosophy.nd.edu/people/all/profiles/van-inwagen-peter/documents/Resurrection.doc.

[17]Lynne Rudder Baker, "The Difference that Self-Consciousness Makes," in Klaus Petrus, ed., *On Human Persons* (Ontos Verlag, 2003), 23ff.

[18]Ibid.

It thus seems clear that a perspective, as understood by Baker, is a not a property but an individual item of some sort, and a perspective is first-personal just when the one that occupies the perspective thinks of herself *as* occupying that perspective. This makes a first-person perspective, as understood by Baker, rather like an arena occupied by a self-conscious being.

In arguing against Baker's proposal I do not want to rest anything on that interpretive comparison; rather, what I have to say rests on the following substantive claim:

> My first-person perspective understood as an individual item can only persist or come to exist again if my perspective does, and this can happen only if this arena, this consciousness (in the sense we have dwelled on) persists or comes to exist again.

Notice that this is only a necessary condition on the persistence or reappearance of a first-person perspective. There may be no informative sufficient condition, and in that sense the persistence of first-person perspectives may be unanalyzable, as Baker suggests.

The substantive claim is hard to deny. If this very arena, this very consciousness, never comes back again then what sense is to be made of the idea of this very perspective coming back again?

But as we shall see, no practically interesting sense is to be made of this very arena or this very consciousness *coming back again*; so also then with the idea of this very individual perspective coming back again. Once we conceive of arenas, consciousness, perspectives, and the like as *individual items of some sort or other* then we shall have to face up to their purely intentional status.

Resurrected Selves?

So what, then, is the problem in principle with the idea of the resurrection of selves and with the associated idea of the re-creation of persons where this essentially involves the re-creation of their first-person perspectives, which in its turn involves the re-creation of a consciousness or an arena?

A materialist or physicalist might be thought to have a ready answer. A materialist might say that the problem in principle with the resurrection of the self lies in the fact that a given arena of presence could not exist without its associated brain existing, because that arena is essentially a product of that brain. This same fact implies that our feats of auto-alienation do not disclose genuine metaphysical possibilities but at most mere conceptual possibilities. For a given self could never extend beyond the life of its brain.

If that is so then the resurrection of the self would depend entirely on the resurrection of its brain. But the resurrection of the brain is something that is already ruled out by our discussion, in lecture one, of perimortem duplicates. For just as two distinct duplicate bodies cannot become one post-resurrection body, two distinct duplicate brains cannot become one post-resurrection brain. So a brain's resurrection cannot consist in the reassembly of its perimortem matter in its perimortem form. But what else could a brain's resurrection consist in?

Nevertheless, I fear that this natural materialist view about the dependence of the persisting self on the persisting brain does not get to the heart of the matter. Indeed, upon reflection, it is a deeply unclear and perhaps even confused view, based as it is on the idea that one's persisting brain *has been* producing the very same arena of presence over time.

The real problem in principle with the idea of the resurrection of the self is that *not even God* could re-create this very arena of presence. (The same could be said of your arena of presence.) God could no more do that than he could re-create Macbeth's dagger or any other *mere* intentional object. Appreciating this will not just finally disable the onto-theology of the afterlife—it must radically change our understanding of *this* life.

Consciousnesses?

It is a commonplace that the very fact of consciousness raises a problem for reductive versions of materialism. The so-called hard problem of consciousness is the problem of reconciling the qualitative feel of experience with a materialist ontology. This problem is typically misposed in terms of a bastard category of *qualia*, thought of as qualitative properties of mental events rather than as qualities and qualitative structures that figure among the intentional objects of both hallucinatory and veridical experience. If we set aside the bastard category of qualia, and recognize that qualities and qualitative structures are among the *intentionalia* of experience, then the "hard problem" of consciousness emerges as just a sub-case of the harder problem of intentionality, the problem of how items can be present to us in our conscious life, a problem whose difficulty has been masked by thinking that some happy combination of description and causation—perhaps augmented by an appeal to reference magnetism—could provide for a reductive account of presence in experience.[19]

A philosophically neutral way of thinking about consciousness might begin by treating it as a remarkable ability or capacity that we have, a capacity to become conscious of this or that, to have items in many categories present to us, and so to have them available for demonstration and as objects of further thought and talk. In such contexts "conscious of" is a determinable expression whose determinates are feeling, reflecting on, perceiving, introspecting, and the like. "Consciousness" is here just a general term for the various kinds of conscious acts.

Then there is philosophically dangerous talk of "a consciousness," as if "consciousness" were a *serious* count noun that divided its reference among individual consciousnes*s*es. Talking this way, we can easily be led to suppose that such individual "consciousnesses" are items with determinate conditions of identity over time. (Then we think: perhaps the reason we cannot state these conditions is that they are unanalyzable.)

In contrast to streams of consciousness, rushes of mental events involving interconnected thought, feeling, narrative, and memories, a consciousness might be supposed to be the mental bed in which such a stream flows. Like any complex process, a stream of consciousness seems to have an objective cross-time identity condition. If the stream has an objective cross-time identity condition then surely the bed in which it flows must also have a objective cross-time identity, no? And so we might be led to ask: What are the objective cross-time identity conditions of an individual consciousness over time? Can they only be secured by the persistence of a brain? Could they hold between a human being in this life and a spiritualized variant on the human being in the next life?

But what if a consciousness, an ostensible mental bed in which such streams run, is a merely intentional object? What if the inner appearance

[19] For more on this way of thinking about the issue, see my "Objectivity of Mind and the Objectivity of Our Minds," *Philosophy and Phenomenological Research* 66 (2007).

of a quasi-container within which mental events occur is a *mere* appearance? What if we are led to speak of a consciousness only because the corresponding stream of consciousness presents an impressive unity both at a time and over brief periods of time? The unity itself might be more than apparent; but consider the appearance that the mental events so unified are bound into a mental whole "in" which the stream of mental events occurs. Could that mental whole be a mere appearance?

With equal justice, these questions just posed of *a consciousness* could be posed of *an arena of presence*, perhaps because these expressions are just two ways of giving voice to the same idea of a mental "container" in which the stream of consciousness ebbs and flows.

We introduced the idea of an arena of presence as the idea of an inclusive mental field, a field comprising the visual, auditory and other sensory fields, the bodily field, and the field of thought and of action experienced from the inside as willed. What are these fields? The visual field is typical, and in a certain way paradigmatic. Recall that one's visual field is a quasi-container in which presentations of objective items in the sector before the eyes co-occur with after-images and hallucinations in such a way that they all appear to stand in quasi-spatial relation to each other. So also with the auditory field in which objective sounds co-occur with the things heard when one is simply "hearing things," that is, suffering from auditory hallucinations. So also with the bodily field, a quasi-three-dimensional volume that includes both bodily sensations and veridical proprioceptions of bodily movement.

The fields that make up an arena of presence are organized around an implied center that is a merely intentional object. What kind of container can be organized around a merely intentional object? A merely virtual container, a container that is itself a merely intentional object.

The arena is made up of fields that apparently encompass both real and unreal items. Press your dominant eyeball and look at your ring finger; you will see an unreal finger apparently alongside it. What kind of container can encompass both real and unreal items, as the visual field manifestly does? A merely virtual container, a container that is itself a merely intentional object.

The boundaries of these fields are odd items. Unlike real boundaries, unlike even real though arbitrary or "fiat" boundaries such as the boundaries of the sector of objective reality now seen from here, there is no good answer to the question of what is on *the other side* of these bound-aries. That question looks suspiciously like the question of what the back of Macbeth's dagger was like. To which the answer is, it was not a real dag-ger but a merely intentional object, that is, an object whose whole char-acterization is determined by how it appeared to Macbeth. What kind of local boundary is such that it is a determinate fact that certain objective questions which it makes sense to ask of real boundaries make no sense when asked of it? The merely virtual boundary of a merely virtual con-tainer, a container whose boundary is itself a merely intentional object.

In these ways we can come to see that the arena is a merely intentional object, an object that has no reality outside the intentional acts in which it appears.

Upon reflection, this should be no surprise. Recall Frege's observa-tion that "I"-thought shows that each of us must have a way of picking himself or herself out that is in principle not available to anyone else. Otherwise you could pick me out as "I," which is absurd. How could we possibly satisfy Frege's constraint if we are restricted to reference to the mutually available stock of real items? Frege's constraint can be satisfied only if one can pick oneself out by way of the merely intentional objects that are available only to oneself.

Yet this must mean that we selves are *creatures* of the unreal.

Deferring to the Victim of Hallucination

The clearest cases of *merely* intentional objects, objects of conscious acts whose whole nature is exhausted by how they present in those conscious acts, are after-images and objects of hallucination. There is no point in looking in the world at large for Macbeth's dagger or for that color patch you are now after-imaging on the wall. Finding an exactly similar col-ored patch on the wall or a dagger exactly like the dagger of Macbeth's hallucination would be entirely irrelevant. Nothing in the world of com-mon experience *could* count as the thing you after-imaged or the dagger Macbeth hallucinated. (Forget the fact that Macbeth is already a fictional character.)[20]

---

[20]I am assuming that Macbeth hallucinated a dagger, but there was not some dagger that Mac-beth hallucinated. This may be unfaithful to Shakespeare's text, at least if we are supposed to under-stand Macbeth as hallucinating the dagger he used to kill Duncan. But I am taking him to just see

In "The Obscure Object of Hallucination" I argued that hallucinations and after-images have a curious character.[21] Either can be an original source of de re knowledge of qualities, patterns, and shapes not yet encountered in veridical experience. For example, hallucinating or after-imaging a very bright green you have never previously encountered might motivate you to actually realize that shade of green for the first time by mixing pigments. Here your hallucination or after-image *gave you* a target shade to think about and aim at realizing. Contrast this with reference to ordinary particulars in the world of common experience; neither hallucination nor after-imaging can provide you with your first basis for referring to such ordinary particulars. Which ordinary particulars you get to hallucinate—your brother, your mother, the town in which you were born, and so forth—depends on your *antecedent* repertoire of singular reference. Hallucination can expand the repertoire of particular colors, shapes, sounds, and the like that we can think about, but it is entirely unoriginal when it comes to ordinary particulars.

Considerations like these lead to the proposal that there are primary and secondary objects of hallucination. The primary objects are what I styled "sensible profiles" or structures of qualities, structures that determine the qualitative character of the hallucination. The secondary objects are the objects determined by how the sensible profile in question strikes the subject, that is, by what the subject immediately takes it to be. To illustrate the use of this terminology, suppose one becomes a connoisseur of one's own drug-induced hallucinations and dwells on their qualities as such. When one simply contemplates one's hallucination it need not strike one as of this or that particular thing. If, in such a contemplative mood, one's hallucination does not strike one as *of* this or that particular thing, then it will not be of this or that particular thing. So even if I had a visual presentation that was in every way just like that enjoyed by a hallucinator of a dagger, I might be hallucinating nothing more than a dagger-like array of visible qualities. I would be enjoying

---

a dagger "out of the blue," that is, with no real dagger in mind. He does say, "Is this a dagger which I see before me." That sounds like a generic dagger, as it were.

W.V.O. Quine famously gave two readings of "I want a sloop." One reading, the referential reading, involves a particular sloop as the object of desire; the other, the notional reading, involves desiring relief from "slooplessness" however that might come about. In speaking of Macbeth and Macduff below, I am supposing that their hallucinations are merely notional in Quine's sense.

[21]Mark Johnston, "The Obscure Object of Hallucination," *Philosophical Studies* 120 (2004): 113–83.

this primary object of hallucination and there would be no secondary object.

How, then, are particular *secondary* objects of hallucination determined as such? Someone could hallucinate a sensible profile just like the one I hallucinated, and it could strike him as a dagger appearing to him. We would then report him as hallucinating a dagger, as it were, deferring to how things struck him. Another person could hallucinate a sensible profile just like the one I hallucinated, and it could strike him as a crucifix appearing to him. We would then report this person as hallucinating a crucifix, again deferring to how things struck him. It is because such a convention of deference operates that a person cannot go wrong in a certain way about what he is hallucinating. At least when it comes to the secondary objects of a subject's hallucinations the convention guarantees that he has got what he is hallucinating right.

Suppose Noddy's aunt has a voice that sounds exactly like the voice of Noddy's mother. On Mondays, Wednesdays, and Fridays Noddy dwells on his mother and her many virtues. On the other days of the week Noddy dwells on his aunt and her many virtues. Noddy also has a tendency to hallucinate, especially when he gets maudlin. So on Mondays, Wednesdays, and Fridays Noddy hallucinates his mother calling his name over and over on the phone. On the other days of the week, Noddy hallucinates his aunt calling his name over and over on the phone. All this could be true even if all the qualities of Noddy's auditory presentations are the same on each day of the week. If one hallucinates a certain sound and it immediately strikes one as one's mother talking on the phone, then it just follows that one has hallucinated one's mother talking to one over the phone. In such cases there is a sense in which one cannot go wrong about just who it is that one is hallucinating. For in such cases who it is one is hallucinating is determined by who one immediately takes it to be.[22] If I waver and ask myself, "Is it my mother or my aunt that

---

[22] "Who one immediately takes it to be" admits of an ambiguity that tracks the distinction between speaker's reference and semantic reference. Suppose someone blissfully ignorant of American politics sees George W. Bush and believes that he is called "George Herbert Bush." He then hallucinates the man. Which man, the son or the father? I suppose that even if his hallucination immediately strikes him in such a way as to lead him to say, "That is George Herbert Bush," his hallucination is of George W. Bush, the speaker referent of his use of "George Herbert Bush" and not the semantic referent. Similar points apply to a variety of other cases in which one is confused about who is who.

I am hallucinating?" no particular person will be determinately the object of my hallucination.

Contrast the case of actually hearing one's mother over the phone. As it turns out, Noddy's family is very close. Both his mother and his aunt are concerned about Noddy's mental state, and they call him regularly. They have an arrangement that divides the labor of calling. Noddy's mother calls on Mondays, Wednesdays, and Fridays, and Noddy's aunt calls on the other days of the week. But one Friday, Noddy's aunt substitutes for Noddy's mother. On that Friday when Noddy's aunt calls, Noddy immediately takes himself to be hearing his mother. It immediately strikes him as his mother talking to him on the phone. But he is wrong about who it is that he is hearing on the phone. It is his aunt and not his mother. The particulars that are the objects of hearing (veridical auditory perception) are not determined by how the qualitative auditory array strikes the subject, in contrast to the particular objects of auditory hallucination.[23]

What of the identity over time of the secondary objects of hallucination? There are two cases, depending on the answer to the question: Is there something real such that he hallucinated *it*, that is, took it to be appearing to him? If Noddy hallucinated his mother, if some visual array struck him as his mother, then she is the secondary object of his hallucination. She is a real object, and her conditions of identity over time are what they are *anyway*, independently of how things strike Noddy. But suppose Noddy hallucinates a motherly presence, that is, a certain hallucinated visual array strikes him as a motherly presence, but in a purely "notional" way,[24] that is, there is no real motherly presence that he takes this to be. In such cases it appears that we follow a certain deferential convention in reporting facts of identity or difference within the hallucination. If Noddy has a similar experience later on, and it strikes him as the very same motherly presence, we will *say* that Noddy hallucinated *a* motherly presence twice. If Noddy has a similar experience later on, and it strikes him as another motherly presence, we will *say* that Noddy hallucinated *two* motherly presences appearing to him.

That is, when we are dealing with merely intentional objects, such as

---

[23] For more discussion of these issues, see my "The Obscure Object of Hallucination."

[24] In the sense of notional as it arises in Quine's distinction between the notional and relational readings of sentences with psychological verbs and noun phrase objects.

a motherly presence that is not any real motherly presence, the identity over time of the merely intentional object is just a matter of how it actually strikes the subject of the hallucination.

I do not mean to say that there exist real objects whose conditions of identity or difference over time are a private subjective matter. There are no such objects. (We could prove that in this way: After a delay in which he was undecided, Macbeth might come to regard the dagger he hallucinated the second time as the same dagger. But there can be no object about which it could *come to be* the case that it was identical with some previously encountered object.)

It is rather that with respect to the reports of the identity or difference of merely intentional objects, we have a convention of deferring to how it strikes the subject of the experience in which those objects appear. Behind the convention the real facts concern the structure of the array or sensible profile that is the primary object in hallucination and how that primary object strikes the subject.

Let us try a couple more examples to get used to this idea as it applies to the case of the ostensible identity over time of intentional objects. Macbeth could hallucinate two very similar sensible profiles, where one hallucination occurs an hour after the other. Macduff could also hallucinate two very similar sensible profiles, with the same time gap in between his hallucinations. Because of the difference in Macbeth and Macduff's antecedent expectations, Macbeth's two sensible profiles might strike Macbeth as the very same dagger, first appearing here and then there, whereas Macduff's two very similar sensible profiles might strike Macduff as a dagger appearing here and then a duplicate dagger appearing there. If so, the correct report of Macbeth's hallucination would be of the same dagger appearing here and then there, while the correct report of Macduff's hallucination would be of two different but similar daggers appearing, one after the other. This could be so even if all four dagger-simulating profiles were qualitatively just alike. The identity or difference of these merely intentional "objects" of hallucination is merely a matter determined by how the primary objects, the sensible profiles, strike the relevant subjects on the relevant occasions.

No doubt you can see where this is heading. A consciousness or an arena of presence, a "container" of a stream of consciousness, is a particular given in inner experience. But reflection on the nature of such "containers" suggests that they are merely intentional objects. For their centers are merely intentional objects, many of their constituents are merely intentional objects, and their boundaries are merely intentional objects. A certain kind of hallucination—that of a container or arena— bounds *even our veridical experience of the world.* The appearance of unity among the mental events that make up a stream of consciousness yields the illusion of a mental unit—an arena, a consciousness—which contains that stream.

So the identity over time of an arena, or a consciousness, is the ostensible identity over time of a *merely* intentional object. As such, it is just a matter of how the unity of the stream immediately strikes the person who is aware of it. As it happens, this unity invariably strikes a person as being a certain kind of whole, an arena or consciousness, as we have been calling it. And for reasons we will turn to, each subject takes this whole, this arena or consciousness construed as a kind of containing whole, as persisting for as long as he or she is conscious.

But there is no substantial issue involved over and above how successive appearances of the apparently unifying container of a stream of consciousness strike the person whose stream of consciousness is in question.

I believe that we were able to get going with a concept of an arena or a consciousness as a persisting thing because our own arenas or consciousnesses have been continually striking us as persisting through time. In this way, we are each like a version of Macbeth who takes himself to be seeing the very same dagger over time. It would then be right to say that Macbeth was hallucinating the same dagger. Likewise, in each case, HERE, whenever I consider the issue it strikes me as the very same consciousness or arena from one moment to the next.

The hylomorphic self, which we argued to be the true focus of feats of auto-alienation and the proper object (if there *is any* proper object) of self-concern, is defined by a unity condition that makes essential reference to a merely intentional object.

This does not mean that *the self* is a merely intentional object. I prefer Phillip drunk to Phillip sober, and I prefer both to Phillip worshiping Baal. Baal, I hope, *is* a purely intentional object, but if we admit qua objects—things like Phillip drunk or Phillip when drunk—then Phillip worshiping Baal, though it is defined relative to an unreal or merely intentional object, will be as real as Phillip sober. Phillip worshiping Baal is a real creature of the unreal, but as such there may be something degenerate about its conditions of identity over time. If Phillip goes through a period where he is ambivalent about whether it is Baal that he is worshiping, then it may be indeterminate as to whether the qua object Phillip worshiping Baal exists during that period.

This is the sense in which our selves are, as I put it, creatures of the unreal. Given that the identity over time of a merely intentional object is a matter of how things strike the subject, so too is the identity over time of a self!

However, at any given time when the question of existence comes up, a self exists, just as Phillip worshiping Baal exists at the relevant times. So whenever the thought "I exist" comes up, it is really true, for "I" in the relevant sense picks out a self, for example, a human being qua at the relevant center of the relevant arena. But as for the thought, "I will exist," things are not so clear.

Why, then, do I trace this arena and this self in the particular way that I do, so that this self's adventures are, de facto, roughly co-incident with the adventures of the human being Johnston? Why does it seem that our self has more or less coincided with our person? It is because we have been brought up inside the narrative of the human being, a narrative which, among other things, tells us roughly how long we can expect to last, at least without recourse to the other world. This narrative, which forms a frame around our collective life, makes what could otherwise strike us as tendentious identifications of a consciousness or an arena *across* periods of deep sleep or unconsciousness seem utterly natural. In making such identifications we make them true or at least immune to refutation. For we are properly reported by way of a convention of deference that takes our reactions as criterial, as settling the matter.

This is because the objects in question—arenas, consciousnesses—are merely intentional objects.

The Vanishing Importance of the Self

Thanks to the convention of deference, the identity of merely intentional objects is merely a matter of how things strike the subject. The responses we as reporters defer to are the subject's *actual retrospective* reactions to the effect that what is now present is/is not the same as what was then present. One day Macbeth "sees" a dagger and the next day he again "sees" a dagger, and he takes it to be the very same dagger. And so we report him as having hallucinated the same dagger on two separate occasions. If the second presentation had struck him as a second dagger, then it would have been correct to report him as having hallucinated two different daggers.

One crucial point is that these identifications are *backward-looking*. What of prospective identifications of merely intentional objects that I now anticipate enjoying in the future? Johnston might now be disposed to regard the future presentations of any arena of presence that he will enjoy as presentations of the same arena as he is now enjoying. But that current disposition of Johnston's is not in itself enough to make his future presentations of an arena count as presentations of the very same arena. For current dispositions can be lost or altered, and even if they persist they can be masked so that they do not manifest in the standard way in the appropriate conditions. Something may distract Johnston, or Johnston may be in a condition of "flow," where he is so absorbed in what he is doing that he has no residuum of self-consciousness in which to consider questions of inner identity. Everything depends on whether Johnston *will in fact* make the backward-looking identifications in question. If Johnston does not, this self will not have that future.

Perhaps, thanks to the way in which Johnston's thought is so deeply shaped by the framing narrative of the human being, I can be confident that whenever the questions of whether it is still "me," still the same consciousness, still the same arena, come up, Johnston will in fact answer those questions in the affirmative, so that this self *will* have a future. But that future must reasonably be taken to be highly intermittent and so nowhere near as continuous as Johnston's stream of consciousness.

So the first thing that follows is that the future lineaments of this self will not correspond to any adequate objects of future self-concern. If Johnston is to be mugged, I can be pretty sure that he will not be making any backward-looking identifications *during the mugging*. After all, being mugged is rather distracting. So Johnston's future during the mugging will not be part of the future of this self. Despite his frenzied capacity for introspection, not even Johnston can sustain the kind of continuous

self-examination required to knit together a seamless self from successive acts of awareness of an arena.

Giving Up on the Self

And, more to the point, WHY SHOULD HE EVEN TRY? For if this is
what self identity turns on it is too trivial a matter to justify future-
directed self-concern. (Recall my concern for my future self as it came
upon me in the booth at Triumph Brewery.) Questions of self identity
will be as thin, and as trivial, as questions of the identity of fictional
characters across different narratives, questions like: Is the Parzifal of
Wagner's nineteenth-century opera the same fictional character as the
Perceval of Chrétien de Troyes' thirteenth-century saga? Wagner, it seems,
intended that it be so, and we may as well leave it as that. The pure question of fictional identity, even if it is not entirely empty, is of no real importance to anyone.

When it comes to hallucination, we have a convention of deferring to
how it strikes the subject of the experience in which those objects appear; we frame our reports of the identity or difference of merely intentional objects accordingly. Behind the convention, the real facts are facts
about the structure of the array or sensible profile which is the primary
object in hallucination and facts about how that primary object strikes
the subject. After describing these facts, we could suspend the convention, and we still would have captured all the important facts. The further reports, as governed by the convention of deference, are of no real
importance to anyone.

But nothing could deserve the name of self identity over time and
be of no real importance to anyone. The "hylomorphic *self*" was badly
named, at least if we were looking for something that would independently justify future-directed self-concern, that is, justify that concern
by way of its distinctive metaphysical nature.

Nothing, it seems, independently justifies future-directed self-concern.
Future-directed self-concern has established itself upon a certain kind of
persistent illusion of a self worth caring about. As William Hazlitt put it,
the bias toward ourselves characteristic of our future-oriented concern
depends on the idea of a persisting self that "habitually clings to the mind

of every man, binding it as with a spell, deadening its discriminating powers, and spreading the confused associations which belong only to past
and present impressions over the whole of our imaginary existence."[25]

Is the Birth of Others as Good as Rebirth?

There are two old questions often supposed to be deeply embarrassing
for the Buddhist theology of the afterlife, combining as it does the doctrine of reincarnation with the claim of *anatta*, the claim that there is no
persisting self that is worth caring about, but at most something like a
variably constituted hylomorphic self, as we might now put it. One old
question is this: If there is no permanent or substantial self, what could
possibly reincarnate? Here the hylomorphic self can in principle stand
in for the permanent self; for there is no straightforward incoherence in
supposing that in one life it can be Johnston at the center of this arena,
in another, a woman or even a parrot.

The second of the old questions is more troubling. I die—this self
dies—and a baby is born. If there are no permanent selves to be reincarnated, why isn't the sequence of my death and the baby's birth *as good as*
what is called reincarnation on the *anatta* (no persisting self worth caring about) view? In our terms, how could something whose persistence
requires the persistence of a merely intentional object make any practical difference, any difference to what is important?

The Incoherence of Non-Derivative
De Se Reasons for Action

Reflection on death, one's own death, brings the arena and hence the self
into clear view. Reflection on the self shows us that the future existence

---

[25] William Hazlitt, *Essay on the Principles of Human Action and Some Remarks on the Systems of Hartley and Helvetius* (London, 1805; repr., with an introduction, by John H. Nabholz, Gainesville, Florida, 1969), 6. It is to Raymond Martin and John Barresi that we owe the widespread appreciation of Hazlitt's work as a deeply insightful anticipation of the contemporary discussion of "what matters in survival." See their "Hazlitt on the Future of the Self," *Journal of the History of Ideas* 56 (1995): 463–81.

Unfortunately, Hazlitt's argument for the conclusion quoted above depends on recapitulating Butler's confusion to the effect that only a merelogically unchanging entity can exhibit "strict identity." This also led to Hazlitt's acceptance of the resurrection as securing "loose and popular identity" and so being as good as what he took to be on offer in this life.

of this self is not of any importance. This discovery should not only change our view of death, it should transform our view of life.

This lecture began with the suggestion that there were two sorts of de se thoughts, one concerned with persons, and the other concerned with selves. Then there is *another* distinction at the level of practical reasons, reasons to prefer and act. There is, for example, a purely impersonal reason to stop making a mess, one that applies to anyone who is making a mess. When John Perry realizes that it is *his* cart that is making the mess in the supermarket and so closes up his leaking sugar bag, he is recognizing that a certain impersonal reason applies to him, as he might put it, "Oops, *I* am the one making a mess, so it is up to me to stop, and clean up." Here Perry is accessing an impersonal reason and recognizing that it applies to *his own* case. He may be said to have a *derivative* de se reason, a reason for *him* to take a certain action, but a reason derived simply from the structure of impersonal reason.

Our attack on the importance of the self leaves the force of these sorts of de se reasons entirely intact, for they can be reconstructed as reasons that persons come to appreciate as they recognize the situations they actually occupy. The uses of "I" involved in the appreciation of what such reasons demand of one in one's concrete situation can be understood as references to the person that one is.

What is threatened are *basic* de se reasons, the reasons of self-interest and the like. If there is no persisting self worth caring about, the premium or excess that special self-concern expects and rejoices in cannot represent a reasonable demand or expectation.

Return to C. D. Broad's characterization of those reasons, which he called "self-referential." Not only do we seek premium treatment for ourselves if the effects on others are not too onerous, but we act as if the interests of our family, our friends, our familiars, our tribe, and our nation somehow count for more. We regard this as somehow rational, and yet we do not believe this because we believe that we ourselves, along with our family, friends, familiars, tribe, and nation are somehow distinguished from the point of view of the universe.

When Ayn Rand advocated ethical egoism, the view that the *only* reasons are reasons of self-interest, even *she* did not advocate this *because* she thought Ayn Rand was marvelously special. No, the reasons recognized by ethical egoism, along with those Broad styled "self-referential," are basic, or non-derivative, de se reasons. It is because it will be *me*, or it is because it will be *my* child, or it is because it will be *my* friend, or it is because it will be *my* country that premium treatment seems rational.

A fundamental question in moral philosophy has been the question of how to balance impersonal reasons with such non-derivative de se reasons. And we are now in a position to answer that question. No issue of balancing arises. There are no non-derivative de se reasons. The relevant considerations are merely apparent reasons, which have been shown to have no force because they depend for their coherence on the persistence of a self worth caring about.

The reasons of prudence, or reasonable self-care, are none other than the reasons of impersonal altruism, applied to one's own case. One's own interests are not worth considering *because* they are one's own but simply because they are interests, and interests, wherever they arise and are legitimate, are equally worthy of consideration.

Consider the command of *agape*, the command to love the arbitrary other as oneself. It is best understood as Janus-faced. It is not just the command to be moved by the legitimate interests of any other just as, and to the degree that, you are moved by your own legitimate interests. It is the command to treat oneself as if one were an arbitrary other, albeit one whose life one is called to live. This command, when properly understood, has invariably, at least from the secular point of view, appeared mad.[26] How could such an absurdly high degree of moral heroism be *commanded*?

But now we have seen that the command of *agape* is extensionally equivalent to the command that we respond to the actual structure of the practical reasons that there are. In that sense it is reason's own command.

In this fashion, the doctrine of *anatta* can be seen to pave the way for the command of *agape*.

A Summary of the Foregoing

Here, then, is a schematic overview of the ground we have covered, itemized as a series of moves or steps. It may be helpful in seeing just where you want to leap from the train before it reaches its destination.

[26] A notable exception is Thomas Nagel in *The Possibility of Altruism* (Princeton University Press, 1976).

1. In lecture two we distinguished my biological death, the death of the human being Johnston, and my subjective death, the death, as we might now put it, of this self. These involve quite different thoughts about me and my fate.
2. This distinction can be made more vivid once we recognize that given the standard view that all uses of "I" are merely indexical and "rigidly" denote human beings, feats of auto-alienation are in a certain way paradoxical.
3. The resolution of this paradox is to recognize that some uses of "I" pick out the person responsible for the use in question, whereas others pick out the self responsible for the use.
4. The notion of the self that is here in play is something readily available to "I"-users, something available to anyone who has the notion of a mind, or a consciousness as an arena with some person at the phenomenological center.
5. If you like to put it in terms of qua objects, the notion of the self is the notion of some person or other, and perhaps a potential succession of persons, qua occupying such a phenomenological center of such an "arena."
6. In cases of auto-alienation, self-concern follows self identity, not personal identity, making it look as though in ordinary cases we care about personal identity because we take it to embody self identity, which is what we most fundamentally care about.
7. If self identity is worth caring about in this way then the persistence of one's self must be worth caring about.
8. But the persistence of oneself is defined relative to the persistence of an arena.
9. An arena is a merely intentional object.
10. The persistence of merely intentional objects is a construal-dependent matter; that is, there is in such cases a convention of deferring to how it strikes the subject.
11. But we could suspend the convention and still describe all the important facts.
12. So, we could describe all the important facts without mentioning the facts crucial to the persistence of selves.
13. Thus we arrive at the doctrine of *anatta*: There are no persisting selves worth caring about.

14. If there are no persisting selves worth caring about then there are no non-derivative de se practical reasons, no de se practical reasons that are not simply the upshot of impersonal reasons applied to one's own case.

15. This means that command of *agape* or radical impersonal altruism is not a call to irrational heroism; it is simply the command to respond to the structure of the reasons that there actually are.

Questions and Replies

Isn't "I"-thought possible in a state of complete sensory deprivation, where we are not aware of the arena and so not thinking of ourselves as at the center of such an arena?[27]

That is not how I think of sensory deprivation. It is not that the arena disappears. It is rather that a certain class of occurrences that are usually found in part of the arena, namely perceptual experiences and sensations in the body-image, are not there. When I enter states of sensory deprivation, there is still thought and what Michael Stocker calls "psychic feelings"—feelings like elation that are detached from any specific bodily sensation—occurring here at the center of this arena.[28]

Perhaps feats of auto-alienation are simply feats of imagining what it is like to be Spinoza or FDR or Britney, as it were, from the inside. One is imagining a certain complex psychological property or type, not one's having it.[29]

That proposal, which is in some ways appealing, will not work for wanting to be Britney, where a girl wants her inner and outer life to be Britney's. Nor am I just imagining a type when I imagine *myself waking up as* a rational parrot. I am explicitly imagining this arena (or so I suppose) being filled with the inner life of an intelligent parrot. In these cases there is not only the imagining of a type of ongoing inner state, there is in some sense an assignment of that state to oneself.

Nor do I think the proposal that we can only imagine the relevant types is suited to capture the content of Sally's dream.

[27] Christopher Peacocke.
[28] Michael Stocker, "Psychic Feelings: Their Importance and Irreducibility," *Australasian Journal of Philosophy* 61 (1983).
[29] An audience member unknown to me.

Here is another kind of imaginary example, an account of a seeming possibility in which one is continuously re-embodied as a parrot. Suppose that for all of us dreaming is fully coherent, just like a kind of waking life. We do know when we are dreaming, however, because this other kind of life, our night life, is quite different. In it we meet, and talk, and live together... but we are all parrots in this "dream" or night world. We carry memories back and forth from the "dream" world to the "waking" world, so we can all talk about what we did in each world. Each remembers being a parrot last night, and what he or she did with the other parrots. Likewise in the "dream" world, each remembers being a human being the day before. Now it seems that there are two worlds—a day world and a night world—and each of us* has two different embodiments in each.

In this scenario, it appears to each one of us that he or she is continuously re-embodied as a parrot person and as a human person. The scenario is fanciful, even ludicrous, and it shows nothing about what is metaphysically or really possible. But in imagining it, we have not fallen into semantic incoherence.

Is it reliance on something like the Neo-Lockean criterion of personal identity that makes it coherent to suppose this? I do not think so. For we can imagine that an epidemic of encephalitis breaks out among the parrots and that many who are infected lose all memory of, and all psychological connection with, having been a human being the day before. They are told by their healthy fellow parrots that this was so, but they find such testimony astounding and unbelievable. It is as if everyone told you that you were a parrot yesterday.

Here we have continuous reincarnation of the self without memory of the person you formerly were.

Again, I am not using this fanciful scenario to make a claim about what is really possible. I am just claiming that in imagining it, I have not fallen into semantic incoherence, I have not lost my grip on the meaning of "I" and its cognates. That is the kind of claim that gets our paradox going.

Aren't you then supposing that there is some kind of soul pellet or separately existing entity that ties a human being in the day world to a particular rational parrot in the night world?[30]

---

[30] A follow-up question.

Chapter Four

What Is Found at the Center?

This lecture, in many ways the most demanding, is based around a philosophical parable. I believe that at least part of what the parable describes is possible, and I shall argue for this. I shall then investigate in remorseless detail just how *it could be possible*. In answering that question we shall discover something very useful about the nature of personal identity, something that will bear directly on the question of surviving death. But before we turn to that, let us make a connection with the previous lectures.

I feel, after a night's reflection, that self-based future-directed concern has not been completely undermined by the denial of a persisting self worth caring about. For I can focus on the person I *presently* find myself to be, and privilege his weal and woe.

And so I find Johnston here now, he is *now* the one at the center of this arena of presence.

That thought about me now is robust, even though thoughts about who I *will* be are not. Johnston is HERE, NOW; that at least seems hard to deny. His now being at the center of this arena of presence puts Johnston in a certain light; he is to be protected, to be privileged, and these experienced demands do not seem tied to a particular time. So I now seem to have prima facie reason to favor Johnston *and* his future. After all, with the demise of the self, he is all I (now) seem to have left.

Johnston is privileged by the structure of my consciousness now. There is, it has been argued, no practically interesting possibility of extending that consciousness into the future, let alone a future in which the one at the center is someone other than Johnston. So it seems that now

This lecture was presented at Princeton's Rockefeller Center for Human Values.

Johnston is the one to be given premium treatment. Later there will be "I"-thoughts associated with Johnston, thoughts that pick him out at the center of some future arena, thoughts that also privilege Johnston as the one to be favored. In fact throughout his life Johnston is susceptible to this mechanism of "I"-thought that presents him as the one to be favored.

Anticipating Johnston's death, I find it to be a special loss to me now. That seems coherent, even given the absence of a persisting self. And the same applies in your own case, with respect to the human being you now are.

So we may have fallen short of our goal of exploding the special concern we have for the futures of *the persons* we now are. The incoherence of self identity over time leaves us with personal identity, the identity of human beings over time. It may still seem rational to care especially for the continued existence of the person, that is, the human being, one now is.

How Did a Human Being Get to Be HERE?

Even so, our finding *human beings* at our respective centers is, from a certain perspective, somewhat adventitious. When we understand just why we do find human beings at our respective centers, things may look very different. There are still more surprises that await us in the philosophy of personal identity.

So consider this question: How exactly does the *human being* Johnston get the guernsey; why does that kind of thing, a human being, satisfy the phenomenological description "the one at the center of THIS"? Of course, carrying on about Johnston is just a way of inviting you to have the same thoughts in your own case. How did your human being get into the privileged position at the center?

After all, there are many things HERE now. There is the human being Johnston, and there is this body, the *H.M.S. Johnston*, something that may exist for a while after Johnston's death, and there is Johnston's stream of consciousness, and there is the Johnston-esque individual personality. All these things are "at the center" in the sense in which we have been using that phrase, that is, they each veridically present as HERE NOW. How did the human being Johnston muscle his way into the role of *the one* at the center?

Clearly, we were all along interpreting "one" in "the one at the center" as a *personal* pronoun and none of these other things—a body, a stream of consciousness, an individual personality is a person. Only a person can have the property of being me. (Recall the bizarre circumstance, described in lecture two, where it becomes plausible that there is no person at the center, so that the apparent evidence counts against *my* very existence.)

Still, the question remains, how do I know that the person HERE is a human being? Of course, dominated as my thought is by the narrative of the human being, this is what most readily comes to mind. I, the one now here at the center of this arena, am a human being. But the narrative of the human being is not inevitable. Other overarching narratives are possible. And these alternative narratives would make different self-identifications seem natural. While these other narratives may be practically assessed as better and worse, we must now recognize that we no longer can claim to have the resources to count them simply as right or wrong.

There are, as we shall see, different kinds of persons. In itself, the personal pronoun "the one" does not discriminate among these. Just how I now get to be one of these kinds of persons is an unsettled, and unsettling, question.

Return for a moment to the conclusions of lecture two, in particular the discovery that there are no superlative selves, which is to say mental substances that could play two roles: that of being the unambiguous and always determinate carriers of our identities, and that of being independent justifiers of our special self-concern.

In rejecting superlative selves, two sorts of considerations were offered. The first had to do with the empirical facts, and the second had to do with the strangeness of the norm that a superlative self is supposed to impose.

A superlative self is supposed be the source of an objective and *yet utterly and essentially privatized* demand for certain responses, namely those associated with special self-concern. But adding superlative selves to the world, one for each person, does not help explain, or even provide a prima facie justification for, this pattern of concern. At best, that addition would put us all on a par metaphysically; each one of us is worth caring about to the same degree because each has a superlative self. This does nothing to explain or even begin to justify each person's sense that he or she is, as it were, entitled to premium treatment, beyond what each of us is owed as one of the others. Yet providing a prima facie justification for precisely this excess of self-concern was part of the defining explanatory role of a superlative self.

So we are left with a vision of the world under the aspect of the absent superlative self. There is not the kind of metaphysical justifier, a substantial self or ego, which could independently determine which parts of nature ought to be the foci of our respective patterns of self-concern. This is the background that I am taking for granted in what follows.

Special self-concern is just a natural fact, no doubt selected for by evolution. More particularly, I have suggested that its deep psychological basis lies in the evolved structure of self-consciousness.[1] But special self-concern is also to some extent under our emotional and rational control. Once we see that the focus and extent of that concern is not justified by any demand outside of the concern itself, we can use our intellectual and emotional resources to elaborate that concern in different ways. Under various circumstances self-concern could come to be directed to quite different parts of nature. The living body, the thing that sits between the gestation and death of a human animal, is one particularly salient kind of thing around which to organize our patterns of self-concern. But there is no general normative fact that says: You must take the bodily envelope to be the boundary of personal identity, and hence as the focus for self-concern, on pain of being out of joint with reality.

Superlative selves represented the best hope for guarantors of such a normative fact, at least if we grant the assumption—who knows where it comes from—that each living body is host to only one superlative self. But since there are no superlative selves, there are no privileged joints which, independently of our actual concerns and tendencies to identify, *already* mark the boundaries of personal identity.

Other Narratives: The Hibernators

Imagine for example, a tribe of human animals, the Hibernators, who have an atypical brain chemistry that keeps them continuously awake for nine months of the year, during which they are enormously productive. Each of the Hibernators falls into a deep sleep for the winter months; upon awaking it takes a week or two for the fog of long sleep to fully dissipate. Each November, the Hibernators leave enormously detailed instructions concerning what is to be done after the next great awakening: construction projects to be taken up again, the beginning of the storage

[1]For more on this idea, and a discussion of how it might figure in a naturalistic account of an insight embodied in the myth of the Fall, see *Saving God*.

of food to be consumed at the very next awakening, and so on and so forth. When we look at these records we discover something remarkable. In their written instructions, the Hibernators of any given year address those who will wake up from the coming winter sleep as if they were *numerically different persons*, who nonetheless could be relied upon to have very similar memories and inclinations. As we would put it, the Hibernators do not realize that sleep, even three months of sleep, is an event that each one of them survives. They are really taken with the analogy between dreamless sleep and death; so taken, in fact, that they regard the analogy as pointing to a valid *equation* of the two states.

What exactly is it that makes the Hibernators *wrong* about sleep? The Neo-Lockeans have a ready answer. After the long sleep, each of the earlier Hibernators has his own unique psychological continuer. But that answer is really an attempt to lay it down that some bundle of experience starting from these experiences now is the proper object of my future-directed self-concern. It is hard to see how such a bundle would fare any better than a superlative self, conceived of as a mental *substance*. How could THIS bundle be the ground of an objective and yet utterly and essentially privatized demand for certain responses, namely those associated with my egocentric concern? If THIS bundle is so good, then shouldn't *you also* feel the demand that it be given premium treatment? This suggests that not only are there no superlative substances, there are no *superlative* bundles either.[2]

If neither mental substances nor mental bundles could play the role of independent justifiers of our special self-concern, then how could our special self-concern be justified? What else could *ground* our special concern for our futures if not such independent justifiers?

STILL ANOTHER NARRATIVE: THE TELETRANSPORTERS

Suppose that as well as encountering the Hibernators, we also knew of another community of humans, a community whose members have, for a generation, been using Teletransportation as a means of super-fast travel. Given the way we trace ourselves, we Human Beings regard Teletransportation as a form of human Xeroxing that has the unfortunate

---

[2]Mutatis mutandis for the interpretation of Neo-Lockeanism as governing sequences of substances. There are no superlative sequences either.

feature of destroying the original. We are inclined to berate the Tele-transporters for ignoring the difference between one person and an-other. At first, it seems to us that the Teletransporters blame and punish people distinct from those who perpetrate crimes, are systematically de-luded about just who had the experiences they seem to remember, and are prepared to commit suicide and even kill their own children by put-ting them into the machine.[3]

However, we might very well discover that the Teletransporters are fully informed about the workings of their Teleporters. They recognize that these machines destroy the human bodies that enter them. They do not suppose that the machines transfer souls from one place to another. Nevertheless, they have come to naturally extend their future-directed patterns of self-concern to the psychological continuers that their Tele-porters produce.

Gradually, dissent breaks out among the Human Beings as to whether the Teletransporters are making a deep mistake. Certain reflex absolut-ists maintain that there is a distinguished relation—the relation of being the very same human being—which in virtue of its independent features demands and justifies the response, on the part of each person, of orga-nizing his or her future-directed concerns and expectations in terms of that relation. The absolutists do not make many converts, in part be-cause the relation of being the same human being seems already gerry-mandered in a way that is responsive to the core concerns and expecta-tions of the Human Beings. It seems that the Human Beings, unlike the human bodies that typically constitute them, can be reduced to the con-dition of mere brains, kept alive in a vat. While the organic lives of human bodies may be relatively natural joints, the lives of the Human Beings need not be so natural. So if anything distinguishes the relation of being the same human being as the relation of personal identity, it is not the solitary work of nature.

---

[3] Just a note on terminology, which will be helpful in what follows. When I capitalize, as in "Human Being," "Hibernator," and "Teletransporter," I mean to pick out those that have been ac-culturated in the relevant way. So, a Human Being is one who has been acculturated in the ways of the Human Beings, and a Teletransporter is one who has been acculturated in the ways of the Tele-transporters. But of course, a Teletransporter at each time at which he exists is—the "is" of constitu-tion—some human being (or human animal), though not necessarily the same human being (or human animal). I shall also write of *the kind human being* and the relation of being *the very same human being*.

If there had been superlative selves, or any similarly independent justifiers of our self-directed patterns of concern, then we would have been
able to formulate just what it is that makes it the case that the Teletransporters have *overextended* their patterns of self-concern. The Teletransporters would have overextended their patterns of self-concern if superlative substances or, as it might be, superlative bundles extended *thus* far,
say, through the lives of individual human beings, and no further.

Wrong in Itself?

Absent such independent justifiers, the situation seems to be this. We
have imagined three distinctive patterns of self-concern, guided by different framing narratives about the extent of a person. Each narrative
plays a relatively fundamental role in the three communities, and so the
same sort of justification could be given for each of these three patterns
of concern. Each community could say: This pattern of self-concern is
basic, and much that we find ourselves justifying is justified in terms of
it. Would it not then be absurdly ethnocentric to insist that only we, the
Human Beings, had got it right thanks to the adventitious history of our
identifications? And for two reasons: First, why should the accidents of
history have decisively favored us? But second, and more pertinent, in
the absence of independent justifiers of future-directed concern, what
could it be for history to have resulted in a specific community getting
the facts of personal identity *right*?

Of course, some patterns of future-directed concern have considerable extrinsic advantages relative to others. The lives of the Hibernators
are short; as a result those lives may also be nasty and brutish. On the
other hand, the Teletransporters can organize their lives around super-
fast travel. Perhaps they also have a way of tweaking their machines so
that the near-duplicate human animal that gets out of the Teleporter is
free of any disease suffered by the human animal that entered the Teleporter. In this way, the Teletransporters come to have both super-fast
travel and practical freedom from disease. Relative to this, the lives of
the Human Beings may seem to be nasty, brutish, and all too short.

What is thus emerging is the radical idea that unless we are focusing
on such comparative extrinsic advantages, no basic pattern of future-
directed identification can be said to be simply wrong. Of course, it may

be unviable, or counterproductive, or less than optimal, and so in any one of these senses *wrong*. What it can't be is *wrong in itself*, wrong because it is out of kilter with the independent justifiers that are the facts of personal identity.

The Evenhanded Treatment

Put aside for now the huge practical advantages that the Teletransporters seem to have; after all, we could have taken the trouble to describe two or more ways of implementing the relation of personal identity that were on a par as to their respective practical advantages.

Having abstracted away from these advantages, let us mean by an "evenhanded treatment" of the three communities one that counts them as each *right on their own terms* when it comes to the question of survival.

Should we aim for an evenhanded treatment? After all, why can't there be facts about how and when personal identity holds that are just there *anyway*, facts that determine which one, if any, of the communities is right. Why should we respect their apparently conflicting opinions about personal identity, any more than we would respect their apparently conflicting opinions about the cross-time identities of swallows or of cobras?

If something is a cobra then it is essentially so; there is no migrating in or out of the relevant condition, and so no chance of finding the thing that was the cobra in a condition in which it is no longer a cobra. In contrast with this, the things that are persons are not *essentially* persons. All the natural persons we know satisfy Locke's characterization "a thinking, reflective being that is able to consider itself as itself at various times and places" not essentially but thanks to characteristic features of some other concrete way of being that is their essence. Such an underlying essence and its consequences due to the laws of nature guarantee the generic emergence in healthy adults of the relevant psychological capacity. So human beings will typically be persons for long stretches of their life, as will dolphins and the higher apes. Yet, as David Wiggins said long ago, there will be no natural essence of a person as such, but each person will have an underlying natural essence as some concrete kind of thing or other.[4]

---

[4] I emphasize natural essence to contrast with the essences of qua-objects like Socrates sitting, an object which is, by construction, essentially sitting. So a human being qua person might be essentially a person, but Wiggins's point is really not affected by this. See his *Sameness and Substance*, p. 172.

However, contrary to what Wiggins thought, it does not follow simply from this observation that you have one and the same human person on two occasions only if you have the same human animal, the same member of the biological species, *Homo Sapiens*, exhibiting the relevant psychological capacity. Animalism, the view that personal identity tracks animal identity, does not follow from the observation that "person" does not denote a kind unified by some natural essence.

We are told that caterpillars are the same biological individuals as butterflies, so that the thing which is a now particular butterfly was in its larval form numerically the same thing as the caterpillar. Now suppose that both caterpillars and butterflies were persons, that is, thinking, reflective beings able to consider themselves as themselves at various times and places. It would not follow simply from the biological facts alone that each later butterfly person is the same person as his earlier caterpillar person.

What further facts would it follow from? If there had been souls that were essentially sites or loci of the power to reflect and consider oneself at various times and places, and the transformation from caterpillar to butterfly preserved the same soul, then it might have been right to take the view that the numerical identity of those persons who are caterpillars and butterflies follows the identity of the biological unit. Contrariwise, if there had been souls that were essentially sites or loci of the power to reflect and consider oneself at various times and places, and the transformation from caterpillar to butterfly did not preserve the same soul, then it might have been right to take the view that the numerical identity of those persons who are caterpillars and butterflies does not follow the identity of the biological unit. Alternatively, if it had turned out that self-consciousnesses were essentially sites or loci of the power to reflect and consider oneself at various times and places, and the transformation from caterpillar to butterfly preserved the same self-consciousness, then it might have been right to take the view that the numerical identity of those persons who are caterpillars and butterflies follows the identity of the biological unit. And contrariwise, if not, not.

What is happening here is that we have a variety of models of what the independent determiners of the facts of personal identity might be, and in thinking of what makes the fact of personal identity hold, we think of these determiners and the lines of identity they delineate.

This is a plausible way to respond because the facts of personal identity are immediately connected with certain norms, with certain facts about how we should react, with facts about how one should be disposed to consider the future person with whom one is identical. That is, the holding of such facts would not only make certain beliefs true, they would make certain patterns of future-directed concern the right ones to have. And those facts, *period, would do this, that is, without the help of further beliefs or desires on one's part.*[5] So, if some future person is you, then you *should* now be disposed to care about him in a certain distinctive way. This conditional is not an enthymeme; that is, it is not true in virtue of some implicit way of filling out the antecedent so that the consequent then follows. For example, it is not that the true conditional that lies behind this conditional is

> If some future person is you, and you are now disposed to care about your future in a certain distinctive way, then you should now be disposed to care about him in a certain distinctive way.

That conditional is more or less trivial, whereas the conditional in which we are interested says something substantive about the facts of personal identity, namely that *they themselves* will justify and require certain patterns of future-directed concern.

Here, then, is the characteristic *practical* role played by anything that deserves the name of the facts of personal identity. In this sense, the facts of personal identity are *justifiers* of certain patterns of future-directed concern. This is one important way in which they differ from the facts of bird identity or reptile identity.

Consider two patterns of future-directed concern. In the first each caterpillar person is disposed to take the anticipatable future interests of the butterfly that emerges from him as his own interests. In the second each caterpillar person is disposed to take the anticipatable future interests of the butterfly that emerges from him as the interests of one of his descendants. Which pattern of concern is the right one, and why?

Our thoughts about the persistence of souls or self-consciousnesses were thoughts about what would make one or the other pattern of concern the right one to have. Those thoughts invoke one or another putative independent justifier of future-directed concern.

---

[5] As Thomas Nagel established in *The Possibility of Altruism* (Princeton University Press, 1976).

But we have seen that there are no independent justifiers of the relevant patterns of concern. There are no souls. There are no superlative mental substances. There are no persisting "consciousnesses" and hence no persisting self-consciousnesses worth caring about. In short, nothing that looks like an independent justifier of future-directed patterns of concern is to be found in the vicinity of any caterpillar, butterfly, or human animal.

You might try to default to the human animal itself and have it break the relevant tie, but unfortunately animalism as an account of the identity of persons has serious disabling features.[6] In any case, as we have seen, mere facts of biological identity don't seem like the sort of facts that would independently justify a definite pattern of future-directed self-concern. The underlying facts of biological identity would not do that for self-conscious caterpillars and butterflies. Why should they then do it for us?

The conclusion, and here we are summarizing the work of the last three lectures, is that there are no independent justifiers of the dispositions characteristic of future-directed self-concern.

Now the Hibernators, the Human Beings, and the Teletransporters exhibit three different patterns of future-directed self-concern. They differ radically in their dispositions to care in the face of the same facts. We might find that one or another set of dispositions has bad practical consequences. But what we cannot now say is that one or another of the differing sets of dispositions is out of kilter with some independent justifier of future-directed self-concern.

Are these different orientations then simply out of kilter with the sheer facts of *personal* identity? Should we still suppose that the sheer facts of personal identity make *at most* one of the three communities right about what it is they survive? If we suppose that, then there is no need for an evenhanded treatment of the three communities, a treatment that counts each community right on its own terms. The following argument counts against this way of avoiding the need for an evenhanded treatment.

It is not plausible that matters of fact such as whether persons would survive dreamless sleep and whether persons would survive Teletrans-

---

[6] See "My Body Is Not an Animal," particularly the discussion of animalism's odd implication that removing your brain from your body and then letting your body die while your brain is kept alive would thereby create a new person.

portation are investigation-transcendent, that is, are such that they could never be discovered no matter how far the issue was investigated. So the Hibernators, the Human Beings, and the Teletransporters should each be such that if they were to take into account all the relevant facts about dreamless sleep and Teletransportation, reflect appropriately on these facts, embed them in larger well-confirmed theories, and explore the consequences, and do all this without any internal epistemic irrationality, *and* continue this process indefinitely they would at some point come to a determination of the relevant facts of personal identity.

Yet it seems that even under such increasingly better epistemic conditions the Hibernators, the Human Beings, and the Teletransporters could rationally persist in their differing implementations of personal identity, no matter how far they investigated the matter. (Remember, we are setting to one side the practical extrinsic advantages of one implementation over the other.)

First notice that it is possible for the Human Beings and the Teletransporters to persist in their differing ways without irrationality even under increasingly better epistemic conditions. The facts relevant to their basic difference over survival concern their own constitution and the inner workings of the Teleporter. Suppose the facts are these: Both the Human Beings and the Teletransporters are never made up of anything more than human flesh. They do not also consist of souls or separately existing entities or immaterial substances or ectoplasm or anything else. Suppose that the Teleporters simply work by reading out all the relevant information about a human body's basic atomic and molecular structure and transmitting that information to a receiving station where a duplicate body is made bottom up from ambient atoms. It is possible that no matter how hard the Human Beings consider such facts, they will hold to their view that they do not survive Teletransportation, and they will hold to this view without making any intellectual error that they could in principle detect. They give the facts their proper weight, they reason well from them, and so on. *They just cannot escape the conviction that the operation of the machine would destroy them.* It is also possible that no matter how hard the Teletransporters consider such facts, they will hold to their view that they do survive Teletransportation, and they will hold to this view without making any intellectual error that they could in principle detect. They give the facts their proper weight, they reason well from them, and so on. *They just cannot shake off the conviction that they literally travel by Teletransportation.* For them, to doubt that would be like our doubting that we can survive general anesthetic. Here we have the sort of thing that Wittgenstein described as a fundamental difference in response, one just like the difference between those who find it most natural to continue 999, 1000, 1001, 1002 and those who find it equally natural to continue 999, 1000, 1002, 1004. (You might say the latter are not *counting*, but so what?)

Perhaps a similar point could be sustained when it comes to the deep difference between the Human Beings and the Hibernators over deep sleep. The Hibernators need be making no correctible factual error about the nature of their deep sleep and what happens after it. It just strikes each one of them as *the end*, and this is a persistent and basic orientation.

So, even under ideal epistemic conditions, the Hibernators, the Human Beings, and the Teletransporters need not deviate from their respective views about what they each would survive. There are two different possibilities here. On the first, at least two of the communities have still missed the relevant facts of survival and will continue to fail to grasp these facts, even as they approach ideal epistemic conditions. On the second interpretation, as each community approaches ideal epistemic conditions, they do discover the relevant facts, and they discover that the relevant facts, for example,

Hibernators do not survive deep sleep, but Human Beings and Teletransporters do.

Teletransporters survive Teletransportation, but Hibernators and Human Beings do not.

leave them each right on their own terms.

On the second possibility there must be some correct evenhanded treatment available, some treatment that shows why they are each right on their own terms. On the first possibility the facts about whether a given person will survive dreamless sleep and Teletransportation are investigation-transcendent; there is no way in which an utterly conscientious epistemic agent, even given world enough and time, could find out if and under what conditions he could survive such events. But treating such facts as investigation-transcendent must count against a theory of personal identity.

That means that we, as theorists of personal identity, should look to develop an evenhanded treatment of these three communities, a treatment that counts them as each *right on their own terms*.

Much will follow from this.

Is Relativism about Personal Identity Coherent?

A smooth transition is often made from an evenhanded treatment of cultural variation to relativism with respect to the differences in question. This is frequently a mistake.

The definitive sign of true cross-cultural relativism with respect to some subject matter is that the respective utterances that appear on the surface to be at odds have a hidden relativity or context sensitivity, which means that the respective communities are *not really disagreeing*.

So, to take a trivial case where relativism is obviously true, when those in Britain say that the equator is to the south and those in Australia say it is to the north, there is no real disagreement because the most natural construal of what is actually conveyed involves a specification of the location of utterance. It is as if the British had said, "To the south from here" and the Australians had said, "To the north from here."

Contrast this with the following case. In the culture in which I grew up, the following was presented as a well-known truth:

It is morally permissible to respond to an insult by asking the person who has insulted you to "step outside," at least if there is a rough equivalence of physical prowess.

In the culture I am now pleased to inhabit, asking—that is, challenging—someone who has insulted you to "step outside" is not morally permissible, and that is presented as a well-known truth.

Whatever one might think about the merits of the issue, it is clear that the two cultures really disagree and that this disagreement cannot be adequately parsed away by discerning a hidden reference to different moral standards from which the conflicting claims follow. For one thing, the respective claims are moral claims and not epistemic or logical claims about what follows from contextually indicated standards. The respective claims are not claims of theoremhood, claims about what you are required to accept given certain moral standards, or anything like that. To see that, notice that their denials are not denials of theoremhood, or anything like that.

However, and this may be of considerable general interest, it seems to me that this rejection of relativism is compatible with an evenhanded treatment of the cultural variation in question. The key idea is to appeal to a higher-order absolutism relative to which the two different ways of responding to insults are each acceptable *implementations* of a common moral ideal.

Suppose that there is an absolute ethic of respect for persons, which holds with equal moral force in all cultures. Even so, there may indeed be communities in which part of respecting another is recognizing as perfectly legitimate his or her courageous readiness to defend his or her honor in the face of an insult. In those communities the overarching ethic of respect would imply that having insulted someone, you thereby made it permissible for them to ask you to "step outside," at least given a rough equivalence in physical prowess. And there may be other communities—ours is one—in which the core implementation of the ethic of respect involves the inviolability of the body of another, so that it could not be morally permissible to ask another to step outside.

Suppose, just suppose, that you thought that the two ways of expressing respect, the one privileging another's courageous readiness to defend his or her honor and the other privileging the inviolability of another's body, are equally legitimate, at least if they are embodied in common knowledge and common expectations. The point is that to think this you would not have to be a relativist in the sense introduced earlier. The right thing to say would be that there is a genuine disagreement between the two cultures, and the claim that

> It is not morally permissible to respond to an insult by asking the person who has insulted you to "step outside," even if there is a rough equivalence of physical prowess.

is false, because wrongly over-generalized from the restricted cases of cultures where a main way of implementing the ethic of respect involves treating the body of another as inviolable.

What is true is

It is not morally permissible to respond to an insult by asking the person who has insulted you to "step outside," even if there is a rough equivalence of physical prowess, so long as the person in question is self-consciously operating in a culture where a main way of implementing the ethic of respect involves treating the body of another as inviolable.

That was not intended as a backhanded defense of duel-brawls! It was meant to illustrate how an evenhanded treatment of cultural variation does not entail relativism in the philosophically problematic sense. (Is this why many arguments over relativism between anthropologists and philosophers seem empty? What the anthropologist is really advocating is an evenhanded treatment of cultural variation, and what the philosopher hears and rejects is relativism?)

Now return to the case of personal identity. Here, if we know what we are talking about, we had better not be relativists about the underlying relation. For personal identity is just the relation of numerical identity, that is, the relation of being one and the same thing, restricted to the case where the things under consideration are persons. Since numerical identity is the relation between a thing and itself, there is no room in principle for another relatum to "relativize" numerical identity.[7] Any relativity in the relation of personal identity must arise from a relativity in what it is to be *a person*.

But how are we to make sense of that? The modern topic of personal identity came from Locke, and Locke defined a person as a thinking reflective being that knows itself as itself in various times and places. No one has shown any tendency to dispute Locke's straightforward characterization, except when that characterization is wrongly employed to preemptively settle the question of the moral status of the fetus, and here it is the use of the characterization that is properly objected to, not the characterization itself.

Locke's characterization does not seem to admit of further relativity.

[7] You could of course follow Peter Geach and define a notion of "relative identity," but it is bootless to do so because the questions we are interested in—questions like "Will I survive?" or "Will any person around after the event be me?"—are questions framed in terms of numerical identity. You would need to argue that numerical identity is incoherent in order to make a notion of relative identity interesting as a successor notion. And that is none too easy a thing to do, for the notion of numerical identity is so simple it is very difficult for its constituent parts to rub together inconsistently.

(I do not say that it is free of linguistic vagueness; that is another matter, not to be confused with the relativity in which we are interested.[8])

This conforms with the fact that (setting aside linguistic vagueness and the related phenomenon of different standards of precision in different contexts) it is difficult to assign a coherent thought to such sentences as

Sam (as he now is) counts as a person in context C, but not in context C*.

Certainly, it is no part of our evenhanded treatment of the Hibernators, the Human Beings, and the Teletransporters to endorse any such relativism.

Any given Hibernator is a person, that is, a thinking reflective being that knows itself as itself in various times and places. It is not that he is a person relative to the standards of the Hibernators, or only in the context of conversation with or among the Hibernators, and fails to be a person relative to standards of the Human Beings, or in the context of conversation with or among the Human Beings. He is a person *period*; for (linguistic vagueness aside) that, that is, *period*, is the only way to be a thinking reflective being that knows itself as itself in various times and places.

This is where the parallel with the discussion of duel-brawls proves useful. Even given an evenhanded treatment of the Hibernators, the Human Beings, and the Teletransporters, there is no implication of relativism about personal identity. Given our evenhanded treatment, the characteristic claim that the Hibernators would make, namely

It is not possible to survive deep sleep.

is false, because wrongly over-generalized from cases where the way of implementing one's personhood over time is built around the relation of being the same hibernator. What is true, given the evenhanded treatment, is

It is not possible to survive deep sleep if your way of implementing your personhood over time is built around the relation of being the same hibernator.

[8]Nor do I insist that being a person does not admit of degree. Once we explain and accept something like Locke's second, oft neglected, clause in his characterization of a person, namely that a person has a "concernment" as he call it, we shall see a way in which some persons can be less than "fully fledged."

Similarly, given our evenhanded treatment, the characteristic claim that the Human Beings would make, namely

It is not possible to survive Teletransportation.

is false, because wrongly over-generalized from cases where the way of implementing one's personhood over time is built around the relation of being the same human being. What is true, given the evenhanded treatment, is

It is not possible to survive Teletransportation if your way of implementing your personhood over time is built around the relation of being the same human being.

An evenhanded treatment of duel-brawls implies that there are different determinate kinds of respect, different ways of implementing the ethic of respect. An evenhanded treatment of the Hibernators, the Human Beings, and the Teletransporters implies that there are different determinate kinds of persons, different ways of implementing our common personhood as Locke correctly described it.

Earlier we argued that an evenhanded treatment of the Hibernators, the Human Beings, and the Teletransporters is forced on us. For there are no independent justifiers of future-directed self-concern, and the answers to questions like "Will I survive deep sleep?" are not plausibly taken to be investigation-transcendent.

So we must find a way to excavate Locke's general characterization of a person to allow that persons might exploit different ways of implementing the more general conditions of personal identity over time. There may be many determinate forms of personhood, each of which satisfies Locke's general or determinable characterization of a person. Recognizing this possibility will leave us with certain questions that did not previously seem thinkable, at least within a naturalistic context, questions like: How did I get to be a mere human being, and must I always and everywhere be merely that?

In order to prepare for the evenhanded treatment, for the characterization of the invariant element in personal identity that allows for different implementations, we need first to elaborate a certain distinction, the distinction between persons and personalities. This will seem at first to be an interlude, but it will provide material crucial to what follows.

Personhood and Personality

There is a certain kind of practical unity required by, and to some extent directly enforced by, temporally extended agency. When that unity is secured within the life of a person, I will say we have a persisting individual personality. I will then go on to distinguish persons and individual personalities, and argue that what we want in survival is not only personal identity but the continuation of our individual personality. This is what we want; however, the basic de se or self-based preference for the continuation of our own individual personality will emerge as problematic, especially so, given the demise of the self as anatomized in the previous two lectures.

The practical unity required for temporally extended agency requires a certain sort of psychological continuity over time. In the Neo-Lockean tradition, psychological continuity is defined in terms of a chain whose links are direct psychological connections. These include what is typically found over short periods of our mental lives, things such as the persistence of beliefs, desires, and other aspects of our dispositional psychology, the connection between an intention and the later act in which the intention is carried out, and the connection between an experience and a memory of that experience. Psychological continuity holds between a person considered at one time and a person considered at another if between them there is a chain whose links are made of such direct psychological connections. (Psychological continuity is thus taken to be the *ancestral* of the relation of direct psychological connectedness.)

We can, of course, define stronger and weaker forms of psychological connection and continuity. What interests me here is the notion of there holding over time, within a person's life, enough psychological connection to enable the development and maintenance of a certain concrete *style of agency*, that which is definitive of what I will call an "individual personality." An individual personality can be thought of as a dynamic aspect of a person, an aspect that persists as long as the person is able to sustain a distinctive style of agency over time, a style of agency that requires the holding of certain psychological continuities and connections, and partly enforces them by way of ongoing commitments to distinctive projects, policies, and relationships.[9]

---

[9] An individual personality is more like an aspect or a process than a substance; when we trace ourselves and each other we are not offloading onto individual personalities.

As moderately rational agents, our actions are not just the vector sum of our desires or drives. They are, at least potentially, the outcomes of our own deliberation about which considerations to throw ourselves behind, and about which courses of action make sense in the light of our ongoing plans and projects. In order to so deliberate we have to imagine ourselves as temporally extended entities, called on to bring some kind of coherence and connection into what we think, do, and feel, so that we can recognize who we are and what we are up to at the various stages of execution of those plans and projects. In this way, our rational agency both presupposes significant psychological connectedness over time and helps enforce such connections, as a condition of our remaining intelligible to ourselves over time.[10]

Crucially, part of the overarching mental activity that sustains rational agency is imagining oneself, in an anticipatable future, enjoying the fruits of one's acts. But this presupposes that there will be a certain persistence of dispositional psychology along with one's plans and projects, so that the one who inherits the consequences of one's present acts will not see them as alien or paternalistic intrusions on his life but as things he himself partly authored by his previous acts.

Typically, this also requires the persistence of some significant part of the particular complex of detailed and manifold social roles (father, lover, friend, leader, supporter, colleague, nemesis, regular customer, etc.) whose default requirements help one give an account of why one is doing what one is doing at any particular time.

By anticipating this kind of psychological connection over the various stretches of time that are taken into the purview of one's practical deliberations, one can reasonably expect to, and so one can intend to, exercise some *prospective control* over the versions of oneself that might figure in the various stages of one's future life. One can bind oneself, reasonably promise things to others, and expect to be able to hold oneself to one's longer-term plans. One can coherently feel direct pride or direct regret for things one has done, look for compensation in one's

[10]In these remarks, I am partly guided by the important work of Michael Bratman on rational agency, intention, and planning. See, in particular, his *Faces of Intention: Selected Essays on Intention and Agency* (Cambridge University Press, 1999). Also seminal, particularly when it comes to the way in which the requirement of finding oneself cross-temporally intelligible can reasonably enforce psychological continuity, is the work of David Velleman; see the preface to his essays collected in *Self to Self* (Cambridge University Press, 2006).

future successes for sacrifices one has made, and admit and feel responsibility for the details of one's life.

These kinds of psychological and practical connections, both presupposed and produced by planning, reflection, and the practice of giving an account of oneself to oneself and to others, will often provide a number of narrative threads by which one can interpret oneself as having evolved in significant part out of the choices of the earlier person one was. *If* one has a narrative temper of mind, one might weave these threads into a more or less coherent story of what one has been up to this week, this year, or, in the most extreme cases, this life.

Still, I do not think that we should suppose that the construction of such a narrative, and the subsequent emergence of oneself as a figure in that narrative, is necessary for the persistence of one's individual personality. One may just reflect and plan, and simply not narrate, let alone articulate to oneself a "practical identity," an overriding sense of who one is and what one is up to that stands hierarchically above one's plans, projects and relationships.[11] One could be just too busy for that and yet still be the same individual personality over time.

These considerations, which I believe many philosophers would accept, force on us a distinction often neglected in the literature on personal identity, a distinction between personhood and individual personality.

"Reincarnation" before Death

There are human beings who have experienced a psychological analog of reincarnation within a single life. We might look for them among the few genuine cases of complete amnesia, or among deposed and banished monarchs, or among defrocked priests driven from the community that they have inhabited since they were children, or among victims of torture and subsequent total mental breakdown who have managed nonetheless to create a new life, or (to revert to history of the old country) among the first convicts who managed to see the fatal shore after surviving the gruesome ordeal of transportation designed for them by a Mother England gone genocidal.[12]

[11] This is one of several respects in which my account of individual personality differs from Christine Korsgaard's impressive account of moral agency and moral personality. See her *The Sources of Normativity* (Cambridge University Press, 1996).

[12] For those who think of this as a dramatic overstatement, I recommend a perusal of the 1822

These are cases where an observer might remark, "He is no longer the person he was." Such remarks are on their face not remarks about numerical identity restricted to the case of persons. For they would then imply that one person has ceased to be and another has come into existence, whereas the intended implication of such a remark is that a particular person has undergone a radical change in personality. After all, to no longer be the person he *was*, *he* had to be there before and after.

Thus we are naturally led to distinguish an individual person and an individual personality. Much of the practically interesting talk about our "identities" concerns the identifications that provide the moorings of our individual personalities. However, it is just a confusion to suppose that such "identifications" determine our natures and temporal extent as *persons*. For the practical task of self-making, the development of a flourishing individual personality, takes for granted the lineaments of personal identity as the frame within which an individual personality will develop.

Even though personhood and individual personality are mostly coincident in ordinary adult life, not all persons exhibit individual personality. So it is with those ravaged by severe mental distortions to the point where they cannot hold themselves to their own intentions, and with those in the end game of Alzheimer's disease. After severe Alzheimer's, it is the same person but not the same individual personality.

Still, the special concern one has for oneself can extend beyond the demise of one's individual personality. If I anticipate being overcome by Alzheimer's, I can now reasonably take special precautions for myself in the later stages of that state, even though I foresee the breakdown of the mental unity constitutive of my individual personality. I here anticipate surviving, without my individual personality surviving. That is part of the tragedy of Alzheimer's.

So when it comes to the question of what it is prima facie rational to care about in caring about survival, the answer is that it appears rational to want a package deal, namely that one continues to exist *and* that one's own individual personality flourishes. The second part of the package

---

Bigge Report to Lord Bathurst, in which John Thomas Bigge laments the way in which the emancipation of convicts and the expenditure on public works within the colony was muddying the clarity of the original British plan for the construction of a gulag on a huge scale.

presupposes the first. An individual personality is a particular person satisfying certain further demanding conditions, and thus an individual personality persists only if the person persists. If this human being is duplicated and then destroyed, my individual personality disappears with me. When the duplicate takes over my life, what I get by way of compensation is just an excellent executor of the projects and plans that were part of the moorings of my individual personality. The duplicate has an individual personality of the very same type, but my token individual personality has ceased to be.

How important having an excellent executor of my plans and projects will seem to me to be will depend on how important I believe those plans and projects are. If I am retired from life, so that most of my desires are for things to fill the life that remains to me (golf and mahjong for example) rather than desires that themselves demand more life so that they can be satisfied (the liberation of the human mind from its natural bondage, making a 155 break in snooker), then my plans and projects may not seem very important to me. In that case, having an excellent executor won't matter much more than having an excellent probate lawyer.

Thus, contrary to Parfit and others, the psychological continuity and connectedness that would be preserved even by Xeroxing me and destroying the original is not in general part of what it is rational to care about in caring about survival. (In the next lecture, we shall look at just what is wrong with Parfit's arguments for his conclusions.) Psychological continuity and connectedness is generally speaking only important when it comes packaged with personal identity. For only then will there be the persistence of an individual personality.

So the second part of the package, the continuation and flourishing of my individual personality, presupposes the first, namely the continuation of the person I am. But it does not replace the first, in the sense that we only need cite the continuation and flourishing of our individual personalities to give an account of what we rationally care about in caring about survival.

For, again, there are situations in which I may correctly anticipate continuing to exist, but at the cost of acquiring a different individual personality. Some of the first convicts who saw the fatal shore may have been in just such a situation, as may a particular defrocked priest or a deposed and banished monarch. Perhaps we need not go so far afield.

Adolescence has gotten so much out of control these days that a sensible child may face it with the sinking feeling that there is little hope that his individual personality will survive, even though *he* will. That is anyway a reasonable way for him to think when he considers the old codger he will eventually become. There may be persistence of certain dispositions of character, but as for the tighter psychological connections that make for the persistence of an individual personality, these will wear out over a long enough life.

Notice that the sinking feeling of the sensible child is different from the feeling of a child facing death, and rationally so. Losing one's individual personality may be felt as something very bad, but there is a further loss in ceasing to be, for that means that there will never be any other individual personality to be or become.

Imagine that the only cure for Alzheimer's that we ever find is a drug that eliminates dementia, increases intelligence and effectiveness, and entirely restores the patient's capacity to remember, *without restoring his actual memories.* Many Alzheimer's patients would then be able to create new and flourishing individual personalities. They would be examples of people who had undergone an analog of reincarnation within a single life. Alzheimer's, though involving a significant loss, would be less of a tragedy than it now is. Much of what it is rational to care about in caring about survival would be secured in properly medicated Alzheimer's, even though the patient's individual personality did not survive.

These reflections suggest that the elements of the package deal that we typically and reasonably want in wanting to survive are complexly related. The two elements are

That the person I am continue to exist

That this (my present) individual personality survive and flourish

There is no getting the second element without the first, and surrogates for the second without the first are of little value. But the first without the second may be of considerable value, especially if one comes to have other individual personalities that flourish.

In the next lecture I shall argue that in the face of death the first without the second is the best one can get, and that the prima facie rationality of caring intensely about the second is only prima facie, at least given the truth of *anatta*. So I shall be arguing we can get much of what it is rational to care about in caring about survival, including of course survival or continued existence itself, even in the face of death.

THE "FORENSIC" IMPORTANCE OF PERSONALITY

At Book 2, Chapter 17, Section 26 of the *Essay* Locke writes

"Person" is a forensic term... appropriating actions and their merit; and so belongs only to intelligent agents, capable of a law, and happiness, and misery. This personality extends itself beyond present existence to what is past, only by consciousness, whereby it becomes concerned and accountable; owns and imputes to itself past actions, just upon the same ground and for the same reason as it does the present. All which is founded in a concern for happiness, the unavoidable concomitant of consciousness; that which is conscious of pleasure and pain, desiring that that self that is conscious should be happy. And therefore whatever past actions it cannot reconcile or appropriate to that present self by consciousness, it can be no more concerned in than if they had never been done: and to receive pleasure or pain, i.e. reward or punishment, on the account of any such action, is all one as to be made happy or miserable in its first being, without any demerit at all. For, supposing a man punished now for what he had done in another life, whereof he could be made to have no consciousness at all, what difference is there between that punishment and being created miserable?

In such passages Locke has been naturally taken to be promoting a certain criterion—same person if and only if same consciousness—by arguing that it captures the forensic aspect of personal identity, namely the idea that the lineaments of responsibility and the lineaments of personal identity coincide.

Now that we have the distinction between persons and personalities, and have noted their different conditions of persistence, we might revisit this claim often attributed to Locke.

First, the forensic context is just the legal context, and the grounds for legal responsibility are as various as the grounds for legal punishment.

Locke, however, seems to have an idea of desert, and of deserving pun-ishment, that potentially transcends any human legal system, namely the idea of desert that should and would guide God on the Great Day. Locke seems to be saying not only that it would be wrong to punish someone who did not commit the crime in question, but it would be wrong to punish someone who had no consciousness of that crime, where here the obvious reading of "consciousness of" is "memory of." And then it is supposed that Locke is to be justly criticized for allowing for an absurd "amnesia defense" against punishment for the crimes one actually committed, as if taking a drug that made you forget could there-by make you innocent.

As against *this* Locke, once we distinguish persons and individual personalities, we can see that some aspects of responsibility follow the lineaments of the latter rather than the former. While the simple amne-sia defense seems absurd, the defense that one was a wholly "different person" then, that is, a very different individual personality, is not ab-surd, at least in blunting some of the grounds that move us to punish.

If Stalin came back as a dog, and you knew this, would you kick the dog? Revenge is an interesting motive, susceptible to symbolic discharge, and so I can understand the impulse to kick the dog, say, on the part of a grandchild of victims of Stalin's purges. But I would not kick the dog, and not because the dog and Stalin fail to satisfy the Neo-Lockean crite-rion for personal identity. If Stalin came back as a delightful child who did remember during nightmares his role in the purges and you knew this, would you call for his incarceration upon reaching maturity? You might hang about looking for certain ominous qualities of character to emerge, but suppose they never appeared? What then?

Or take the cases of psychological rebirth within a life, cases that might actually occur. Suppose my crimes in my earlier life are many. In my old age, I am devastated by Alzheimer's, and I lose not only my mem-ory but my personality. But then I am cured by the marvelous new treat-ment, and during my recovery I live in a monastery by night and become a Red Cross relief worker during the day. As time goes by I become, as they say, another person. I build a new individual personality and ex-hibit a new style of agency, one oriented toward the needs of others.

I believe that when I find out about the things I did in my previous life, I should feel shame and agent-regret. As for my few good acts, I would still take some pride in them. After all, I performed those acts. But should I now be punished for the bad acts? Doesn't the fact that I am now "a different person," that is, another individual personality, mean something? You might hang about looking for certain ominous qualities of character to reemerge, but suppose they never did? What then?

Of course I can understand why a legal system interested in systematic *deterrence* would not respect different individual personalities in these ways. That said, it is just not clear that the forensic issues should always neatly respect the lineaments of personal identity as opposed to individual personality.[13] Personal identity provides the frame within which individual personalities arise, but when a new individual personality comes to inhabit the frame, questions of responsibility are considerably muddied.

What Is Invariant?

If personal identity provides the frame within which individual personalities arise, how in our case does that frame get to be the frame of the Human Being? If the Hibernators and the Teletransporters would be as right as we are about personal identity, how did we get to where *we are*?

The following conclusion emerged from consideration of the three communities: Since there are no independent justifiers that settle the appropriate lineaments of personal identity, and since each community can reasonably continue in their ways in the face of all the relevant information, we need an evenhanded treatment of the disagreement among the Hibernators, the Human Beings, and the Teletransporters. Yet in doing this we must not lapse into an implausible relativism about personal identity.

How is it possible to provide an evenhanded treatment of the Human Beings, the Hibernators, and the Teletransporters without lapsing into an incoherent relativism about personal identity? More concretely,

How could the Teletransporters survive Teletransportation when the Human Beings and the Hibernators do not, and how could the Teletransporters and the Human Beings survive deep sleep when the Hibernators do not?

[13]Here I am diverging from my previous discussion of these matters in "Relativism and The

The key is to find some common invariant that is differently implemented among the participants in the disagreement. Our suggestive hint
of what an invariant would look like was given by the supposed common
ethic of respect for persons in the evenhanded treatment of the disagreement over duel-brawls. What is the relevant invariant in the case of personal identity? What do the Hibernators, the Human Beings, and the
Teletransporters have most fundamentally in common? If we can find
that common and invariant factor, we might then see how these might
be three different but legitimate ways of implementing this common,
invariant factor.

Whatever the common and invariant factor is, it must be connected
with the special status of persons as such, namely their having a worth
that does not reduce to their degree of usefulness in the plans and projects of others. Why are persons, however they conform their identities,
fundamentally worthy of the kind of respect that sets boundaries on what
can legitimately be done with and to them?

To be sure, normal adult Hibernators, Human Beings, and Teletransporters each satisfy Locke's characterization: each is a thinking, reflective being that is able to consider itself as itself at various times and places.
But if we consider reflection as mere de se thought, then a person's sheer
capacity to take him- or herself as a topic of thought and talk gives us
little hint as to why persons deserve respect.

What then of the fact that anything human (or animal) that satisfied
Locke's characterization would find itself at the center of an arena of
presence that affectively privileges it over its environment and fellows?
(Recall the imbalance discussed earlier, the profound asymmetry of affectively disclosed value as between HERE and THERE.) So far from
this arena-based structure of reflective consciousness being the source
of the demand that we respect all persons, it instead seems to be the root
cause of each person's requiring premium treatment for himself. As
such it is not only a persistent illusion but an important part of what
makes us natural enemies of each other and of morality itself. What
Kant called the radically (that is, naturally) evil element in humankind
thus seems partly built into the structure of any animal consciousness
that has been raised to the level of reflection, so that it can acquire what

Self," in M. Krausz, ed., *Relativism: Interpretation and Confrontation* (Notre Dame University Press, 1990).

seem to it to be basic de se reasons from the asymmetric structure of an arena of presence.

What, then, is so good or important or valuable about persons? It only begins to come into view when we turn our attention to the practical side of being a reflective, thinking thing that can consider itself as itself at various times and places. The awareness that I (this person who is here now) am present at various times and places is not just the bare awareness of my persistence through time. I could have that kind of awareness of myself over time and be no more *engaged* with myself than with a stone I keep constantly wrapped in the palm of my hand.

A person is not a thinking, reflective being that is just aware of his extended life as the persistence of some sort of thing or other; a person is crucially aware of his life as something *to be lived*. This is the fundamental demand or call that is constitutive of the experience of personhood, the demand that one *live* the life that one is more or less continuously aware of; that one give it some shape in accord with what seems to be interesting, reasonable, appropriate, beautiful; in short, in accord with what seems to be *good*.

It is because persons are thinking, reflective beings who thus experience the demand to *live* their lives, to give their lives shape according to their idea of the good, that they deserve a kind of respect that no mere thing, however appealing, does. And this is so even if a person's particular idea of the good is way off, or even perverse.[14]

The experience of the constitutive demand that one guide one's life by one's grasp of the good is not to be confused with more concrete demands, which require different degrees of sophistication and particular cultural settings in order to arise or even make sense. Making something of yourself, having meaningful projects, living out an exciting or interesting narrative, being moral, doing good—these are all demands that may represent particular ways of responding to the fundamental demand. But none in itself is the fundamental demand.

The experienced demand that one live one's life, that one give it shape in accord with one's grasp of the good, can only have the status of an obligation if one has the capacity to reason practically, that is, to weigh considerations for and against courses of action, and evaluate means to

---

[14]In thus emphasizing the constitutive demand of personhood, the demand that one live one's life, that one guide one's life by one's conception of the good, we connect with something like Locke's "second clause" in his characterization of a person, namely that a person have a "concernment."

those courses of action, in the light of an idea of the good that discriminates practical considerations or reasons as better or worse considerations for doing this or that. So a fully fledged person, one who is able to respond to the demand that he live his life, will be a practical reasoner.

In a fully fledged person, practical reasoning is not just, and not even primarily, a way of maximizing the satisfaction of present desires. It is a practical orientation toward shaping one's life understood as a temporally extended thing with a future that one can to some degree anticipate and to some degree influence. That practical orientation cannot simply consist in present desires that one's future desires be satisfied, since even in the absence of such desires, the practical orientation will count one's anticipatable future interests as providing present reasons to act in certain ways.[15] So the characteristic manifestation of a person who is responding to the demand to live his life, rather than merely satisfy his present desires, is to anticipate what he will need and want. And, further, to the extent that he regards these future needs and wants as legitimate interests that he will come to have, they will now figure as default starting points in his practical reasoning about what courses of action to take and avoid. The considerations that shape what such a person does arise as much from his anticipatable interests as from his present desires and interests.

The examples are easy to think of. Just to take one: Suppose in my forties, I anticipate living on into my sixties and recognize that in my sixties, I will have a legitimate interest in not having to hobble around as a result of the accumulated sports injuries piled up through an overextended career as an amateur Australian Rules Football player. That means I now have a reason (perhaps not an overwhelming reason, but certainly what the lawyers call a *pro tanto* reason) in favor of hanging up my boots. I have this reason now even if I thoroughly dislike what I reasonably can infer about my sixty-year-old self; for example, that he has come to hate sport and wants to sit around writing philosophy all day. It is not thanks to my admiration or liking for him that I have this reason now. It seems that it is simply because *I am he* that I have this reason. How can that be?

The Radical Reversal

It is thus characteristic of a fully fledged person that his anticipatable future interests figure among the default starting points in his present

---

[15] As Thomas Nagel convincingly argued in *The Possibility of Altruism*.

practical reasoning. But this means that he must have some idea of his actual and possible extent through time, that is, he must have some conception of personal identity over time, which determines what futures, and what future interests, could turn out to be his as opposed to someone else's. How does a person then learn the appropriate extent of this future-directed concern? How does he learn to extend it over the life of a Hibernator, or of a Human Being, or of a Teletransporter?

Not, as we might have thought before we entered upon these reflections, by turning his attention to what we naturally and obviously are, for example, animals of a certain species. None of the three communities, not even the Human Beings, has a concept of personal identity that exactly coincides with the life of a human animal. The Hibernators find *many* persons within the life of a *single* human animal, the Human Beings suppose that any one of them could in principle *outlive* his "animal" at least if his head or brain is kept alive and functioning, and the Teletransporters bundle together *many* human animals into the life of a *single* person.

Instead it seems that a person learns the appropriate extent of his future-directed concern by being brought up within an unquestioned (even if not fully determinate) narrative of personal identity, a frame taken for granted by the community in which he comes to self-awareness. The narrative of personal identity will not so much be a *story* we tell our children but an unquestioned frame that shapes and bounds the stories we tell our children, even the transgressive stories in which people turn into frogs and snakes and dragons.

An evenhanded treatment of our three communities, a treatment that counts them each right on their own terms, must somehow explain how the absorption of such a narrative is, in a certain way, self-validating. That is, it must explain why the fully fledged persons that arise in the three communities each turn out to be roughly right about the kind of future they will have.

Now there can be nothing magical about a community as such. It is far from a general truth, and it may be close to a general falsehood, that a community's framing narratives are self-validating. Rather, it must be that the narratives of personal identity *cause* developing persons to do something that itself settles their actual and possible extent over time.[16]

---

[16]This again is a change in view from that expressed in "Relativism and the Self."

What are we thereby led to acquire, which in its turn fixes the boundaries of our identity? Presumably, it somehow must be that thanks to the framing narrative we acquire some basic future-oriented disposition that helps fix the kind of future we *can* have. As the details of this disposition vary, there will be different kinds of available futures determined. That, in the broadest outline, is how the fully fledged persons that arise in the three communities turn out to be roughly right about the kind of future they can have.

Even before we proceed to fill out this idea, we should see how radical it is. For it amounts to the view that personal identity, far from being an independent justifier of certain future-oriented dispositions, something that requires and justifies those dispositions, is in a particular way "response-dependent," that is, partly determined by certain dispositions a person has at a particular time. This is nothing less than a *radical reversal* of the natural, and to that extent intuitive, order of justification and explanation. Yet, just such a radical inversion seems to be the best way to provide an evenhanded treatment of our three communities.

Consider the paradigm case of a claim of response-dependence in the wake of an error theory about the subject matter in question, the case of the colors, or more exactly the properties of having this or that shade as your surface, volume, or radiant color. The colors present as qualities that pervade surfaces, volumes, and certain kinds of light. So in the case of surface cherry red, being surface cherry red is most naturally understood as having the quality cherry red spread out over your surface. This is the naive view of being colored. It comes closest to how the having of surface color looks or visually presents. As it were, the colors present like very thin paints, and your surface gets to *be* colored by having one of these paints cover your surface. (Even so, the "paints" or qualities are not used up by being spread upon the objects, as normal paints are.) However, we seem pressed to give up this simple view of color *properties* thanks to another central condition on the property of being cherry red and the like. Being cherry red is a visible property, which entails that it must enter differentially into the causal explanation of our visual experience; something's being cherry red must causally explain its standardly appearing so. Yet when we look into the actual causal explanation of our experience as of cherry red we have no model of causation and causal explanation that would allow us to invoke as causally explanatory the property of being cherry red.[17] Why really seems explanatory are the dispositions of surfaces to produce experiences as of cherry red, dispositions had by surfaces thanks to their micro-physical and hence light-reflective properties.[18] Thus, by a continuation of such reasoning that need not distract us here, we are led to say:

A surface has the property of being cherry red if and only if and because it has the disposition to look red to standard perceivers under standard conditions.

Here we have a reversal relative to the naive or simple view. On the simple view, our responses—our visual experiences as of the color properties of things—are to be judged correct or incorrect *because of* how things independently are with respect to color. On the response-dependent reversal there is no such independent criterion of correctness or incorrectness of our responses. Rather, it is our responses that determine how things are with respect to the colors that we see. Moreover, thanks to the reversal, another animal's visual experience as of the colors of things cannot be said to be simply wrong because it does not chime in with ours. The standard responses of any kind of animal with a highly developed visual system bid fair to determine a range of color-like properties, understood as the dispositions of objects that correlate with the responses the animal is typically disposed to make. There is no room for the thought that it is the human beings and not, say, the birds who are getting on to the real color properties had by things.

We are now about to contemplate a corresponding reversal about personal identity, likewise prompted by the discovery of a pervasive

---

[17]For more detail on this argument, see Mark Johnston, "How to Speak of the Colors," *Philosophical Studies* 86 (1992): 221–63, reprinted in A. Byrne and D. Hilbert, eds., *The Philosophy of Color* (MIT Press, 1997). For an interesting account of how one might deny this and save the simple view, see John Campbell, "A Simple View of Color," in John J. Haldane and Crispin Wright, eds., *Reality: Representation and Projection* (Oxford University Press, 1993). Almost all work on the philosophy of color, my own early work included, ignores the crucial distinction between cherry red and being cherry red, i.e., between the quality that is the shade or color and the property that is having that shade as your surface, volume or radiant color. I hope to rectify this widespread conflation in the future, but for some preliminary discussion of the issue, see "Objectivity of Mind and the Objectivity of Our Mind."

[18]The appeal to the micro-physical and light-reflective properties themselves would have been the best explanation if those properties had exhibited some kind of uniformity with respect to the determination of color experience, but notoriously they do not. See, for example, Larry Hardin, *Color for Philosophers: Unweaving the Rainbow* (Hackett, 1988).

error in our ordinary way of thinking. Whereas the naive intuitive view is that the holding of the relation of personal identity independently justifies certain future-directed dispositions, the radical reversal will have it that, within certain limits, those dispositions make it the case that one or another restriction of identity counts as personal identity for a given community!

THE IDENTITY-DETERMINING DISPOSITION*

What is this identity-determining disposition, which may take different concrete forms and so determine one or another restriction of identity as the relation of personal identity for a given community? What is it a disposition to do, such that as a result of doing that thing differently the Hibernators, the Human Beings, and the Teletransporters have different kinds of futures?

The identity-determining disposition is obviously not a disposition to desire that one will survive certain events, for such desires are not self-validating. They are not satisfied just thanks to the fact that one has them. And it is not a disposition to believe that one will survive certain events, for such beliefs are not self-validating; they are not made true just thanks to the fact that one has them.

The only kind of disposition that seems even to be a candidate for the status of an identity-determining disposition is a disposition to somehow deeply and consistently identify with some future person. Of course, there are many forms of identification with future people. Because of how I feel about my friends I can identify with my friends' futures, but that does not make me come to exist as them.

What pattern of identification with some future person is of the right kind to "make for" personal identity? First, it should be a pattern of identification we would recognize as coinciding with personal identity in the normal range of cases. However, there is room for some movement here, since we should expect that the radical reversal has some revisionary implications, so that it does not leave everything as it was. For example, given the radical reversal it will be hard to see how persons who are very far from being fully fledged in the sense introduced earlier could have fully determinate futures. Perhaps there is a metaphysical truth in the claim that we have to treat young children as if they were already Human Beings in order to get them to be Human Beings.

Second, the pattern of identification should be determined by a disposition that antecedently, that is, before we were led to the radical inversion, we would have taken to be required and justified by the holding of the relation of personal identity. For what we are being asked to contemplate as a result of the radical inversion is that certain fundamental attitudes we took to be required by the facts of personal identity are, in reality, part of what determine those facts.

The constraints I will now lay down in order to characterize the relevant disposition are the upshot of my brief attempts to meet these last two requirements. I am more convinced of the requirements than of the details of their application given below. And I should be very happy if others do better, particularly in ways that preserve some of the conclusions that will follow.[19]

1. *Practical absorption of future interests.* We should begin by saying what the disposition to identify in the relevant sense is a disposition to do. It is the disposition to absorb the anticipatable legitimate interests of a future person into your present practical outlook, so that you are now disposed to promote those interests.

2. *Coordination of the disposition.* The relevant disposition is not a mere disposition to absorb the future interests of a person as he is at some future time; the disposition has to be wedded to that person whenever and wherever you take that person to exist. Suppose a person is now disposed to practically absorb the future interests of a person C considered at some time *t* in the future. Then the requirement of coordination has it that the original person now has the disposition to identify in the relevant sense with C only if he is also now disposed to practically absorb the future interests of C at all times at which he takes C to exist. This means that spurts of altruism directed toward the needy futures of others won't meet the standards for the relevant form of identification. (As for radical and consistent altruism, see the sequel.) The relevant dispositions go far beyond the products of episodic whims, or even of adopted projects.

---

[19] For a different development of these ideas, in part prompted by "Relativism and the Self" see David Braddon-Mitchell and Caroline West, "Temporal-Phase Pluralism," *Philosophy and Phenomenological Research*, LX, 2001, and David Braddon-Mitchell and Kristie Miller "How to Be a Conventional Person," forthcoming in *The Monist*. In a series of unpublished lectures given at Oxford

3. *Non-mediation of the disposition.* It is important that the disposition be in a certain way unmediated, that it not depend for its felt intelligibility on an antecedent liking or admiration of the future person in question, still less on the holding of some special intimate relation like parenthood. Nor is identification in the relevant sense mediated by an antecedent value judgment to the effect that the future person in question is particularly good or worthy or important. I can identify with a person as my "future self" and yet find him dull and repellent. (I might have a very dark view about how badly people with my genes age.) Contrast the kind of identification we are trying to bring into view with, say, the identification that a Celt might have for other Celts; he cuts a fellow Celt a special break *because* he thinks that there is a distinctive value in being a Celt. I need not think that there is a distinctive value to be found in some future person to identify with that person as my future self. There is something crucially unmediated in the kind of identification in which we are interested. I recognize a person has certain future interests, and that in itself, and without any such further thought like this is my fellow Celt, or my friend, or my child, or my beloved, leads me to absorb his future interests into my present practical outlook. At least that is so if I have the relevant disposition toward him.

4. *The disposition is not necessarily bounded by individual personality.* You can have the disposition to identify with a person in the relevant sense *even* if that disposition is not essentially dependent on that person's continuing to exemplify your present individual personality. There is a kind of case in which your presently absorbing some anticipatable future interests would likely be an expression of your attachment to the individual personality whose interests they are. But my concern for my future self is not like that. Consider: Alzheimer's has begun to set in, but I am told that the effective treatment that will more than restore my memory is more than a year away. By that time I will have lost all the memories that support the moorings of this individual personality. The treatment, though wonderful, has one defect. It will

---

University, Dean Zimmerman has explored various ways of embodying the thought that personal identity or more exactly its implementation is a response-dependent matter.

restore my *capacity* to remember but not my memories. I can get on with a practical form of life after my recovery, but it will not be this form of life. A functioning individual personality may emerge, but this individual personality will be lost. I face a version of psychological rebirth within this life. Even so, the kind of future-directed concern that goes with personal identity does get engaged here. Anticipating all this, it would be natural for me to now plan around the anticipatable needs of that new individual personality. The relevant disposition gets a purchase on the person with the new individual personality.

5. *Only persons have interests in the relevant sense.* In the sense of interest at hand, the sense that is relevant to identifying with some person as my "future self," only persons, that is, reflective intelligent beings that can consider themselves as themselves at various times and places, have interests. (This is not meant to exclude other things that predicatively are persons, such as individual personalities, that is, persons that satisfy certain further conditions.) The relevant disposition could not get a purchase on spiders, rainforests, crystals, or the like. On the other hand, for all I say here, the higher animals could well be persons with interests.

6. *Masking does not defeat the disposition.* Certainly depression and self-loathing can at times smother a person to such an extent that he *manifests* no disposition to absorb any of his anticipatable future interests. Or a person may be given to bouts of self-destructive recklessness, where nothing seems to matter to him. Dispositions can be masked, and when they are masked they are not lost; their manifestations are suppressed by other factors. Fragility is roughly the disposition to break when struck. When the inside of a fragile glass is packed tightly with paper this works to cushion the structure-deforming impact of a blow so that the glass may not break when struck. But it is still fragile; it still has the disposition to break when struck. The disposition is simply masked—its manifestation is suppressed—by the paper stuffed into the glass. Many cases of depression, self-loathing, and recklessness will be cases where the disposition to absorb future interests is masked. Imprudence does not eliminate one's future; it is invariably a masker of an underlying disposition to take that future into account.

7. *A failure in the disposition need not eliminate one's future.* But now take a case where the disposition to practically absorb future interests *is* lost. Is such an unfortunate person then devoid of any future? Not necessarily, for if he is still a person he *will* have interests, and those interests could be such that his earlier "self"— he himself earlier—*was* disposed to practically absorb those interests. If he continues to be a person he will continue to have interests, and those interests could be such that his earlier self was disposed to practically absorb those interests. He now has a future secured by the dispositions of his earlier self. In general, the disposition "makes for" identity, but a subsequent failure in the disposition, a subsequent unfortunate failure to be disposed to absorb the future interests of a given person, is not enough to guarantee non-identity between the unfortunate and the person in question.

8. *"Making for identity" is not making identity happen.* As emphasized all along, identity does not hang about waiting to see what two things it will be caused to hold among. Identity, the relation between a thing and itself, never holds between any two things and never holds temporarily or accidentally. The disposition does not affect the holding of the relation of identity; it determines what kind of thing, with what temporal extent, counts as the person in question. It selects a more specific relation to be the implementation of the relation of personal identity.

You can see what I am doing here; I am attempting to characterize a certain dispositional structure that is ordinarily secured by the conviction that one is capable of having a certain sort of future, and then invert its ordinary role, so that it is instead understood as the thing that determines or selects the kind of future in question. As evidenced in the case of the color properties, this is the characteristic kind of move behind revisionary discoveries of response-dependence.

The Solution to Our Problems

We are now in a position to solve our earlier puzzlement as to the somewhat adventitious character of finding human beings at our respective centers. The questions that expressed that puzzlement were:

What makes it the case that each one of *us* finds a human being at the relevant center?

How is it possible to provide an evenhanded treatment of the Human Beings, the Hibernators, and the Teletransporters without lapsing into an incoherent relativism about personal identity?

Or more concretely:

How could the Teletransporters survive Teletransportation when the Human Beings and the Hibernators do not, and how could the Teletransporters and the Human Beings survive deep sleep when the Hibernators do not?

The key to the solution is this: As the radical reversal implies, different patterns in dispositions to identify, that is, to absorb future anticipatable interests, select different relations as the relevant implementations of the relation of personal identity.

Like you, I have been brought up in the narrative of the human being; among other things, this has solidified in me a particular coordinated and unmediated disposition to absorb certain anticipatable future interests into my present practical outlook. Operating within the framing narrative according to which my life is the life of a human being, I consider some human being in some anticipated future. The question of his being me reduces to the question of whether he is the human being Johnston. If I decide he is the human being Johnston then I treat his anticipatable interests as my own, that is, *as default starting points in my present practical reasoning.* It is this kind of unmediated future-directed concern that exhausts my identifying with him in the relevant way, the way that involves regarding him as me.

Consider what it is like to be a Teletransporter. In order to configure your identity around the relation of being the same Teletransporter, you have to radically identify with the person who will get out of the machine, the person who then has a duplicate of your present brain and body. You would have to fear his death as you would fear your own, you would have to treat his anticipatable interests as you would treat your own, that is, *as default starting points in your present practical reasoning.*

On the view being proposed, it is not that the facts of personal identity independently justify our dispositions to identify. Rather, those dispositions to identify help constitute the relevant facts of personal identity, which in turn justify those concerns and expectations. This is the radical reversal that comes with the explanatory hypothesis that personal identity is a response-dependent matter.

There is a difference between an intellectual discovery and a change in how things look or immediately present. Even after we learn that there is no absolute sense in which the sun goes around the earth, the sun still *looks to be* going around the earth. It has moved across the sky this afternoon, hasn't it? The earth still seems to be the center, because that is where we are.

Given what was emphasized in lecture two, namely the apparently centered structure of presence, it is profoundly difficult to maintain a vivid sense that we are, as I like to put it, "ontological trash," that we are nowhere near being *primary phenomena*, that we are not superlative selves whose natures provide independent justifiers for self-concern. These claims are not going to be intuitive. They are forced on us by argument. For a moment one's sense of being a primary phenomenon can be stunned by argument. But soon, it will return.

Similarly, it will be profoundly difficult to maintain a vivid sense that the implementation of the general form of personal identity is a response-dependent matter. That personal identity is response-dependent is not presented as an initial intuitive reaction. It arises only in the wake of what philosophers call an "error theory" about the self. That is, it emerges as an option only after the discovery that we made in lectures two and three, namely that our subjective life is based around an illusion.

A FALSE SENSE OF OUR ESSENCE

Here, then, is the explanation of how it is that the Hibernators, the Human Beings, and the Teletransporters can each be right on their own terms. Each human animal is also a person, a reflective self-conscious being who must embody his or her identity in one or another concrete way. At the deepest level, this involves the organization of his or her future-directed concerns. How that stands at a time determines what kind of person is available to the reflective self-conscious being that has so organized its future-directed concern, and this determines what kind of events the reflective conscious being will survive.

What, then, is the essence of a person as such, the essence that would be shared by the Hibernators, the Human Beings, and the Teletransporters, despite their different ways of implementing this essence? To answer that question we have to consider what would happen if one were to refigure one's identity-determining dispositions so that those dispositions came to focus on a different way of implementing this common essence.

Would one person cease to be and be replaced by another, or would the first person simply open himself up to possibilities that already lay in his essence?

Imagine a tribe of human beings in which a common genetic disorder inevitably leads to their dying in their twenties. When they come in contact with old people from other tribes they are stunned and first treat these elders as different kinds of beings from themselves, for they think of a human being as *essentially young*. They are then astonished to find that these elders take themselves to have once *been* young. Finally, they are cured of their disorder and they themselves live to ripe old ages. The members of the tribe thereby discover that they had made a profound mistake about their essences. They had treated a lifelong phase consisting of childhood and youth as if it represented a limit fixed by their essence as persons, but they came to learn that they could live through this phase.

Is something like that possible for us?

REFIGURING ONE'S BASIC DISPOSITIONS

Given where we now are, it would seem entirely reasonable for a Human Being who has come into the guardianship of a waif not yet acculturated in the ways of the Human Beings, the Hibernators, or the Teletransporters to decide to place his charge in the hands of the Teletransporters. At least that would be the right choice if the Human Being had already accepted our evenhanded view of his differences with the Teletransporters. For as we are imagining them, the Teletransporters have super-fast travel and practical freedom from disease. And there is nothing *inherently* wrong with their way of organizing their identity-determining dispositions.

Having engaged in this reasonable act of transcending his own ethnocentric prejudices for the sake of another, our Human Being begins to wonder about himself. Are the benefits of super-fast travel and practical freedom from disease in principle available to him? It may seem not, given the way his identity-determining dispositions were originally organized. His present practical outlook is just not engaged by his contemplating the interests of any potential human being who would be generated from him by Teletransportation. Accordingly, given that the facts of personal identity are determined by these dispositions, he would not survive as any human being generated from him by Teletransportation.

However, he has also heard that those broadminded Teletransporters now offer a kind of boot camp for Human Beings, a camp whose purpose is to get the Human Beings who attend to undergo a profound change of outlook so that they do come to have unmediated and coordinated dispositions to identify with the human beings that are produced from them by Teletransportation. Our Human Being decides to attend the camp. But then he finds out that part of the transformative process involves attending a series of long and tortuous lectures on personal identity and the unreality of the self. That is not his cup of tea; indeed he regards it as a fate worse than death! So he changes his mind and tries to return to a modest state of comfort with his lot as a Human Being.

But what if? What if he had attended the camp and his dispositions had been transformed in the desired way so that they came to be just like those of lifelong Teletransporters? Would he have simply acquired the delusory conviction that he could and would survive Teletransportation, or would he be more like a member of the tribe of always young humans who had a potentiality for survival that had been hidden from them suddenly open up?

I believe that there is only one adequate way of extending our thought that personal identity is partly response-dependent to this kind of case. And it implies that our Human Being would not be suffering a delusion if the boot camp had worked on him in the intended way.

For consider a Human Being now contemplating the boot camp in prospect. He thinks of himself on the last day of the camp with his dispositions then refigured, so he now has dispositions that correspond to those of the Teletransporters. It is thanks to those dispositions that the Teletransporters survive Teletransportation, so why shouldn't that person on the last day of the camp be such that he survives Teletransportation? But that person on the last day of the camp would be the same person as the Human Being contemplating him in prospect. For by hypothesis, the Human Being is now disposed to absorb that person's interests into his present practical outlook, and this disposition is coordinated and unmediated. For example, he may agonize over whether that person (that is, he himself) will then be deluded, and so in need of being protected from stepping into a Teleporter for the first and last time. So the Human Being is identical to that person on the last day of the camp (given the response-dependence of personal identity), and that person on the last day will survive Teletransportation, just as the original Teletransporters do. But survival is here identity, and identity is transitive, so our Human Being *will come* to survive Teletransportation thanks to having his dispositions refigured in the appropriate way.

The natural assumption made here is an assumption of temporal invariance: If some time is such that your coordinated and unmediated dispositions at that time determine what you will survive, then there is nothing special about *that time*. It is the dispositions that are doing the work, and if they change in certain ways, then what you can survive may well change.

If that is right, we are now in a position to state the invariant essence of persons that allows us to understand the Hibernators, the Human Beings, and the Teletransporters as each having their own way of implementing personal identity.

What we have discovered is that we *are* in a certain way like the tribe of always young humans who supposed that old age is not available to them thanks to the metaphysics of the situation, thanks, that is, to their supposed essence. Like them, our identities are more flexible than we have taken them to be. The tribe treated a lifelong phase as if it were fixed by their essence. We Human Beings have been doing the same thing. We are both victims of a false sense of necessity.

Persons Are Protean

If refiguring our identity-determining dispositions can open us up to, or close us off from, certain forms of survival, then there is a sense in which our natures are Protean. As with Proteus, who could assume the forms of a lion, a leopard, a serpent, or a pig, our essence could allow changes in our form of embodiment. The concrete embodiment of our identities as persons is in a certain way up to us to fill out; what we can survive, and the resultant facts of personal identity, are in a certain way response-dependent. So much emerges when we recognize that there are no independent justifiers of our self-directed concerns.

The fact that our Human Being can come to survive Teletransportation by having refigured his identity-determining dispositions in the appropriate way indicates the kind of invariant we have been seeking.

Here, then, is the invariant part of our natures as persons, the invariant the three communities implemented in their different ways.

A person considered at some time *t* is (at *t*) capable of surviving a later event *e* if that event is not at odds with the person's identity-determining dispositions at *t*. That will be so if there would be a person around after the event *e* whose anticipatable interests are such that the person at *t* is appropriately disposed to incorporate them into his practical outlook at *t*. (Note that this condition is only intended as a sufficient condition. The appropriate disposition is the one characterized earlier. For example, it must be unmediated and coordinated.)

Let us call this the thesis that persons are Protean, for it implies that if we could refigure our identity-determining dispositions then what we are (in the relevant sense) *capable of surviving* would change. If and when a person refigures his dispositions, something only apparently essential changes, and something really essential remains true of him; he remains the sort of thing that is capable of surviving some event if that event is not at odds with his identity-determining dispositions.

We can now say what the thesis that we are Protean implies about our three communities. A member of a given community would be correct to take identity restricted to the kind K (as it might be, the kind hibernator or the kind human being or the kind teletransporter) to set down his limits of survival just in case he was organizing his identity-determining dispositions around the relation of identity restricted to K (as it might be, being the same hibernator, or being the same human being, or being the same teletransporter). What makes it the case that a given relation is the implementation of the relation of personal identity for the members of a given community is just that the members of the community standardly organize their identity-determining dispositions around that relation.

The identity-determining dispositions are in a certain way self-validating. What counts as the correct implementation of personal identity is a response-dependent matter. Nonetheless, the fact that we are Protean, namely that the terms of our survival depend in this way on our dispositions, is an independent and essential fact about our natures as persons. Strictly speaking, it is the implementation of personal identity that is a response-dependent matter, which can vary blamelessly across communities. Personal identity, the identity over time of the Protean beings we in fact are, is a response-independent matter.

Thus we arrive at the desired evenhanded treatment of the Hibernators, the Human Beings, and the Teletransporters. They are *each correct on their own terms*. None has made a mistake at odds with the commonly available facts about the lives of human animals, unless it is the common mistake of being in the grip of an illusion of necessity about their way of implementing or embodying personal identity.

As reflective beings, who can identify ourselves as ourselves at various times and places, we must also have some concrete ways of embodying our identity, that is, some concrete way of organizing our fundamental future-oriented dispositions. We cannot be simply Protean; we also need some specific way of embodying that Protean nature by way of some specific identity-determining dispositions.

Now we see why it is that *we* seem to find a particular sort of person at the center (if I am right about *us*, a human being). The relation around which we have been organizing our specific identity-determining dispositions is identity restricted to the kind human being. This is no surprise, since we were all brought up within the narrative of the human being, and this shaped our fundamental dispositions. What is a surprise is that the kind human being is not a substance kind, not a kind that unites its members by way of a shared essence. We have discovered that it is a phase kind, one we could in principle migrate out of, if we were to radically refigure our basic dispositions.

Every time a person, an embodied being that can consider itself as itself at various times and places, uses "I" the essence-characterizing kind for that being is the kind Protean Person. When a Human Being thinks "I cannot survive Teletransportation" the truth nearest to what he is thinking is that he, as he then is, cannot survive Teletransportation. But this does not mean that there can be no situation in which he, the Protean person, survives Teletransportation.

At the beginning of this lecture, I said that I found the human being

Johnston here at the center. That is true, but misleading. What fundamentally occupies centers, and so what certain uses of "I" pick out, are Protean persons. A human being gets to be there at a center because of the identity-determining dispositions of the Protean person that is there.

That is not to say that there are two persons here at the center, the Protean person and the human being Johnston. This is not a case of co-occupancy. Johnston is, and is essentially, the Protean person, and this Protean person is now a human being. Johnston's being a human being has turned out to be more like his being a permanent resident. Being a human being is a phase we could potentially grow out of.

All this pushes us toward the question of whether there is any *psychologically available* way of implementing personal identity that would be better than our present way of doing so, stretched as it is over the lives of human beings. Existing as just a human being, surviving only what a human being would survive, is *that* the best way for essentially Protean beings to organize their identity-determining dispositions?

That question will assume center stage in the next and final lecture. For the fact of our deaths, a fact in part constituted by our identity as human beings, makes the question all the more pressing.

ANOTHER ROUTE TO THE CONCLUSION*

Here is an alternative route to the conclusion that we are Protean, one that does not require us to take the *Hibernators* seriously, at least in the sense of supposing that their claims to be tracing persons will remain tenable, even under ideal epistemic conditions.

That claim of persistent rational tenability is considerably more plausible in the cases of the Human Beings and the Teletransporters. For their "dispute" exactly mimics the longstanding and apparently irresolvable dispute in the philosophy of personal identity as to whether persons can survive Teletransportation. It unlikely that the philosophers engaged in such a dispute over the last thirty years have missed the decisive argument, one way or another, that renders one side's position rationally untenable. So we have considerable evidence for this premise.

> The respective claims of the Human Beings and the Teletransporters to be tracing persons will remain rationally tenable, even under ideal epistemic conditions.

Given this premise there are a number of possibilities. One is that personal identity is an investigation-transcendent matter, so that there is a fact of the matter, forever unknowable, which makes it the case that one or both of the respective claims is false. This is in effect the unattractive view that we can never find out what we are, what our conditions of persistence are, even though we seem to face no such principled obstacle with reptiles or birds or dogs or cats.

If we set that view aside then there seem to be two remaining possibilities. The first is the conclusion we are aiming for, namely that both of the respective claims are correct thanks to the fact that both the Human Beings and the Teletransporters have organized their dispositions around an admissible implementation of the relation of personal identity. The second remaining possibility is that all the rationally irresolvable dispute between the Human Beings and the Teletransporters shows is that we have a case of conceptual indeterminacy. On this view, the concept of personal identity is not fully determinate, that is, it does not determine every event involving a person as either definitely a case of that person continuing to exist or definitely a case of that person ceasing to be. Specifically, it does not decide the issue of Teletransportation, even given all the facts of the case.

On this second possibility, the Human Beings and the Teletransporters present equally legitimate ways of making the not fully determinate concept of personal identity determinate when it comes to the case of Teletransportation. The Human Beings say you do not survive, and the Teletransporters say you do. That is why their dispute remains rationally irresolvable. There is no determinate fact of the matter as to whether a person survives Teletransportation.

This second possibility was actually the starting point of another argument I gave long ago for the view we are Protean, an argument that I think I can state here in a relatively streamlined way.[20] In effect, the argument is that the second possibility, namely that this is a case of two different ways of legitimately resolving an indeterminacy in the concept of personal identity, actually collapses in favor of the first possibility, namely that the Human Beings and the Teletransporters have organized their dispositions around admissible, though different, implementations of the relation of personal identity.

[20] In "Relativism and the Self."

To begin on the argument: numerical identity is not an indeterminate concept, so any indeterminacy in the concept of personal identity must derive from indeterminacy in the concept of a person, in particular indeterminacy in the possible temporal extent of the things we call "persons." Given the permissive hylomorphic account of entities developed in lecture three, we will have entities that cease to exist when their brains and bodies are destroyed (say, organisms) and we will have entities capable of surviving Teletransportation (say, certain successions of organisms). The only question is whether the first or the second class of entities best deserves the name of persons. Given the second possibility, the answer to this question is that both classes of entities equally but not perfectly deserve the name of persons, and there is no better deserver of the name.

Typically when there are two different groups that are equally good claimants to be Fs, then on one way of making things determinate one group of claimants are the Fs while on the other way of making things determinate the other group of claimants are the Fs. But there is a further constraint in the case of persons that does operate in the typical case. Anything that is as good a claimant to be a person as something that is already being counted as person should also be counted as a person. (Think of this as in effect what supervaluationists call a "penumbral" truth, a truth that must be upheld on an acceptable way of making things determinate.[21])

This constraint holds because the nature of the status *person*, and the way in which we are obliged to extend that status to things that are sufficiently person-like. So the persons recognized by the Human Beings and the persons recognized by the Teletransporters are *all simply persons*, on any legitimate way of making the concept of a person fully determinate. So the second possibility was not a real possibility, the concept of a person cannot be indeterminate in exactly the way it implies. For on all legitimate ways of making that concept determinate there are persons that survive Teletransportation and there are persons that do not.[22]

That means that the persons recognized by the Human Beings and

---

[21] A suggestion made by Jamie Tappenden.

[22] Epistemicists typically explain what they regard as the kind of ignorance that goes under the heading of indeterminacy by appeal to the existence of many candidate meanings that differ just a little in meaning. One, and only one, of these gets picked by how we use a word, thanks to hypersensitive rules about how use determines meaning. So, on this view, what we describe as vagueness or indeterminacy is our inability to see or discover just what we mean and where what we mean

the persons recognized by the Teletransporters have different conditions of persistence. The best explanation for this is that there are different *sorts* of persons. So, again, we do need an evenhanded treatment of the Human Beings and the Teletransporters, a treatment that sees them as working with two different but legitimate implementations of the relation of personal identity. And upon further analysis—here we revert to the previous line of argument—it appears that the best evenhanded treatment implies that persons are Protean.

Is the Persistence of Personalities Response-Dependent?*

That our true essence is Protean, that the correctness of a way of implementing our Protean natures is a response-dependent matter, is tenable only in the wake of a diagnosis of profound error in our ordinary ways of thinking about self identity and personal identity. There is no way that nature or supernature can conform itself to provide for some independent justifier that would make one way of implementing personal identity *the* correct way. And there is no sense to be made of persisting selves, which might privilege one or another candidate to be *the* relation of personal identity, say, by persisting as long and only as long as that relation holds. That was the burden of the last two lectures.

We have been driven to a strongly revisionary metaphysics of selves and persons, a view to the effect that there are none of the first worth caring about and that the second have a Protean essence. We have nonetheless offered a merely descriptive account of individual personalities, which tries to capture something that still seems to be left intact in our ordinary ways of thinking about ourselves.

An individual personality can be thought of as a dynamic aspect of a person, one that persists as long as the person is able to sustain a distinctive style of agency over time, a style of agency that requires the holding of certain psychological continuities and connections, and partly enforces them by way of ongoing commitments to distinctive projects, policies, and relationships.

---

draws the crucial line. But if we recognize the so-called penumbral truth then we should not think of the difference between the Human Beings and the Teletransporters in *that* kind of way. (A point made to me by Dean Zimmerman.)

Just to fix ideas, recall Robert Louis Stevenson's *Strange Case of Dr. Jekyll and Mr. Hyde,* a case of two very different personalities, the one good and the other evil, intermittently taking over the life of a single person. The medical researcher Jekyll seeks a healing potion that would isolate and remove the evil part of human nature. Experimenting on himself, he creates instead another personality entirely, one that goes about under the name of Mr. Hyde. Hyde represents the intensification of Jekyll's evil impulses; he is free of the pangs of conscience, and sets on a course of rape and murder. After a period, Jekyll's original personality returns, and by inference from certain signs Jekyll discovers what Hyde has done. The two personalities, Hyde and Jekyll's original personality, exhibit very different memories, styles of agency, projects, and policies. Each for a time is unaware of the other's existence.

It might be thought that the Neo-Lockean account of personal identity is in some danger of misclassifying persons and personalities in this case. Hyde and Jekyll's original personality are presented as so psychologically disconnected that they seem to violate the Neo-Lockean necessary condition on being the same person. But the coherent, and it seems successful, intent of Stevenson was to describe a single human being *Jekyll,* who brought about an extreme split of personality in himself. After the split, there were two personalities manifesting themselves in a single person's life.

Cases like this suggest that the Neo-Lockean necessary condition on identity, the condition of significant psychological interconnectedness, is better suited to individual personalities rather than persons. The same is suggested by the imagined case of my psychological rebirth after being cured of Alzheimer's disease. Despite my cure, psychological connection is broken between my earlier and later personalities, since the memories that provided the moorings of my earlier personality never return.

Be that as it may, for we are not going to rest much on an appeal to our intuitions about personal identity in an imaginary case. Nevertheless, as such cases bring out, the holding of the psychological connections that make for the persistence of the same individual personality is an objective psychological matter. It is not a response-dependent matter, one to be determined by our dispositions to identify with later phases of some individual personality. There is an objective, though sometimes vague, fact of the matter as to whether a certain style of agency, which requires and partly the holding of certain psychological continuities and connections, has persisted over time.

So far there is supposed to be nothing revisionary in this. And I believe that there is nothing revisionary in the idea that since an individual personality is an aspect of a person, it survives only so long as that person survives. There are conceivable cases where despite the obliteration of my individual personality, the same type of individual personality continues on in another. But these are not cases where my individual personality survives; at best they are cases where I will have an excellent executor of the plans and projects that were partly constitutive of my individual personality. That is what happens when a Human Being (one still acculturated in the ways of the Human Beings) steps into the Teleporter. He is destroyed, and a duplicate is created at the receiving station. That duplicate represents at most an excellent executor of the plans and projects of the individual personality that was destroyed with the destruction of the Human Being. So much, I think, just follows from the idea that an *individual* personality is a (token) aspect of a person and not just a type of agency.

Still, this is enough to show how the response-dependence of the correctness of a way of implementing personal identity will make the persistence of an individual personality *partly* a response-dependent matter. For a given individual personality survives only if a given person survives, and the survival of a person is, we have argued, partly a response-dependent matter.

This will be important in what follows.

The Other World as an Ethical Epiphenomenon

Recall that I am not *dogmatically* anti-supernaturalist; for me the issue of supernaturalism is an empirical question, and I take it that the massive preponderance of the detailed empirical evidence counts against supernaturalism. But first and foremost, I am a methodological naturalist, in part because I believe that the right starting point in the foundation of ethics and the philosophy of religion is this: Is it possible to ransom any of the genuinely salvific ideas of the major religions from their supernaturalist captivity, and what price do we have to pay for the ransom? This question is forced upon us by our need for salvation, that is, our need for an adequate response to the large-scale structural defects of human life, and the fact that believing in the speculative and inevitably dodgy claims of supernaturalism cannot be, morally and religiously speaking, necessary (let alone sufficient) for salvation.

But if I am right that personal identity, and to that extent individual personality, are partly response-dependent then it is possible that when it comes to surviving death, supernaturalism is even more irrelevant than has ever been supposed.

As Aquinas held, and as the promise of *bodily* resurrection itself suggests, even if there were immaterial souls, we would not be not *identical to* those immaterial substances or souls. There would still be the need for an account of why a person lives on either as his immaterial soul or as that soul re-embodied. And it falls within the purview of philosophy to investigate and discover what that account is.

As we have seen, the relevant philosophy is full of surprises, for we begin with a quite mistaken view of our nature. There are no selves worth caring about and the persons that we are have a Protean nature. This means that we could allow for the existence of exactly the supernaturalist apparatus depicted in *The Entombment of Gonzalo Ruiz* and *yet regard it as nothing to us.* For all the supernaturalist apparatus would give us is the familiar sequence of individuals described in Catholic theology, first a living human being, then during the interregnum between death and the Great Day his soul, a remnant of the human being, and finally after the General Resurrection an individual consisting of that soul animating a spiritualized human body. The last "spiritualized" individual could carry on the same *type* of individual personality as that embodied in the human being who once lived. But what would make it continue the very same (token) individual personality? Nothing but the facts of personal identity, facts which are partly response-dependent, and would remain so in the supernatural scenario being considered.

Even given the supernatural apparatus depicted both in *The Entombment* and in Aquinas's theology of death, the person that I am might not survive after death in either heaven or hell. It all depends on just how, in this life, I configure my identity-determining dispositions.

You might think that in the face of the supernaturalist apparatus in question I had jolly well *better* configure these dispositions in the appropriate way so that I survive as my soul and then the spiritualized individual who comes into being after the resurrection. That would at least be a plausible thing to say if you were a universalist about salvation, holding that we all get to heaven in the end. Otherwise, the risk of eternal damnation born by the spiritualized individual who inherits my soul might rationally dissuade me from configuring my dispositions so as to identify especially with *him*.

But—and here is my main point—configuring the relevant dispositions so as to *especially* identify with the spiritualized individual who inherits my soul would actually be inconsistent with the central salvific idea of Christianity, namely the idea of *agape*, the very form of love we are commanded to adopt.

My point will be, and it will be the burden of the final lecture to show this, that given the response-dependent element in personal identity, living out the ideal of *agape* would make us live on in the onward rush of humankind and *not* (or not especially) in the supernatural spaces of heaven, even if such spaces existed and were inhabited by inheritors of our souls.

Even if supernaturalism about death, say the existence of soul-inheritors in an afterlife, were literally true, this would be morally and religiously speaking a kind of distracting, if not irritating, epiphenomenon. Our morally urgent postmortem future would remain here on earth in the onward rush of humankind.

A Summary and a Bridge to the Last Lecture

That was a lot of material to have covered. It may be helpful to rehearse the overall argument, and provide a bridge to what is to come.

Drawing on the results of lectures two and three, we can now assert the following:

1. There is not the kind of metaphysical justifier, such as a self or a soul or ego, which could independently determine which parts of nature *ought* to be the foci of our respective patterns of self-concern.

Given 1, we can draw our first intermediate conclusion.

C1. It is possible to have quite different implementations of personal identity, say those of the Hibernators, the Human Beings, and the Teletransporters, where none of these implementations is out of kilter with the identities of selves or souls or egos, or indeed anything that could be understood as an independent justifier of self-concern.

Are these different implementations then simply out of kilter with the sheer facts of *personal* identity? Should we still suppose that the sheer facts of personal identity make *at most* one of the three communities right about what it is they survive? If we suppose that, then there is no need for an evenhanded treatment of the three communities, a treatment that counts each community right on its own terms. What I called the "alternative route" and the following argument each count against this strategy for avoiding an evenhanded treatment.

a. It is not plausible that matters of fact such as whether persons would survive dreamless sleep and whether persons would survive Teletransportation are investigation-transcendent, that is, could never be discovered no matter how far the issue was investigated.

b. So, the Hibernators, the Human Beings, and the Teletransporters should each be such that if they were to take into account all the relevant facts about dreamless sleep and Teletransportation, reflect appropriately on these facts, embed them in larger well-confirmed theories, and explore the consequences, and do all this without any internal epistemic irrationality *and* continue this process indefinitely, they would at some point come to a determination of the relevant facts.

c. Yet even under such increasingly improving epistemic conditions, even as the investigation into the facts gets better and better, the Hibernators, the Human Beings, and the Teletransporters could rationally (at least from the epistemic point of view) persist in their differing implementations of personal identity no matter how far they investigated the matter. (Remember, we are setting to one side the practical extrinsic advantages of one implementation over the other.)

d. So, we do in fact need an evenhanded treatment.

Our second intermediate conclusion should therefore be:

C2. We need to find an evenhanded treatment of the three implementations, a treatment that counts each right on its own
terms.

But,

2. No sense is to be made of relativism about personal identity.

So,

C3. We need to see the three implementations as different expressions of an overarching relation of personal identity, expressions somehow due to the different psychologies characteristic of the three communities.

But,

3. The basic relevant difference between the three communities is
a difference in identification, where this comes to a difference
in their respective dispositions to immediately take certain anticipated future interests as default starting points in their present practical interests.
4. It is these differences that appear to select one or another implementation of personal identity.
5. The best explanation of 4 is that we are Protean.
6. But if we are Protean, in the sense defined, we can in principle
refigure our present implementation of personal identity by refiguring our dispositions to take anticipated future interests as
default starting points in our present practical reasoning.

So,

C4. By refiguring our basic dispositions in this way, we could
come to be able to survive events (e.g., Teletransportation)
that previously we were not yet in a position to survive.

Now,

7. The command of *agape* is the command to refigure one's basic
dispositions so that one becomes disposed to take all anticipat-

able future interests as default starting points in one's practical reasoning.

Hence,

C5. Given that we are Protean, following the command of agape would mean that we would thereby implement personal identity in such a way that we would survive wherever and whenever interests are to be found. We would, quite literally, live on in the onward rush of humankind.

But, as was established at the end of lecture three by appealing to the fact of *anatta*,

8. The command of *agape* or radical altruism is simply the command to live in accord with the practical reasons that there actually are. And that is all "goodness" in the practical realm can be reasonably taken to mean.

So now we see how it could be that

C6. The good, that is the *really good*, survive death.

THE LIFE TO COME

I know that some Christians in the audience (and among my readers) will regard this as a snare and a delusion. They will adhere to the Pauline stance. They will say that unless Christ is supernaturally risen from the dead, *and unless we are to follow him in this*, then Christianity is empty, not a means of salvation at all. And perhaps they will go further and follow Paul when asserts at 1 Corinthians 13:32, by way of recapitulating the argument of the Wisdom of Solomon, that *agape* would then be sheer foolishness.

I believe that this view of what Christianity essentially is embodies a terrible mistake, and it wrongly places a millstone around the neck of the truly faithful. I have argued against it elsewhere.[23] But, obviously, the assent to that argument will fall short of being universal. (To put it mildly.)

There will be Christians who accept the philosophical considerations that show that the mortalist Protestant ambition has failed, that neither

[23] *Saving God.*

the bodily criterion nor Neo-Lockeanism nor the persistence of selves can effectively underwrite the possibility of resurrection. If they adhere to the Pauline stance, they will have one last refuge, in effect the theology of *the Entombment*, the belief in the immaterial and separable soul and in its re-embodiment at or before the General Resurrection.

After all, the strongest thing that an intellectually responsible person can say against this refuge is that the massive preponderance of the de-tailed empirical evidence is against it. That may seem to leave room for faith that the Pauline stance may still be sustainable, and that (contrary to what Paul himself seemed to think) its promise will be made true thanks to the existence of souls that can survive death.

All I would add is that this particular form of faith is not *itself* faith in the importance of goodness, it is the faith that allows itself labile epis-temic standards in order to provide what it takes to be necessary to maintain faith in the importance of goodness.

Even with that said, even with that difference or profound divide be-tween us fully registered, there is still something surprising here for those who hold to belief in the soul in order to allow for supernatural survival. Thanks to the nature of personal identity and the character of *agape*, the life to come is more complicated than is usually imagined. There is more—much more—to assimilate about your postmortem future.

You could not at your death deserve heaven *without also remaining here on earth, multiply embodied in the onward rush of mankind.*

Questions and Replies

How do the Hibernators and the Teletransporters manage to trace each other? Clearly, they are not offloading onto substances such as human an-imals.[24]

That is right, and neither exactly are we. We are attempting to trace em-bodied selves by offloading onto the human animals that invariably con-stitute them. In the light of our later beliefs about the brain, and so forth, we naturally suppose that the mere survival of a brain might be enough to secure the survival of an embodied self. That is why we are properly located among the Human Beings. Perhaps a way to understand the

[24] An audience member unknown to me.

Teletransporters is to think of them as needing to go in for the extra cognitive labor of explicitly checking who came from what machine when.

Would not Nancey Murphy's view be a coherent thing for the Teletransporters to accept? Suppose you are a Teletransporter and a transmitting station blows up as you enter it. Still it will be possible, in the broadest sense of possible, that you will be resurrected on the last day. God remembers exactly what you were like and, as it were, stands in for the receiving station![25]

Theology aside, it would be coherent for the Teletransporters to accept that as a possible way for them to live on in the next world, if there were a next world. That is not because the Teletransporters necessarily believe in the Neo-Lockean view. They might believe in the correct view and simply understand themselves as implementing personal identity in a particularly effective way. Your point is that given the way their future-directed dispositions are organized the jump to the next life should not strike them as very different from the jump from one Teleporter station to another.

But the Teletransporters would have a better option. They can refigure their basic dispositions so as to live on in this world, and not just as their products by Teletransportation.

Once we see that there can and should be an evenhanded treatment of different implementations of personal identity, we see another reason why resurrection by body duplication cannot be a viable theological idea. For suppose we *were* Teletransporters. In developing a reasonable theology of resurrection we would have to accommodate the resurrection of the Human Beings as well. God is not going to grant the Human Beings lifelong moral holidays by leaving *them* in the grave forever, is he? But how can he possibly resurrect them given their identity-determining dispositions?

Perhaps he undetectably whisks them away from their death beds to a boot camp course on personal identity.

Is there not an enormous difference between the connections that hold within the lives of the Hibernators, the Human Beings, and the Teletrans-

---

[25]Sarah-Jane Leslie.

porters on the one hand and the connections that hold among me and arbitrary others—the objects of agape—on the other hand?[26]

Yes, within the lives of the Hibernators, the Human Beings, and the Teletransporters there is typically psychological continuity and a kind of direct psychological connection that allows for some prospective control over how that life develops. There is typically, as I put it in the lecture, the survival of the very same individual personality.

The first thing to note is that although the survival of the individual personality is from the self-interested point of view part of what matters in survival, it is not necessary for personal identity. After all, in the case of my recovery from Alzheimer's, my original individual personality does not survive, but I do. (I am not here using that case as an intuition pump, but just as an illustration of a difference.)

In general I believe that it would be wrong to say that unless one can exercise prospective control over the life of some future person, one will not be identical with that person. That surely is too strong a requirement. The child in those old familiar photos is the same person as me, whatever the changes in outlook, personality, ability, and mental disposition that have taken place since then. The child who imagines the old codger he will become is not committed by the logic of personal identity to believing that he can exercise prospective control over the life of that old codger.

Now turn to the question of what matters, what it is rational to care about in caring about survival. I allow that *granting* the self-interested point of view I reasonably want not only personal identity but the survival of *my* individual personality. So from the self-interested point of view there seems to be all the difference in the world between surviving as a Hibernator or a Human Being or a Teletransporter and surviving in the onward rush of humankind. In the last case one's very own individual personality does not survive.

However, in lectures two and three we saw in detail that the self-interested point of view, the point of view that regards a particular person and a particular individual personality as worthy of premium treatment because he is *me* or because it is *mine*, is not a coherent point of

[26]Philip Pettit.

view. That is, the distinctive reasons that arise within it are not really reasons at all.

Moreover, the only candidates for living on in the onward rush of humankind are those who have completely abandoned the self-interested point of view and come to have the dispositions characteristic of *agape*. For *them*, the fact that there is a form of survival that does not preserve their *very own* individual personalities involves no great loss.

Recall the "epistemicism" about vagueness pressed by Roy Sorenson and by Timothy Williamson. They say that "bald" is our term and we are disposed to use it in certain ways, and as a result it comes to be associated with a definite concept that determines a definite property, call it P. Now it follows from classical logic that any head you might like to consider either has P or does not have P, whether or not we know it or can find it out. Now surely "personal identity" is our term, we Human Beings are disposed to use it in certain ways, and as a result it comes to be associated with a definite concept that determines a definite relation, call it R. Now there will be a fact, whether or not we know it, as to whether R holds across Teletransportation or not. So either the Human Beings or the Teletransporters or both will be wrong about personal identity. So there is no room for an evenhanded treatment of personal identity.[27]

Good. That argument brings out an assumption that does not clearly get a purchase in the present case. The assumption is that our concept of personal identity determines a definite relation, call it R, which *independently of the practical dispositions of the persons involved* either holds across Teletransportation or does not. That is, it ignores the possibility of a response-dependent parameter within the relation that is R. But the relevant relation R is the relation of being the same Protean person, and that does include a parameter within it that is set by our dispositions to identify.

Why postulate that sort of parameter in the case of "same person" and not in the case of "bald"? Once again, the postulation comes in the wake of a detailed error theory about our conception of personal identity. But second, although it may be somewhat plausible, at least given the global "epistemicist" response to vagueness, that alleged cases of indeterminacy with respect to bald are cases of investigation-transcendent facts, that is,

---

[27]Eden Lin.

that there might be no way even in principle to find out if a person within the region of indeterminacy is bald, the corresponding move in the case of personal identity is much less plausible. That is, it counts against a theory of personal identity that it treats matters like the survival of Teletransportation or deep sleep as investigation-transcendent.

Isn't "personal identity" our term, that is, the Human Beings' term, so that the Hibernators and the Teletransporters are not really focused on personal identity, but on something else?[28]

The fact is that there is a massive functional symmetry between what they care about when they look to their futures and what we care about when we look to ours. But as your remarks suggest, there is another way of proceeding here, which would leave everything the same as far as the conclusion goes. Call the relation of being the same Protean person the "P-like relation." An evenhanded treatment of the three communities might then consist in finding them each to be respecting the P-like relation. What we Human Beings have been calling "personal identity" is just an implementation of that relation. Considered in itself, it is no better an implementation than the other two implementations. Effects aside, it is no more rational to employ the one implementation rather than the other two. Once we see that, we can also see that what it is basically rational to care about in caring about survival is the holding of the P-like relation. (It does not matter that one implementation is called "personal identity" by us.) You should care about the holding of some implementation of this more general relation because it is an implementation of the more general relation.

Compare adopting the dispositional theory in the case of color, and then choosing between two ways of thinking of the color properties to which the birds are sensitive. On the first way of thinking, color properties are relative, where the relativity correlates with just which population's dispositions are in question. On the second way of thinking, the color properties are just the properties defined relative to *our* dispositions, and the birds are sensitive to "color-like" properties. Here is no great matter.

You have an argument against animalism, the view that persons are essentially self-maintaining organisms, that says that you cannot make a

---

[28] An audience member unknown to me.

person come into being by removing the flesh and bones of a body, and keeping the brain alive and functioning. Since the functioning brain then constitutes a person and is not a self-maintaining organism, the animalist must say that this remnant person has just come into existence or was doubled up all along with the organism who was a person. You take it that we know that this is not a way of making a new person, so that animalism is false. So why can't we just lay it down that waking up after there has been three months of sleep is not a way for a person to come into existence? The Hibernators are just wrong too.[29]

You might think that the self-styled "animalists" have chosen a poor name for their view. No one sensible denies that we are *predicatively* animals, that the predicate "is an animal" is true of us in our present dispensation. You get to be an animal by having a certain sort of body, and it is not a matter of serious dispute that we all now have the right sort of body to count as animals of a certain species. We are not plants, for example. The real issue is whether a person is identical with his or her body, and hence is essentially an animal. The animalists, if they are to have a distinctive position, will assert that we are identical with our bodies and hence are essentially animals. This implies that we cannot survive being reduced to the condition of a mere head or brain artificially kept alive and functioning. That would be the end of us, because it would be the end of our body. Animalism, at least when it admits that its natural opponents will all agree that we are, as presently constituted, animals, just seems to be the old view that a person is identical with his or her body or "human organism."

I therefore stick to the argument against animalism.[30] A brain or head artificially kept alive and functioning could be the organic locus of a person, a thinking reflective thing that can consider itself as itself at various times and places. But it is not a body or human organism, only an organ or body part, and so the person in question is not an animal. The animalist has no good account of this kind of "remnant person," and worse, he has no good account of *where that remnant person has come from.* We don't bring a person—a thinking reflective being—*of any sort* into existence by removing tissue, unless that tissue has been suppress-

---

[29] Sarah-Jane Leslie.
[30] As it occurs in "My Body is not an Animal."

ing an otherwise ready capacity for mental life. This principle seems to be plausible, given all that we know about how consciousness is realized. It is not a mere appeal to an intuition about a particular case.

That is why I did not consider a tribe of Animalists. I lack the relevant sympathies for their views, and so could not say that those views are sustainable even to the end of rational inquiry into the matter. But I have still some sympathy with the Hibernators, for total loss of consciousness is a very considerable subjective occurrence. We think of it as an intimation of death, but why should it not be simply, death, that is, ceasing to be? You can see why Descartes' view that we are always conscious even in sleep was not regarded as a strange view.

Still, at the end of the day, you may be right. I *would* ask a tribe of Animalists to take into account the facts about how a person does not come into existence simply by the removal of tissue, and if they did not and persisted in their ways I would not regard their way of organizing their concerns as in the end rationally defensible. So, perhaps as you say, I should regard the proposition that a person does not come into existence by waking up, or more exactly by becoming conscious in a body that has been unconscious, as just a fact, a fact about persons of any sort. Then the Hibernators cannot stick to their way of organizing their basic dispositions without neglecting certain facts about the restricted variety of ways in which a person can come into being. They would not then be an admissible example in the discussion that motivates the view that we are Protean.

There is an asymmetry between alternative putative implementations of personal identity that make for lives that are *less* expansive than the lives of Human Beings, as in the case of the Hibernators, and implementations of personal identity that make for lives that are *more* expansive than the lives of Human Beings, as in the case of the Teletransporters. We Human Beings are likely to find ourselves with convictions about which processes do not bring people into existence, convictions which if true will defeat the claim that the less expansive implementations are rationally defensible in the light of all the facts. But notice that the Teletransporters are not committed to strange claims about when persons come into existence. They may simply disagree with us about when people *continue* to exist, and hence about when people come to an end.

They *need not* deny our view that a completely new, fully conscious human animal and so a new human being can be created by processes like those happening at their receiving stations. They can recognize that a person could be made by running the receiving program on a design plan that is a pure invention and so is not extracted from anyone who got into a transmitting station. Still, they can consistently take themselves to be the higher-order person constituted by the human being who gets in and the distinct human being who gets out.

The basic disagreement between us and them about when people *continue to exist* is robust, that is, it can continue even as each community gets more and more responsive to the available facts. Unless, that is, each view comes to adopt the view that persons are Protean.

So all I really need to motivate the view that we are Protean is the rationally irresolvable dispute between the Human Beings and the Teletransporters, at least if resolution is conceived of as granting victory to one side. And, after all, that dispute, or a dispute just like it, has remained the central unresolved dispute in the philosophy of personal identity pretty much since its inception.

If I make this concession that the Hibernators are a sort of expository ladder that can be kicked away, then we need another condition on a pattern of identification if it is truly to be identity-determining, namely that it be admissible, that is, that it not imply that persons come into being in situations where *no person of any sort* comes into being. I have to say that sort of thing about the tribe of Animalists, anyway.

This still allows as admissible dispositions that are more expansive than those of the Human Beings, such as those of the good. Even given the extra constraint, they will count as identity-determining, that is, they will determine a specific implementation of the relation of personal identity.

Chapter Five

A New Refutation of Death

Let us begin with an anticipation of the central idea to be defended in this lecture. Here is John Stuart Mill on what he calls, after August Comte, the "Religion of Humanity":

> I am now speaking of the unselfish. Those who are so wrapped up in self that they are unable to identify their feelings with anything which will survive them, or to feel their life prolonged in their younger cotemporaries and in all who help to carry on the progressive movement of human affairs, require the notion of another selfish life beyond the grave, to enable them to keep up any interest in existence, since the present life, as its termination approaches, dwindles into something too insignificant to be worth caring about. But if the Religion of Humanity were as sedulously cultivated as the supernatural religions are (and there is no difficulty in conceiving that it might be much more so), all who had received the customary amount of moral cultivation would up to the hour of death live ideally in the life of those who are to follow them.[1]

In this lecture, our discovery that we are in a certain way Protean will be deployed to give *literal content* to Mill's metaphor of the unselfish living on in the lives of those who are to follow them.

Before we do that, let us survey the terrain we have already covered. We began with an ancient worry—which was tellingly reformulated by Kant—that a purely naturalistic understanding of death threatens the importance of goodness by severing even the generic connection between goodness and just desert, the very connection that goodness itself demands, not as a motive to be good but as a condition of moral coherence.

[1] John Stuart Mill, "The Utility of Religion," in *Three Essays on Religion* (Hackett, 1998), 119.

As Kant went on to note, given the naturalistic view of death, the good are left entirely unprotected from the brutal edge of human life, they are in constant danger of becoming fodder for the bad, and absent a system of real justice they will in effect be patsies, victims of the bad, because of their goodness. From this realistic view of human history, Kant was prepared to draw a dire conditional conclusion about morality, as when he writes in the *Lectures on Ethics,*

> We are obliged to be moral. Morality implies a natural promise: otherwise it could not impose any obligation upon us. We owe obedience only to those who can protect us. Morality alone cannot protect us.

If Kant is right here, and I believe he is, then given our commitment to a naturalistic view of death, we must not only make naturalistic sense of goodness being its own reward; we shall also have to see how that reward can be some kind of *protection.*

This would be an unbearable burden, were it not for the fact that the naturalistic understanding of death must be conditioned by certain dramatic surprises that await us in the philosophy of personal identity. Those surprises are:

There are no persisting selves worth caring about.

There are no independent justifiers of our future-directed self-concern.

The implementation of personal identity is a response-dependent matter, so that we are, in a certain way, Protean.

In the course of these last few lectures, a number of audience members have asked whether in defending these theses, I have in effect gone over to the views of Derek Parfit, despite my previous firm rejection of those views. The answer is no, and understanding why will be helpful in approaching our main argument.

A Comparison with Parfit

That there are no persisting selves worth caring about is a thesis I share with Derek Parfit, who arrives at it in a very different way. It would be better to say that we both share this thesis with the ancient Buddhist tradition. For the thesis that there are no persisting selves worth caring about is the general thesis of *anatta*, which is given importantly different twists by different schools of Buddhism. Parfit has tried in a number of places, and most famously in his very influential work *Reasons and Persons*, to use the doctrine of *anatta* to discredit the idea that persons matter.

He supposes, following certain schools of Buddhism, that when we look to what we call "our" futures, the only things worth caring about in caring about our survival are the future bundles of states and events that happen to be psychologically connected to our present mental lives. And in some moods, as when he defends what he calls the Extreme Claim, Parfit finds that not even these bundles are especially worth caring about.

Parfit's view comes in three stages. There is first a general line of argument from what he calls Reductionism about personal identity, the thesis that personal identity does not consist in the persistence of separately existing entities distinct from brains and bodies but rather in the holding of patterns of physical and psychological continuity. This first line of argument depends on what I once dubbed "the argument from below"; in effect it claims that since the value of something constituted in this way must be found entirely in what it consists in, the value of personal identity cannot outrun the value of the more particular continuities. But we can secure these more particular continuities without securing personal identity, so personal identity is not really what matters.

Parfit has a second line of argument to the conclusion that the more particular continuities are the things worth caring about. He claims that this is clearly so in certain strange cases, such as his Combined Spectrum in which personal identity seems vague, or at least turns on very slight underlying differences, and the case of fission, where we would be said to survive twice over but for an apparent entailment of the logic of identity. Parfit's strange cases can be psychologically, and I think rationally, quarantined behind this cordon sanitaire: They have never actually occurred, and if they were to occur, it would be more rational to adapt and extend our identity-based concern to such cases rather than completely junk it in favor of concern for the holding of the more particular relations of bodily and psychological continuity. We might think of our present reactions to Parfit's imagined cases as representing *an anticipation* of that adaptation and extension, and not as the revelation that identity is never what matters.[2]

Parfit still disagrees with that response to his second line of argument, and I hope to take up that disagreement elsewhere.[3] But more to the present point, Parfit's ingenious arguments from the strange cases are, of necessity, rather delicate, and so they admit of equally delicate responses and counterresponses.[4] That lies in the nature of the terrain, for the philosophy of personal identity is a very complicated subject. More than this, I have come to believe that Parfit's argument from his master case of fission can be entirely disabled, once we realize that anything capable of fission is already a higher-order individual, that is, one capable not only of variable but of multiple embodiment. Surviving twice over is only apparently at odds with the logic of numerical identity. The Tiger survives in Bengal and in North Africa. This is "twice over," since either lineage, occurring on its own, would have represented the whole of the continued existence of the Tiger.

Be that as it may. There remains the crucial disagreement between us over the status of persons, and of personal identity, in any rational ethical outlook. Parfit thinks, and this is the third distinctive element in his view, that talk of persons and personal identity is entirely dispensable in such an outlook, for all the relevant facts can be captured by a description of the underlying physical and psychological continuities.

As against the Parfitian position, unless we keep persons and personal identity in view, there will be little left for an ethical outlook to be an outlook *on*. This is because any reasonable ethical outlook must find a place for the central notion of an interest, something different from a mere whim, or even a desire. A desire is something an interest might make sense of, and typically only when some interest does make sense of a desire is that desire a source of reasons for others. The notion of

---

[2] For an elaboration of this point, see Mark Johnston, "Reasons and Reductionism," *Philosophical Review* 101 (1992). For copyright reasons much of the same material of this essay had to be reworked in a different form for J. Dancy's volume, *Reading Parfit* (Basil Blackwell, 1996), where it appears as "Human Concerns without Superlative Selves."

[3] See my "Human Concerns without Superlative Selves," Parfit's ninety-page reply at http://www.ammonius.com/, and my reply that will soon be posted there.

[4] See, e.g., D. K. Lewis, "Survival and Identity" and "Reply to Parfit," in his *Philosophical Papers*, vol. 1 (Oxford University Press, 1987), along with Ernest Sosa's probing examination of Parfit's position in "Surviving Matters," reprinted in R. Martin and J. Barresi, eds., *Personal Identity* (Blackwell, 2003).

something about a person's condition being a source of reasons for others is a foundational notion in the ethical domain, and so the notion of an interest is foundational in that domain. The paradigm bearers of interests are persons, and they have these interests in part because of who they are over time, because of the various ways in which their developing individual personalities encounter challenges and opportunities.

Mere short-lived bundles of beliefs and desires are not bearers of interests; interests arise only where there is a sense of an ongoing life to be lived or, in the last act, to be brought to an end. That is, interests arise within the lives of persons and, more specifically, within the lives of individual personalities. Such interests count as sources of reasons only if persisting individual personalities matter, and matter *as such*. Recall our earlier discussion of the important practical difference between the persistence of an individual personality and the acquisition of an excellent executor. But a persisting individual personality only matters in this way if the facts of personal identity matter.

The thing to see is that there can be such further significant facts of personal identity without those facts consisting in the persistence of souls, or the persistence of separately existing entities distinct from our brains and bodies, or the persistence of superlative selves, or indeed of the persistence of anything that would make the facts of personal identity independently justify our future-directed concern. Or so I said almost twenty years ago.

Several commentators, most notably Roy W. Perrett, have observed that in saying this, I was effect allying myself with the more conservative schools of Buddhism, which insist that the doctrine of *anatta* does not remove persons and personal identity from the landscape or make them merely verbal or conventional entities, which could be left out of a complete description of reality.[5] Parfit, however, accuses me of being bewitched by language, and insists that all talk of persons and personal identity could be left out of a complete description of reality. Thus he aligns himself with the more radical elaborations of the doctrine of *anatta*.

The issue between us comes most clearly into focus with Parfit's general argument from below, his argument that personal identity cannot

---

[5] Roy W. Perrett, "Personal Identity, Minimalism and Madhayamaka," *Philosophy East and West* 52 (2002). There Perrett also has some worthwhile things to say about Parfit's first reply to "Human Concerns without Superlative Selves."

distinctively matter; that is, it cannot matter more than what it consists in, on his view, the holding of facts about the underlying physical and psychological continuities.

For example, about the case of Teletransportation, Parfit writes,

[T]he fact

(a) that my replica will not be me

would just consist in the fact

(b) that there will not be physical continuity

and

(c) that, because this is so, R will not have its normal cause....

Since (a) would just consist in (b) and (c), I should ignore (a). My attitude should depend upon the importance of facts (b) and (c).[6]

Parfit then argues that since it cannot be important that R—the holding of relations of psychological continuity and connectedness—has its normal cause, the difference between my surviving and my merely having a replica cannot really matter. Hence personal identity cannot really matter.

I pointed out long ago that this form of argument, an argument that supposes that the importance of a fact is to be found in the facts in which it consists, is not in general reliable. For if it were, it would provide an all-too-quick argument from materialism to nihilism. Materialism is the view that all the facts consist either in facts about the paths of fundamental particles through space-time or in facts about the distribution of fundamental magnitudes over space-time. Considered in themselves, these facts about the paths of particles or the distribution of magnitudes do not matter. But then if we argue from below, if we accept the principle that the value or significance or importance of a fact must be found in the facts it consists in, it follows that nothing matters. This, I said, is not a proof of nihilism from materialism; it is a reductio ad absurdum of the general validity of the principle behind the argument from below. I concluded that there can be constituted facts whose value is not a simple sum or upshot of the value of the facts that constitute them. For the value

[6]Derek Parfit, *Reasons and Persons* (Oxford University Press, 1986), 285–86.

of the constituted facts can come from their place in our lives, and not just from their constituent facts. That is how it could be with the facts of personal identity. So, twenty years ago, I asked: Why in the case of personal identity could we not instead argue "from above"? Why not argue that what looks like a trivial difference between cases in which I survive and cases in which I don't survive can nonetheless acquire derivative significance precisely because it makes for a difference in what matters, namely personal identity?[7]

In saying that, I was not asserting the general validity of the argument from above. I was saying that there was as yet no reason to respect the argument from below in the case of personal identity.

Recently Parfit has published, as a prize essay on the Web site of the Ammonius Foundation, a ninety-page article, which is mostly concerned to resolve once and for all the differences between us. Parfit there accepts that the argument from materialism to nihilism is a bad one, and hence that the argument from below is not in general a good argument.

He then offers a few cases where he suggests that the relevant argument *from above* is unintuitive. Like others who have looked at these cases, and the ones he published earlier,[8] I find that they involve confounding variables that make it unclear whether it is the argument from above that is at fault. But in any event, the relevance of these cases is obscure to me, for I was not asserting the general validity of the argument from above.

What would be really helpful would be the articulation of a plausible criterion of when the argument from below is good and when it is not, a criterion that would separate off the case of inferring nihilism from materialism as a bad application of the argument from below. In his ninety-page reply, Parfit has now offered just such a criterion, advancing the debate beyond the previous standoff in which we found ourselves—where he says "Below" and I say "Above."

This is not just a local scholarly dispute about the soundness of certain arguments; it bears directly on just what form of the doctrine of *anatta* one should endorse. And that will have enormous practical consequences.

---

[7] Johnston, "Reasons and Reductionism."
[8] See Derek Parfit, "Why Our Identity Is Not What Matters," in R. Martin and J. Barresi, eds., *Personal Identity* (Blackwell, 2003).

Parfit's New Criterion

Parfit's new criterion, which I am inclined to accept, is that the argument from below only works when the equivalence between the constituted fact and the constituting facts *holds as a conceptual matter*. This certainly blocks the bad argument from materialism to nihilism, the argument we both agree is bad. For even if materialism, the claim that all the other facts are constituted by facts about fundamental particles or fundamental magnitudes, is true, it is obviously not a conceptual truth. It is a thesis only made tenable by the general drift of the empirical sciences. You could not have ruled it in, or out, by what was known in, say, 1405. It is a posteriori, that is, not determined as true by the way we use words or employ our concepts. No investigation simply into the way we use words or deploy our concepts could itself settle the truth of materialism.

The appeal of Parfit's new criterion is this. When a claim of constitution is made true by the way we use our words or by which concepts we deploy then *we surely have the option of using other words or other concepts*. And if we eschew the battery of concepts that just serve to describe the constitut*ed* facts, we can still fully describe the constitut*ing* facts, and our diminished description of the world will still be complete in one clear and important sense. It will as a conceptual matter fix all the facts, even those we could go on to describe using the battery of concepts we had set aside. Parfit's view is that since our diminished description of the world captures all the facts in this sense, it ought to capture everything that is important. For just by choosing to speak in a certain way, we cannot create things with distinctive value (other than certain speech acts or tracts).

Here, as usual, Parfit comes up with a nicely chosen example, the example of a copse. A copse, the dictionary tells us, consists of some small bushes or trees growing together. Before you knew of that dictionary equivalence, you could perfectly adequately describe the distribution of small bushes or tress. But you would not have counted the world as containing any copses. Still, even without employing the concept of a copse you would have captured all the facts about copses in your description, in a very strong sense of "capture," namely this sense—the dictionary definition of "copse" is enough to show your description of the distribution of small bushes and trees entails all the facts about copses. This is what Parfit means when he says that the truth of the claim that facts about copses consist in facts about the distribution of small trees and bushes is just a matter of how we use words.

In such a case, it does seem clear that an argument from above would be bootless; there could be no distinctive value in facts about copses that was not found in the constituent facts about trees and bushes and their arrangement. We could drop all talk about copses and still capture everything that is valuable about them at the level of the arrangement of trees and bushes.

So Parfit's criterion has it that the argument from below fails when the relevant claim of constitution is true not as a conceptual matter but true a posteriori—as in the case of materialism—and that the argument from below works when the relevant claim of constitution is true as a conceptual matter—as in the case of the copse.

To run the argument from above in the case of a copse *would be* to be bewitched by words or concepts; it would be to think that using a word or a concept could itself add something of distinctive value to the (non-literary) world.

Hence Parfit's suggestion that I am bewitched by words in holding onto the idea that personal identity can still matter, that is, still be a component of what it is rational to care about in caring about survival, even though there are no separately existing souls distinct from our brains and bodies.

As I say, I take it that Parfit has here clearly articulated the issue between us in a principled way. So I consulted various dictionaries in an attempt to find an entry like the following:

> Person, common noun: a person is a thing whose persistence through time just consists in the holding of various relations of psychological and/or physical continuity and not in the persistence of souls or entities capable of existing separately from bodies.

But to no avail, I am afraid.

That is, of course, unfair—in one way to Parfit's view and in another way to mine. It is unfair to my view because even if there were a dictionary entry of this sort, it would not follow that the case of persons is like the case of the copse. Many "dictionary definitions" are meant to be really informative; they are not intended as a priori equivalences, in the sense of equivalences understood by everyone competent with the term. In many cases, "dictionary definitions" are not nominal definitions, definitions of a word or concept, but characterizations of the thing or phenomenon picked out by the word or concept, where the characterization involves information known a posteriori, even if the a posteriori knowledge in question is ready to hand. This is a way in which dictionaries can be like very terse encyclopedias. The dictionary entry for "copse" is one kind of case, where the definition does look merely nominal; that is why it is helpful for Parfit's purposes.

On the other hand, to rely on the deliverances of dictionaries to exhaust the merely conceptual equivalences is unfair to Parfit's view. There may be things that are in a certain way a priori, in a certain way conceptual truths, that it is no part of the role of a dictionary to list. The equivalences provable in elementary logic may be an example.

In any case, what decisively settles the issue between Parfit and me is a fact ready to hand. Any claim like

> Facts about whether a person has persisted through a period of time wholly consist in facts about the holding of various relations of psychological and/or physical continuity

is obviously a posteriori if true. It cannot be known just thanks to reflection on our concepts and their relations. It does not hold just in virtue of our use of words. In fact, as Parfit himself repeatedly insists throughout the early sections of part 3 of *Reasons and Persons*, it comes, if it comes at all, in the wake of an empirically motivated rejection of what he calls the Cartesian View or Non-Reductionism about personal identity, the view that the persistence of persons consists in the persistence of souls or separately existing entities distinct from our brains and bodies.

That is just how it should be. Recall our review in the second lecture of the empirical material that bears on the question of whether there are souls capable of a distinct existence. It consisted in part of results from neurophysiology and from the study of ostensible out-of-body experiences. And even now, I dare say that the empirical question is not *entirely* closed. Against all the odds, the soul could come back into contention *if* certain postmortem out-of-body reports gave information that could only be gleaned from a certain "elevated" point of view, and the best explanation was that a person had left his material body to occupy that point of view.

This fact, that the existence or nonexistence of immaterial souls animating human bodies is an empirical matter, is a controlling point for the philosophy of personal identity. If there were souls, they would be strong pretenders to be things whose persistence, at least in part, makes for personal identity over time. That means that the correct way of filling out the right-hand side of the schema

x, existing at t, is the same person as y, existing at t, if and only if xSy

must result in a statement that is knowable only a posteriori, that is, in the light of our total empirical knowledge, and its bearing on the issue of immaterial souls. That is very bad news for those who rely simply on the a priori method of cases to determine the correct specification of S, as it might be in terms of bodily and/or psychological continuity. Our empirically uninformed imaginative reactions cannot be sufficient to determine the correct instantiation of the schema, the correct view about what the facts of personal identity consist in.

The a posteriori character of personal identity should be obvious so long as we do not fall into the temptation of treating the well-grounded empirical convictions of our culture circle as a priori, that is, available merely by sound reflection on our concepts. This is not bewitchment by words, but it is a sort of bewitchment nonetheless.

Thus, the case of personal identity obviously falls on the same side of Parfit's own divide as the case of materialism. It is precisely not like the case of the copse. Indeed, it may be that we arrive at the correct view about personal identity on grounds very similar to the grounds supporting materialism.

So Parfit should now agree that by his own lights, and by his own criterion, the argument from below does not apply in the case of personal identity, any more than it applies in the case of materialism.

This means that we can admit the doctrine of *anatta*, in the sense that there are no persisting souls or selves worth caring about, and yet still allow that personal identity and the persistence of individual personalities matter. These latter are not merely conceptual additions to a world that really would be the same without them.

Nor does the merely verbal or conceptual nature of personal identity follow from the fact that the implementation of personal identity is a response-dependent matter. That does not mean that personal identity is a creature of our concepts or beliefs; it means instead that certain of our dispositions select just which relation objectively holding in the world is the relevant concrete implementation of personal identity.

So Death Is Something to Us

The least revisionary or the most purely descriptive account of what it is rational to care about in caring about survival is a package deal consisting of

self identity, that is, the continued existence of the self one is

and

the persistence and flourishing of one's individual personality

where it is possible to have the first without the second, as in the cases of those who are psychologically reborn within a single life.

Relative to this package deal, personal identity is important because its continuing to hold is the practically necessary, and perhaps even the metaphysically necessary, way in which self identity can be secured.

The doctrine of *anatta,* in the sense defended here, does prompt a revision to this account. It is not rational to care about self identity, for there is no persisting self worth caring about. Indeed one's ownmost death is impossible, because radically undefined. (Recall the arguments of lectures two and three.) However, as we noted at the beginning of lecture four, this does not entail that there is no coherent first-personal way of privileging a particular person as me now, and then caring especially about him, his future, and his individual personality. I can focus on the person I *presently* find myself to be and reasonably privilege his weal and woe. And so I find Johnston here now; he is *now* the one at the center of this arena of presence. That means that Johnston is now presented in a special light, in a way that makes it *seem* rational to be especially concerned about him.

So we are left with a revised package deal. What it is rational to care about in caring about survival is a combination of personal identity, that is, the continued existence of the person one now is

and

the persistence and flourishing of one's individual personality

where, again, it is in principle possible to have the first without the second, as in the cases of those who are psychologically reborn within a single life. That is a surprising transformation, one we might rationally hope to avoid. But it is not as bad as death, the cessation of one's own existence, for it offers the possibility of developing a different individual personality in the time to come.

How much of the apparent rational appeal of the revised package is affected by the discovery that we are Protean, and that the implementation of personal identity is response-dependent? Those discoveries prompt a number of thoughts. First, what counts as survival is not something fixed in a uniform way by our natures as persons. For the kind of person we find at our respective centers can vary, depending on our identity-determining dispositions. Second, were we to have sufficiently inclusive identity-determining dispositions, we might reasonably have to contemplate what is in effect reincarnation within a single life; that is, we might reasonably anticipate a life in which a series of different individual personalities are exhibited by the person we are. Facing that prospect, there seems little rational appeal in privileging one's present individual personality over the others one can anticipate coming to have. Why rest so much on *this* individual personality, rather than the many others that the person that I am will come to exhibit? To be sure there is the bare possibility of a form of de se concern that is doubly indexed to the present, the concern for the person that I now am and the individual personality that he *now* is. But that seems rational only to the extent that one has a more general concern for the person one now is and for each of the individual personalities that person will come to have.

We therefore seem pushed to a further revision in our account of what it is rational to care about in caring about survival. One should want the doubly revised package, the package consisting of

personal identity, that is, the continued existence of the person one now is and

the flourishing of one's individual personalities, if many there be.

Recall the Teletransporters, who as a result of their practical freedom from disease have to deal with the tedium of extreme longevity. Every young Teletransporter is told not only that he is likely to have many jobs and marriages through his lifetime but that he is also likely to come to have different personalities at various stages of his long life. Faced with that prospect, doubly revised concern seems to be rational. It is rational to care about personal identity and one's present and future individual personalities. And this entails that it is rational to care about the continued existence of the person one now is.

The central ambition of these lectures is to meet the generic threat of death to the importance of goodness, in effect by making something of Socrates' hope "that there is something for us in death, and as was said of old, something better for the good than for the bad"—and to do this without recourse to supernaturalism. On any naturalistic view, death obliterates one's individual personality, so if there is something especially for the good in death, it might be that the loss of one's individual personality is less bad for the good than it is for those who are not good. The good must be better placed to face down death, even though their individual personalities are obliterated by death.

There is a further, more surprising possibility. Another thing that is better in death for the good may be found at the level of personal identity; the good survive death in a way that is not open to those who are not good.

My argument will be that reasonably good people are less attached to their own individual personalities; to the extent that they are good they care about the flourishing of individual personality as such, and they recognize that this is a likely outcome in many of the lives of those who will outlive them and be born after them. So the obliteration of their own individual personalities is less of a loss to reasonably good people. In this sense, a reasonably good person is more able to face down or overcome death.

But I shall also argue that if there are *really good* people, they are not only able to face down death, that is, face the obliteration of their own individual personality without feeling it to be a tragic loss, they are also able to literally survive death.

On Being Higher-Order

Given that we are Protean, each of us in principle has access to a higher-order identity. We can begin to make this higher-order identity vivid by accessing one of our available schemas for thinking about things, the schema of the higher-order individual. The clearest application of this general schema is in the case of species and in the case of word types.

The Tiger, along with the Lion, the Jaguar, the Snow Leopard, and the Leopard, is in the genus *Panthera*. That is to say that the Tiger is a sub-kind of the kind *Panthera*. *Panthera*, in its turn, is a sub-kind of the family Cat. So the Tiger is a kind of Cat. As it happens, the Tiger is also the mascot of Princeton University. Being the mascot of Princeton University, the Tiger is depicted by kitsch Princetoniana, the paraphernalia of football games, reunions, and other alumni events.

The same could not be said of the property something has to have in order to be a Tiger, to wit, Tigerhood. Tigerhood is not a kind of Cat. Tigerhood is not the mascot of Princeton University. (How weak would that be, having a *property* as a mascot?) Kitsch Princetoniana includes cuddly little Tiger dolls, but no cuddly little property dolls. (What on earth would they be like?)

The Tiger is an endangered species and could become extinct. That would involve there ceasing to be examples of that kind of Cat. But the property Tigerhood is not the sort of thing that could become extinct. Even though a property could cease to be had by anything, no amount of environmental neglect could make a property extinct. Yet it would be a ludicrous argument against the effort to preserve species to point out that the corresponding properties will always be with us.

It appears that the Tiger came into existence in northern Asia during the Pleistocene epoch. Nevertheless, the property Tigerhood did not come into existence in northern Asia in the Pleistocene epoch. Properties just exist; they do not exist at some times and not others, so they do not come into being. Unless, that is, they are properties that have temporal individuals somehow built into them, such as the property of Being Napoleon. Perhaps the property of being a member of the kind Tiger *could* be said to have come into existence when the kind Tiger came into existence, but that property is obviously not the kind Tiger.

The Tiger moved from northern Asia to Bengal, although no first-order individual tiger made the whole journey. Neither Tigerhood nor the property of being a member of the kind Tiger moved from northern Asia to Bengal. Properties don't move, and not because they are immobile in the ordinary way. Yet, move is precisely what the Tiger did.

Further to the difference between kinds and properties, the Tiger propagates by sexual reproduction; its litter usually consists of six or seven cubs. And no property has a litter or propagates itself by sexual reproduction. Properties are somehow above that sort of thing. It lies in their nature to be chaste.

That last argument may be cute; but for semantic reasons, it can be resisted. Someone might say that the truth that the Tiger propagates by sexual reproduction is the same truth as is expressed by the bare plural

Tigers propagate by sexual reproduction

which only commits us to the existence of tigers, not to the existence of the kind Tiger, something that then is shown not to be a property by the fact that no property goes in for sexual reproduction.

Just so, there may be something in that idea. The best way to argue for the existence of kinds distinct from their corresponding properties is to concentrate on what linguists call "D-generics," generics whose predicates can only be truly predicated of a kind and not its members, and then observe that those predicates cannot be truly predicated of the corresponding properties either. Here are examples of true "D-generics," which would do the work we need done.

The Dinosaur is extinct.
The Blue Whale was recently placed on the endangered species list.
The Pit Bull is the most vicious of the dog breeds.
The Koala is scattered throughout the temperate regions of Australia.
Last year, the Kangaroo destroyed a hundred thousand miles of fencing.

Because there are true D-generics like these, we need to recognize that we are referring to kinds in a good deal of our informed thought and talk. Considering the range of true D-generics, we can also see that species like the Tiger have their own distinctive spatio-temporal path and profile. They come into existence at a certain place and time, they move across distances that none of their examples could cover, they survive for longer periods of time than any of their examples, and they are in danger of going extinct. These facts suggest that we should conclude that a species like the Tiger is a higher-order individual, an individual constituted at different times by different "first-order" individual tigers, or different populations of individual tigers.

Whenever you are in the presence of an individual tiger, you are in the presence of the species. "Look son, here is the Tiger, it is found in Bengal." Individual tigers are examples of their species; they stand to it in roughly the way that a word token stands to a word type.

That is another case of what I have in mind. Whenever you are in the presence of a word token, the word type is also there. Consider this blackboard pattern, which I once had to erase before my own class.

A TYPE AND TWO TOKENS
THE
THE

Philosophers say that there are three things, indeed three words, there below the title, two word tokens and one word type. The third word, the one doubly exemplified, came into existence at a certain time and entered the English language at a later time. It may one day fall into disuse. None of those remarks can sensibly be reconstructed as being only about tokens of the word, at least within the constraints of equivalence provided by the science of linguistics.

Let us consider one more example, closer to the terrain of personal identity.

The Clone

When we philosophers teach bioethics and cloning comes up, we have a standard way of dealing with the initial, "naive" reaction that the clone is the original person again, so that cloning is a form of continued existence for the original person. We patiently explain the distinction between matching similarity and numerical identity; between having your intrinsic properties in common and being one and the same item. The signs at airport luggage carousels warn, "Many suitcases are identical." This warning can be true only in the first sense of matching; obviously the many very similar token suitcases cannot be numerically one and the same token suitcase. Cloning, we then say, is at best a form of delayed twinning; and identical twins are two and not one. After all, here is the one twin, and there is the other twin; they are wearing different clothes, they are thinking different thoughts, they have different bodies. They are two. Therefore, they are not one! So we say.

With all that said, there remains the possibility that there is still something naive in our "sophisticated" response. Having our students imagine cloning may have activated their schema for conceiving of higher-order individuals, in effect leading them to think of the original person as having a higher-order identity, one that allows a person to be embodied by different human organisms at different times, and at some times by two or more different organisms, as when one is cloned twice.

It raises the question of whether the ban on cloning works to prevent the continued existence of people who might survive as clones.

The Phoenix

In further defense of the existence of the psychological schema of the higher-order individual, I turn to a famous mythical case. This is the case of the Phoenix. The Phoenix is first mentioned by Herodotus as a fabled bird of Egypt. Four hundred years later, the myth reaches its canonical form in Ovid's *Metamorphoses*, a collection of stories about the preservation of the identity of animals, men, and gods through radical changes in form. *The Metamorphoses* thus concerns itself with stories of identity over time, stories that significantly stretch, but do not quite break, our schemas for tracing individuals. As far as I can discern, in telling his stories and constantly flirting with the physically impossible, Ovid never forces anything conceptually incoherent upon us.

As it happens, Ovid reserves a special place for the story of the Phoenix, a story told, most suitably, by a character called the Philosopher. The Philosopher's prologue makes the familiar Ovidian point.

> Nothing retains the shape of what it was,
> And Nature, always making old things new,
> Proves nothing dies within the universe,
> But takes another being in new forms.

What is called birth is change from what we were,
And death the shape of old left behind.
Though all things melt or grow from here to there,
Yet the same balance of the world remains.
How many creatures walking on this earth
Have their first being in another form?

But then the Philosopher adds something new to the ubiquitous theme of *The Metamorphoses*.

Yet one exists that is itself forever,
Reborn in ageless likeness through the years.
It is that bird Assyrians call "the Phoenix,"
Nor does he eat the common seeds and grasses,
But drinks the juice of rare, sweet-burning herbs.
When he has done five hundred years of living
He winds his nest high up a swaying palm
And delicate dainty claws prepare his bed
Of bark and spices, myrrh and cinnamon
And dies while fire lifts his soul away.
Then from his breast—or so the legend runs
A little Phoenix rises over him,
To live, they say, the next five hundred years.[9]

The object of the myth or legend is thus made quite clear. The fabled Phoenix is not a species of bird that happens to have a strange method of reproduction by means of self-immolation; the Phoenix is a bird that exists forever, or at least for a very long time, "*reborn* in ageless likeness through the years." The Phoenix is not a property or universal; it is a higher-order bird, a bird variably constituted by different first-order birds at different times, as it might be Phoebe, Phoenicia, Photion, and Pho on and Pho forth.

That this is the proper understanding of the Phoenix is evidenced by its role in medieval law, in particular by the way it was used to explain the institution of the *corporation sole*, a long-lived, variably constituted

---

[9]From *The Metamorphoses* by Ovid, trans. Horace Gregory (Viking Press, 1958), 425–26.

entity distinctive among corporations in being constituted only by a single person at any given time. The Phoenix's role in providing an analogy for the corporation sole is incompatible with understanding it as a universal or a property potentially had by many things. A corporation sole is not like that at all.[10]

The British monarch is a corporation sole, with Elizabeth Windsor as its present occupant or embodiment. The monarch has certain prerogatives, which Elizabeth Windsor exercises on its behalf, and not her own, and certain property (such as the Crown Jewels) she uses for its sake, but does not own. I have heard it argued that in the utterance "The monarch is dead, long live the monarch," the first title refers to the recently deceased embodiment of the monarch and the second to the ongoing corporation sole.

Of course, the British monarch differs from the Phoenix in a number of ways. Those who come to embody that institution have an earlier life during which they did not embody it; and the changing of the guard is usually less spectacular than in the case of the Phoenix.

In the interests of full disclosure, I should admit that the Phoenix is the totem animal of the ancient Johnston clan of Caskieben, and the clan's associated motto is "Vive ut postea vivas," a rough translation of which is "Live now so that you will live again in the future." The eerie thing is that I found this out while revising these lectures for publication. I knew nothing of this when I first presented the Phoenix as a way to introduce the possibility of a higher-order existence.

Truth *is* stranger than fiction.

How Could a Mere Bird Survive as the Phoenix Does?

Suppose one particular first-order bird in the sequence that constitutes the Phoenix, say, Phoebe, had learned of the story of the Phoenix and so wanted to be immortal, or at least as long-lived as the Phoenix, the second-order bird of which Phoebe is an example. How might it do that?

There is no hope of Phoebe becoming identical with the Phoenix. The Phoenix predates Phoebe. But perhaps Phoebe can become Phoenix-

---

[10]See Ernst Kantorowicz, *The King's Two Bodies: A Study in Medieval Politics and Theology* (Princeton University Press, 1997), for the relevant history of the corporation sole and the myth of the Phoenix as its analogy.

Vive Ut Postea Vivas

like, even though Phoebe, at the very least, *starts out* as a particular avian organism. A mere *bird* is stuck with that. Still, if we pretend that Phoebe is also an embodied self-consciousness with no superlative self to fix its temporal boundaries, then we may suppose that Phoebe, like us, is Protean. Phoebe, when taken to be a person, is not necessarily stuck with her original constitution as one particular avian organism.

Imagine, then, that Phoebe radically identifies with the genuine interests of the first-order birds that embody the Phoenix at different times. As it were, it loves the other birds as it loves itself. It treats their anticipatable interests and needs as it treats it own, as default starting points in its practical reason. In this way, it comes to see the first-order bird that it once found at its center as merely one bird among many, all equally deserving of future-directed concern. It comes to care for that first-order bird as just another bird, one whose interests just happen to present in a particularly immediate way. It comes to organize its identity-determining dispositions not around the relation of being the same first-order bird, but around the relation of being the same bird sequence. So it then survives whatever the Phoenix survives. It is now a thing that will be present wherever and whenever the Phoenix is present.

But again, Phoebe is not the Phoenix. Phoebe's essence is not the essence of some essentially second-order bird. It is instead the Protean essence of an embodied self-consciousness, an essence that has Phoebe survive any event that is not at odds with the holding of the relation around which it is then organizing its identity-constituting dispositions.

You might say that Phoebe comes to be Phoenix-like in that it comes to be constituted by a series of birds over time, a series of birds that is itself part of the history of the Phoenix. Before Phoebe refigures its concerns and expectations it is constituted by a particular avian organism; afterward it is variably constituted by a series of different avian organisms.

This is *anastasis*, the raising up of one's identity to that of a higher-order entity. So, if there are beings with Protean identities they are capable of *anastasis*, that is, they are capable of coming to be variably constituted by a series of different individuals over time.

This is how examples of the Phoenix, as it might be Phoebe, Phoenicia, and Photion, can piggyback on the longevity of the Phoenix. Notice that this possibility did not require the Phoenix itself to be anything other than a second-order bird, a bird wholly constituted by a series of birds. We need not think of the Phoenix as any kind of higher or deeper self. In fact all we need is the series of birds itself.

Suppose the next bird, Phoenicia, follows Phoebe in identifying with all subsequent birds in the sequence. Then Phoenicia, too, will come to be variably constituted by a series of different birds. Still, Phoebe and Phoenicia will be distinct higher-order individuals. They will differ in their original constitution. Phoebe will have been originally constituted by the bird she could easily have mistaken herself for, the bird that came before Phoenicia, the bird we lazily called "Phoebe." That was lazy because Phoebe is not identical with that bird but only originally constituted by it. For as we now are assuming, Phoebe is person. And no person is identical with an organism. There is a substantial and interesting account to be had of just when an organism gets to be the embodiment of a person.

So far, we have only told a consistent story, about a self-conscious bird, that is, a person who is (first) embodied as a bird, a particular avian organism. The question is whether there is an interesting case of *anastasis* available for us.[11]

Could we, for example, come to be one of those things that will be present wherever and whenever human organisms with their associated individual personalities are present?

In asking whether we could come to survive as a person variably constituted by different organisms or bodies, by refiguring our basic disposition, I do not mean to suggest that our basic disposition is under the direct control of our wills. I do not mean to suggest that Phoebe could just get up and decide to have the coordinated and unmediated disposition to absorb the anticipatable legitimate interests of any future bird that descends from it in the characteristic way. That kind of disposition is not under the short-term control of the will; for it is in part constitutive of the will, at least if we understand the will as a particular disposition to a style of practical reasoning and to the performance of actions that follow from that practical reasoning.

Nonetheless, one's basic practical dispositions can change as a result of self-examination, modeling, and training. The process is more like becoming an extraordinary pianist than like choosing to see things a certain way.

So far, we only have the abstract possibility of "re-incorporating" oneself so as to be constituted by a sequence of organisms or bodies. But as the case of a species brings out, higher-order individuals admit not only of variable constitution over time but also of multiple constitution at times.

Is *that* a possibility for a Protean person?

TELEPORTERS OFTEN "MISFIRE"

I should say that I have been holding something back from you in my account of the Teletransporters. The shocking fact is that their receiving stations have never worked properly, and rather than fix this "problem" the Teletransporters have just organized their life around it.

[11] Nothing, of course, should be read into the fact that this Greek word *anastasis* that is so well suited for describing the process of assuming a higher-order identity is the word used by Paul in his epistles to describe the resurrection.

The embarrassing "problem" is one of duplication. All invariably goes well at the transmitting station: one individual steps in, all the information about his brain and body is recorded, and in the recording process the brain and body are destroyed, nearly instantaneously and certainly painlessly. The problem happens at the receiving station. Often two individuals, each with a brain and body that duplicate the original, step out.

Each remembers the original's experiences, and each has the same orientation toward the future. The practical complications are enormous, for each is prepared to take over the original's whole place in the world—his spouse, his family, his friends, his job, his relationships, his wardrobe, his checking account. The Teletransporters have managed to adjust to this sort of outcome. They use bigamy as the model on the personal side and divorce as the model on the financial side. That is, to deal with such cases they employ a combination of time-sharing and splitting of assets.

They do this not just to resolve practical problems but because they have come to regard duplication as providing the original person with a *multiple* embodiment at a later time, in the fashion of a higher-order individual such as a word type or a species.

So whereas one-one Teletransportation provides variable embodiment over time, in the fashion of the Phoenix, one-many Teletransportation provides for multiple embodiment over time. A single higher-order individual who was constituted by the original human organism comes to be constituted by two human organisms.

Don't say that this higher-order individual is not a person. As it happens, a Teletransporter is disposed to immediately identify with the anticipatable interests of each of the potential products of his Teletransportation. The Teletransporters thus organize their future-directed concerns and expectations around a relation that holds throughout the life of a higher-order individual. *That* is how they actually implement the relation of personal identity, the relation of being the same Protean person.

As a result, a Teletransporter survives fission twice over, *and with no violation of the one-one logic of numerical identity.* There is a single person who is around before and after; the only thing is that afterward that person is doubly embodied—he is constituted by two human organisms, which will diverge psychologically with the passage of time.

Policing the Dispositions

One of the few gifts of aging is a growing detachment from one's own individual personality. The Teletransporters live a very, very long time. They have overcome disease, but not aging, so that the oldest Teletransporters disappear like old soldiers; they fade away. As a result, when it comes to preserving their identity as Teletransporters, many of the very old Teletransporters have a certain psychological problem. For it is hard, after living for many centuries, for a Teletransporter to maintain an intense proprietary attachment either to his individual personality or to his type of individual personality. Very old Teletransporters find themselves caring more and more for individual personality as such and for their own individual personalities merely as examples of it. So with time, their identity-implementing dispositions generalize and drift.

The worst cases exhibit the following psychological syndrome.

1. *Practical absorption of all future interests.* They have an indiscriminate disposition to absorb the anticipatable legitimate interests of *any present or future person* into their present practical outlook, so that they are presently disposed to promote those interests.

2. *Coordination of the disposition.* The relevant disposition is not a mere disposition to absorb the future interests of any given person as he is at some future time; the disposition is wedded to the person whenever and wherever they take that person to exist. The relevant dispositions go far beyond the products of episodic whims, or even of adopted projects.

3. *Non-mediation of the disposition.* The disposition is in a certain way unmediated; it does not depend for its felt intelligibility on an antecedent liking or admiration of the future person in question, and not on the holding of some special relation like sharing the same token or type of individual personality. Nor is identification in the relevant sense mediated by an antecedent value judgment to the effect that the person in question is particularly good or worthy or important. The disposition extends even to people they find dull and repellent.

The philosophically informed among the Teletransporters understand just what this syndrome amounts to. For they understand that persons are Protean, and hence that the common identity around which the Tele-transporters have built their life is profoundly threatened by this general-ization of the crucial dispositions. After all, the victims of the syndrome bid fair to live on *whenever and wherever an individual personality is found*. And if this is widely known, others may come to regard Teletrans-portation as a snare that actually occludes one's wider possibilities for survival. In its turn, this realization might well undermine the mission-ary effort among the Human Beings. (Recall the weeklong boot camp with its endless lectures on personal identity.) After all, there are many Human Beings who also feel a certain detachment from their individual personalities. Why should they refigure their fundamental dispositions in the fashion of the Teletransporters when an even more inclusive iden-tity is available to them?

So the Teletransporters set about policing the dispositions of the old; they try in various ways to intensify the attachment of old Teletransport-ers to their individual personalities. They ban the performance of plays and operas that depict the tedium of extreme longevity. *The Makropolis Case* and *The Flying Dutchman* are among the most stigmatized. None of this works very well.

Finally, those who would police the dispositions of the old discover a more effective psychological technique. The victims of the syndrome have another, related, characteristic; in the battle between their individ-ual personalities and the world they have come more and more to take the side of the world. This is in part because they have noticed that a single individual personality is not suited to survive and flourish in the face of certain large-scale defects that are an essential part of being in the world. "But what if," the policers ask, "we were to advertise another world entirely free of these defects, in which each individual personality could continue to thrive, and do so forever? A Teletransporter can enter this world after death, so long as he has been virtuous in the ways of the Teletransporters. Might that not be a marvelous way to cement people in their attachment to their individual lives, thereby suppressing the ten-dency to generalize the crucial dispositions?"

The policers try this, and it works very well, at least for those who have not yet acquired the syndrome. In this way, the policers preserve the distinctive identity of the Teletransporters. But they do it at the cost of suppressing something very close to goodness.

THE POINT OF THE ALLEGORY

All that was philosophical allegory, employed to illustrate that a certain conception of the dispositions characteristic of the good, when wedded to our thesis that persons are Protean, would count the good as living on in the onward rush of humanity.

A person comes into being in the usual way, he is embodied by a particular human organism, and his fundamental dispositions develop over time, along with the development of his individual personality. But if that person becomes good, that is, if his practical outlook is an expression of *agape*, then he becomes generally embodied; his constitution is made up of the constitution of all present and future beings with interests. This is how, when death brings the destruction of his initial individual personality, he continues on in the onward rush of humanity.

Overlap in constitution does not make for identity. The Reptile and the Bird are higher-order individuals that partly share their constitution, for example, in those dinosaurs that are both reptiles and birds. But the Reptile and the Bird are distinct higher-order individuals, for they otherwise differ in their constitution.

Likewise the good are not one, but many. Though each good person is partly embodied by all the human organisms that embodied the others who lived with him and after him, each good person has a distinct human organism as his or her initial embodiment.

Suppose that somewhere in the world there has once been a good person. He is now partly embodied by the human organism that embodies you. Still, that does not make him identical with the person you are. Suppose that you firmly stick to selfishness, so that the only anticipatable future interests that you can incorporate as default starting points in your practical reasoning remain fundamentally those of your first and only individual personality. Then you will cease to exist when the human organism that embodies you dies. If there ever has been a good person, his extensive future embodiment is not threatened by this limitation in your embodiment. He is not identical to you. He is temporarily embodied by the human organism that also embodies you. He is generically reincarnated in the onward rush of humanity, and you are not.

WHAT IS A GOOD WILL?

Here, then, is our first pass at characterizing what it is to be a good person, and why the good are in a position to survive death. A good will is a certain kind of fundamental disposition manifested in one's style of practical reasoning and action. More specifically, a good will is a disposition to absorb the legitimate interests of *any* present or future individual personality into one's present practical outlook, so that those interests count as much as one's own. A good will is likely to find the present interests of the person whose will it is to be more accessible and vivid than the interests that are more remote in time and space. But it does not treat those more remote interests as less weighty or significant.

Having a good will is thus utterly at odds with seeking premium treatment for oneself. A good person has come to see himself as one among the others, all of whose legitimate interests count equally.[12]

As a first pass, then, we could say that a good will is a disposition to absorb the legitimate interests of *any* present or future person into one's present practical outlook, so that those interests count as much as one's own. Of course, the very specific interests of remote and future individuals will be unknown to the good person, just as his own remote future interests will not be accessible in all their specific detail. But there are generally predictable, legitimate interests that future persons will have, interests in having the psychological and material resources required for the development and flourishing of their individual personalities, and those of their family, friends, and familiars. In his practical reasoning about the remote present and the future, a good person focuses on these interests.

Moreover, when it comes to presently existing individual personalities that he encounters and gets to know, the good person is disposed to treat their specific interests, where they are legitimate, as on a par with his own. This disposition is not limited in its scope to those he actually encounters and gets to know, as is shown by the fact that as that group expands over time, the disposition gets engaged in each new case. Indeed this is the basis for attributing to the good person an *open-ended* disposition, one not restricted to the interests of those known by or even

---

[12]Here I am echoing Thomas Nagel's remarks about altruism in *The Possibility of Altruism.*

contemporaneous with the good person. The disposition a good person actually exhibits is indefinitely extended in its scope. It is a disposition to absorb the legitimate interests of *any* present or future personality into his present practical outlook, so that those interests count as much as his own.

Is Goodness Bounded?*

That is one conception of goodness. But here is another, naturally associated with the idea that the dispositions that constitute goodness are a rationally driven generalization of the dispositions that originally made for *reciprocal* altruism. A person may be very good, but his disposition to incorporate in his practical reasoning the interests of others as on a par with his own may manifest a certain bound, even when it comes to those around him. For he may be convinced that among those around him are people who are irredeemably closed to goodness, people incapable of allowing the interests of others to truly permeate their own practical reasoning unless that serves their own interests. How he becomes convinced of this, and whether he is right to be convinced, does not matter. What matters is that he is not disposed to incorporate into his own practical reasoning the interests of those irredeemably closed to goodness. When he believes another is of this sort, his benevolence does not extend to them. He nonetheless supports and would fight for juridical and political equality for such people; but as he sees them, they are so irredeemably wrapped up in themselves that they do not deserve the *special* solicitude of those who have turned toward others. He thereby manifests a bounded disposition to practically incorporate the interests of others. Why is this kind of disposition not representative of a good will?

Now, as a matter of fact, I believe that it may be almost always morally wrong to view any specific living person as irredeemably closed to the good. But that is not the point here. One might have the bounded disposition, without the bound ever actually constraining one's benevolence, precisely because one took it to be morally wrong to view any person in this way. Our question is another one entirely. Is the good will better represented by the unbounded or by the bounded disposition?

How could one get a purchase on such a question? Recall the plausible Kantian thought, appealed to in lecture one, that a good will cannot be a practically irrational will, not even conditionally. That is, a person with a good will ought to be able to rationally maintain that will as the disposition it is, in the face of learning any relevant fact. This thought provided one route to understanding how death (and life's other large-scale structural defects) might threaten the importance, and perhaps even the coherence, of goodness. (Recall Kant's remarks about Spinoza.)

This Kantian thought will inevitably interact with the radical reversal and its consequences. For if persons are Protean then a good will plays a certain selective role in determining which implementation of the relation of personal identity governs the conditions of survival of the person with that good will. The selective effects of a good will on the conditions of survival of the person whose will is in question is now a highly relevant fact. Can such a will maintain itself, without irrationality, in the face of *that* fact?

The onward rush of humanity may not present a wholly pleasing prospect to the good. It would be rational for a good person to find repugnant the prospect of partly sharing the embodiment of those that are irredeemably closed to the good. This suggests that it is the bounded, not the unbounded, disposition that better represents the good will. Construing the good will as the unbounded disposition leads to paradox, in this way.

1. A good will is an unbounded disposition, a disposition to absorb the legitimate interests of *any* present or future personality into one's present practical outlook, so that those interests count as much as one's own.
2. A person with a good will ought to be able to rationally maintain that will as the disposition that it is in the face of learning any relevant fact.
3. Persons are Protean.
4. There will be individual personalities who remain so locked in their selfishness that they are irredeemably closed to the good. (Asserting this true *general* premise is not morally wrong.)
5. The prospect of partly sharing the embodiment of those that are irredeemably closed to the good is rationally repugnant to a person with a good will. That is, he cannot will that he come to have such embodiments, or will the means to coming to have such embodiments, without irrationality.

6. But given that persons are Protean, the very disposition that we are taking to constitute a good will involves willing the means to coming to have such embodiments.

7. In learning this fact, a person with a good will cannot maintain that will as the disposition that it is, short of irrationality, that is, short of willing a means to an end he rationally finds repugnant.

Here we have a contradiction as between 2 and 7, a contradiction to be blamed on 1.

This means that instead of thinking of the good as living on in the onward rush of humanity, we should think of them as living on with those that are not closed to goodness.[13]

THE DISPOSITIONS OF THE GOOD

Humankind, someone said, is the species that distinguishes itself from the Wolf by being a wolf unto itself. If that seems harsh or overstated, we need only review the atrocities of the last century, atrocities that we, as a species, now seem poised to outdo. To some extent the worst of what has happened has been the product of thoroughly evil wills swept into positions of enormous power by circumstance and by their own demonic determination. But their collaborators have been many, and these were in the main ordinary people driven to collaborate by no more than concrete variations on the motive of seeking premium treatment for themselves in straightened and competitive circumstances. This aspect of the banality of evil, the ordinariness of those who collaborate with evil, and the ordinariness of the motives that led them to collaborate, suggests that was something in Kant's dark view that we are "radically" or naturally evil. In claiming this Kant meant that by nature we are disposed to seek premium treatment for ourselves, and so by nature we are potential enemies of each other and of goodness. (Perhaps a crucial part of that natural condition is the immediate affective sense of evaluative asymmetry, as between HERE and THERE, given in an arena of presence, so that the fact that we are naturally evil is in part due to an illusion built into the structure of self-consciousness.)

Kant held that although we are naturally evil, we are not bad to the

---

[13]Others may contemplate more restrictive bounds on the dispositions of the good, bounds forced by stronger variants on premise 5, but this is as far as I am prepared to go here.

bone; we can acquire good wills. The survey of history that makes humanity look worse than the wolves may also seem to count against this claim. But it is a biased survey; it is a survey of battles, fraudulence, and betrayal, a survey of kings and queens, of presidents and dictators, of nation-states, and of powers and principalities. None of that would be possible without something the survey omits—a recurrent part of human history, which although miraculous makes for much less memorable stories. I mean the collective miracle of the nurturance of the young of our species, who begin life so pathetically dependent and remain that way for so long. Who can fail to be astonished at the enormous amount of distributed good will required to provide them with the material and psychological resources that gives them a chance to develop flourishing individual personalities. This, combined with the fact that there are flourishing individual personalities, moves Jonathan Lear to conclude that the human world is, as he puts it, a *good enough* world. Despite our recurrent failure to love, the fact that we are to some degree psychologically stable individuals testifies to the existence of an enormous fund of good will that helped nurture us.[14]

The good, I would argue, have a collective interest in making the human world a *better* world, a world in which it is easier for individual personalities to become open to goodness. Among other things, in working for this, they are determining the quality of their future embodiment.

The good have a collective interest in making history be in part the history of the improvement of human dispositions in the direction of increasing openness to the good. It is not very mysterious how that interest is addressed in practice: attend to the nurturing of children, meet basic needs, offer reasonable ideals of goodness, create a sense of shared fate embodied in a sustainable scheme of distributional justice.

How Does "I" Work, If We Are Protean?

All this talk of shared embodiment may encourage the thought that our identities will get thoroughly confused if persons are Protean and some

---

[14]See his brilliant work, *Love and Its Place in Nature* (Yale University Press, 1999). And philosophical discussion of the theme of natural hope, utterly important if there is ever to be such a thing as a naturalistic discussion of salvation, cannot but take Lear's *Radical Hope: Ethics in the Face of Cultural Devastation* (Harvard University Press, 2006) as a master text.

people have had a genuinely good will. How, for example, does "I"-thought work in such a circumstance?

The use of "I" at a given time is best understood as picking out the person at a given center at that time. As we have seen, this is partly a revisionary doctrine, since many uses of "I" in thought would have been best understood as directed at persisting selves worth caring about, if there were such things.

So, we are left with a construal of "I"-use as picking out persons at given centers of arenas or consciousnesses, even though the persistence of such arenas or consciousness is just the persistence of merely intentional objects.

But once we take the view that many persons may be embodied by the body or organism whose brain functioning is responsible for the appearance of an arena and its center, how do we tell *which* person to count as *at* the relevant center?

The least revisionary proposal is to take it to be the person whose conditions of survival are determined by the dispositions that have their material basis in the human organism in question, that is, the human organism whose brain functioning is responsible for the appearance of the relevant arena and center. For that is the person who appears at the center.

So the person that I am is the person at this center, and that person is the one whose present conditions of survival are determined by the present dispositions that have their material basis in this human organism or body, namely the *H.M.S. Johnston*. So I am the person Johnston, even if others are also partly embodied by the *H.M.S. Johnston* and have their present ethical condition partly expressed by Johnston's individual personality.

However, it now appears that I no longer have the only urgent interest in the ethical quality of that individual personality! All the good that there have ever been share my present constitution as part of their constitution and must suffer my individual personality as part of the expression of their present ethical condition. (Unless . . .)

SELF-OWNERSHIP AND THE INTERESTS OF THE GOOD*

A number of theorists in ethics have remarked on the importance of the idea of "self-ownership," the conviction, as I would express it, that this body and individual personality are mine and mine alone, and hence that I have a special proprietary interest in their development, flourishing, and general comportment, even unto death.[15] This means that another cannot own me; another cannot legitimately exercise fundamental control over my body and individual personality. Perhaps it also means that I have a *pro tanto* right to obliterate this body and individual personality when their continued existence have become intolerable to me.

However, the view that because this body and individual personality are *mine* I therefore have a proprietary right in them and their development and comportment can now be seen to bundle together two different claims. These claims pull in different directions.

The first is the claim that the person that I am has a proprietary right over how things go with this body and individual personality.

The second is that a person who is now embodied by this body, which gives rise to and maintains this individual personality, has a proprietary right over how things go with this body and individual personality.

Each of these two claims articulates a plausible ground for the feeling of self-ownership. But they are distinct claims, and distinct grounds. The first ground has to do with a person's legitimate interest in not having his control over his body and the development of his individual personality interfered with by the actions of others. The second ground has to do with a person's legitimate interest in the ethical aspect of his embodiment, an interest in what kind of individual personality comes to be associated with the body that makes him up.

In effect, we all had been taking it that the person that one is just is *the* person who is now embodied by the body or human organism that provides the material basis for one's individual personality. But now we can see just why this identification may fail. Every one of the good that there have ever been are persons now partly embodied by the body or human organism associated with this individual personality.

There remains something to the idea of self-ownership, for my having a proprietary right over how things go with this body and individual personality. In fact we can articulate an extremely compelling ground for some such right. The dispositions of this personality determine the

---

[15]See, in particular, Robert Nozick, *Anarchy, State and Utopia* (Basic Books, 1974), and G. A. Cohen, *Self-Ownership, Freedom and Equality* (Cambridge University Press, 1995).

very conditions of my existence. This consideration supports protections of my capacity to control my self-constituting dispositions and supports non-interference in what might be real options in the extension of my conditions of survival. (Perhaps the government ban on cloning oneself is thus, morally speaking, deeply problematic.) Others have no right to impose my self-constituting dispositions on me, or arbitrarily limit them, for then they would be making or remaking me.

The second ground for self-ownership was that a person has a legitimate interest in controlling that aspect of his embodiment that determines and expresses his ethical condition, the aspect that is his individual personality. This may seem to license a certain fundamental freedom from any obligation to others when it comes to developing one's individual personality. I stand to this personality in a way that no one else could: this personality presently expresses what I am, what is good and bad about me, and it will continue to do that at any future time at which it exists.

We can now see that last thought is thus built around a false presupposition, one of uniqueness. Your present individual personality is not an expression exclusively of *your* embodiment; you share that embodiment with each of the good if any there have ever been.

That thought may help you turn toward goodness, for the good collectively may hold more shares in your individual personality than the solitary share you hold. The good can be expected to vote as a single bloc on the question of how this individual personality should develop. For they have a collective interest in the appearance of future embodiments appropriately expressive of their original good wills.

So when I ask myself, "In what direction should I steer the development of my individual personality?" I should weigh my dominant interests alongside those of the good. For the good are all here now. Things that I might not find too shameful or too base would be simply shameful and simply base to them. In this way, by means of compassion for the interests of the good, the conscience of humankind may properly weigh upon us at crucial moments, and thereby help move us toward goodness.

Here we find an essential part of the point of any institution that would deserve the name of the Religion of Humanity. Such an institution would explicitly articulate and attempt to implement the longstanding interests of the good. Their votes would begin to get counted.

ARE WE GOOD ENOUGH?

I could go on defending the consistency of this conception of what we are and can become against apparent philosophical paradoxes, but that does not seem to be to the point. First, the conception of the kind of individual that is continually re-embodied in the onward rush is no great variant on the notion of a species properly understood, and that notion is consistent.

Second, there will be an extensive question period, where the question of consistency will come up. And third, I hope to set out the conception in more detail elsewhere.

More relevant to our purposes here, one might feel that even if the conception is consistent, it will still be entirely inapplicable thanks to actual human psychology.

So all of our work may leave everything as it was; for a life that is not driven by special self-concern, by the demand for premium treatment, may be practically impossible, whether or not it is justified.

Even given my less than rosy views about human nature, I don't believe it. Many of us who are poor candidates to be listed among the good nevertheless do come, over our lifetimes, to exhibit the beginnings of a trajectory whose long arc tends toward goodness.

Special self-concern has evolved as part of a larger pattern of self-referential concern for oneself and one's kin. Not only do we seek premium treatment for ourselves if the effects on others are not too onerous, but we act as if the interests of our family, our friends, our familiars, our tribe, and our nation somehow count for more. Yet as we mature, a thought begins to break through, a thought that our family, friends, familiars, tribe, and nation are not *independently* distinguished as *the ones to care for*. We come to regard our self-referential concerns as disclosing values that people and groups have *anyway*, independently of our relation to them. So also—at least if one is lucky enough to have one's basic needs satisfied, or to find the strength of living with their lack of satisfaction—one comes to love oneself in a more objective way, namely as one person among others, all of whose real and legitimate interests are sources of reasons for preferring and acting. Of course, one knows much more about the person one happens to be, one stands to him or her in the special relationship of having to live his or her life. But the narrative of that life becomes less the search for premium treatment and more the attempt to use one's gifts, such as they are, to be as helpful as one can be.

In this way, a significant weakening of the sense of the self as a justifier of special self-concern is something many of us have lived through, as we discovered in practical terms what it is to be one person among many, all of whose real interests are sources of reasons for preferring and acting. This weakening of the centripetal force of the self is not the realization that persons do not matter as such or that personal identity does not matter. Still less are we left with a utilitarianism that finds the determiners of right and wrong action merely to be the states of pleasure and pain that might be found in momentary slices of our mental lives. What does emerge is the discovery that one is oneself just one of the others, one among many whose needs are equally real and pressing.

To the extent that many of us move in that direction, we become good enough to feel some detachment from our own individual personalities and manifest a corresponding increase in our attachment to individual personality as such, and so to the many loci where real interests arise. To this extent, we are better placed to face death down, to see through it to a pleasing future in which individual personalities flourish.

This way of seeing things is available to those who are good enough; they can see through death in a way that the utterly selfish cannot. For the utterly selfish, however, the obliteration of their individual personalities is the obliteration of everything of real importance to them.

Who Has a Good Will?

So much for the good enough. Then there are the good, the ones whose wills are genuinely good. We have argued that they survive death, living on in the onward rush of humanity.

Who, then, is good? Our enormous capacity for rationalization, and for self-deception, makes utterly opaque the true answer to this question as applied to one's own case. The only place to begin that provides any chance of self-understanding is under the standing accusation that one's own will is not a good will, along with the horror and self-disgust that this entails.

Have I not spent my life with my finger on the scales, with a certain definite desire for premium treatment, even in all the acts that conformed perfectly to the requirements of morality, ordinary decency, kindness, professionalism, patriotism, and support for the "good" causes?

Absurd! Am I not a strident and authentic supporter of the correct causes, have I not done my altruistic bit, have I not been decent, am I not widely known as such a person? Perhaps, maybe, okay. Am I not then good?

Probably I am not, is Kant's point, here openly plagiarizing the New Testament. Even if my record were stainless, to the point of being lily-white, it would very likely be sepulchral. For very often these good things I have done are precisely consistent with the narcissistic strategy by which a bad will avoids facing its own self-dealing by secretly reveling in its ability to meet or exceed the standards of conventional moral expectation. Stop the rationalizations that an intelligent mind can invent ad nauseam and recognize that the interests of those you are prepared to favor, thanks to their special relations to you—your friends, your familiars, your family—get traction because they swell and satisfy your narcissistic preference for yourself.

Still, some of us who do not have a good will have had the wonderful fortune to have encountered genuinely good wills, and the memories of those persons live on with us, as both a balm and an accusation. And in my experience, contrary to Nietzsche's misunderstanding of the good, these people were not life deniers; they were the most fully alive because they were not quarantined from any part of life by the boundaries of their own individual personalities. The essential signs of this were their self-directed irony, their endless playfulness, their capacity for forgiveness, and their enormous interest in life.

My point is only that philosophical reflection reveals that these people, because of the largeness of their identifications, are present, here and now, embodied now as we are.

A Comparison with Schopenhauer

I said at the outset that what followed would be novel, and perhaps I have done enough to have delivered on that promise. Still, the idea that a good will opens up a new identity is really a very old idea. You can find it in Buddhism, and in Christianity, and you can find it in the Vedantism of

Schopenhauer—both in *The World as Will and Representation,* and in *The Basis of Morality.*

I read Schopenhauer's *World as Will and Representation* as following Vedanta in claiming that we are *already* the Will of the World, and that only the illusion of the separate self, which Schopenhauer sees as the upshot of our belief in a false principle of individuation, prevents us from seeing this as our essential identity.

Schopenhauer openly admits his debt to Vedanta: He tells us, "I owe what is best in my works to the impression made by Kant's works, the sacred writings of the Hindus, and Plato," and again, "I confess that I do not believe that my doctrine could have come about before the Upanishads, Plato and Kant could cast their rays simultaneously into the mind of one man." (The Upanishads bring to completion the doctrine of the Vedas, or books of knowledge, and for this reason their collective content is known as "Vedanta" or the conclusion of the Vedas.)

According to the version of Vedanta with which Schopenhauer was familiar, there is a real World behind the world of *maya*, the play of appearances. There is also a real Self, *Atman*, to be found at the source of all the mental acts of the illusory particular selves associated with individual human beings. Reincarnation, the cycle of birth and rebirth, is merely the business of illusory particular selves and so is a dead end as far as salvation goes. Salvation consists in discovering that one is not an illusory particular self but rather *Atman*—the World Self—who is none other than *Brahman*, the creator and sustainer of the world. The enlightened or saved person can express the content of his transformed understanding of reality by the utterance "THAT (demonstrating external reality) is what I am," in effect the claim that the deepest principle of external reality is one and the same as the deepest principle of inner reality.

Schopenhauer read the Vedantic doctrine through a Kantian prism. There is a single noumenon or thing-in-itself, which Schopenhauer identifies with the Will. This single Will is the sustainer of the World; individual appearances, including phenomenal selves, are manifestations or objectifications of this Will. This single Will is also the noumenal Self common to all, a Self revealed to us through the forms of art, through the felt content of a radically altruistic morality, and through mystical experience. Accordingly death, for Schopenhauer, is a release from the illusion of the separate self and the pointless struggle of this self against the ways of the world. Thus death is a sanctification and a deliverance, a natural door to Nirvana. Indeed, rightly understood, death is the purpose of life.[16]

This is Schopenhauer's notorious pessimism, which resonates more with the Buddha's First and Second Noble Truths ("Life Is Suffering" and "The Cause of Suffering Is Self-Regarding Desire") than with anything in Vedanta. And it ignores the Fourth Noble Truth, which sets out a good way of life in which self-caused suffering is overcome. The truncated Buddhistic element in Schopenhauer, the emphasis on the perversely self-frustrating mechanism of desire, and the consequent sense that life is constant suffering, punctuated if at all only by cycles of boredom and aesthetic feeling, obscures the true Vedantic ideal, which is that death should not catch us "unannihilated," that is, still in the bondage of the separate self.

Contrary to Schopenhauer's deepest convictions, there is no good reason why one should not love and cherish the world of illusory play, just so long as one does not get wholly lost in it. Unfortunately, then, what is still the most serious attempt in Western philosophy to assimilate Vedanta remains poisoned by a pessimism that is wholly extraneous to that ancient doctrine.

Even so, Schopenhauer's genius adds something new to Vedanta. In *The Basis of Morality* he grafts onto Vedanta a radically altruistic ethic, a more vivid conception of the good will than even Kant allowed himself, by identifying the good will with "loving-kindness... or *agape*" (163). Schopenhauer takes loving-kindness or *agape* to be independently justi-

---

[16] Schopenhauer writes:

If suffering has such a sanctifying force, this will belong in an even higher degree to death, which is more feared than any suffering. Accordingly, in the presence of every person who has died, we feel something akin to the awe that is forced from us by great suffering; in fact every case of death presents itself to a certain extent as a kind of apotheosis or canonization. Therefore we do not contemplate the corpse of even the most insignificant person without awe, and indeed, strange as the remark may sound in this place, the guard gets under arms in the presence of every corpse. Death is certainly to be regarded as the real aim of life; at the moment of dying everything is decided which through the whole course of life was only prepared and introduced. Death is the result, the resume of life, or the total sum expressing at one stroke all the instruction given by life in detail and piecemeal; namely that the whole striving, the phenomenon of which is life, was a vain, fruitless and self-contradictory effort, to have returned from which is a deliverance. (*World as Will and Representation*, vol. 2, trans. E.F.J. Payne [Dover, 1969], 636–67)

fied by the fact that behind the illusion of many separate agents there is a single Will self-same in all.

The intuitive recognition of the identity of the inner nature of all conscious life is what Schopenhauer calls "compassion," and he insists that it is this, and not Kant's rationalistic Categorical Imperative, which is the true ground of morality. Here, for example, is Schopenhauer's panegyric on compassion.

> Boundless compassion for all living things is the firmest and surest guarantee of pure moral conduct, and needs no casuistry. Whoever is inspired with it will assuredly injure no one, will wrong no one, will encroach on no one's rights; on the contrary he will be lenient and patient with everyone, will forgive everyone, will help everyone as much as he can, and all his actions will bear the stamp of justice, philanthropy, and loving-kindness.[17]

In feeling compassion for another's suffering, I no longer experience the other as simply an object of my perceptual awareness, "as something strange and foreign, as something entirely different from me." On the contrary, Schopenhauer writes, "I share the suffering in him, in spite of the fact that his skin does not enclose my nerves. Only in this way, can *his* woe, *his* distress, become a motive for *me*."[18] But this is not mere sentimentality, an infection of feeling, in which I merely feel sorry for a version of myself, imagined into his condition. What compassion reveals is that this very distinction between my empirical self and his is merely a matter of appearance. Here, Schopenhauer insists, we have at last hit upon the metaphysical basis of ethics, its true justifying ground. He writes:

> Accordingly, if plurality and separateness belong only to the phenomenon, and if it is one and the same essence that manifests itself in all living things then that conception that abolishes the difference between ego and non-ego is not erroneous, but on the contrary the opposite conception must be. We find also that this latter conception [the erroneous one] is described by the Hindus as *maya*, i.e. illusion, deception, phantasm, mirage. It is the former view

---

[17] *On the Basis of Morality*, trans. E.F.J. Payne (Hackett, 1998), 172.
[18] Ibid., 166.

which we found to be the basis of compassion; in fact compassion is the proper expression of that view. Accordingly, it would be the metaphysical basis of ethics and consist in *one* individual's recognizing in *another* his own self, his own true inner nature.[19]

The radical nature of what Schopenhauer calls compassion should not be underestimated; it is not empathy, it is not ordinary fellow feeling, and it is not conventional benevolence. The most dramatic examples of Schopenhauerian compassion are epiphanies in which a fundamental aspect of reality is revealed, with immediate motivational consequences. So a woman strolling on the beach sees a man drowning. Forgetting herself, she jumps in; seconds later she just finds herself in the water, struggling to drag him to shore. Or two men are locked in a murderous hug, each desperately trying to strangle the other to death. All of a sudden, when each is nearing success, both recoil, because each has seen in the eyes of the other his own terror. Schopenhauer's idea is that in these kinds of cases compassion involves a shudder of recognition, not just of the full reality of the other but of his underlying identity with one's deepest self.

These, however, are episodes, flashes of recognition of an alleged noumenal truth. The real question is whether the episode prompts a change in one's basic disposition or will.

The Mistake in *Tristan und Isolde*

To underline that difference, take the most famous musical-dramatical case, the one precisely designed by Richard Wagner to illustrate Schopenhauerian compassion, albeit in the problematic context of erotic love. Tristan and Isolde drink what they each take to be a death potion. But they do not die. There is then one of the most remarkable musical-dramatical moments found in any opera: the shudder of mutual recognition between Tristan and Isolde. After this shudder of mutual recognition, it is not that Isolde feels empathy or fellow feeling for Tristan. She knows she is Tristan, or more exactly that they are each manifestations of a common identity. The next act is sprinkled with the lovers' Vedan-

---

[19] Ibid., 209.

tic pronouncements, as when they express their love by singing together such lines as, "I am the world."

There is no mistaking the Schopenhauerian point. In 1858 Wagner, who was still a devoted acolyte of Schopenhauer's philosophy, went so far as to compose a letter in which he tries to persuade the philosopher that erotic love is not always blind narcissism but that, as the libretto of *Tristan und Isolde* shows, it can be a context in which true compassion arises.[20] The letter was not sent; we know what Schopenhauer, who wrote of lovers as unwitting collaborators in a great game of bait and switch perpetrated on us by the Will for the sake the species, would have made of it. Schopenhauer would have found no place for *agape* in the context of erotic love.

It was probably just as well that the letter was never sent. (And of course, even though Wagner did send him an early text of *Der Ring*, Schopenhauer continued to admire Rossini's operas most of all, a wise choice for a pessimist.)

Despite Wagner's pleading, the love of Tristan and Isolde is not an ideal example of compassion, or of the good will. The compassion that is

---

[20]Wagner, then in Venice, composed the letter, titled "The Metaphysics of Sexual Love" ("*Geschlechtsliebe*") to Arthur Schopenhauer in December 1858. Here is a translation, due to Boris Kment.

There was each year some case or other of joint suicide of two people who were in love with each other but prevented [from marrying] by external circumstances. Concerning such incidences, it has come to seem inexplicable to me why those who are certain of each other's love and [can] expect to find the highest degree of happiness through it, would not rather take extreme measures to withdraw from their [social] relations and endure any kind of suffering than to give up their lives, and thereby renounce a kind of happiness greater than any other they could conceive.

I am tempted to assume that you have not found an explanation of this [phenomenon]; for I would like to flatter myself by following up on this point and telling you about a view of my own, according to which the natural tendency [*Anlage*] to sexual love represents a way to salvation, to self-knowledge, and to self-negation of the will, and precisely not only of the individual will.

You alone give me the conceptual resources through which it becomes possible to communicate my opinion philosophically, and when I try to express the view clearly I can do so only by trusting in what I have learned from you. Please pardon my lack of practice, and perhaps of talent, in dialectics that showed itself in the fact that I had to proceed in a very tortuous way and by first describing the archetypal and highest form of the disposition of the will [*Willensentscheidung*] I have in mind, in order to explain the case to which you have drawn attention, which I can only take to be an imperfect and low degree of that disposition of the will.

the expression of a good will is not an episodic spasm and does not involve hysterical identity-confusion. (Though they share future embodiments, the good are many, not one.) The compassion that opens up a higher identity is a standing condition, a stable, livable outlook, which doesn't tear at the social fabric but heals it. In many ways, the true exemplar of compassion in *Tristan and Isolde* is King Marke, at least in the last scene of the music-drama, where he stands betrayed by his wife and closest friend, and yet forgives them, and mourns their fate, out of a deep and abiding sense of common humanity.

Two Problems with Kantian Vedantism

For Schopenhauer, compassion and the agapeistic morality it supports is supposed to be justified by, and grounded in, "Kantian Vedantism," the doctrine that behind each individual consciousness there lies *Atman*, a single noumenal self, the one who is dreaming the dream of waking life, including the dream of the separate selves that appear to inhabit waking life.

There are two things wrong with Kantian Vedantism, and the second is worse than the first. The first is the highly conjectural metaphysics, not a claim about some emergent entity, which are ten-a-penny and easily constructed from any principle of unity,[21] but instead a claim about what is fundamentally real, namely a single noumenal Self *behind* the illusory separate selves that embroil us in our everyday egoism.

There need be no such thing. The "illusory" separate selves could simply inhabit the psychologies of human animals. They need be no more than the virtual objects implied by the seeming convergence of the perspectival modes of presentation these animals are continually accessing. (To invoke the ideas developed in lectures two and three.) We do not need a Self of all selves to explain the central illusory element in each person's experience of himself. That is the first difficulty, the totally conjectural status of *Atman*, the noumenal Self supposedly behind all phenomenal selves.

The second difficulty goes deeper, and it would remain even if we admitted a single noumenal Self behind the billions of phenomenal

---

[21] A theme of my "Hylomorphism."

selves that there have ever been. *Atman*, however impressive, would be in the end *just another ingredient of reality*. We are being asked by Schopenhauer to treat *Atman* as, in effect, an independent justifier of loving-kindness, or *agape*—an aspect of reality that in itself demands these responses.

Recall that we were unable to find anything of this sort that grounds our egocentric concerns, even in a world augmented with individual mental substances; even they could not justify the essentially privatized privileges—"premium treatment for me"—demanded by egocentrism. Schopenhauer asks us to imagine that all the conscious beings that have ever lived are the expression of a single principle, something that lies at the true center of each person's mental life. Why should that fact, if it were a fact, demand and thereby justify *compassion* for all conscious beings?

What Schopenhauer offers is a metaphysical shell game in which the very same pea turns up inside every cup: "You care intensely about yourself, right? Well, it turns out that I am identical with you, so you should in all consistency care intensely for me, right? And what's true of you and me is true of you and everyone, so you should in all consistency care intensely for everyone, right? So the fact of *Atman* demands and thereby justifies *agape*, right?"

Wrong—that is not the only consistent response to the fact of *Atman*. Upon discovering that the thing I cared so much about has always been there behind the billions of conscious lives there have ever been, I might just cease to care about it. Or I might evenly and thinly spread out my concern among the teeming billions, so that it makes no difference in action.

Schopenhauer formulates the requirements of compassionate goodness with a moving simplicity: *Neminem laede, imo omnes quantum potes, juva* ("Injure no one, but on the contrary, help everyone as much as you can"). The requirements of goodness are just these: justice and charity. (Surprise, surprise; of course, they must be the requirements of goodness. As Kant observed, who could plausibly pretend to any originality here!) But not even *Atman* could rationally force those requirements upon us. It takes goodness to see the appeal of goodness, just as it takes egocentrism to hallucinate the appeal of egocentrism. The putative independent justifiers are fifth wheels.

This World, Not the Other World

Forget *Atman* and the metaphysical shell game that treats *Atman* as an independent justifier of radical goodness or *agape*. Suppose you *are* good in this simple but utterly demanding sense: you injure no one, but on the contrary you help everyone as much as you can. You love your neighbors, the arbitrary others, as yourself, and in that way you learn to love yourself with proper impersonality, namely, merely as another, one whose needs you learn of in a particularly immediate way.

Then our radical reversal in thinking about the relation between future-directed concern and personal identity has prepared for you a protection and a reward. It is not a reward you sought or even conceived of, but one you nevertheless deserve.

Given your pattern of concern you will have filled out your identity as a Protean person in a particular determinate way; in identifying fundamentally with the interests of the arbitrary other you will have become something that is present whenever and wherever embodied individual personality is present. You will live on, as Mill put it in his remarks about the Religion of Humanity, "in the onward rush of Mankind." You will live on in the onward rush not metaphorically as Mill intended it, but literally.

If persons are Protean this will not be a merely surrogate or spectral form of survival, one without consciousness, deliberation, or action. For if persons are Protean, then a person is conscious at a time if at that time he is constituted by a body that is then a site of consciousness; a person is deliberating at a time if at that time he is constituted by a body in which brain processes grounding deliberation are going on; and a person is acting at a time if at that time he is constituted by a body that is then engaged in voluntary movement. So the good after death are conscious, they deliberate, and they act—all of this in and through the multitude that come after.[22]

This is the "reward" of *agape*; but in giving this reward, *agape* has remained its own "reward." It is not, as Paul suggests in his epistles, that

---

[22]What is true, of course, is that the initial individual personalities of the good do not exercise any distinctive prospective control over the deliberation and action of the individual personalities associated with the future bodies or organisms that come to constitute them.

agape earns you heaven after the *anastasis*, Paul's own word for the resurrection.

Instead, *agape* constitutes the *anastasis* of the good, their rising up to acquire a higher-order identity, an identity as a thing that is present wherever and whenever others are present.

Thanks to their higher-order identity, every time a child is born and begins to develop into an individual personality, the good acquire a new face.

And so, even if something very like a good person's individual personality were in fact to be continued in another world, as in *The Entombment of Gonzalo Ruíz, Count of Orgaz*, that would be a mere sideshow. The good person's real life would continue here on earth, along with the community of the good and the good enough.

Thus, for the good, the other world, even if it exists, is an irrelevance, perhaps even an irritation.

Paul was nonetheless right about one thing: the wages of sin, which he identified as the obliteration inherent in death. If goodness is *agape*, then all we can really mean by "sin" is the condition of those of us who cannot make our way beyond our egocentrism. We are then left only with our small individual personalities, and they are, indeed, obliterated by death.

Perpetual Return

We all remember that Nietzsche regarded *agape* with utmost suspicion. For example, he saw its valorization in Wagner's *Parzifal* as a desperate groveling before the Cross, and before the ascetic or "monkish" virtues he believed had strangled true life, and the possibilities for its affirmation. Contempt for *agape* was on Nietzsche's part a self-conscious repudiation of Schopenhauer's pessimism and alleged hatred of life.[23] But Schopenhauer's intellectual defense of pessimism was based on a mis-

---

[23] Perhaps the best exploration and defense of this theme is given in Christopher Janaway, *Beyond Selflessness: Reading Nietzsche's Genealogy* (Oxford University Press, 2007). See also his "Schopenhauer as Nietzsche's Educator," in Nicholas Martin, ed., *Nietzsche and the German Tradition* (Peter Lang, 2003).

By the way, all the signs are that Schopenhauer was much more fun to be with than either Nietzsche or Wagner. Pessimism has its distinctive charms.

understanding of Vedanta, which actually celebrates the blissful affirmation of life that comes with awareness of the truth of *maya*, *anatta*, and the identity of *Atman* and *Brahman*.

Schopenhauer's profound mis-assimilation of the best of Eastern philosophy into the Western tradition helped make Nietzsche possible, by giving him his main intellectual foil, a detailed philosophical defense of an etiolated ethic of self-sacrifice.

Are we then reviving that old self-denying ethic and simply providing it with a novel ontological framework?

You will also recall that Nietzsche employed a certain spiritual exercise—the contemplation of the myth of perpetual return—in part to illustrate just how demanding the affirmation of life is.

> What if some day or night a demon were to steal after you into your loneliest loneliness and say to you: "This life as you now live it and have lived it, you will have to live once more and innumerable times more.".... Would you not throw yourself down and gnash your teeth and curse the demon who spoke thus? Or have you once experienced a tremendous moment when you would have answered him: "You are a god and never have I heard anything more divine."[24]

But just how much love of life does one need to affirm the perpetual return of the actual life lived by one's own individual personality? There are two cases. One is the case of a person like the Sun King, Louis XIV, who spent large parts of his day simply stunned by his own impressiveness. For such beings the contemplation of perpetual return is not a test of affirmation of life at all. They would joyfully embrace perpetual return simply because they fancy themselves so much. Compare Ayn Rand, who once said "the true name for God is 'I.'" Given what we know of her life, it is natural to construe Rand as being *in the relevant respect* a monotheist, and hence really meaning that "I" was *her* name. How could anyone in that frame of mind fail to wish for their return over and over again?

Obviously, this kind of affirmation of perpetual return does not exhibit a noble love of *life*. Rand and the Sun King did not love life as such. They were just, as we say in the old country, "up themselves"—they sim-

---

[24]Friedrich Nietzsche, *The Gay Science*, trans. Walter Kaufmann (Random House, 1974).

ply took themselves to be objectively wonderful, and could not have but rejoiced in their perpetual return.

What, then, is the *other* case of affirmation of return that *does* show a noble *love of life* as opposed to an adoration of one's individual personality? Nietzsche's view is that noble love of life is the expression of a healthy *egoism*, a healthy *self*-regard, and that one can have this without having delusions of grandeur, as with the Sun King or Rand. Unfortunately for that view, the established fact of *anatta*, the fact that there is no persisting self worth caring about, entails that the affirmation of the perpetual return of my individual personality, just because it is *mine*, is not a reasonable affirmation.

There remains one coherent basis for the affirmation of one's own perpetual return, indeed the perpetual return of each human life, namely love of individual personality as such. There can be healthy and coherent self-regard, but it is the regard for one's own individual personality as one among many equally real. And this, to love individual personality as such at least wherever it is not irredeemably closed to goodness, is the basic orientation of the good.

Notice just how far this orientation is from the life-denying strictures of asceticism and the monkish virtues.

For now the demon (or is it the angel?) is saying to the good:

Each life that will be lived, you will also live in all its grandeur, squalor, and mediocrity, with the only exception being those lives that remain closed to goodness.

Nietzsche called the contemplation of the myth of the perpetual return "das schwerste Gewicht," the heaviest burden. Yet here, it seems, is a *heavier* burden. Those who take it up are the true affirmers of life.

THE INTERESTS OF THE GOOD

Nietzsche presents the contemplation of perpetual return not only as a test of life affirmation but also as a way of fixing one's focus on the importance of the choices that will shape the only life you will ever have: "Imagine living with those choices and their consequences over and over again!" This is meant to be galvanizing. (For some, that imaginative act is not galvanizing; it produces paralysis.)

What the demon/angel says to the good person should be galvanizing to that person. The good are disposed to promote the good, but like all of us their basic dispositions are sometimes masked by fear, by depression, and by anxiety. The thought about one's future incarnations may weaken the effects of these maskers. In that sense the good may be galvanized by what the demon/angel says.

The good are those with an unmediated disposition to promote the interests of individual personalities, at least those personalities not irredeemably closed to goodness. (This leaves, along with the future good, all of the good enough and those who are capable of being good enough.) Given that this disposition determines the future incarnations of the good, the good must then look to the condition of their future incarnations. They are likely to be galvanized to promote the flourishing of individual personality wherever it arises. They will also try to spread the disposition of goodness, so that more of their future embodiments are good. In this way, what a good person lived for in his or her first incarnation will come again, and in the best case goodness will finally be found conjoined with human happiness, that is, the flourishing of individual personalities.

If, *if*, these interests of the good—

The flourishing of individual personality wherever it arises,

The propagation of the dispositions characteristic of goodness,

The conjoining of goodness and human happiness—

were to be secured to some significant degree, then we would have what used to be called the kingdom of heaven on earth. I would rather style it the moral adulthood of humanity. That circumstance would be a vindication of the whole project of goodness and a vindication of the good themselves.

Is it a reasonable hope that some approximation to this will appear in human history, or in the history of embodied self-consciousness, at some time or other?

I can't say. All I can say is that *this is* the hope that properly goes with *agape* and with faith in the importance of goodness. In this way, the so-called theological virtues converge and support each other.

Supernaturalism provides a way of transforming something like this hope into a guarantee, a concrete but fantastic guarantee that the good will be vindicated in *another* world. But as we have seen, we can't get to the other world from here, which suggests that it is not a genuine destination. All that supernaturalism does is replace the virtue of hope with a *fantasy* of otherworldly reward and vindication.

Perhaps that is not all that it does. It diminishes this world by representing it as merely a place of testing. It encourages the vengeful fantasies of eschatological apocalypse, of the final settling of all the old scores. And in doing all this, in allowing so many to celebrate in the thought of the end of all things, it takes on the great risk of hastening the destruction of humanity and its home, the earth.

To this extent supernaturalism is of no help to the good. In its more virulent forms it may be the deadly enemy of the good, as it works to allow the thinking of the unthinkable, the obliteration of the very future in which the interests of the good could be secured.

RECONSIDERING THE THREAT OF DEATH

These lectures were concerned with the apparent threat of death, understood in naturalistic terms, to the importance of goodness. The threat arose because of the unreliable, even haphazard, connection within single lives between being good and being happy, that is, between being disposed to treat oneself as one person among others and flourishing as a human being.

Given naturalism, and the resultant unavailability of the afterlife, death as a generic phenomenon may seem to undermine the rational appeal of goodness, because goodness does deserve to be paired with happiness, and the good do not deserve to be fodder for the predatory bad. The supernaturalist thought is that this can only be corrected in the next life, where the good receive their reward. But the facts of personal identity show that we cannot get to the next life; it is not a life for us. So the threat remains.

The threat of death to the importance of goodness is itself a generic threat. The threat would not be met by pointing to quite a few cases where good people do in fact flourish. Nor would the threat be vindicated by pointing to quite a few cases where good people never flourish. The task is to make out some generic and hence non-adventitious connection between goodness and flourishing.

In these lectures I have said nothing about certain advantages the good have just by virtue of being good. Being disposed to treat oneself as one person among others opens the good person to genuine love and friendship. Being disposed to treat oneself as one person among others frees the good person from the complex defenses that selfishness requires, and thus facilitates a turn toward reality, with a consequent escape from the controlling influences of one's fantasies. In these ways the good, and to some extent the good enough, are more likely to flourish.

When it comes to facing death, the characteristic disposition of the good is very helpful. A good person, however well endowed by nature and nurture, does not see himself as a Sun King, one whose death would remove everything of paramount importance. Nor does a good person feel that his own individual personality is of special importance because it is *his*. The good value individual personality as such, and they see it continued in their younger contemporaries and in the lives of all those who follow them. In this way the good, and to some extent the good enough, are less threatened by death. Where death looms less over a life, there is more chance that that life will be a genuinely flourishing life.

To these thoughts I have added two more considerations. The first is that the good have a larger identity; they live on in the onward rush of humankind, variably and multiply embodied in the embodiments of those that follow them. Generically speaking, individual personality is a good thing, enjoying more of it rather than less is to be strongly desired. Even a good enough individual personality has a reasonable chance to flourish, and this fact and the higher-order identity of the good may decrease the variance that makes the connection between being good and being happy seem haphazard or adventitious.

In suggesting that, I am not trying to explain how the good receive their proper *just deserts* within a naturalistic framework. I am not counting the benefits of a larger identity as just rewards for the good. For how large the benefit is depends on where in human history a good person finds his first incarnation. Justice does not reign here. But generically speaking the good are very far from being patsies. It is those who remain locked within themselves who now look pathetically stupid, even if in particular times and places they may meet the standard of a flourishing life.

Finally, I have contemplated the possibility of an actual historical condition, the moral adulthood of humanity, in which the interests of the good—the flourishing of individual personality, the propagation of the dispositions characteristic of goodness, and the conjoining of goodness with human happiness—are secured to some significant degree.

In the *Système de politique positive* (1854), August Comte wrote of the "Great Providential Being" consisting of "all those who have cooperated in the great human task, those who live on in us, of whom we are the continuation, those whose genuine debtors we are." Comte meant the Great Providential Being to stand in for the True Church or the Extended Body of Christ in his (Comte's) positivist variant on Christianity. For our part, we could drop talk of *a* Being and talk instead of the good, who live on embodied as we now are, of whom we are the continuation, and whose genuine debtors we are.

In the moral adulthood of humanity we would explicitly recognize our debt to the still present good who have passed. Consequently, there would be a widespread recognition of the deep falsehood in the ordinary idea of pure self-ownership of one's individual personality. The person who ordinarily comes to mind, the person whose identity is determined by the dispositions of THIS individual personality, is one person. The persons whose ethical condition is presently expressed by this individual personality are many; they include the person who ordinarily comes to mind and all the good who have gone before. Each of these persons has a reasonable claim on how any given individual personality should develop and comport itself. And of course all of the good who have passed and are still present will here vote as one. The moral adulthood of humanity would be a situation in which the claims of the good effectively count.

This explicit and properly institutionalized respect for the good, who are here with us even to the end of humanity, would help us all be better. This would be the vindication of the good, and it is their natural hope.

Yet, even forgoing this last possibility, the possibility of humanity eventually entering moral adulthood, and putting all the rest together, we have enough to see that even in the face of death, goodness remains a reasonable form of heroism. And there is no complete reasonableness short of this heroism.

Questions and Replies

What you are describing as surviving death is not individual personal survival.[25]

I understand what you are saying; there is something that is normally there that is missing. There is no survival of one's very own individual personality, but there can be clear cases of individual personal survival without the survival of the individual personality, as in the case of my recovery of my memory without recovering any of my memories.

You may say, with some justice, "I don't care much about a form of survival unless it involves the survival of my individual personality." But that is a remark about yourself, one that is strictly irrelevant to the issue at hand. (I might share your attitude, but that, too, is irrelevant to the issue at hand.) The only candidates for the form of survival under discussion are those who have internalized the dispositions that are characteristic of *agape*. And they are people who care about individual personality as such, and treat the interests of individual personalities as on a par, no matter whose individual personalities are in question. So for them, there is little loss in this form of personal identity or continued existence.

And once again we have the surprising result that comes from moving from *anatta* to *agape*: here their attitude, not ours, is the rational one given that there is no persisting self worth caring about.

We could put it this way. There is something that supernaturalist survival secures that this kind of survival does not. It is the survival of one's own individual personality. But the good are not actually very interested in that, and rationally so.

Isn't the survival of the individual personality the remaining putative advantage of supernaturalist survival?[26]

Yes, at least on the surface of things that seems right. However, when we look to the details of supernaturalist survival we find some serious fudging on the issue of the survival of the individual personality. There is reincarnation, in which, for example, Elijah or Jeremiah is supposed to come back as Jesus, where these are clearly distinct individual person-

---

[25] An audience member unknown to me.
[26] A follow-up from the previous questioner.

alities. (Compare the apostles' answer to the question "Who do people say that I am?" at Matthew 16:14: "Some say John the Baptist; others say Elijah; and still others, Jeremiah or another one of the prophets.") Then there is Nirvana where individual personality is literally "blown out" like the flame of a candle. Then there is the Beatific Vision, where one enters into the inner life of Divinity. None of these forms of afterlife clearly admits of the survival of the individual personality. And the same is arguably true of the heaven in which there is "no giving and taking in marriage." Uh huh, and what else *isn't* there? In fact, all these forms of "afterlife" seem to be presented as *better than* the continuation of our individual personalities.

That said, supernaturalist survival *as popularly conceived* may still seem to offer us more of what we typically want, namely the continuation of "the precious"—our own beloved individual personalities.

This concession about what we typically want leaves further questions. Should we want this? Is it rational to want this? Is the normal cessation of one's individual personality in itself something that one should rationally reject? Working on maintaining a rich individual personality is a form of very serious play, requiring significant effort and skill at self-control and managing one's own interests in the context of ongoing plans, policies, and projects. For some, indeed for some in this audience, it may amount to a work of art. But it lies in the nature of this genre of art for its examples to be used up in the living of a life.

It would be confused to *mourn* the bottle of Chateau Margaux 1982 (which is something of a work of art) one has just put away, as opposed to wishing that one had another and another and another. That last wish, as it were for the perpetual return of Chateau Margaux 1982, will not remain very stable in the face of all the other wines one might try. Rather than wish for the perpetual return of Chateau Margaux, one might more reasonably prefer to sample a wider selection. One might be led to the same view about individual personalities.

One would, I admit, have to be *led* to that view. For typically the seriousness required to manage one's individual personality over time strongly reinforces the desire that one's own individual personality continue on, so that one of my fundamental values, underlying all the efforts I expend on my plans and projects, becomes the persistence of this individual personality. So I can easily feel that any time or world that is without *it* is to that extent barren. Is this not the paradigm case of what the psychologists call "effort justification"—of projecting a great value into something because of the great effort one has invested in it?

I admit that one has to be led to the view that it would be better to sample a wide range of individual personalities than have one's own again forever. But these lectures were designed to lead you to that view.

That pure desire for the persistence of *my* individual personality can only be adequately captured by means of what we were calling a subjective use of "I" and its cognates. My attachment to my individual personality and my attachment to Johnston's individual personality are not the same attitudes. From the basis of our own self-interested outlook, the first attitude seems non-derivatively rational, and the second attitude only derivatively so, consequent upon my recognizing that I am Johnston and that his individual personality is the one I have constructed. To represent the first attitude as differing from the second only in its indexical mode of presentation of Johnston makes our fundamental orientation toward ourselves superficially incoherent. It makes us akin to the drunk who, mistaking modes of presentation for what they present, believes the lampposts get bigger as he moves toward them and shrink in size as he moves away.

To avoid reconstructing our basic orientation as in this way superficially incoherent, we need to construe one's attachment to one's own individual personality as *truly subjective*. It is the individual personality associated with this persisting subject of experience, or persisting self, or persisting arena of presence, or continuing consciousness that I especially value, and value as such. Yet, to summarize the previous argument, when we try to fill out the content of the relevant subjective thought that is supposed to justify the special self-concern that would support the attachment to our very own individual personality, we run foul of the fact that the associated sortal employed in picking oneself out, as it might be *self*, or *subject of experience*, or *arena of presence*, or *consciousness*, is a busted substance sortal. The pure desire for the continued existence of *my* individual personality, which makes any time or world that is without *it* seem barren, may not be superficially incoherent. But it is deeply incoherent. It is individual personality *as such* that must matter, if my concern for my own individual personality is to have any rational force. And after my death, there will be plenty of individual personality around.

Letting go of our own individual personality in the face of death is easier if we value individual personality as such and recognize that the world is full of it. This pattern of valuation is typical of the good. As a result, other things being equal, death is less of a loss for the good. To this fact, I have added an account of how the good might indeed live on in other individual personalities. Perhaps letting go of our one's particular individual personality is made still easier if one not only values individual personality as such but reasonably believes that we live on in other individual personalities.

And so once more, even with no recourse to the other world, we may follow Socrates in saying:

> I am in hope that there is something for us in death, and as was claimed from old, something better for the good than there is for the bad. (*Phaedo* 63c)

Isn't it strained to think of oneself as capable of multiple embodiments at a given time?[27]

Strained? Perhaps it is a *strange* thought, but our everyday understanding of ourselves is in its own way very strange too, and indeed it is so deeply erroneous that the truth must inevitably surprise us. So we are no longer moving within the domain of the intuitive, the commonsensical, and the everyday. That domain is busted.

More specifically, I thoroughly agree that the thought that we are capable of multiple embodiments at a given time is a surprising, even strange, thought, but I believe that it is one that we are pushed to anyway, independently of the thesis that we are Protean.

That we are capable of multiple embodiments is also shown by the fact that each of us is susceptible in principle to *a certain kind* of splitting, a fission where each fission product, considered in itself, has a real claim to be the person who split.

I do not mean that we are, even in principle, like amoebas. For when an amoeba splits it ceases to be and is replaced by its "daughters." And if only one of the daughters were to have proven viable that would not be a case in which the original amoeba is identical with the one remaining

---

[27] An audience member unknown to me.

daughter. It would be a case where the original amoeba gives rise to just one offspring.

The same is true for the bodies or human organisms that constitute us. If they were to split, it would take so much internal reorganization of matter and form that neither branch of the splitting process would be such that, had it happened on its own, it would have secured the survival of the original body or organism. Consider Dean Zimmerman's imagined case of bodily organic fission, described in the first lecture. Set aside the case where the body miraculously sloughs off a pseudo-corpse, while the body itself chugs along in the normal way. Concentrate on Zimmerman's "equal" fission case. There the *avowedly miraculous* processes involved on both sides of the fission are so unlike the life processes of an organism that neither fission product has a real claim to be identical to the original organism that split. For neither involves a body chugging along in the normal way. As in the case of the amoeba, the radical "gestational preparation" for the offspring is not something that the original organism survives.

By contrast, each of us is in principle susceptible to a kind of fission in which we would have survived as one or the other of the fission products, if that product had been the unique product.

David Wiggins was the first to describe how this kind of fission might occur in the life of a human being, but the point comes out most clearly in the case of the Teletransporters.[28] For purposes of argument then, suppose for a moment that we would survive Teletransportation.

So recall how it went in the lecture. You step into the transmitting machine and things misfire at the receiving station so that two people, each with a brain and body that duplicate yours, step out. Each remembers your experiences, and each has just your orientation toward the future. As noted in the lecture, the upshot is a practical nightmare; each is prepared to take over your whole place in the world—your spouse, your family, your friends, your job, your relationships, your wardrobe, your checking account.

Obviously, the Teletransporters have to make some sort of conventional adjustment for this sort of outcome. Suppose they use bigamy as the model on the personal side, and divorce as the model on the finan-

[28] David Wiggins, *Identity and Spatiotemporal Continuity* (Oxford, 1967), 51ff.

cial side. That is, some combination of time-sharing and splitting of assets provides them with a practical way of dealing with these cases. Even so, as a French diplomat famously said in connection with a proposed UN solution to the crisis in Algeria, "That's all very well in practice, but will it work in theory?"

That is, we may have a way of sorting out relationships and goods, but as yet we have no answer to the question of who is who. Clearly the post-Teletransportation products are not identical; one emerges on the right, the other on the left, and they differ in their spatio-temporal pathways through the world, in the subsequent environments they inhabit, and in the thoughts that they come to think. So Lefty (short for "the one who emerges of the left") and Righty (short for "the one who emerges on the right"), as we might call them, are two distinct first-order individuals. So you, the one who got into the transmitting machine, cannot be strictly identical with both of them. And it would be arbitrary to choose one and designate him as the one who is you. For whatever psychological relations you stand in to Lefty, you stand in to Righty, and vice versa.

It is even worse than that. Consider the process that issued in Lefty, as it were, the left-hand side of the process that issued in both Lefty and Righty. If that process had occurred and was in all intrinsic respects just as it was, and yet was the only process that provided you with a psychological continuer, then that process would have been ordinary one-one Teletransportation. And, falling in with the Teletransporters, we are counting that as a form of survival. You would have survived thanks to the left-hand process.

Now consider the process that issued in Righty, as it were, the right-hand side of the process that issued in both Lefty and Righty. If that process had occurred and was in all intrinsic respects just as it was, and yet was the only process that provided you with a psychological continuer, then that process would have been ordinary one-one Teletransportation. And falling in with the Teletransporters, we are counting that as a form of survival. You would have survived thanks to the right-hand process.

But when both processes occur together it seems that you do not survive, for you cannot be identical with both of Lefty and Righty, and in the absence of bare haecceitistic facts about persons it is entirely unclear what fact would make it the case that you survive as one rather than the other. A double success thus adds up to an abject failure.

That is not just puzzling. It is paradoxical when we add the following principle:

> Necessarily, if some process secures your survival then it secures your survival in any possible situation in which it, the numerically same process, occurs and is intrinsically just the same.

This principle is itself more plausible than any specific sufficient condition for personal identity. *Whatever* might be sufficient for a person to survive in a given situation, and however this might be secured by underlying bodily, or brain, or psychological processes, *including processes involving thoroughgoing identification with some future person*, if all of that were to occur in another situation then the very same person would survive.

However, the principle leads to what I once called the paradox of fission,[29] at least when we add the basic fact highlighted by the fission case, namely this:

> It is possible that a process that would secure your survival could co-occur with a distinct and separate process that would also secure your survival.

Given a case in which the two processes co-occur it then follows that you would survive as two distinct people, the one whose survival is secured by the first process, and the one whose survival is secured by the second process. But you may feel, in my view with perfect right, that you are not the sort of thing that could be wholly present in two places at once. Perhaps universals, for example, whiteness, can display such behavior; perhaps whiteness can be *wholly* here and *wholly* there (pick the places of two white things). But anything that deserves the name of *an individual* cannot be *wholly* present in distinct, non-overlapping places. So haven't we run out of consistent ways of describing what takes place in the case of fission?

Philosophers have long relied on a standard answer, an answer that subsequently received its canonical formulation in the work of Robert Nozick.[30] Nozick deals with the paradox of fission by insisting that per-

---

[29] For a more complete discussion of the paradox, and a solution I am now less happy with, see my "Fission and the Facts," in J. Tomberlin, ed., *Philosophical Perspectives*, vol. 3 (University of California Press, 1989).

[30] Robert Nozick, *Philosophical Explanations* (Harvard University Press, 1981), 29–70.

sonal identity is, after all, an extrinsic and partly negative matter. On Nozick's view, personal identity involves the winning by one person of a certain kind of competition. Of all the beings who might continue you in the future the one who continues your bodily and/or mental life most closely is the one who *is* you. If there is a tie, as in fission, then you have no *closest* continuer. So we can get cases in which you cease to exist only because the duplication process worked so evenhandedly that the relevant Lefty and Righty continued you absolutely equally well. On Nozick's view, if there had been a slight lapse on the left side, so that Lefty could not remember your phone number, then you would have been Righty. (Remember I am using "Lefty" and "Righty" as shorthand for the corresponding definite descriptions.)

Thus on Nozick's view, your continued existence always partly involves a negative fact, namely that there be no better continuer than the continuer who is you. So when answering a question about whether you survived some process we are not considering enough of the world in order to determine whether you survived, if we just examine all the details of that process. How much of the world would have to be considered to settle that there was not a better continuer than the one who continued on as a result of that process? Well, actually, the whole of the world. That is how it is with negative existential facts.

Nozick's view has caught on, not because it is intuitive but because it is a way out of paradox. What has not been noted is that there is a clear counterexample that shows that Nozick's Closest Continuer Theory cannot be accepted as he intended it, namely as a *general* account of the identity of composite individuals. For it obviously yields the wrong result in the case of higher-order individuals.

Returning to the Tiger, we can consistently suppose that after the Tiger originated, in, say, Bengal, half of an early population that included all the original tigers died off, and the remainder began the long journey to Africa, a journey completed only by their successors. Here the persistence of the species that is the Tiger is wholly constituted by what we might call the journey to Africa. Alternatively, we can consistently suppose that only the *other* half of that original population of tigers died off, and the remainder began a long journey to China, a journey completed by *their* successors. In this scenario, the persistence of the species that is the Tiger is wholly constituted by the journey to China. Clearly the two scenarios have been constructed so that they could occur together, and then the right thing to say would be that the Tiger ends up in *both* Africa and China. But that cannot be said on the Closest Continuer Theory, for either it is the case that one of the two continuations of the Tiger is closer, in which case it alone represents the persistence of the Tiger, or there is a tie, in which case neither continuation represents the continued persistence of the Tiger. Here, with the analog of fission in the case of a higher-order individual, the Closest Continuer Theory gives the wrong result. (If you try to fiddle with what it is to be a continuer in this case, then there will be a question of why we can't or don't allow the corresponding fiddle in the original case of personal fission.)

Nor does Nozick's principle appear particularly plausible when it comes to persons. Certainly it yields results at odds with what we care about in caring about survival. We do care about the holding of relations of personal identity. So we should and would care derivatively about any means that secures the holding of such relations. But, as a matter of fact, when friends of the Closest Continuer Theory are asked to imagine duplication by Teletransportation, and then asked if they would pay a significant sum to have the relevant Lefty missing a few memory cells so as to produce in him some subsequent forgetfulness, thereby guaranteeing unequal fission and survival as Righty, the uniform reaction is that they would not pay such a sum. From the point of view of what matters, equal fission seems like a double success; you seem to be getting what matters twice over in a case of equal fission.

Should we then conclude, with Derek Parfit, that personal identity is not what matters, not what it is rational to care about in caring about survival? No, we should not. We should try to make sense of the fact that fission provides a double dose of what matters, without invoking the Closest Continuer view. We should try to make sense of the idea that in fission the original person would be equally, but not wholly, present on the left and on the right. But how are we to make sense of that?

This, by now standard, line of puzzlement, like the discussions of species as if they were properties, just misses an option. The so-called paradox of fission only yields the result that you are present where Righty is and you are present where Lefty is. True, that is not possible for a first-order individual. But it is possible for a higher-order individual. Recognition of the existence of higher-order individuals not only provides a counterexample to the Closest Continuer Theory, it also provides a way out of the resultant paradox of fission!

Here, then, is my claim: Fission would indeed be a double success. In your fission, you, a higher-order individual, would be embodied on the right and on the left. That is, as a result of your fission you come to be multiply embodied. In general, anything that could split in the appropriate way, and is such that its identity is an intrinsic matter, is more like a species than like an atom. Anything that could split in this way, and is such that its identity is an intrinsic matter, is a higher-order individual, one capable of being constituted by different lower-order individuals at different times.

In the fission case there are four things, and the survivor is the fourth thing, the higher-order thing.

This, then, is how one individual can literally *become* two individuals—not in the fashion of David Lewis's suggestion about fission, where it ends up true that there have been two people all along,[31] but by being a higher-order individual first constituted by one thing, and then by two.

In real life you have never had any motive to distinguish yourself from the organism that embodies you. But in your fission you would come to have *two separate* organic embodiments. You would be embodied by two (newly created) human bodies. You were one, and you became two, but this is not the impossible circumstance of one thing becoming identical with two. The solution to the so-called paradox of fission is that fissionable individuals are capable of multiple embodiment at a time.[32]

The same should be said if the output of the Teleporter were thousands of duplicates. In that case you, the higher-order individual who entered the Teleporter, were constituted by one individual; now you are constituted by many.

Notice that one-many survival of this sort would be personal survival. And given that what survives is a higher-order individual, this would also be *individual* survival. You, the higher-order individual, would survive *as* all those lower-order individuals. That is, you would come to be constituted by them. Despite the radical change in your constitution, the

---

[31]Lewis, "Survival and Identity."

[32]Does this provide a solution to the problem of perimortem duplicates? No, it does not. There we have two people dying at different times, not one person who was multiply embodied and who then becomes singly embodied at his resurrection by reassembly.

change from being singly embodied to being multiply embodied, you would literally continue to exist.

How, on your view, does agape *differ from a kind of global selfishness?*[33]

There is a superficial paradox associated with any doctrine like Vedanta, which finds all persons to be, at their metaphysical core, one. Such a monism of the personal threatens to obliterate our moral separateness, a basic phenomenon around which much of our practical life is organized. So I take my neighbor to court to sue him for the return of my donkey, and he says that he is me, that what is mine is therefore his. And then the judge, who we may also suppose is also persuaded by the doctrine of the one Self in all, chimes in to assert his claim over the donkey as well. Is this not a reductio ad absurdum of the idea that one Self, *Atman*, is at the source of all the mental acts found in the lives of human beings?

No, it isn't. In our terms, the Vedantist can distinguish personhood and individual personality, and then coherently maintain that in denying the metaphysical separateness of persons, he is not denying the separateness of individual personalities. Once that distinction is made, the Vedantist needs to add that the practical relations of responsibility, ownership, and commitment all follow the lineaments of individual personality and not deep personhood. The morality that goes under the heading of "Respect for Persons" is then best described as respect for individual personalities. These remain separate, despite the radical doctrine of personal identity.

Although the proposal of lecture five was premised on a rejection of the Vedantist doctrine of *Atman*, it may still seem to be saddled with similar paradoxes. If we are Protean persons, who survive any event that is not at odds with the holding of the relation selected by our identity-determining dispositions, and if *agape* in fact involves directing such dispositions to all those who do and will exist, so that one comes to be constituted by all who live on in the onward rush of mankind, doesn't it follow that *agape* is in the end a kind of grand selfishness?

No, it doesn't. The distinction between altruism and egoism can be plausibly redrawn at the level of individual personalities. *Agape* does not obliterate the distinction between individual personalities; it lies in its

---

[33] An audience member unknown to me.

nature to respect those very distinctions, for the individual personality is the locus of real interests. And egoism or selfishness consists in a certain way of holding to one's individual personality, demanding premium treatment for it, as if it were somehow privileged by its being one's own. The radical altruist, the one who lives out the command of *agape*, is clearly not in this way selfish.

Is it then a worse thing to kill a totally self-involved person than to kill a good person, since a good person lives on in the onward rush of humankind and the self-involved person does not?[34]

There are two questions behind what you ask. One is the moral question. Here, as just noted, once we distinguish personhood and personality, and understand what is involved in both, then the absolute moral side-constraints on our pursuit of any beneficial outcome are best construed as side-constraints on how we treat individual personalities. And there is an absolute moral side-constraint that takes murder off the table as a means to any outcome, however beneficial. So it is equally morally wrong to kill, or more exactly murder, any individual personality.

The other question is the question of value, the question of good and bad outcomes, and of how to compare them. When a good person is killed, something very fine is destroyed, namely the individual personality that embodies the disposition that is *agape*. From the point of view of the destruction of what is fine or excellent this is, other things being equal, much worse than the destruction of the individual personality of an ordinary self-involved person.

Why add the qualification that other things should be equal? Nothing said so far counts against the view that certain forms of human excellence can be found in very self-involved personalities.

Of course, as you say, if the argument of lecture five is correct then in killing a good person you do not bring that person to an end. He lives on embodied with other individual personalities. But you do destroy his individual personality; that is morally bad, and from the point of view of what is valuable the destruction of a good individual personality is a worse thing than the destruction of the individual personality of a bad or morally indifferent person.

[34]Thomas Kelly.

Still, a good person's death matters *less to him* than a bad person's death matters *to that bad person*. But, since a bad person's death matters more to him because of his irrational selfishness, this difference does not give *us* a reason to prefer the death of the good over the death of the bad.

Doesn't your view make for a certain form of injustice, for those who have been good all their lives and those who turn to goodness on their deathbed both survive death?[35]

I myself am a great fan of the deathbed conversion, and I hope for it in my own case. But it is not that easy. We need to distinguish episodic and standing attitudes, and the disposition that is constitutive of identity is a standing attitude, not something that consists in an episode of now wanting to be good. On the other hand, it might be that on the deathbed one's underlying benevolent disposition, which has been for sometime masked by circumstance, comes to manifest itself. The irrelevant case is one in which a person out of vulnerability in the face of death simply behaves *as if* he had, or had just adopted, the benevolent disposition. Is this not the crucial difference between the genuine case of Verdi's Violetta and the more dubious case of Waugh's Lord Marchmain?

On the larger question of injustice, there has always been some moral discomfort over the parable of the workers who come late in the day but who end up receiving the same compensation as those who have been laboring since the morning.[36] And yet we are told that the kingdom of heaven is like unto that!

It is not that the afterlife of the good is an extrinsic compensation for goodness, a compensation for the sacrifices made in the name of goodness. Goodness is its own reward means that the reward of goodness is intrinsic to being good. By being good, a good person achieves a different ontological status, one in which the death of his individual personality does not threaten the importance of goodness. And this is equally true for those who are good from the beginning of their first incarnations and for those who turn to goodness later in their first incarnations.

Having said that, there is nonetheless something else that distinguishes the two cases. When it comes to death (and a similar thing applies to the confrontation with other large-scale defects of human life),

[35] An audience member unknown to me.
[36] Matt. 20:1–16.

there is a further advantage for those who have been good for a long time. This advantage lies on the psychological side of overcoming or seeing through death, not on the ontological side of surviving death. Those who have been good for a long time have had more chance for their other-regarding motivation to pervade their whole personality—their thoughts and their feelings have become more and more expressive of the objective relation that they have to themselves. In the face of death, the impending loss of their own individual personality will *move* them less. They will be able to take a vivid pleasure in the thought that there will be so many individual personalities flourishing in the future. They will also be able to draw some strength from the reasonable hope that among these many some will be good, so that what is finest in their own individual personalities will recur again.

The relation of identity is reflexive, symmetric, and transitive, but isn't it possible that a person A identifies in your sense with a person B and with a later person C, but that B does not identify with C? So B is not C. But A is B and C, so C is B. This is a contradiction. Even more simply, it can be that a person A can identify with a person B but not vice versa. If identification of the right sort makes for identity and non-identification makes for non-identity, then A is B and B is not A. This is another contradiction.[37]

Yes. Those are contradictions. But they are not implied by the view in question.

It is simply part of the logic of identity that one person cannot become another person. So it is simply part of the logic of identity that one person cannot become another person by radically identifying with the interests of that person's individual personality. That is not what is being proposed. What is being proposed is that as a result of one person's radically identifying with the interests of another person's individual personality, the first person comes to be partly constituted by the human organism whose associated mental states and dispositions make up that individual personality.

It is our constitution across time that is variable and determined by our patterns of identification, not *which person one is identical with.*

The idiom of constitution is crucial here. The good are those persons

[37] Elizabeth Harman and Walter Sinnott-Armstrong.

whose initial individual personalities are good or become good. As a consequence of this, the persons in question will come to be *constituted* by the bodies associated with all those individual personalities that are not irredeemably closed to goodness. The patterns of identification among *those* individual personalities may be as they are. This does not affect the multiple constitution or embodiment of the good.

So, for example, if A identifies with B in the appropriate way, A's total embodiment includes B's original embodiment, in the typical case a human body or organism, as a proper and discrete part. If B does not identify with A in the appropriate way then B's total embodiment does not include A's original embodiment as a proper part.

You say that a person is conscious at a time if at that time he is embodied by something, some body, that is conscious, and I suppose that you would also say that a person is conscious at a place if at that place he is embodied by some body that is conscious. Why can't I refute your view in this way? I call up a good person and ask him what he can see from here; he thinks I am mad, since he can see nothing from here![38]

That, what you take to be the obvious thing, is actually what the view implies, *not* a consequence at odds with it. The view is not that a good person comes to be a sort of World Soul peering out through each individual consciousness and somehow having it all presented to him in one consciousness. Not at all. The multiple embodiments of the good are separated embodiments; they are the bodies that are the loci of distinct conscious lives and distinct individual personalities. There is no suggestion that the good somehow concatenate the conscious experiences of all those bodies into, as it were, *one* arena of presence.

Compare trying to object to the view of fission just presented by observing that Lefty doesn't know what Righty is thinking or feeling. Of course he doesn't; consciousness is a body-based phenomenon, and it remains so, even under conditions of multiple embodiment.

One distinctive feature of the view as it applies to the premortem embodiment of the good is that one can be conscious at a place without being *at the center* of any arena or consciousness that is embodied at that place. Another distinctive feature of the view as it applies the postmor-

[38] An audience member unknown to me.

tem embodiment of the good is that one can be conscious at a time at which one is no longer *at the center* of any arena or consciousness. That was not to be expected, I admit.

But remember the crucial result from lecture three. Being at a center (and hence being *me* or being *you*) turns out to be an utterly shallow matter. It is occupying an illusory or merely virtual position; that is all there is to it.

Doesn't the view that persons are, at least potentially, higher-order individuals that are variably and multiply constituted by successions of individual personalities wrongly treat tightly knit groups or dynastic families as single persons?[39]

Not quite. Take the Kennedys, and very significantly idealize the actual situation by supposing that each Kennedy is disposed to identify with the future interests of all the Kennedys, down through the generations.

Now here is the reason why the structure of higher-order persons is not realized even in the case of the idealized Kennedys. The relevant pattern of identification on the part of a Kennedy is crucially mediated by the further thought that the other person is a Kennedy and by a deep clannish admiration for the Kennedys as such.

That is not how it works with indentifying with persons or individual personalities in the way that includes them in one's future. When I look to the future interests of my post-Alzheimer's individual personality I am disposed to take those interests as default starting points in my present practical reasoning in a way that is utterly unmediated by thoughts like "He is a member of the clan" or "He is very admirable." That is why, in the specification of the relevant dispositions to identify, we required that the disposition be unmediated, that is, that the disposition's condition of manifestation simply be the recognition of an anticipatable future interest.

Group identities are very interesting things, but they are not what is being described here.

You keep saying that given that we are Protean then if a person A identifies in the appropriate way with a person B he comes to be partly constituted

---

[39] Justin Alderis and Hedrik Lorenz.

by the organism that constitutes B. Why not simply say the he comes to be partly constituted by the person B?[40]

There are a number of ways of seeing why that cannot be right. Here is one. Suppose there is a perfect communion of A, B and C, such that each has come to identify with the other two. Then we would have that A is partly constituted by B and B is partly constituted by A, which would imply that A is partly constituted by something which is itself partly constituted by A. This is impossible, even if we do not infer from this that A is a proper part of itself.

Instead what happens is that the constitution of the person A is first the body whose coming into being and maturation resulted in A, and then, given the development of A's good will, A's constitution comes to also include the body whose coming into being and maturation resulted in B, and the body whose coming into being and maturation resulted in C. The constitution of the person B is first the body whose coming into being and maturation resulted in B, and then, given the development of B's good will, B's constitution comes to include the body whose coming into being and maturation resulted in A, and the body whose coming into being and maturation resulted in C. (Similarly for C.)

So in this case of perfect communion all that is implied is that three higher-order individuals come to have the same constitution, after having had a different original constitution.

So too, all the good who have passed come to have the same *future* constitution, there in the onward rush of humankind. They do not become identical. There is no becoming identical.

Then there is the metaphysically possible case of the always perfect communion, three contemporaneous beings who have always had good wills, and who therefore have always shared the same constitution. Since constitution is not identity, they can indeed be three distinct beings that are one in constitution.

Of course, if you ask me to contemplate a science fiction in which my body is made up of smaller persons who can enter into perfect community with me, then I will say that the extent of the embodiments of these "smaller" persons is not a mere matter of stipulation.

[40] An audience member unknown to me.

If you are ethically pretty ordinary, if you cannot get all the way to agape, *why do you have any motive in trying to be good, any motive not undermined by the arbitrariness of death and suffering, and the other "large-scale defects" of human life?*[41]

Talk of *motive* aside, it is a penetrating question. I do not want it to turn out that goodness is important, but only for the good. I do not want it to turn out that the threat of death to the importance of goodness is only met by the good, so that goodness is important, but only to them.

That is why I emphasize the role of goodness not only in surviving death but in overcoming or "seeing through" death. We are good to various degrees. A few meet the very high standard of incorporating in their individual personalities the disposition that is characteristic of *agape*. Many of us are good enough; we have turned toward the real interests of others to the degree necessary to do our bit in sustaining a good enough world, a world in which there is found the enormous collective benevolence required for the nurturance of the young and the maintenance of the sick and old in some kind of decent condition. Many however will remain selfish and self-involved, so that the interests of others will figure in their practical reasoning only instrumentally, that is, when attending to them serves their own interests. These latter, who remain parasites living off the accumulated benevolence of the good enough world, are wholly indentified with the interests of their individual personalities. The death of their individual personalities will seem to them the loss of everything that is really important, unless they practice a worthless detachment, which is not in its turn a form of attachment *to* anything.

For those who are good enough, death will appear differently. To the extent they are good they will find that death, although it obliterates their individual personalities, leaves much that is fundamentally important behind. In that case there remains, even in the face of death, something to rejoice in.

So here, too, we have met the condition set out by Socrates; there is something in death that is better for the good enough than it is for those who are forever closed in upon themselves.

[41] An audience member unknown to me.

What about the heat death of the sun and the last persons who face this as a fate? The good among them do not live on.[42]

Yes, that is right. Everything complex that has a beginning in space and time is susceptible to having an end. So it is with the phenomenon of embodied self-consciousness. Given naturalism, we must see the emergence of embodied self-consciousness as something that happened because of lucky conditions that arose on a planet in a backwater of the universe. Even if embodied self-consciousness turns out to be a phenomenon with a much wider scope than the history of humankind it will come to an end, certainly with the next collapse of the universe. If the universe is cyclical, the phenomenon may appear again. Or it may not.

If it does not, then even the higher-order individuals who are the good will come to an end. The good will survive death, but they will not be immortal. They will not live forever. Still, the good will have larger identities; they will be with us to the end.

However, the considerations I have amassed to answer the *generic* threat of death to the importance of goodness are not undermined by the finiteness of human history or of the history of embodied self-consciousness—they will still be in place. They did not depend on the supposition of eternal life. Nor did the generic threat simply consist in the observation that sometimes, in some situations, the good are without any recourse at all.

Are not the last ones, even the good among them, likely to be demoralized by the immanent end of humanity? And, we are supposing, they have no prospect of a larger identity.

Even if their demoralization is to be expected, the point remains. This generic statement remains true: Goodness is a reasonable form of heroism even in the face of death and the other large-scale defects of human life. Most coherent general claims about what is reasonable are generics, and this is no exception. And generics are not rendered false by local exceptions.[43]

But forget about the main thesis of the lectures. What about *them*, the

[42]Michael Forster and Ade Artemis.

[43]On the nature of generics and generic thought, see Gregory Carlson and Francis Jeffry Pelletier, eds., *The Generic Book* (University of Chicago Press, 1995), and Sarah-Jane Leslie, "Generics: Cognition and Acquisition," *Philosophical Review* 117 (2007), "The Original Sin of Cognition," forthcoming in the *Journal of Philosophy*, and her forthcoming book with Oxford University Press.

last ones who are good, and who are facing the end of all things? Is there anything that they could know that could reasonably prevent them from demoralization?

It partly depends on how human history has gone. Suppose at some point the good were partially vindicated, so that for a time goodness and happiness were conjoined. The last of the good might look back on this with legitimate pride. For some time the flag of the good flew, justly, over some of the kingdoms of the earth. Knowing this, or something like this, the last of the good might continue to tend to their fellows, even to the end.

We can also expect that some of the last of the good will tend to their fellows and will resist demoralization, without the need for this backward-looking consolation. And who can say that they would be wrong in this?

Index

after-images, 225, 226

agape: as *anastasis* of good people, 351; and *Atman,* 349, 350; and degrees of goodness, 375; and future-directed concern, 49; and good will, 344–45; and heroism, 238; and identity, 14; as identity-constituting, 49; and individual personality as such, 358; and interests of good people, 354; and life in onward rush of human-kind, 293, 300, 331; and Nietzsche, 351; and overcoming death, 50; and refiguring of basic dispositions, 295–96; reward of, 350–51; and Schopen-hauer, 344–45, 347, 348; and self as arbitrary other, 236; and selfishness, 368–69; and universal impersonal concern, 49

agency: and psychological continuity, 259–60; style of, 259, 266, 289, 290–91; temporally extended, 259; and thought, 155; and unity, 259

altruism, 49, 275, 333, 344, 368, 369

Alzheimer's disease, 262, 264, 266, 276–77, 290, 299

amnesia, 266

anastasis, 327, 351; defined, 326

anatta, 237, 265; and *agape,* 236, 296, 358; defined, 234; and Nietzsche, 353; and Parfit, 307, 309, 311; and personality and personal identity, 315; and self identity, 316; and

tracing selves, 212; and Vedantism, 352. *See also* self/selves

animalism, 249, 251, 301–4

Anscombe, G.E.M., 20

Apocalypticism, 128–29, 137

apperception, unity of, 167, 207

Aquinas, Thomas, 91, 93, 213–14, 292

arena, of presence and action: as all-inclusive psychological field, 182; and asymmetry of evaluational affect, 157–58, 159, 161; and brain, 208, 222; centered structure of, 280; center of, 138, 168–69, 207, 208, 209, 230, 241–42; and contingency, 151–54; continuation of, 168–69, 174–75, 180; and death, 164, 179; defined, 139–41, 181–82; human being as center of, 213; "I" as center of, 139, 140–41, 142–45, 151, 152, 153, 154, 156, 157, 158, 161–62, 164–65, 192, 193; and indexical use of "I" vs. subjective uses of "I," 151, 154; as individual item, 221; as intentional object, 141, 165, 229–30, 231, 237; as mere appearance, 224–25; and morality, 268–69; persistence of, 179, 208, 230, 237, 337; and persis-tent vegetative state, 161–62; and perspective, 153; prospective iden-tifications of, 232; and radical evil, 335; recreation of, 221–22; same as existing later, 165; and self, 165–68,